RIGHTEOUS DISCONTENT

RIGHTEOUS DISCONTENT

The Women's Movement in the Black Baptist Church 1880–1920

Evelyn Brooks Higginbotham

Harvard University Press
Cambridge, Massachusetts
London, England

First Harvard University Press paperback edition, 1994

Library of Congress Cataloging-in-Publication Data

Higginbotham, Evelyn Brooks, 1945–
Righteous discontent : the women's movement in the Black Baptist
Church, 1880–1920 / Evelyn Brooks Higginbotham.
p. cm.
Includes bibliographical references and index.
ISBN 0-674-76977-5 (alk. paper) (cloth)
ISBN 0-674-76978-3 (pbk.)
1. Afro-American women—History. 2. Afro-American Baptists—
History. 3. National Baptist Convention of the United States
of America—History. I. Title.
BX6447.H54 1993
286'.133'082—dc20
92-19345
CIP

For Leon

Contents

Acknowledgments   *ix*

1 The Black Church: A Gender Perspective   *1*
2 The Female Talented Tenth   *19*
3 Separatist Leanings   *47*
4 Unlikely Sisterhood   *88*
5 Feminist Theology, 1880–1900   *120*
6 The Coming of Age of the Black Baptist Sisterhood   *150*
7 The Politics of Respectability   *185*

   Notes   *231*
   Index   *297*

Acknowledgments

Just as the church owes its strength and sustenance in the black community not merely to the minister, but to many unheralded people, I owe the publication of this book to the many people who aided me in tangible and intangible ways. It is with sincere appreciation that I acknowledge those who generously offered information, expedited my research, read and commented on drafts of the manuscript, provided funding, and extended sympathy and support. I am also indebted to the millions of church women who left a legacy of cooperative efforts, resources, and faith, providing inspiration and strength to future generations of African Americans like myself.

Longtime leaders of national, state, and district Baptist conventions as well as leaders of local churches were especially helpful in sharing their memories of some of the experiences and personalities mentioned in this book. Some described growing up in poor, segregated southern communities and attending church-operated elementary and secondary schools—often the only schools open to African Americans. Some worked as maids in the homes of white people, while serving as prominent leaders in the churches of their own communities. They all made me aware of the great sacrifice and communal spirit of black church women in building schools, conducting social service programs, and extending aid to the needy during the era of Jim Crow. I would like to thank especially Dr. Mary O. Ross, President of the Woman's Convention, Auxiliary to the National Baptist Convention, for sending me her published autobiographical writings. Others with whom I corresponded and spoke deserve mention: Ethel Gordon, Historian of the Woman's Convention; Isola Richardson, a delegate for many decades to the annual meetings of the National Baptist Convention; the Reverend William Harvey, Executive Secretary of the Foreign Mission Board of the National Baptist Convention; and the leadership of the Nannie Helen Burroughs School in Washington, D.C.—namely, Aurelia Downey, Mattie A. Robinson, and Alice Smith.

My cousins Leah V. Lewis and Lucille Frazier, who are sisters and both in their nineties, enriched my knowledge of church life and school life at Hartshorn in Richmond during the early twentieth century. Discussions with local church leaders and their willingness to reveal written documents proved invaluable sources of information. I am grateful to Etta Booker (deceased) and the Reverend Jerry Moore of the Nineteenth Street Baptist Church in Washington, D.C.; Dorothy J. Moore of the Shiloh Baptist Church in Philadelphia; the Reverend Henry C. Gregory, III (deceased) of the Shiloh Baptist Church of Washington, D.C.; and the Reverend William J. Shaw of the White Rock Baptist Church in Philadelphia.

I am grateful to a number of persons who read part or all of the manuscript at various stages. I benefited from the breadth of knowledge and advice of Eugene D. Genovese, Elizabeth Fox-Genovese, Stanley L. Engerman, and Winthrop S. Hudson. I shall never forget the warmth and hospitality shown to me by the Genoveses and the Engermans whenever research trips took me in their vicinity. Stanley Engerman deserves immeasurable praise for his careful reading of the manuscript after it was revised for publication.

In the process of revision, I benefited from the comments of Houston Baker, Jacqueline Jones, and Susan Rabiner. Carroll Smith-Rosenberg and Paul Hanson enriched my knowledge of cultural studies and left an imprint on the pages of this book. Elsa Barkley Brown, Randall Burkett, Sharon Harley, Gerald R. Gill, David L. Lyons, John Ingham, and Dorothy Porter-Wesley represent the best in scholarly collegiality. While engaged in their own research, they were willing to share findings related to my work. The members of the Northeastern Seminar on Black Religion, particularly Randall Burkett, Jualynne Dodson, Peter Paris, Albert Raboteau, James Washington, Preston Williams, and David Wills, represented an important and critical community in which to introduce and test my ideas over a period of years.

Steven Niven tirelessly and painstakingly proofread the manuscript, followed up on my research queries, called my attention to incongruities, rechecked notes, and offered editorial advice. His devotion to the project will be forever cherished.

I am indebted to the many library and archival staffs who facilitated my research: Beverly Carlson in the American Baptist Archives Center in Valley Forge, Pennsylvania; James Lynch in the American Baptist–Samuel Colgate Historical Library in Rochester, New York; Bill Sumners of the Southern Baptist Historical Library and Archives in Nashville; Brenda Holland of the Sunday School Publishing Board of the National Baptist Convention, U.S.A., Inc. in Nashville; Beverly Guy-Sheftall and Brenda Banks of the Spelman College Archives in Atlanta; Tom Owen of the University Archives Division of the University of Louisville; Audrey Walker, who processed the Nannie Helen Burroughs Papers at the Library of Congress; and Esme Bhan of the Manuscript Division of the Moorland-Spingarn Research Center, Howard University. I would like to express a special word of thanks to Janet Sims-Wood of the Moorland-Spingarn Research Center. I would also like to acknowledge the staffs of the Smithsonian Institution; the Franklin Trask Library of Andover-Newton Theological School in Newton Centre, Massachusetts; the Washingtoniana Room of the Martin Luther King Public Library in Washington, D.C.; the Valentine Museum as well as the archives of Virginia Union University in Richmond; and the archives of Shiloh Baptist Church in Washington, D.C.

I would like to acknowledge the generosity of the W. E. B. Du Bois Institute at Harvard University and the Women's Studies Program of the Divinity School at Harvard for dissertation fellowships. I received the following postdoctoral grants: the J. Franklin Jameson Award in 1985 from the American Historical Association and the Library of Congress; a grant from the National Research Council in 1987–1988 for aid in exploring the suffragist activities and political involvement of black Baptist women leaders; and research money from the University of Pennsylvania.

Anita Jackson Wieck, Stephanie Camp, and my daughter, Nia Higginbotham, brought both efficiency and a sense of humor to the task of reading page proofs. I would also like to mention my gratitude for the photographic services of M. Rudolph Vetter and the secretarial services of Paulette Didion, Kathryn Clark, and Martha Rosso.

I could not have found a better group of persons with whom to work than my editors and other staff members at Harvard University Press, particularly Margaretta Fulton, Aida Donald, and Mary Ellen Geer.

I have reserved my final and most heartfelt expression of appreciation for my family. My mother, Elaine C. Wells, and my sister, Elaine A. Brooks, buttressed me with their love and support throughout the years. Moreover, it was my mother who planted the seeds for this study. Well before I entered graduate school, she suggested that I investigate the life of Nannie Helen Burroughs. Burroughs had been a member of my grandfather's church and was a hero in our household. I began my study of Burroughs partly in the hope of learning more about my grandfather, the Reverend Walter Henderson Brooks. Their stories led me to the larger movement about which this book is written.

I would like to acknowledge my debt to my father, Albert N. D. Brooks. A history teacher and secondary school principal, my father simultaneously worked for many years with Carter G. Woodson in the Association for the Study of Afro-American Life and History; and he instilled in me a commitment to uncover the African American past. Although he never lived to see me finish college, much less write this book, it was because of him that I pursued the discipline of history.

On many occasions, Nia and Karen Higginbotham encouraged me when I needed it most. Finally, this book is dedicated to my husband, A. Leon Higginbotham, Jr. A jurist, scholar, and teacher, he always found time in his incredibly busy schedule to listen to my ideas, read drafts, and offer constructive criticism. Leon offered a rare sensitivity and appreciation for my subject matter, for he has always taken pride in the fact that his mother, while a domestic for white people, was a pillar of strength for her family and church community. This book is a testimony to his encouragement.

RIGHTEOUS DISCONTENT

1

The Black Church: A Gender Perspective

> As I look about me today in this veiled world of mine, despite the noisier and more spectacular advance of my brothers, I instinctively feel and know that it is the five million women of my race who really count. Black women (and women whose grandmothers were black) are . . . the main pillars of those social settlements which we call churches; and they have with small doubt raised three-fourths of our church property.
>
> W. E. B. Du Bois, *Darkwater* (1918)

Much has been written about the importance of the black church in the social and political life of black people. Much less has been written about black women's importance in the life of the church. This book is a study of women in the black church between 1880 and 1920—a period that has come to be known simultaneously as the "woman's era" and the "nadir" in American race relations. I argue that women were crucial to broadening the public arm of the church and making it the most powerful institution of racial self-help in the African American community. During these years, the church served as the most effective vehicle by which men and women alike, pushed down by racism and poverty, regrouped and rallied against emotional and physical defeat.

In some instances, church women contested racist ideology and institutions through demands for anti-lynching legislation and an end to segregation laws. They expressed their discontent with both racial and gender discrimination and demanded equal rights for blacks and women—advocating voting rights or equal employment and educational opportunities. Black women even drew upon the Bible, the most respected source within their community, to fight for women's rights in the church and society at large. During the late nineteenth century they developed a distinct discourse of resistance, a feminist theology. More often, however, their efforts represented not dramatic protest but everyday forms of resistance to oppression and demoralization. Largely through the fund-raising efforts of women, the black church built schools, provided clothes and food to poor people, established old folks' homes and orphanages, and made available a host of needed social welfare services.

This study attempts to rescue women from invisibility as historical actors in the drama of black empowerment. Since women have traditionally constituted the majority of every black denomination, I present the black church not as the exclusive product of a male ministry but as the product and process of male and female interaction. In offering a corrective to the near exclusion of women in most studies of the black church, my book departs from the more recent and positive discussion of exceptional women, the early women preachers.[1] Research on women preachers, while of great value, does not capture the more representative role of the majority of women church members. If taken alone, such discussion continues to render women's role as marginal. Left obscured is the interrelation between the rising black churches in the late nineteenth and early twentieth centuries and the indefatigable efforts of black women's organizations. Left unheard are women's voices within the public discourse of racial and gender self-determination. In short, the focus on the ministry fails to capture adequately the gender dimension of the church's racial mission. Ultimately, my study provides a vantage point for viewing the interplay of race, gender, and class consciousness, for it presents the church, like the black community it mirrors, as a social space of unifying and conflicting discourses.

I have focused my attention on the movement that brought into existence the National Baptist Convention, U.S.A., Inc. This movement represented and continues to represent the largest group—religious or secular—of black Americans. To persons not versed in church history, the term "convention" might bring to mind an annual meeting or tangential association. In the history of black Baptists, however, "convention" has almost the same meaning as "denomination." The black Baptist convention is distinct from that of white Baptists and emerged only because otherwise autonomous black Baptist churches voluntarily and freely came together.[2] Their collective association, beginning first at the state level and eventually embracing a national constituency, effected an unprecedented arena for public discussion and mobilization of resources on the part of African Americans.

Although conventions did not originate with late nineteenth-century black Baptists, their profound importance rests in their deployment as vehicles of black identity and empowerment. Ironically, it was the issue of slavery in 1844 that divided white Baptists into northern and southern conventions.[3] The close of the Civil War did not heal the rift among white Baptists, but it did give black Baptists the opportunity to forge a national unity and identity of their own. The decision to form a black national convention was motivated by discriminatory policies on the part of white Baptists, as well as by the growing support among African Americans in general for racial self-determination.[4]

James Melvin Washington's *Frustrated Fellowship: The Black Baptist Quest for Social Power* (1985) remains the most comprehensive discussion of the racial tensions that spurred the evolution of the black Baptist movement. Washington and others have described its separatist, indeed nationalist character as informed by philosophies of racial self-help and racial self-determination. But in chronicling the events that led to the development of the black Baptist church as a potent national force, they have focused overwhelmingly on the contributions of outstanding ministers within male-dominated state and national conventions.[5]

Black Baptist churchmen certainly recognized the importance of women's active support for the denomination's efforts toward racial self-help and self-reliance. Yet male-biased traditions and rules of decorum sought to mute women's voices and accentuate their subordinate status vis-à-vis men. Thus tainted by the values of the larger American society, the black church sought to provide men with full manhood rights, while offering women a separate and unequal status. As we will see in the chapters that follow, however complex the black Baptist women's own ideas were concerning separate roles for men and women—or the appropriate sexual division of labor—they would not lightly accept their own subordination in the struggle of their people.

The Black Church during the Nadir

The nationalist consciousness of the black Baptist church came of age during the years of heightened racism that followed Reconstruction. In 1880, when black Baptists took the first step toward creating a permanent national structure, the halcyon days of voting and political ferment among southern blacks had given way to growing disillusionment.[6] By 1890, it had become preeminently clear that the black community would have to devise its own strategies of social and political advancement. In that year Mississippi adopted a disfranchisement plan that served as a model to the rest of the South. Disfranchisement formed part of the larger process of "depoliticalization": literacy tests, poll taxes, and other state election laws, along with social and psychological sanctions such as economic reprisal, violence, and threats of violence, effected the mass removal of blacks from the nation's political life. Political institutions and representative government became simply inaccessible and unaccountable to American citizens who happened to be black.[7]

Black men lost more than the ballot on election day. They lost many other rights, which theoretically the constitution and federal civil rights laws protected: the right to hold public office, sit on juries, allocate tax dollars for schools and other social services, protect their women and themselves from insult and victimization, and share in other basic human and citizenship rights. Black women, like all American women, had never shared political equality with their men. Once black men were denied the suffrage, however, black women became ever more powerless and vulnerable to southern racial hostility.[8]

As southern state after state during the 1880s and 1890s set in motion a barrage of discriminatory laws that routinized the separate and inferior status of blacks, violence and intimidation solidified the "Negro's place" in the New South. Between 1884 and 1900 more than 2,500 lynchings of blacks were recorded. American race relations reached an all-time low—the "nadir," as Rayford Logan termed the disquieting times.[9] Jim Crow, as segregation was called, quickly pervaded every part of life and made itself felt even in death. In employment, housing, places of amusement, public transportation, schools, hospitals, and cemeteries, segregation daily produced and reproduced racial identities, power, and disempowerment. During the "nadir," black communities turned increasingly inward. They struggled without the aid or protection of the federal government; worse yet, they suffered its policies of betrayal. In 1883 the Supreme Court had declared unconstitutional the federal Civil Rights Act of 1875, a law prohibiting racial discrimination in places of public accommodation. In 1896 the Court announced its sanction of the "separate but equal" doctrine.[10]

Powerless to avert the mounting tide of racist public opinion, black people struggled to maintain family and community cohesiveness in an environment that sought to tear both asunder. African Americans, looking now to themselves to educate the masses of their people, care for the needy, facilitate economic development, and address political concerns, tapped their greatest strength from the tradition of their churches.[11] From the early days of slavery, the black church had constituted the backbone of the black community. Truly African American in its origins, it provided a spiritual cohesiveness that permitted its people to absorb, interpret, and practice the Christian faith—to make it their own. As the "invisible institution" of the slaves, the church had long promoted a sense of individual and collective worth and perpetuated a belief in human dignity that countered the racist preachings of the master class.[12] In the decades following Reconstruction, the church's autonomy and financial strength made it the most logical institution for the pursuit of racial self-help. It functioned not only as the house of worship but as an agency of social control, forum of discussion and debate, promoter of education and economic cooperation, and arena for the development and assertion of leadership.

Recognizing its diverse roles, E. Franklin Frazier termed the black church a veritable "nation within a nation."[13] At the individual level, but especially when collectively joined in association, black churches represented not an escapist and other-worldly orientation but the only viable bastion of a community under assault. If for many of its members the black church remained a focus for the perpetuation of community identity, for many of its leaders it became the vehicle for consolidating every existing strength into a concerted campaign for racial self-reliance. Those who sought to make the church the flagship of black dignity espoused strong race-conscious views concerning the preservation of the black community, and, just as important, they sought to shape the community so that preservation could become progress.

Race consciousness reached its apogee with the creation of the National Baptist Convention, U.S.A. in 1895. Determined to create a forum through which black people could voice their spiritual, economic, political, and social concerns, the convention's leaders equated racial self-determination with black denominational hegemony. These ideas were not unique to the black Baptist church. The African Methodist Episcopal Church had emerged as a separate denomination during the dawning years of the nineteenth century.[14] By the late nineteenth and early twentieth centuries all the black denominations had established community institutions and advanced the philosophy of racial self-help. But it was in the black Baptist church where this philosophy found its largest following.

Black Baptists constituted the most numerically significant attempt to counter the debilitating intent and effects of American racial exclusivism, and thus their story broadly characterizes the black church and black community. The National Baptist Convention, which existed apart from the powerful white Northern Baptist Convention and Southern Baptist Convention, constituted the largest and most representative sample of the black churchgoing population. In 1906 it had 2,261,607 members, while the second largest denominational membership, African Methodist Episcopal, had only 494,777. The National Baptist Convention included 61.4 percent of all black church members in the United States.[15] By 1916 National Baptists numbered 2,938,579. The convention was larger than any other black religious group and larger than either of the two major white Baptist groups, namely, the Northern Baptist Convention with 1,232,135 or the Southern Baptist Convention with 2,708,870.[16] The numerical power of the black Baptist convention appears even more dramatic when compared against the other white denominations. In 1916 it ranked as the third largest religious body in the United States—trailing only the Roman Catholic and Methodist Episcopal churches.

The great majority of the convention's members, like the great majority of blacks themselves, lived in the South and in areas with populations under 25,000. But its leaders hailed from towns and cities, and thus the bulk of its programs were there. The convention's urban presence steadily increased as blacks began to migrate in larger and larger numbers to southern and northern cities. In 1906 the National Baptist Convention constituted the largest denomination, black or white, in Atlanta, Memphis, and Richmond. By 1916 it took the lead in Birmingham and Nashville, while continuing to dominate in Memphis and Richmond. In Louisville, Washington, D.C., and New Orleans, it was second only to the Catholic church, while its numbers grew exponentially in Philadelphia, Pittsburgh, and Chicago.[17] By sheer size alone, the black Baptist church formed a microcosm of the black population in America and included men and women from all social classes and geographic regions.

The Black Church as Public Sphere

By law, blacks were denied access to public space, such as parks, libraries, restaurants, meeting halls, and other public accommodations. In time the black church—open to both secular and religious groups in the community—came to signify public space. It housed a diversity of programs including schools, circulating libraries, concerts, restaurants, insurance companies, vocational training, athletic clubs—all catering to a population much broader than the membership of individual churches. The church served as meeting hall for virtually every large gathering. It held political rallies, clubwomen's conferences, and school graduations. It was the one space truly accessible to the black community, and it was this characteristic that led W. E. B. Du Bois, long before E. Franklin Frazier, to identify the black church as a multiple site—at once being a place of worship, theater, publishing house, school, and lodge.[18]

The church also functioned as a discursive, critical arena—a public sphere in which values and issues were aired, debated, and disseminated throughout the larger black community. The black Baptist convention movement facilitated the sharing and distribution of information through periodic statewide and national meetings, where thousands gathered and discussed issues of civic concern. Since black women constituted two-thirds of this movement, they had a crucial role in the formation of public sentiment and in the expression of a black collective will. Particularly through women's efforts, black com-

munities with very limited income raised funds sufficient to build and
sustain churches, schools, and social welfare services. At times in
concert and at times in conflict with their men, black women initiated
race-conscious programs of self-help.

The very nationalist discourse that unified black men and women
betrayed inherent gender conflict. As a deliberative arena, the National Baptist Convention sought to speak for both men and women,
but it did not encourage expression from men and women as equals.
The convention's masculine bias was evident in its institutional structures and discourses. Positions of authority and power were monopo-
lized by men. Thus women sought to develop their own voice and
pursue their own interests, which at times overlapped and at other
times contested the men's. Rising gender consciousness was part of a
complex of ideas that informed black Baptist denominational work as
a whole.

In 1900 women succeeded in forming an alternate sphere of deliberation within the larger denominational context of the National
Baptist Convention. The Woman's Convention, defined as an auxiliary to the NBC, summoned a sisterhood more than one million strong
and culminated nearly three decades of work by women's organizations
at the local and state levels. Through their convention, black women
shared knowledge of their state and local activities. They governed
their own members, initiated their own agenda, elected their own
leaders, and developed criteria that won respect and emulation from
other women. In 1909 the convention boasted of having established
the first school for black women that black women themselves owned.
Through their school and their national convention, black Baptist
women challenged many of the real and symbolic barriers that others—white Americans in general and even black men—sought to
impose upon them in the church and larger society.[19] Rather than
diminishing racial solidarity, rising gender consciousness made possible
the effective drive toward a national black Baptist identity.

Through a racial and gender-based movement, black women confronted and influenced their social and political milieu, and they did
so through the mediating influence of the church. According to Peter
Berger and Richard Neuhaus, "mediating structures" constitute part of
the public realm. They stand between private citizens and the large,
impersonal institutions of public life, such as the government, and

produce meaningful value systems as well as concrete mechanisms for ordering people's lives and addressing needs.[20] More effectively than any other institution, the church stood between individual blacks, on the one hand, and the state with its racially alienating institutions, on the other. The church's ability to sustain numerous newspapers, schools, social welfare services, jobs, and recreational facilities mitigated the dominant society's denial of these resources to black communities. And it was primarily the fund-raising activity of black women that undergirded the church's mediating function.

In characterizing the black church as a public sphere, my analysis moves in a different direction from such conceptual models as "civil religion" or "public religion." The concept of civil religion, made popular and controversial by Robert N. Bellah, calls attention to the character and role of religious symbolism in American political life. It locates religious symbols outside the confines of the church and asserts their life and meaning in expressions of patriotism, the general understanding and articulation of American national identity, and in public rituals and ceremonies such as holidays and presidential inaugurations.[21] Instead, my book stresses the public character and role of the black church. This is no small difference. The religious symbolism of the nation's public life—its collective thanksgivings and civic piety—held problematic and contradictory meanings for African Americans.[22] Frederick Douglass conveyed this point eloquently before a crowd of white Americans on the Fourth of July in 1852. Contrasting their celebration of liberty with the enslavement of his own people, Douglass called the Independence Day festivities "sacrilegious" and proceeded with his jeremiad: "Your prayers and hymns, your sermons and thanksgivings, with all your religious parade and solemnity, are to Him [God], mere bombast, fraud, deception, impiety, and hypocrisy."[23]

For African Americans, long excluded from political institutions and denied presence, even relevance, in the dominant society's myths about its heritage and national community, the church itself became the domain for the expression, celebration, and pursuit of a black collective will and identity. At issue here is the public dimension of the black church, not the religious dimension of the public realm. The question is not how religious symbols and values were promoted in American politics, but how public space, both physical and discursive, was interpolated within black religious institutions. Indeed, scholars of African American religion do not tend to utilize the concept of civil religion. For example, James Melvin Washington inverts Sidney Mead's usage of Chesterton's phrase—the "nation with the soul of a church"—by describing black Baptists as having a "church with the soul of a nation."[24]

In the closed society of Jim Crow, the church afforded African Americans an interstitial space in which to critique and contest white America's racial domination. In addition, the church offered black women a forum through which to articulate a public discourse critical of women's subordination. A gender perspective on the black church facilitates understanding the church's public dimension, since, in emphasizing discursive interaction between men and women, such a perspective more accurately portrays the church's extensive activities and influence at the grass roots level. I describe the black church not as the embodiment of ministerial authority or of any individual's private interests and pronouncements, but as a social space for discussion of public concerns. During the late nineteenth and early twentieth centuries, the church came to represent a deliberative arena, whose character derived from the collective nature of the church itself, namely, as a body of many diverse members, and from race-conscious feelings of nationalism.[25]

My analysis of the black church finds conceptual utility in the scholarly literature that has been inspired by Jürgen Habermas's formulation of the "public sphere." Habermas identified the public sphere as a historically situated and institutionalized discursive realm. It mediated between private citizens (civil society) and the state and afforded an arena for the rational formation and functioning of information, in other words, public opinion. In the collective effort to arrive at a "common good," public opinion emerged, Habermas posited, as "the tasks of criticism and control which a public body of citizens informally—and, in periodic elections, formally as well—practices vis-à-vis the ruling structure organized in the form of a state."[26] Thus separate and independent of the state and also the market economy, the public sphere operated as a realm where all citizens interacted in reasoned discourse, even in criticism of governmental authority.

Critics of Habermas question his idealization of the liberal or bourgeois public sphere, and they especially criticize his failure to explore more fully competing, non-bourgeois publics.[27] They pluralize the "public sphere" concept in order to represent, at specific historical moments, a number of groups and interests that stand in oppositional relationship within societies stratified along racial, class, and gender lines. These numerous "publics" may overlap, but more often conflict—becoming oppositional or "counter-publics."[28] While these scholars focus upon neither the black church, nor black women, their critiques of Habermas are especially illuminating for asserting a variety of public arenas in which people participate.

When E. Franklin Frazier termed the black church a "nation within a nation," he conveyed the meaning of a "counter-public sphere." Frazier's metaphor of the black church as nation suggests a public distinct from and in conflict with the dominant white society and its racist institutional structures. The church-sponsored press played an instrumental role in the dissemination of a black oppositional discourse and in the creation of a black collective will. As black literacy rose from a mere 5 percent in 1860 to 70 percent in 1910, the church served as a major site of print production in black communities. Penelope Bullock's study of the black periodical press notes that churches, particularly the Baptist, A.M.E., and A.M.E. Zion churches, took the lead in the publication of general magazines in the post-Reconstruction era. For example, the anti-lynching newspaper *The Free Speech and Headlight* of Memphis, which was made famous by Ida B. Wells, was a black Baptist–owned newspaper.[29] Black Baptist state conventions, men's and women's, figured prominently in newspaper publication during the late nineteenth century. In 1900 black Baptists at the local and state levels published forty-three newspapers, the great majority of which were located in the South.[30] This role of the church cannot be overstated, since there were no black newspapers with massive national distribution; nor were the ideas and activities of blacks considered newsworthy to the white press except in the most derogatory and repressive way.

The role of publishing was vital to the creation of a black civic vision. The *National Baptist Magazine*, publication of the National Baptist Convention, defined its scope as "devoted to the interests of the Negro Race in general."[31] The magazine featured articles and editorials on a variety of subjects, including black history, lynching, presidential elections, industrial education, and segregation on railroads. The publishing board of the National Baptist Convention reported a circulation of more than 13 million issues of various tracts and booklets between 1900 and 1903. The press published religious materials, but it also conceived of its mission as "moulding the doctrines and opinions and shaping the destiny of the future church and race." The National Baptist Convention unquestioningly viewed itself as a public in opposition to white America, and it referred to the importance of its press in this context: "The Negro Baptists of this country . . . must discuss, produce or provide literature capable of keeping the identity and increasing race pride of the rising generation or they must be entirely overshadowed by the dominant race of this country."[32]

The formation of the National Baptist Convention, U.S.A. and its auxiliary women's convention afforded black men and women social space in which to critique openly the United States government, its laws, and its institutions. In fact, the level of public discussion caused one of the leaders of the Woman's Convention to come under government surveillance.[33] There were also subtle, perhaps more far-reaching political implications. The Baptist convention offered black men and women a structure for electing representatives, debating issues, and exercising many rights that white society denied them. Benjamin Mays and Joseph Nicholson, pointing to this surrogate political role, stated that the "local churches, associations, conventions, and conferences become the Negro's Democratic and Republican Conventions, his Legislature and his Senate and House of Representatives."[34] Through their conventions, African Americans refuted notions of their inability or unreadiness for equal political participation. Among women, this understanding heightened support of women's suffrage. The political rhetoric espoused at black women's annual meetings included the demand not only for voting rights, but for full inclusion in American public life.

The black church constituted a public that stood in opposition to the dominant white public, and yet as the case of women illustrates, it did not form a monolith. Nor did it reveal values completely independent of white America. A gender perspective on the church lends clarity to this matter, since it locates different sites in which black women both embraced and contested the dominant values and norms of northern white Baptists, white women, and even black men. For example, during the 1880s and 1890s southern black and northern white Baptist women worked in a cooperative fashion rare for the times.[35] Their cooperation was not based upon identical motives and interests, but it indicated that divergent motives did not preclude mutual goals. Together, black and white women spread the Gospel, supported one another's organizations, financed black education, and alleviated the plight of the poor. The women's movement in the black Baptist church imagined itself both as part of the black community and as part of an evangelical sisterhood that cut across racial lines.[36] That black women voiced the race-conscious interests and agenda of the male-dominated movement precluded neither interracial cooperation with white women nor conflict with black men.

Church Women's Multiple Consciousness

During the late nineteenth and early twentieth centuries, laws and changing social attitudes were chipping away at barriers to women's right to property, to education, to the professions, and even to suffrage in the western states of Wyoming in 1890 and in 1896 in Utah, Colorado, and Idaho.[37] During the latter decades of the nineteenth century white and black women joined in religious associations and secular clubs to bring about social reform. They fought for temperance, educational opportunity, suffrage, and a variety of gender-related issues. "To be alive at such an epoch is a privilege, to be a woman then is sublime," proclaimed the black educator and feminist Anna J. Cooper during the heady times of the "woman's era."[38] Cooper's exhilaration expressed nothing less than the black Baptist women's rising expectations.

The years between 1890 and 1920 witnessed significant strides for women. The number of all women with professional degrees rose by 226 percent.[39] Hazel Carby notes the increase of black women writers during the decade of the nineties. Anna J. Cooper published her feminist critique *A Voice from the South* (1892); other publications included Ida B. Wells, *On Lynchings* (1892) and Gertrude Mossell, *The Work of the Afro-American Woman* (1894). Black women established their literary presence in novels: Amelia E. Johnson's *Clarence and Corinne* (1890) and *The Hazely Family* (1894); Emma Dunham Kelley's *Megda* (1891); Frances Ellen Watkins Harper's *Iola Leroy* (1892); and Victoria Earle's *Aunt Lindy* (1893). Moreover, black women's writings drew attention and praise in the burgeoning field of journalism, as was reflected by the chapter devoted to them in I. Garland Penn's *The Afro-American Press and Its Editors* (1890).[40]

The cynical era of Jim Crow and the optimistic woman's era stood entangled one with the other—their imbrication giving shape to the black Baptist women's nationalist, yet feminist appeal. The complexity of the racial and gender meanings of the age suggests both the multiple consciousness and multiple positioning of black women, and also the complexity of the black church itself—an institution overwhelmingly female in membership. The church, like the black community, cannot be viewed solely through the lens of race. A gender perspective on the black church reminds us that the history of African Americans cannot be excluded from the important effort to identify and study social relations between men and women.

The history of black Baptist women discloses not only the gender dimension of the church's racial mission, but its class dimension as well.[41] The leadership of the women's convention movement formed part of an emergent class of school administrators, journalists, businesswomen, and reformers who served an all-black community. This educated female elite, frequently consisting of teachers or wives of ministers associated with educational institutions, promoted middle-class ideals among the masses of blacks in the belief that such ideals ensured the dual goals of racial self-help and respect from white America. Especially in the roles of missionary and teacher, black church women were conveyers of culture and vital contributors to the fostering of middle-class ideals and aspirations in the black community. Duty-bound to teach the value of religion, education, and hard work, the women of the black Baptist church adhered to a politics of respectability that equated public behavior with individual self-respect and with the advancement of African Americans as a group. They felt certain that "respectable" behavior in public would earn their people a measure of esteem from white America, and hence they strove to win the black lower class's psychological allegiance to temperance, industriousness, thrift, refined manners, and Victorian sexual morals.

On the one hand the politics of respectability rallied poor working-class blacks to the cause of racial self-help, by inspiring them to save, sacrifice, and pool their scant resources for the support of black-owned institutions. Whether through white-imposed segregation or black-preferred separatism, the black community's support of its middle class surely accounted for the development and growth of black-owned institutions, including those of the Baptist church. On the other hand, the effort to forge a community that would command whites' respect revealed class tensions among blacks themselves. The zealous efforts of black women's religious organizations to transform certain behavioral patterns of their people disavowed and opposed the culture of the "folk"—the expressive culture of many poor, uneducated, and "unassimilated" black men and women dispersed throughout the rural South or newly huddled in urban centers.[42]

The Baptist women's preoccupation with respectability reflected a bourgeois vision that vacillated between an attack on the failure of America to live up to its liberal ideals of equality and justice and an attack on the values and lifestyle of those blacks who transgressed white middle-class propriety. Thus the women's pronouncements appeared to swing from radical to conservative. They revealed their conservatism when they attributed institutional racism to the "negative" public behavior of their people—as if rejection of "gaudy" colors in dress, snuff dipping, baseball games on Sunday, and other forms of "improper" decorum could eradicate the pervasive racial barriers that surrounded black Americans. The Baptist women never conceded that rejection of white middle-class values by poor blacks afforded survival strategies, in fact spaces of resistance, albeit different from their own. Equally important, while the female leaders of the black Baptist church sought to broaden women's job opportunities and religious responsibilities, they revealed their conservatism in their unquestioning acceptance of man's sole right to the clergy.

Legacy of Resistance

Despite the limits of their movement, black Baptist women left an impressive record of protest against the racist and sexist proscriptions of their day. Eugene Genovese has written that "the living history of the Church has been primarily a history of submission to class stratification and the powers that be, but there has remained, despite all attempts at extirpation, a legacy of resistance that could appeal to certain parts of the New Testament and especially to the prophetic parts of the Old."[43] Exposing the black church's public dimension does not invalidate the centrality of its spiritual dimension in the private lives of black people or in the life of the black community. However, my interpretation of the church and black church women stresses the imbrication of the social and the spiritual within a context akin, but not identical, to what C. Eric Lincoln and Lawrence Mamiya call the "dialectical model of the black church." For Lincoln and Mamiya, this model postulates the black church to be in "dynamic tension" within a series of dialectical polarities: priestly versus prophetic functions; other-worldly versus this-worldly; particularism versus universalism; privatistic versus communal; charismatic versus bureaucratic; and accommodation versus resistance.[44]

I characterize the church as a dialogic model rather than dialectical, recognizing "dynamic tension" in a multiplicity of protean and concurrent meanings and intentions more so than in a series of discrete polarities. Multiple discourses—sometimes conflicting, sometimes unifying—are articulated between men and women, and within each of these two groups as well. The black church constitutes a complex body of shifting cultural, ideological, and political significations. It represents a "heteroglot" conception in the Bakhtinian sense of a multiplicity of meanings and intentions that interact and condition each other.[45] Such multiplicity transcends polarity—thus tending to blur the spiritual and secular, the eschatological and political, and the private and public. The black church represented the realm where individual souls communed intimately with God and where African Americans as a people freely discussed, debated, and devised an agenda for their common good. At the same time that church values and symbols ordered the epistemological and ontological understandings of each individual and gave meaning to the private sphere of family— both as conjugal household and as "household of faith"—church values and symbols helped to spawn the largest number of voluntary associations in the black community. It follows logically, then, that the church would introduce black women to public life. The church connected black women's spirituality integrally with social activism.

Although women's historians tend to focus overwhelmingly on the secular club movement, especially the National Association of Colored Women, as exemplary of black women's activism, clubwomen themselves readily admitted to the precedent of church work in fostering both "woman's consciousness" and a racial understanding of the "common good." Fannie Barrier Williams, a founding member and leader of the National Association of Colored Women, acknowledged in 1900: "The training which first enabled colored women to organize and successfully carry on club work was originally obtained in church work. These churches have been and still are the great preparatory schools in which the primary lessons of social order, mutual trustfulness and united effort have been taught. . . . The meaning of unity of effort for the common good, the development of social sympathies grew into woman's consciousness through the privileges of church work."[46]

The club movement among black women owed its very existence to the groundwork of organizational skill and leadership training gained through women's church societies. Missionary societies had early on brought together women with little knowledge of each other and created bonds of sisterly cooperation at the city and state levels. Not only Baptists but black Methodists, Presbyterians, and women in other denominations came together in associations that transformed unknown and unconfident women into leaders and agents of social service and racial self-help in their communities. For black Baptist women during the 1880s, the formation of state societies nurtured skills of networking and fund-raising. For more than a decade before the founding of the National Association of Colored Women, church-related societies had introduced mothers' training schools and social service programs, many of which were later adopted into the programs of the secular women's clubs.

More than mere precursors to secular reform and women's rights activism,[47] black women's religious organizations undergirded and formed an identifiable part of what is erroneously assumed to be "secular." The black Baptist women's convention thrust itself into the mainstream of Progressive reform, and conversely such clubs as those constituting the secular-oriented National Association of Colored Women included church work as integral and salient to their purpose. This complexity precludes attempts to bifurcate black women's activities neatly into dichotomous categories such as religious versus secular, private versus public, or accommodation versus resistance.

Even such quotidian activities as women's fund raising, teaching in Sabbath schools, ministering to the sick, or conducting mothers' training schools embraced a politically subversive character within southern society. In many respects, the most profound challenge to Jim Crow laws, crop liens, disfranchisement, the dearth of black public schools, and the heinous brutality of lynching rested in the silent, everyday struggle of black people to build stable families, get an education, worship together in their churches, and "work the system," as Eric Hobsbawm terms it, "to their minimum disadvantage."[48] Arguments over the accommodationist versus liberating thrust of the black church miss the range as well as the fluid interaction of political and ideological meanings represented within the church's domain. Equally important, the artificiality of such a dichotomy precludes appreciation of the church's role in the "prosaic and constant struggle" of black people for survival and empowerment.[49] Edward Wheeler persuasively argues for the paradoxical implications of social uplift and accommodation: "Accommodation, which of course had a submissive tone, also had a subversive quality. On the one hand, uplift meant accommodation and surrender to the concepts, principles, and ideals of the dominant society. On the other, uplift was a denial of what white society meant by accommodation, for it spoke of a possibility to move beyond the limits prescribed by the dominant society."[50]

In the 1909 Atlanta University study of social betterment activities among African Americans, Du Bois attributed the greater part of such activities to the black church and specifically to church women.[51] In the final analysis the women's movement in the black Baptist church may be likened more to Harriet Tubman's repeated, surreptitious efforts to lead slaves step by step away from bondage than to Nat Turner's apocalyptic, revolutionary surge. Women's efforts were valiant attempts to navigate their people through the stifling and dangerous obstacle course of American racism. Committed to the causes of racial self-help and advancement, the convention movement among black Baptist women contributed greatly to the church's tremendous influence in both the spiritual and secular life of black communities. But the women's movement did something more. It gave to black women an individual and group pride that resisted ideologies and institutions upholding gender subordination. The movement gave them the collective strength and determination to continue their struggle for the rights of blacks and the rights of women.

2

The Female Talented Tenth

> The earnest well trained Christian young woman,
> as a teacher, as a home-maker, as wife, mother, or
> silent influence even, is as potent a missionary
> agency among our people as is the theologian; and
> I claim that at the present state of our develop-
> ment in the South she is even more important
> and necessary.
>
> Anna J. Cooper, *Voice from the South* (1892)

The convention movement in the black Baptist church was led by a race-conscious vanguard imbued with the class values of Victorian America. In the decades following Reconstruction, the movement expanded its ranks with growing numbers of educated men and women, the majority of whom had been trained in southern black schools and colleges. There was little doubt in their minds that education stood second only to religion in enabling their survival and salvation in America. The evidence of education's value appeared irrefutable to men and women denied legal access to learning under the slave regime. With 95 percent of southern blacks unable to read or write at the outbreak of the Civil War, illiteracy proved a bitter fruit of bondage. African Americans were quick to identify literacy with personal fulfillment and upward mobility. The testimony of ex-slaves repeatedly noted how significant it was to read the Bible, write one's name, compute one's earnings, and teach others to do the same.

Despite the value of education to individual advancement, its larger, more lasting service was perceived in terms of collective empower-ment. Education, especially higher education, was considered essential to the progress of African Americans as a group. It is no wonder, then, that the black church's social and political influence expanded with both the rise in black literacy and the rise of a leadership class that came increasingly to embody college-trained men and women. The growth in church women's visibility and influence throughout the last quarter of the nineteenth century was directly related to the growth in the number of educated women. To a significant extent, the convention movement among black Baptists was sparked by the educational philosophy of the colleges that were founded in the postbellum South by white northern Protestants. The schools owned and supported by northern Baptists advocated the development of an educated elite. College-educated black women, a group I call the Female Talented Tenth, disseminated middle-class morals and values among the masses and, at the same time, generated financial support for the black church and its educational and numerous social service programs.

The concept of the Talented Tenth gained widest currency through the eloquent and incisive pen of W. E. B. Du Bois, who in 1903 began to challenge the authorial voice of Booker T. Washington as spokesman for black people.[1] While Washington valorized the kind of education that fit the masses for the American industrial order, Du Bois championed the same breadth and depth of higher education that served the nation's leadership. The Talented Tenth symbolized the best and brightest in all societies, African American not exempted; and it was to this exceptional minority that societies owed their progress. Du Bois argued that liberal arts colleges and universities served as the training ground for the educated vanguard, which advanced its own civil rights and, in addition, those of the inarticulate masses. In upholding the preeminent role of the Talented Tenth, he rejected any acquiescence to the "Negro's place"—specifically the separate and subordinate position of all blacks within the South and the nation. For Harvard-trained Du Bois, the salvation of blacks en masse lay in the hands of men like himself—the talented few, upon whom higher education bestowed not only the "intelligence, broad sympathy, knowledge of the world" necessary to demand respect, but also the social consciousness necessary to "guide the Mass away from the contamination and death of the Worst, in their own and other races."[2] Thus Du Bois's message of racial equality held implicit class assumptions. As the guiding force "away from the contamination of the worst," the Talented Tenth expressed middle-class goals.[3]

The Talented Tenth's female component should not be overlooked. During the late nineteenth and early twentieth centuries, educators and religious leaders accentuated women's roles and, in quite explicit terms, deemed them essential, even paramount, to African American progress. Through public schools, hundreds of private schools, churches, and home visitation, the Female Talented Tenth served as a conduit of race pride and white middle-class culture. This chapter focuses on the nexus between the church and educational institutions. Conceptualization of the Female Talented Tenth provides an opportunity for exploring the process by which middle-class values were introduced and promulgated among the freedpeople, as well as interpreted and, in some cases, resisted by them. For both blacks and their white philanthropic supporters, the goal of higher education embodied conflicting motives, pedagogies, and ideological meanings.

Opening School Doors to Women

Northern white efforts, specifically those of the American Baptist Home Mission Society (ABHMS) and its women's auxiliaries in New England and the Midwest, played a seminal role in the development of educated black leaders. In 1862, in the midst of the Civil War, the ABHMS pledged to provide the emancipated slave with "Christian instruction." In its report in 1865, the ABHMS designated the training of black men for the ministry as the "most direct, accessible and effective way of teaching the mass of colored people." In less than a decade the society broadened its goal to include the collegiate training of black women. In 1872 Shaw University in North Carolina, a Home Mission school, opened its doors to women. The other ABHMS schools moved quickly to become coeducational. By 1880 the white Baptist educators owned and supported eight schools for blacks—only two of which were exclusively male: Richmond Institute (male), Richmond, Virginia; Atlanta Baptist College (male), Atlanta, Georgia; Shaw University, Raleigh, North Carolina; Benedict Institute, Columbia, South Carolina; Nashville Institute, Nashville, Tennessee; Natchez Seminary, Natchez, Mississippi; Leland University, New Orleans, Louisiana; and Wayland Seminary, Washington, D.C.

School reports for 1880 affirmed the commitment of the ABHMS to women's education. The reports juxtaposed women and ministers as vital contributors to racial uplift. The report of the Reverend Charles Ayer, president of Natchez Seminary, declared: "Give us the ministers and the women and we will lift the masses of our free people."[4] G. M. P. King, the white president of Wayland Seminary in

Washington, D.C., appealed to the nation's guilt when he professed that white America owed black women an education. He argued that the Old South's denial of education to slaves resulted in the inability of black mothers to read the Bible to their children. An educated womanhood, according to King, endowed the roles of wife, mother, church worker, and schoolteacher with special influence.[5] Benedict Institute maintained similarly: "No one can measure the importance of educating and training the females of this race." The report requested an expansion of college accommodations for women. Leland University in New Orleans recommended a women's dormitory and additional courses in home management, since one-third of the school's students were women who commuted from the rural outskirts of the city. In July 1880 the ABHMS committee on the freedmen unequivocally asserted the importance of a trained ministry, but offered as "scarcely less important" the preparation of black women as homemakers and teachers.

Blacks themselves urged the Home Mission Society to open the doors of its schools to women. In the early 1880s black churches in Atlanta and Richmond pledged money for women's education, since northern Baptists had provided only for men in the two cities. Their financial as well as verbal support proved a persuasive argument. In April 1881 the Reverend Frank Quarles, Atlanta leader and pastor of Friendship Baptist Church, turned over the basement of his church to Sophia Packard and Harriet Giles of the New England–based Woman's American Baptist Home Mission Society. The two women had come to Atlanta in order to establish a school of higher education for black women and had learned of Quarles's interest in this cause. Within a few days of their meeting Quarles rallied the local black ministers, who vigorously publicized and facilitated the school's opening by printing and distributing flyers. The church basement served as the founding site of Atlanta Baptist Female Seminary (renamed Spelman), and for two years the church housed the school.

In the critical first year of Spelman's existence, black Atlantans raised funds sufficient to confirm their commitment to its success and attract further support from northern white Baptists. The black Baptist state convention and especially leaders such as William J. White, a minister, newspaper editor, and prominent figure in the founding of Atlanta Baptist College (renamed Morehouse), committed proceeds from the sale of valuable property to the Atlanta women's school. During this early period Reverend Quarles took time from his busy ministerial schedule to tour the north in order to solicit donors.[6] In the course of his otherwise successful tour, Quarles caught pneumonia and died soon after returning to Atlanta—thus literally giving his life to the cause of Spelman. Henry Morehouse, field secretary of the ABHMS, noted twenty years after the school's founding that "it was cradled and nursed by the Colored Baptists of Georgia."[7]

Richmond blacks similarly promoted the higher education of black women. In 1880 black churches, represented in the Virginia Baptist State Convention, begged the ABHMS to alter the all-male policy of its Richmond Theological Institute so that women could be admitted and housed on the campus. The black minister Anthony Binga of Virginia urged northern Baptists to establish educational opportunities for black women. Asserting that "mothers will give caste to society," Binga considered an uneducated mother, no matter how devoted to her children, unprepared to meet the demands of the age.[8] Other black Virginians employed arguments based on gender fairness. In 1881 the black Baptist minister Walter H. Brooks pleaded in a white northern Baptist magazine for the Richmond Theological Institute to broaden its ministerial focus and include college courses comparable to those at the black universities Howard and Fisk. Women's education figured decisively in his argument. Brooks found parallels between racial and gender discrimination and called attention to the contradiction and injustice of addressing one without the other: "But we ask for no educational advantages for our sons which we do not ask for our daughters. If our sons have reason to complain of the exclusive spirit of certain institutions of learning in this state, our daughters have more, for they have not even a place in the Richmond Institute, the only Baptist institution in Virginia which furnishes academic training to colored pupils."[9]

Two years after Brooks's plea the northern white Baptists established Hartshorn Memorial College for the singular purpose of educating black women. Like Spelman, the college was initially housed in a black Baptist Church—Ebenezer Church in Richmond—although it eventually purchased eight and a half acres of land and buildings in the northwestern section of the city. Hartshorn's curriculum entailed much more than preparation for wifehood and motherhood. Its liberal arts program never failed to mention women's domestic duties, but it emphasized a wider range of educational and professional options. The school's charter read: "An institution of Christian learning of Collegiate grade for the education of young women, to give instruction in science, literature, and art, in normal, industrial and professional branches."[10]

In 1883, the year of Hartshorn's founding, the American Baptist Home Mission Society proclaimed that if "we had it in our power to educate one hundred, we would educate fifty men and fifty women rather than one hundred men."[11] The growing significance attached to women's education on the part of the northern Baptist school founders reflected their recognition of influential roles besides the ministry. They were convinced that black women left an indelible imprint on the character of society, whether they worked as wives and mothers in their own homes, or indirectly influenced other homes through work as teachers and missionaries.[12]

By 1892 the impact of women's education was discernible among both students and teachers at the Baptist Home Mission schools. A comparison of schools in 1880 and 1892 illustrates not merely growth in the number of students and teachers, but a dramatic growth in the number of female students and teachers. In 1880 the ABHMS conducted eight schools. Male enrollments more than doubled female: of 1,191 students, 852 were men, while only 339 were women. The teaching staff was more evenly distributed by sex, with 21 male teachers and 16 female. In 1892 the ABHMS counted 202 teachers in 13 schools of higher education—82 were men and 120 women. Of the 5,167 black students enrolled in 1892, 2,219 were men and 2,948 women. Women were concentrated, for the most part, in the normal departments, which specialized in teacher training. Nor did training for the ministry continue to hold precedence over teacher training: in 1892 ABHMS colleges included 458 students preparing for the ministry and 1,829 preparing to teach.[13]

Northern Baptist Reflections

The ABHMS characterized its educational work for the southern freedpeople as that which produced leaders. So convinced were the northern Baptists of the need for black women's higher education that they termed exclusionist policies toward women "short sighted and suicidal."[14] Departure from the "suicidal" policy of only educating men reflected the complex motives that underlay the ABHMS's work among the freedpeople. These motives, both egalitarian and self-serving, came to be articulated through the concept of the Talented Tenth. Indeed the very concept came to life with the rise of black Baptist colleges and represented the philosophical basis upon which the missionary educators sought to transform black America.

In 1896, one year after Booker T. Washington's famous Atlanta Compromise speech, Henry Morehouse, executive secretary of the ABHMS from 1879 to 1893 and from 1902 to 1917, coined the term Talented Tenth in order to distinguish the work of his society from that which catered to average or mediocre intellect. Maintaining that black advancement depended largely on well-trained leaders, Morehouse proclaimed:

> I repeat that not to make proper provision for the high education of the talented tenth man of the colored colleges is a prodigious mistake. It is to dwarf the tree that has in it the promise of a grand oak. Industrial education is good for the nine; the common English branches are good for the nine; that tenth man ought to have the best opportunities for making the most of himself for humanity and God.[15]

Through the Talented Tenth, northern white Baptists hoped to transform—albeit indirectly—the illiterate and impoverished black masses into American citizens who valued education, industriousness, piety, and refined manners.[16] Rather than tackle the cost of mass education, the ABHMS channeled its energies into the formation of a black elite that would serve and lead its own community. And the society did so with the self-conscious acknowledgment that blacks worked more effectively in segregated black communities than did white missionaries. For the ABHMS, the explicit goal of preparing blacks for citizenship entailed an alliance with black leaders who had imbibed white middle-class values and commanded the respect and following of their own people. In 1898 George Sale, a white man and the president of Atlanta Baptist College, bluntly told a white teachers' association in Georgia: "A white man, northern or southern, may go to their gatherings; they will treat him with all respect and will listen to all he has to say, but they will follow the lead of their own men, and if we will do anything for or with the Negro we must do it through Negro men and women."[17]

Sale's candid acknowledgment stood at the core of the northern Baptists' conception of the Talented Tenth. Through the black educated elite, the degraded masses would be introduced to the values of white, middle-class Protestant America. The Talented Tenth would guide the black masses along the journey up and away from the heritage of slavery. This constituted the very goal of uplift—a goal at once progressive and conservative. Its progressive, in fact subversive, side remained obvious to southern and most northern whites, who frowned upon ideas that presumed for blacks the identical educational standards and cultural practices of middle-class whites.[18] In contrast to the elitist character of liberal arts education, industrial training appeared far less threatening to the etiquette of Jim Crow and the "race problem" in general. However, the American Baptist Home Mission Society believed just the opposite to be true. According to northern Baptists, it was the men and women of the Talented Tenth who assured race management—that is, control of the masses—and consequently the well-being of the nation.

Despite the ABHMS's liberal impulse, conservative motives—class and racial self-interest—clearly informed the northern Baptists' analysis of black higher education. In 1871, the society stated that the work of establishing schools was beneficial "not to the colored race alone, but to the white race of this land."[19] From the northern Baptists' perspective, a well-educated black vanguard constituted a buffer between white society and the black masses. It appeared axiomatic that properly trained black leaders held the key to the "peaceful solution" of the race problem. According to George Sale, the Talented Tenth was intellectually and socially broader than uneducated or half-educated demagogues who appeared more inclined to a militant and extremist position vis-à-vis white America.[20] Morehouse concurred in the effort to create what he termed the "colored American Yankee." He advocated racial equality while ever mindful of blacks' potential for violent retaliation against continued injustice. "For the sake of the land we love," he pleaded on behalf of higher education, "we must finish this work, or the problem will be, not, 'What shall we do with the negro?' but 'What will the negro do with us?'"[21]

T. J. Morgan, executive secretary of the ABHMS from 1892 to 1902, also associated a liberal arts education for blacks with national security. Like other officers of the ABHMS, he encouraged a balance between academic and industrial instruction. Yet he appealed to white self-interest in denouncing philosophies that restricted blacks to the latter. Morgan posited that only "broad intellectual culture" sharpened the senses and aroused the mind to become rational, perceptive, and analytical. More specifically, the influence of the Talented Tenth promised to temper heightened emotions and redirect anger and frustration on the part of the masses. In the event of rebellion, the Talented Tenth would serve as a critical mediating force between several million oppressed blacks and white America. Morgan warned:

> By sheer force of numbers, they can make or mar the peace and welfare of the nation. For their sake, as well as for our sakes, there ought to be among them a class of men and women who have the best opportunities for securing breadth of culture, along economic, historical, political, education, and social lines in order that they may be helpful in creating among the Negroes a wholesome public sentiment, and that they may be a restraining force to hold them in check in any time of racial disturbance or public excitement.[22]

Morgan's juxtaposition of "wholesome public sentiment" with racial "public excitement" tempers the progressive image of the society's work—capturing instead the connection between race management and its educational goals. Trained to think, act, even dissent in a rational rather than violent way, the Talented Tenth would propagate its values— ergo, the northern white Baptists'—among the masses of black people. In 1881 the ABHMS reported that, as a "general rule," it did not approve of educating large numbers of blacks in northern colleges. This position, which also suggests fear of mass black migration, reflects the important "buffer" role of the Talented Tenth itself. Whites worried that the northern setting would cause physical and emotional distance between the Talented Tenth and the black masses "for an unduly long period of time." Assuming that such a separation would create a cleavage between the educated and the uneducated, the report urged contact between college students and the common people "during all the years of their education."[23]

The Female Talented Tenth became essential to the northern Baptists' program. Indeed, it was the conscious motive of self-preservation that led them to describe their earlier all-male policy of education as "short sighted and suicidal." In 1891 Malcolm MacVicar, superintendent of the board of education for the ABHMS, emphasized the role of the Female Talented Tenth over that of ministerial students. Arguing that women played the more direct and pervasive role in spreading "correct" values throughout black communities, he consequently urged the establishment of missionary departments in at least four of the largest black colleges. These departments were to train women to work in schools, in churches, and through house-to-house visitation.[24]

The northern Baptists envisioned their colleges as assimilating apparatuses that would render the black elite "thoroughly homogeneous" with white middle-class culture. Herein lay the dialectic between the conservative and progressive implications of their educational philosophy. When they compared their southern schools to the University of Chicago or to Vassar and Wellesley, as they often did, they signaled a progressive challenge to both racism and sexism and thereby encouraged their male and female students to take pride in their intellectual capabilities. For example, Hartshorn maintained noble aspirations for its students, stating that it did not prepare young women to be servants. In 1898 Lyman Tefft, president of Hartshorn, raised the possibility of eventually broadening the school's teacher training focus to include a women's medical school.[25]

T. J. Morgan addressed the Talented Tenth's female constituency in egalitarian fashion. He believed that women's education ought to be as thorough and as rigorous as men's, and that higher education developed greater abilities and aspirations in women, affirming women's equal footing within humankind. Morgan deemed black women no less capable of high intellectual and cultural attainment than white men, black men, or white women. He insisted upon equality of instruction and standards identical to those of such white women's colleges as Mount Holyoke, Vassar, and Wellesley, and such coeducational universities as the University of Chicago and the University of Michigan. Higher education, Morgan projected, would permit future generations of black women to enjoy unfettered development of their abilities, for it strengthened the black woman's analytical skills, refined her tastes and sensibilities, and cultivated within her an appreciation for art and music.[26]

His perception of an educated black womanhood did not question women's domestic roles. On the contrary, Morgan stressed domestic duties—arguing that properly trained black homemakers were essential to racial uplift. Higher education prepared even the poorest to maintain orderly, intelligent homes. It prepared them to teach their children to read, appreciate knowledge, and develop self-discipline and lofty ideals. Yet higher education also equipped black women to earn a living—an especially important function since, as Morgan noted, economic necessity forced large numbers of them to work. Venturing an optimistic prediction of widening employment opportunities, he contended that college training would prepare black women to keep pace with changes in the upcoming decades.[27]

The concept of the Talented Tenth was rife with northeastern chauvinism. Members of the ABHMS hailed the great institutions of learning in the Northeast and considered them models for emulation. Baptist missionary educators presumed the superiority of the North's public school system, endowments, colleges, theological seminaries, and technical schools. Since they defined northeastern culture as the correct standard for all Americans, they identified the northern liberal arts colleges as the source of America's cultural and intellectual progress. In the eyes of the ABHMS, a curriculum that trained men and women simply to earn a living could not produce greatness and, more important, could not produce men and women steeped in the reigning values of white America. The society stipulated an identical standard for black and white schools—identical textbooks, teachers' qualifications, courses of study, discipline, buildings, libraries, and furniture. In 1900 Morgan asserted that northern philanthropy must assume the responsibility for instituting the most modern instructional techniques in black Baptist schools, so that these schools might replicate the finest white institutions.[28] The white Baptists' efforts to replicate their own ideals in black colleges were based on the belief that intellectual development was as critical to black progress as it was to white.[29] Although segregated, they reasoned, blacks would be taught to mirror whites in their behavior, values, and modes of work.

Nor did northern Baptist educators distinguish between black and white women when integrating lessons of refinement and other "lady-like" proprieties into the liberal arts curriculum. Their concern for black women's higher education, in the form of women's schools and coeducational colleges, closely paralleled the history of white women's collegiate training. For example, Vassar's founding in 1865 marked the emergence of an explicit policy of providing women with the same types of college courses that were available to men; yet the development of refinement and grace loomed as significantly in the college's objectives as scholarly accomplishment.[30] Black women's higher education stressed the same goals. This is significant when one considers white public opinion toward black women at the time. Jacqueline Jones vividly exposes the ridicule and hostility directed at southern black families when wives and mothers attempted to attend to their own households in the years following the Civil War. In contrast to the domestic ideal for white women of all classes, the larger society deemed it "unnatural," in fact an "evil," for black married women "to play the lady."[31]

Despite the much lower income level of their students, black schools preached the gospel of manners and morals and charged women with the special mission of promoting clean and cultured homes. In 1886 the white teacher Belle Pettigrew of Shaw University in Raleigh typified this philosophy when she stated: "I want my girls to feel that it is possible, while engaged in daily toil and in poverty even, to exalt home life into a thing of beauty." A letter from E. B. Battey to the *Two Republics*, a daily newspaper published in Mexico City, praised Spelman women for exhibiting table manners no different from those of Vassar and Wellesley women.[32]

Most important, the transformation of ex-slaves into "black Yankees" or "Anglo Africans" entailed the education of the "head, heart, and hand." The trilogy framed the context of the northern Baptists' pedagogy. For the white northern Baptists, moral training took precedence over everything else; it gave meaning to education as a civilizing and acculturating process. Officials of the ABHMS termed thorough instruction "Christian education."[33] They argued that slavery had deprived blacks of positive role models and reiterated time and again the need for self-control and moral discipline.[34] Annual reports for each of the Home Mission schools listed the number of religious conversions as proudly as they noted the intellectual and professional achievements of their students.

All the schools of higher learning incorporated industrial education in greater or lesser degree. It was considered necessary for teaching the dignity of labor, but it was also integral to the schools' boarding system. Without adequate staffing, endowments, or sufficient revenue from tuition, Home Mission schools found manual labor, while under the pedagogic rubric of "industrial training," to be a necessary expedient for daily cleaning, cooking, and campus upkeep. "Education of the head, heart, and hand" became the favorite cliché for all sides: industrial school and liberal arts devotees, whites and blacks, men and women. When extolling the virtues of liberal arts over industrial education, advocates of the Talented Tenth rarely indicated an either-or position, in the strictest sense, but rather an emphasis within a three-sided focus.

The Spelman Model

Among the ranks of white Baptists, the strongest support for black women's higher education came from women themselves. In 1880 the then three-year-old Woman's American Baptist Home Mission Society, based in New England, narrowed its general purpose of evangelization to the education of women among the freedpeople, immigrants, Indians, and settlers on the western frontier. The New England women's most lasting accomplishment, and the effort to which they attached their greatest pride, was the establishment of Atlanta Female Baptist Seminary in 1881, renamed Spelman Seminary in 1884. From its humble beginnings more than a century ago, Spelman has represented the epitome of black women's collegiate education. On 11 April 1881, when the school opened in the basement of Friendship Baptist Church, it had a student body of eleven women—the majority of whom were adult. After summer vacation, the basement school reopened the following October and during the course of the school year enrolled 175 students of varying ages, including mothers and daughters. At least one-third of the first year's class consisted of women between the ages of 25 and 50. All the students required basic elementary education. The younger women attended in order to prepare themselves for a future vocation, while older women primarily sought religious instruction and the rudiments of reading and writing.[35]

For two years Friendship Baptist Church housed the school, which benefited, in turn, from the church's prominent place in the black Atlanta community. According to the historian Howard Rabinowitz, Friendship had a membership of 1,500 people in 1882—growing to 2,500 within the next decade.[36] With rudimentary support, the teachers and growing student body had to improvise an educational setting. Lacking blackboards, students added and subtracted on the floor. Three recitation classes were heard at once in opposite corners of the basement, while a fourth enjoyed greater privacy in the coal bin. The early conditions were "not inviting," reminisced Henry Morehouse a decade later. According to Morehouse the basement was "dark, damp, so full of smoke at times that a visitor declared it was difficult to tell, across the room, who were white and who were black."[37] And yet the students continued to flock to the basement seminary in growing numbers. In 1883 the school moved out of Friendship Baptist Church and acquired property befitting its expanding faculty and student body. Its educational goals were officially stated at this time: "To train the intellect, to store the mind with useful knowledge, to induce habits of industry and a desire for general information, to inspire a love for the true and the beautiful, to prepare the pupils for practical duties of life."[38]

Strengthened enormously by the largesse of the Rockefeller family in 1884, the school adopted the maiden name of Laura Spelman Rockefeller, wife of the oil mogul John D. Rockefeller. Spelman Seminary, named for Laura Rockefeller's abolitionist family, continued to receive repeated Rockefeller gifts and witnessed dramatic growth after the initiation of its boarding system. As early as 1885 Spelman boasted 250 boarding students and a total enrollment of 645. The great demand for the seminary led to overcrowded conditions. The report for 1886 noted that six to seven young women were packed into a single dormitory room, with as many as three in a bed.[39] The seminary's student population varied from teenage women to those in their fifties. The students reflected diverse socioeconomic backgrounds as well: some were described as coming from crude log cabins, others from houses with modern comforts.[40] Throughout the 1880s and much of the 1890s Spelman functioned as an elementary and secondary school rather than a college. The racist denial of public school facilities to the great majority of Georgia blacks retarded the appearance of Spelman's collegiate curriculum. Indeed, black Atlantans remained without a public high school until 1924.[41] Throughout the latter decades of the nineteenth century, private schools, sponsored mostly by churches and taught by students and graduates of the missionary-founded colleges, were largely responsible for upgrading the level of students entering Spelman and elsewhere. In 1887 the seminary awarded diplomas to the first class to complete the higher normal courses (academic work equivalent to high school instruction).

Spelman introduced Latin and college preparatory classes into its curriculum in 1894. By the mid-1890s women entered the school with stronger academic backgrounds. In 1891 only one in seventy students came prepared to take courses at the high school level; by 1895 one in nine enrolled at that level. In 1901 Spelman conferred its first baccalaureate degree.[42] Moreover, the socioeconomic status of entering students appeared to rise over time. According to information for 1905, among the 300 women coming from outside the Atlanta area and boarding on the Spelman campus, 70.5 percent came from families who owned their homes, 10.5 percent from families in the process of buying their homes, and 19 percent from families who were renting. Atlanta residents who commuted to Spelman for day classes were less affluent: only 43 percent of these students' families owned homes, 10 percent were buying, and 47 percent rented.[43]

At Spelman, as at the other Baptist schools, industrial training constituted an important but not preponderant aspect of the curriculum. Industrial training was viewed as enhancing, not diminishing, the school's overall academic direction. Founders Sophia Packard and Harriet Giles believed that the legacy of slavery left blacks indolent and in need of proper work habits, and they insisted that an academic education without an internalization of the Protestant work ethic proved more harmful than beneficial. Under the title "domestic training," the industrial component, begun in 1883, offered practical lessons in sewing and dressmaking, housekeeping, laundry work, chamber work, and cooking. The school catalog for 1883 indicated that domestic training taught each student "to preside intelligently over her own household, or to do good service in any family."[44] In 1885 Spelman installed a laundry large enough to accommodate eighty students at one time. Packard described it as one of the largest in the country. In the same year Spelman received a printing press through the auspices of the Slater Fund. Students learned the technique of typesetting in printing classes, which served the school in the publication of its own catalogs, programs, holiday cards, and its newspaper, the *Spelman Messenger*.[45]

Spelman began its nurse training program in 1886. It was organized by Dr. Sophia Jones, a black woman and graduate of the University of Michigan medical school. Nurse training required two years of physiology and the theory of nursing, in addition to English courses. In the third and final year, student nurses donned uniforms and devoted themselves entirely to the practical side of the profession by administering to the sick in the school ward and in the larger urban community.[46]

The Atlanta school for women provided its students with heavy doses of religious instruction. Packard and Giles considered the religious component so important that they dismissed the benefits of higher education if devoid of missionary spirit. Committed to the belief that religion must inform and direct secular training, both industrial and academic, Spelman's founders integrated religious training into the overall curriculum. Spelman adopted as its motto, "Our whole school for Christ," and consistently reported a larger number of religious conversions than any of the other Baptist schools.[47] Spelman students proselytized outside the seminary as they visited homes, distributed tracts, organized temperance bands, and taught in Sunday schools.

Similar to other northern white missionaries in the South, Spelman's founders voiced concern over the expressive character of black religion. They spoke of their work as if they had embarked upon a foreign mission field, and frequently referred to the "heathenism" in both Atlanta and Africa. They strove to rid black worship of emotionalism. Viewing the homes of their students as a retrogressive and debasing influence, Packard and Giles argued for the necessity of boarding school facilities. They sought to surround their students with refined manners, "correct" Baptist doctrine, and "proper" religious and social deportment. In 1883 Packard expressed her satisfaction with Spelman's accomplishment: "There is no excitement, which is very remarkable among this emotional people, but there is a steady, quiet work of grace."[48] On campus, students gathered in social purity meetings, Christian endeavor societies, converts' meetings, and the Young Women's Christian Association with its missionary and temperance bands. On a daily basis, students were required to attend devotional exercises as well as a class in the systematic study of the Bible. Lucy Upton, a teacher at Spelman and the third principal after the death of Harriet Giles, described Sunday as the "best day of the week." At 8:30 a.m. the students gathered for chapel devotions, after which the older girls went into the Atlanta community to teach in various Sunday schools. At 11:00 students had a choice between silently reading the Bible or meeting in religious organizations. In the afternoon they attended Sunday school, which was followed by the preaching service. On Sunday evening the women held missionary and prayer meetings.[49]

Heeding the call of the ABHMS superintendent of education, Malcolm MacVicar, for formal missionary training, Spelman founded a separate missionary training department in 1891. In 1894 the WABHMS appointed Emma De Lamotta, a former Spelman student, field superintendent. A two-year course of study with five months of field work experience, the missionary training program graduated seven women at the completion of its first two-year period. Missionary training commenced after the student had mastered the academic department. The program endeavored to train women to live among their people in the most destitute areas of the South. They were to impart to poor and uneducated blacks knowledge of the Bible, personal hygiene, temperance, family and household duties, and habits of punctuality, thrift, and hard work. Working in Alabama, Tennessee, and Georgia, the trained missionaries spread the Spelman message through a variety of activities: addressing churches; organizing Sunday schools and sewing classes; distributing clothing, Bibles, and hymnals; and assisting ministers and teachers.[50]

Teacher training formed the core of Spelman's academic work. Yet its goals were hardly secular, since students were taught to function in the dual capacity of teacher and missionary. As far as the WABHMS was concerned, the two roles were inseparable. As early as 1883 students learned the rudiments of teaching methods in the school's normal department. In that year Spelman established a Model School in which elementary school children were taught by student teachers under the supervision of the faculty. Practice teaching was required of the students, and graduates of the teacher training component affirmed the proficiency of Spelman's program as they opened their own schools throughout the South. The school's annual report in 1883 to the Woman's American Baptist Home Mission Society, the New England–based sister organization of the ABHMS, recorded that 200 women were preparing for careers in teaching. Referring to the increasingly rigorous examination for Georgia teachers' licenses, Giles noted in 1889 that the higher standards prompted more women to seek thorough training before establishing their own schools, or before prematurely embarking upon the teaching profession.[51]

Harriet Giles's leadership (1891–1909) introduced Spelman students to the most current teaching methods in the country. In 1893 Elizabeth V. Griffin, a graduate of Potsdam Normal School, reorganized the normal practice school at Spelman, and under her supervision student teachers received instruction in the latest teaching techniques. Spelman's new normal training school patterned its curriculum on the model of the Normal School at Oswego, New York—a forerunner in shaping normal school methods at the turn of the century. In 1895 Spelman reported that the corps of instructors in the teacher training department were graduates of colleges and normal schools in New York, Pennsylvania, Massachusetts, and Maine.

Spelman's new curriculum included the theory of teaching along with daily practice teaching under the scrutinizing eye of experienced teachers. Teacher training programs such as Spelman's led the northern Unitarian minister and educational reformer Amory Dwight Mayo to write of southern women's education in the early 1890s: "Until recently there has been more valuable instruction in pedagogies in the superior schools for the colored than for the white race in the South." Henry Morehouse, too, described the program as a modern departure from methods in the South and, in fact, superior to the teacher training programs of white southern schools. At a time when few whites actually held teaching licenses, a Spelman graduate in 1894 became the first black person in twenty years to receive a first grade license from her county commission in Georgia. In 1902 G. R. Glenn, the state school commissioner, commended the exacting standards of Spelman and noted that its graduates would be the race leaders and teachers of the future.[52]

Spelman students in the higher normal courses devoted their summers to teaching throughout rural Georgia and other parts of the
South. Between 150 and 200 Spelman women taught each year during
their four-month summer vacation. Since the teachers averaged forty
pupils per class, Spelman boasted that it "spread out her wings to brood
over at least six thousand children" during the summer season.[53] Often
the schools established by the student teachers were the first in a
particular location, and for many parts of Georgia these schools would
be the only educational opportunity for blacks during the year. A few
even captured the attention of the local press, as in the case of Carrie
Walls's summer school in Hunter's Chapel. Walls was featured in the
Gazette after a visit by James Clark, a wealthy white man living in the
area. Clark, who described himself as a "friend of the race," dropped
in on examination day and marveled at Walls's studious and obedient
class: "The recitations, the singing, the speaking, reading, spelling,
arithmetic and all else were well nigh perfect." He was especially
intrigued with the students' harmonious rendition of the multiplica-
tion tables.[54]

In most instances, however, Spelman students conducted their summer schools with little public acknowledgment of their hard work and
sacrifice. Letters of student teachers described long working hours
under difficult conditions. They taught in makeshift schools, log cabins
with pine boards for chairs. The young teachers reported that they
walked miles to their schools—opening them at 8:00 A.M. and closing
at 5:00 P.M. The students taught regular school on a daily basis and
Sabbath school on weekends. Since children were needed on farms,
the Sabbath school usually served the largest number of people of all
ages. It was not uncommon for them to average over 100 students. In
the Sabbath school pupils learned religious lessons and also reading,
writing, and the "Yankee" values of hard work, thrift, punctuality,
refinement, and discipline.[55] Nora Gordon, who would later become a
missionary to Africa, spent the summer of 1885 in Appling, Georgia.
Gordon's was the first school for blacks in the area. Her weekday school
held thirty "scholars," but her Sabbath school held fifty-five. In the
following summer Gordon went to Long Cave, Georgia, where she
enjoyed admittedly her most pleasant and successful experience. Her
day school comprised 126 students. For two months, she also conducted women's prayer meetings at the local church.

All of the student teachers attempted to impose upon the rural folk the values learned at Spelman. They taught from the literature supplied by the northern Baptist women—using the same lesson cards and other guides given to them at Spelman. The Spelman women strove to change cultural patterns in communities where they established schools. Nora Gordon noted her success in stopping the use of tobacco among her people. Rosella Humphrey's backwoods school organized the community against its former Sunday habit of card-playing and ball-playing.[56] Emma De Lamotta, graduate of the Spelman missionary department, was typical of others when she linked racial self-help with her campaign against drinking, gambling, and chewing tobacco. Between May and August 1890 she visited 1,050 homes—going from house to house, reading the Bible, handing out literature, praying with families, and instructing on proper behavior. She spoke candidly about everything, from snuff-dipping to hair-combing. Not least was her insistence upon respect for black womanhood. At a three-day conference of black Baptists in the northern part of Georgia, she admonished her audience: "We shall never be a people until our men respect our women and girls."[57]

It was not uncommon for the Spelman women to meet with resistance, however. Some blacks rejected their Victorian ideals and viewed their "assimilationist" goals as divisive in families and communities. Student teacher Gertrude Murray spoke of her difficulty in banning the use of snuff and tobacco. Emma De Lamotta visited a black community in the quarries of Georgia where the residents had never had a Sabbath school and were opposed to education. "They say we have a factory at Spelman," De Lamotta wrote to Packard, "where we make girls work." After talking to a crowd for about an hour on the subject of temperance, a missionary in South Carolina attested to the difficulty of converting her listeners. "None of them considered themselves drunkards," she bemoaned, "for they never drank enough to lay them in the gutter, or at least not very often and a moderate drinker is, in their minds, a long way from a drunkard." During vacation from school, students often met resistance from their own family members when they returned home and endeavored to alter long-established patterns. A missionary reported that the students were called "big-headed" or "too fine" because of their tireless efforts to sway parents from smoking and drinking.[58]

Undaunted, college-bred black women were convinced of their critical position of leadership. They envisioned themselves to be spiritual and intellectual beacons to their people. Spelman student Rosella Humphrey articulated this sentiment, while reminding her sisters of their collective importance as both leaders and symbols: "You are the best of our race. You form a great chain; and if one of you falls, you disgrace the whole."[59] From the point of view of the Woman's American Baptist Home Mission Society, Spelman thus fulfilled the meaning of the Female Talented Tenth.[60] The New England Baptist women and their agents in Atlanta argued that by educating the few, Spelman reached countless black people indirectly, since its students and graduates wielded influence over their people in ways impossible to either white women or black men. A survey of Spelman alumnae, conducted in 1906, confirmed the wisdom of their argument: 87 percent of all graduates had engaged in teaching since leaving college; 41 percent were actively teaching at the time of the survey; 17 percent were homemakers; 7 percent were continuing their studies. Of Spelman alumnae, 58 were teachers in ABHMS-aided schools, 40 were public school teachers in Atlanta, and 6 were missionaries in Africa.[61]

Spelman co-founder and principal Harriet Giles explicitly advocated the concept of the Talented Tenth as part of the school's educational philosophy. Giles viewed Spelman's laudatory history as prophetic of its evolution into a great "university where every facility may be found for the thorough training of colored women who may become wise and God-fearing leaders, the 'Talented Tenth,' as Dr. Morehouse so fittingly styles them, bearing comparison with their sisters of the more favored race."[62] She concluded that if the broadest culture and intellect were necessary for white women, then they were even more necessary for blacks, whose slave forebears had been denied an education.

At the twentieth anniversary of Spelman Seminary, T. J. Morgan hailed the school for being an expression of patriotism. Projecting that African Americans would approximate whites in number within the next century, he urged amicable race relations based on mutual respect and economic opportunity. Without respect and opportunity, Morgan forewarned, the black masses would be led to desperation. Thus Spelman became a significant national force to the ABHMS because it sought to mitigate racial friction. Henry Morehouse praised the seminary's first twenty years from a similar perspective. He proudly

observed that Spelman had sent more than 5,000 young women out
of its halls as contributors to the public welfare. For Morehouse,
Spelman's value rested not merely in intellectual training, but in
teaching discipline and specifically "respect for authority, proper regard
for the rights of others, correct deportment, self-control, habits of
application to given tasks and the harnessing of life's energies to noble
and useful ends." Fearful of inevitable danger if such discipline were
not taught, Morehouse praised Spelman for creating leaders able to
mold the masses of former slaves into a productive and stable working
class.

The text of Morehouse's speech captures the liberal-conservative
dialectic that informed the northern Baptists' conception of the Talented Tenth. The Talented Tenth undermined the validity of racial
caste, while it simultaneously functioned as a "conserving influence"
with regard to the unskilled masses. Black women, especially as teachers and missionaries, facilitated class stability within the South, just as
educators in northern public schools integrated and assimilated immigrants into the northern industrial order. "For the same reason that
the North gives its disciplinary education to the children of these
swarming millions from other lands," Morehouse asserted, "the South
should give a similar education to the increasing swarms of children
of the Negro race already numbering nearly nine millions, and certain
to number fifteen millions a generation hence, when the menace will
be greater than now, unless the remedy is at once applied."[63] The
Talented Tenth, particularly its female component, was perceived as
the remedy.

Teachers and Preachers

If the dawning of the twentieth century confirmed the northern
Baptists' goal to advance women's higher education alongside men's,
the new century also confirmed that 1 percent, not 10 percent, of black
working women entered professional service. Only 1 percent enjoyed
a middle-class status distinguishable from the economic and social
status of female agricultural laborers and domestic servants—the vast
majority of employed black women. And this was true for blacks as a
whole. One percent fell under the category "professional service" in
1910; and thus despite a large numerical increase, the relative propor-

tion of professional to all working blacks remained the same as in 1890.[64] This 1 percent represented the unbridgeable chasm between the ideal of the Talented Tenth and the harsh realities of job discrimination and the lack of black public schools in the South. Clearly the Talented Tenth as a proportion of the work force existed only in theory. White Baptist educators and blacks themselves nonetheless hailed the professional advancement of thousands as extraordinary progress for a people only one generation removed from slavery. They attributed this advancement to the benefit of higher education.

The progressive role of education affected women's placement within the black middle class. Although the Talented Tenth in reality hardly rose above 1 percent for the entire time between 1890 and 1910, the proportion of professional black women to men changed dramatically. During these two decades the number of black women engaged in professional service rose by 219 percent, while their male cohorts rose by 51 percent. The number of all black women workers grew dramatically—by 107 percent—during this period, but the number of black professional women grew at twice this rate.[65] The growth testified to the increasingly visible presence of the Female Talented Tenth. In 1890 women constituted merely 26 percent of all black professionals, whereas by 1910 they stood at a prominent 43 percent. This growth was overwhelmingly attributable to the rise in the number of women teachers.

As teaching assumed a feminine identity at the start of the twentieth century, higher education tended to widen the division of labor between black professional men and women. The dual priority of training men for the ministry and women for teaching revealed unmistakable trends. Preachers and teachers dominated the ranks of the black middle class. According to census figures, the number of ministers increased from 12,159 in 1890 to 17,996 in 1910, while teachers increased from 15,100 in 1890 to 29,772 in 1910—thus constituting 27 percent and 44.9 percent, respectively, of all black workers falling under the category "professional service" in 1910.[66] In 1900, 86.7 percent of all black women in professional employment were teachers, in contrast to only 24.4 percent of all professional black men.

Higher education steered greater numbers of black men into other professional fields between 1890 and 1910. Male-dominated professions such as medicine and particularly the ministry witnessed increases as men abandoned teaching. Although the black teaching force nearly doubled, growing faster than any other category including the ministry, male teachers declined in absolute number. Out of a total of 15,100 black teachers in 1890, male and female teachers were rather evenly represented, with 7,236 men and 7,864 women. By 1910 the number of black teachers had risen to 29,772, of which 22,547 were women and only 7,225 were men.[67]

In the field of teaching, black women found respectable, relatively well-paying employment despite a job market that generally denied equal access to blacks and to women. Jacqueline Jones argues that teaching carried with it an implicit form of "social and political activism," since its goal of endowing blacks with literacy and other skills for social advancement defied the racial caste intentions of the New South order. Black women teachers, motivated by racial consciousness and commitment to their local communities, served as a counterweight to crude school facilities, the poverty of their students, the shortened school year, and white hostility. They labored under harsh conditions, not least of which was an inequitable pay scale. Their teaching salaries averaged less than half of those of white male teachers, and less than those of white women and black men as well. For some black women teachers, the end of the school term marked not vacation, but employment as laundresses and seamstresses in order to make ends meet.[68]

Teaching proved by far the most viable professional option for educated black women, but this was true for educated women regardless of race. For white women, normal schools and colleges such as Vassar reinforced the demand for qualified teachers in the nation's public schools. At the turn of the twentieth century, women constituted 74.4 percent of the 327,206 teachers in schools and colleges in the United States.[69] An increasingly female teaching force influenced the American Baptist Home Mission Society's preconceptions about the Talented Tenth. Moreover, the society's New England representation and bias reinforced this direction. In 1900 women constituted 85.1 percent of all teachers in New England.[70]

Class and Culture

As educated black women took places of leadership beside black men, their number augmented the ranks of the black middle class and heightened growing cultural differences within African American society. The Civil War and emancipation initially set cultural tensions in motion when northern missionary educators introduced the former slaves to new and alternate values, namely those of the dominant American society. Self-consciously as well as subconsciously, many blacks increasingly linked the new values with upward mobility and the old with backwardness. Unquestioned assumptions and values within the slaves' cultural world collided fiercely with the new standards, promoted by Yankee missionaries, black schools, and churches. In the late nineteenth and early twentieth centuries, black male and female leaders taught that individual advancement, as well as the advancement of the entire black community, demanded a lifestyle that stood at odds with many of the older cultural practices.[71] Gaining respect, even justice, from white America required changes in religious beliefs, speech patterns, and manners and morals.

During the last three decades of the nineteenth century, the Home Mission schools had trained men and women to become cognizant of cultural bifurcation within the black church itself. The men and women of the Talented Tenth acknowledged that one cultural form, which they themselves represented, embraced educated ministers and laypersons who sought to employ intellect and skill on behalf of the race. The second, represented by the illiterate masses, consisted of "crude and undeveloped" believers who adhered to emotionalism and "superstition" and exhibited no knowledge or interest in temperance, education, and Victorian morality.[72] Attempting to win over the masses, the educated black Baptist ministry and laity distinguished their goals and their message of salvation from those of the untrained ministry. Howard Rabinowitz observed that the shift from the illiterate "old time preacher" to the college-trained minister was particularly notable among black Baptists because of schools founded by the ABHMS.[73]

In some instances, the "old time preacher" challenged the rising influence of trained ministers and women teachers. For example, the popular former slave preacher John Jasper rose to national fame in 1878 with his sermon "The Sun Do Move." In 1887 Jasper boasted a Baptist congregation of some 2,000 people, although "'higher-class' Negroes . . . felt that his efforts actually lowered the dignity of the race and confirmed white charges of black ignorance."[74] In rural areas and even in such cities as Memphis, the untrained ministry rejected the black elite's emphasis on higher education and bitterly opposed women's organizational work.[75] By conforming to the Baptist doctrine taught in the schools of higher learning, educated ministers and women teachers and missionaries adhered to the same beliefs of most white Baptists and rejected conjuring, belief in ghosts, voodoo, and practices of "superstition" that carried over from slave religion. The educated ministry and laity in the late nineteenth century commonly encouraged a less demonstrative worship style than the "shout," bodily movement, or moaning and clapping prevalent among the folk.[76]

The Talented Tenth sought to subvert the power of illiterate leaders by privileging the written word: the Bible itself and other published writings. College-trained men and women participated in this endeavor. The Reverend Sutton Griggs, a graduate of the ABHMS's Virginia Union University and a novelist, typified those who stressed print discourse—thus implicitly devaluing the interpretive authority of illiterate leaders. Griggs argued that published writings, not direct personal appeals, had the power to reach and influence countless people throughout the nation. He equated the spiritual and intellectual advancement of blacks as a group with the expansion of a reading public, and he maintained further that "to succeed as a race, we must move up out of the age of the voice."[77] The Female Talented Tenth was no less committed to a community of readership. College-bred women, like their male counterparts, interpreted scripture, contributed to and published newspapers, and promoted tract literature among the masses.

Indeed the educated ministry and laity established access to correct doctrine through literacy and rational discourse. They upheld the legitimacy of their leadership and authority in theological interpretation through preaching, teaching, and writing. An anthology of essays entitled *The Negro Baptist Pulpit* (1890) represented this very effort on the part of educated black Baptist men and women to establish a written record, a discursive legitimation of their leadership and views. The black minister and university educator Edward M. Brawley edited the anthology, which was published by the ABHMS. In the book's preface, Brawley captured the importance of writing and publication to the Talented Tenth: "Much has been done by the living voice to train and lead the people, but the time has come when the pen must also be employed. Our trained leaders must write." He also distinguished the emotional style of preaching that predominated before the Civil War from that of the new wave of educated leaders, criticizing the former style as being "more sound than sense."[78]

The Female Talented Tenth played a decisive role in linking literacy to the dissemination of middle-class values and religious proselytization. Women worked extensively throughout black communities and directly with poor and uneducated households. Students at Hartshorn College became an influential force in Richmond after organizing the society "Home Workers." The Hartshorn women went from house to house throughout the city's black neighborhoods, teaching literacy through religious lessons and distributing second-hand clothing to needy families.[79] The students, like their sisters in the other Home Mission schools, led "industrial schools," which taught a variety of skills to black women and children of all ages. These schools sprang up throughout the South in churches and private homes. Sewing classes were those most often conducted. The industrial schools afforded the poor an opportunity to clothe themselves and their families, while gathered in a setting that promoted fellowship, self-help, and intellectual development. In 1888 Hartshorn students led an industrial school of older women who met each Friday to sew and learn "Bible-reading" and physiology. Poor blacks in Richmond offered their alley dwellings to the students, and in one such "alley" school Hartshorn women taught sixty-three boys and girls, ranging in age from four to fourteen. During 1889 the Hartshorn women taught the youngsters sewing, reading, and the cause of temperance.[80]

Without doubt, the Talented Tenth reproduced and disseminated the reigning values of middle-class Protestant America, but it nevertheless expressed a race consciousness that united black men and women in a struggle for racial dignity and self-determination. While whites referred to the nation's safety when calling for black collegiate education, black leaders spoke about the importance of higher education to race survival and empowerment. A white missionary alluded to this spirit: "Yet in almost every community are some [blacks] who have had a taste of higher education than that afforded by the common school, and who have a righteous discontent with the old order of things."[81]

The men and women of the Talented Tenth took seriously the liberal impulse of the white northern Baptists, and set out to undermine attitudes and practices of paternalism and racism on the part of the white South and on the part of the American Baptist Home Mission Society as well. Black Baptist leaders championed the benefits of black-owned and controlled institutions, and they established their own denominational schools and conventions. Within this larger racial agenda, the Female Talented Tenth empowered itself by establishing separate missionary and educational organizations for work they believed only women could do.

3

Separatist Leanings

It goes without saying that if we are to develop,
expand, improve, or advance, we must launch out
for ourselves, and help ourselves. . . . We must do
as others have done before us: make a way for
ourselves through the ranks of opposing forces—
peaceably, if we can, but none the less firmly. We
must fill our place in the world if we are to furnish
our true and complete parallel to its history.

Amelia E. Johnson, *National Baptist Magazine* (1899)

During the closing decades of the nineteenth century, the church
became the most influential force for collective self-help and self-determination in the black community. Since the time of slavery, the
church had provided an emotional and spiritual bulwark against individual demoralization and defeat. In the 1880s and 1890s—at a time
of disfranchisement, segregation, and rampant racial violence—the
church came increasingly to represent an ideological and social space
for articulating group needs and implementing programs for their
fulfillment. The black church constituted an arena in which poor,
racially oppressed men and women assembled, freely voiced their
opinions, and exhibited a sense of national community.

In the 1880s and 1890s men and women in the black Baptist church
discussed and debated strategies for racial advancement. They succeeded in establishing a denominational identity and voice separate
from those of either white southern Baptists or white northern Baptists. The church's leaders functioned in the conceptual sense of Antonio Gramsci's "organic intellectuals," since they identified with their
group of origin (in this case, their racial group) and, more important,
were rooted in a cultural heritage and in institutions and social relations that both defined and united them with the black masses.[1]

Through the institution of the church, male and female leaders attempted to transform the race-conscious ideas and values of the poor, unlettered, and politically powerless black masses into an assertive collective will. As the voice of that will, the leadership championed black denominational hegemony and mobilized support for its realization. While contextualized in a religious movement, their actions opened new terrain upon which to pursue broader goals of racial solidarity and empowerment.

The black Baptist convention movement formed part of an emergent black nationalism that resonated throughout the African American population and invoked feelings of racial pride and self-determination. Studies of black nationalism reveal that calls for racial solidarity and self-help have recurred throughout American history and especially during periods of declining civil rights and hence widespread black disillusionment with American "democracy."[2] This was especially true in the late nineteenth and early twentieth centuries. As race relations worsened in the post-Reconstruction years, the resurgence of racial doctrines of self-help, uplift, black pride, economic solidarity, and other forms of collective action found spokesmen as ideologically far apart as Booker T. Washington and W. E. B. Du Bois. Optimism about civil rights and political inclusion yielded to cynicism. Blacks strove as best they could to derive power from their otherwise separate and unequal status. The milieu encouraged black religious leaders, like black leaders in other walks of life, to adopt a race-conscious discourse.

The historian Wilson Moses describes the late nineteenth century as "the golden age of black nationalism" because of the proliferation of various separatist strategies. In a few instances, blacks called for repatriation to Africa, but more often they advocated the ownership of black schools, churches, and newspapers. Moses asserts that the advocacy of black-owned institutions constituted not an escape from the larger American society but "an alternative structure, a functional tradition created for the purpose of publicizing black aspirations, giving them political force, and institutionalizing them in forms that might ultimately transform American civilization."[3]

Black Baptists' activities clearly proceeded from such an orientation, but they evolved within the context of conflict with northern white Baptists. In the 1880s blacks grew to resent the American Baptist

Home Mission Society's policies and denounced what they believed to be racism and paternalism in the society's educational and publication work. Southern black colleges represented sites of intense racial contestation. Black Baptists challenged white domination of colleges and universities on the ground that the growing number of educated black leaders merited greater representation in faculty and administrative positions. When their demand for inclusion in the white-controlled schools met resistance, their cry for racial separatism heightened. Racial tensions mounted further when black Baptist state conventions established their own secondary schools and colleges. Increasingly blacks perceived themselves to be a constituency with interests opposed to those of whites.

Church doctrine and religious symbolism did not prove to be divisive issues. It was race consciousness alone that prompted black Baptists to re-define and re-present themselves differently from white Baptists. Blacks fostered an ideal of community that affirmed mutual identification and self-determination. Their sense of community approximated Benedict Anderson's discussion of nationalism,[4] where he defines nation as "an imagined political community—and imagined as both inherently limited and sovereign." In the case of black Baptists, the "imagined community" was racially bounded and its sovereignty was perceived as free of white control—hence black denominational hegemony. Across the South and the nation, black men and women of different ages and classes, and personally unknown to one another, perceived and sought to realize a common destiny distinct from that of whites. Their community was also imagined, since tensions and conflicts between black men and women coexisted alongside assumptions of a "deep, horizontal comradeship." Through statewide organizations, lectures, conferences, newspapers, and journals, black church men and women promoted the message of racial unity.[5]

The ability of the church to establish schools, newspapers, and other institutions of racial self-help has often been applauded but rarely analyzed. In portraying the church's role, historians tend to rely too heavily on the speeches and actions of outstanding ministers. Too often, "minister" functions as a metonym for church and as the embodiment of the church's public identity and influence. Such an interpretation fails to capture the collective character of the black church. Focusing on the church as a social space of male and female interaction, on the other hand, illuminates the process by which the church came to wield broad influence in the black community, for it offers clearer insight into how church-founded institutions, particularly schools, were established and supported. Women's missionary and financial efforts were decisive to the success of the black Baptist church in rallying the impoverished masses for the staggering task of building and sustaining institutions independent of white control. One cannot overstate the importance of black women in shaping a public opinion conducive to racial self-help. Such a focus reveals racial solidarity and racial self-determination; it also reveals gender conflict and women's assertions of female solidarity and gender self-determination. The process of discursive interaction between church men and women discloses what Nancy Fraser terms in another context "intrapublic relations," or an interaction "governed by protocols of style and decorum that were themselves correlates and markers of status inequality."[6]

The black Baptist women's quest for equality proved at once their distinct yet integral relationship to the larger racial struggle. Rising gender consciousness formed part and parcel of a complex of ideas that informed black Baptist denominational work as a whole. For women, these ideas reflected the paradox of opposition to male domination and at the same time cooperation with ministerial-led conventions. They reflected as well the paradox of desiring autonomy from white control while at the same time collaborating with white Baptist women. Instead of diminishing racial solidarity, the rising gender consciousness of black women made possible the effective drive toward a national black Baptist community. The evolution of the women's movement in the black Baptist church during the late nineteenth century represented an amalgam of separatist leanings inspired by the nexus of race and gender consciousness.

The Struggle over Schools

During the 1870s and 1880s tensions rose to fever pitch over hiring policy at the American Baptist Home Mission Society's schools. The reluctance of the ABHMS to hire black faculty and administrators served as a continual insult to growing numbers of blacks. The society, like other northern Protestant founders of schools during the post–Civil War years, expressed reluctance to hire black teachers and administrators or to entrust blacks with the responsibilities of financial management.[7] Except for Howard University, the schools established by the various Protestant denominations employed only one or two African Americans on their faculties during the early 1880s. Even Congregationalist-founded Howard refused to promote John Mercer Langston from acting president to president after the death of Oliver O. Howard. Langston's stellar reputation as an Oberlin graduate, dean of the Howard law school, and role as acting president did not convince the white founders, who refused to appoint Langston to the position despite the demand for him on the part of black trustees and the student body. Reports of northern Protestant societies often emphasized that blacks were in the childhood stage of racial development and were people of "low civilization."[8]

Similar attitudes were prevalent among northern white Baptists. The philosophy of the Talented Tenth had not caused them to practice full equality between the races. Attempting to balance the egalitarian aspects of their work with the reality of southern racism, the schools of the ABHMS learned to coexist with segregation and endeavored to win support from the white South's "better classes."[9] In a memorandum to the heads of the Home Mission schools, Henry Morehouse counseled that the schools should attempt to compromise with white and black Southerners by neither offending the prejudices of the whites, nor insulting the pride of the blacks. The racial assertiveness and self-help philosophy of the educated black leaders made the compromise difficult to attain.

African Americans waged power struggles in all of the schools established by the northern white Protestant denominations, but Baptists suffered the greatest dissension. In 1872 black ministers in Virginia demanded that the ABHMS hire black teachers at the Richmond Institute. In South Carolina Edward M. Brawley, while on the faculty at Benedict Institute, agitated vociferously for more black teachers and repudiated the school's white president, Charles Becker, for his racial chauvinism. In 1883 the ABHMS quieted the clamor at Benedict by establishing an interracial board of trustees.[10]

Racial turmoil at ABHMS-controlled Roger Williams University in Nashville in 1887 and at Bishop College in Marshall, Texas, between 1889 and 1891 led to such fiery student protests that the two school presidents were forced to resign.[11] Such events served to intensify the separatist spirit among blacks, who increasingly called for control of black institutions and for the appointment of black presidents to the Home Mission schools. Even the example of Booker T. Washington failed to persuade the ABHMS. Although Washington had studied at the Home Mission Society's Wayland Seminary in Washington, D.C. during the 1870s and had gone on to establish Tuskegee Institute and to exhibit unmatched skill in amassing philanthropic support, his example, like that of other graduates of Home Mission schools, did not bring about greater faculty and administrative appointments as much as did black protest and confrontation.[12]

Racial conflict especially disrupted work at Wayland Seminary. During the 1880s the seminary exploded in heated controversy when twenty-six black Baptist churches in the District of Columbia, Alexandria, and vicinity leveled charges against the school's white president, G. M. P. King, "for his repeated assaults upon female students and his ungentlemanly bearing toward them." In an official list of grievances against King in 1885, the convention of churches called for his resignation. Charging him with a series of incidents against women students, the black ministers claimed it their duty as men to "resent, in the most positive and unmistakable terms, everything that even looks toward our degradation in destroying manhood and womanhood rights." They chronicled years of physical abuse by King. In 1878 King lost his temper and pushed "forcibly" Anna M. Mason, a member of the school's singing troop, during a performance in Redbank, New Jersey. The same year another student, Maggie Washington, interrupted King during his lunch hour; he became incensed when she would not immediately leave his office and reportedly led her down the stairs at a very rapid rate, jerking her to the point that he injured her side.[13]

The case of Wayland student Mary E. Williams in 1882 caused the school's alumni and the black Baptist community in Washington to rise up in an uproar against King. Citing the sworn testimony of Williams, who was described as a "member of good and regular standing" in a Baptist church in Washington, the black Baptists recounted King's excessive abuse, which left her with bruises all over her body: "He seized her by the arm; jerked her loose from the balusters; forced her backward into her room; her cries filling the entire building, he closed the door; forced her down into a chair, and placed his knee in the lower part of her stomach to keep her there."[14] The convention took the case to the ABHMS, but the society, after an investigation, found no grounds for dismissal, though King was urged to apologize to the local black ministers. Twenty students left the school as a result.[15]

During the winter of 1884–1885 King again incurred the wrath of the black Baptist community because of corporal punishment against a twenty-three-year-old student, Lillie Williams. Dismayed, an increasing number of black Baptists began to believe it impossible to continue harmonious relations with the American Baptist Home Mission Society. Walter H. Brooks, pastor of the Nineteenth Street Baptist Church in Washington, reflected a growing separatist spirit among black ministers. Responding to the ABHMS's refusal to dismiss the Wayland president, Brooks proclaimed: "We, like our brethren in the African M.E. Church, must rise and build, and take management of our own schools."[16]

Racial Self-Determination

Underlying the tensions between black and white Baptists were feelings of racial self-determination, which preceded the Civil War but grew much more rapidly afterward. With emancipation from slavery the freedpeople deserted the white-controlled churches that had previously commanded their membership. Leon Litwack captures the euphoric feelings associated with the ability of the freedpeople to acquire churches and hire ministers from among their own people. No longer were blacks forced to hear sermons on obedience to white masters. An ex-slave jeered the oft-repeated message of the southern white ministers: "The Lord say, don't you niggers steal chickens from your missus. Don't you steal your marster's hawgs."[17]

Under black-controlled churches, ministers not only preached the message of human equality and the dignity of the individual, but they increasingly mobilized an offensive drive against the socioeconomic forces and attitudes contributing to their people's oppression.[18] In the 1860s and 1870s black ministers allied their churches in statewide conventions, for the purpose of harnessing traditional feelings of mutuality with new assertions of self-respect and self-determination. These assertions were implicitly if not explicitly at odds with the racist prescriptions of the white South and also with the paternalistic

attitudes and policies of northern white religious power, such as the
American Baptist Home Mission Society.

From the first days of freedom, black communities also sought to
establish and administer their own schools. In such places as Augusta
and Savannah, blacks took pride in the "secret schooling" that had
survived nearly a century of slavery.[19] During the era of Reconstruction
blacks and Yankee missionary teachers frequently stood at odds over
the freedpeople's determination to educate themselves.

Historians of black education call attention to schools established
independent of white support during the Reconstruction period. Jacqueline Jones notes that about two hundred black men and women
led schools in Georgia between 1866 and 1870.[20] In 1865 John W.
Alvord, national superintendent of schools for the Freedmen's Bureau,
acknowledged the prevalence of "native schools" in Fortress Monroe,
Savannah, Alexandria, and New Orleans prior to the arrival of missionary educators. Sabbath schools constituted another example of
independent efforts to promote black literacy during and after the
Reconstruction era. Products of the black church, these schools were
usually run by women in the evenings and on weekends and provided
instruction in both religion and reading. Sabbath schools and other
church-housed and sponsored schools continued to offer needed academic and industrial training as public schools literally lost ground
throughout the late nineteenth and early twentieth centuries.[21]

Black private schools had long provoked a dilemma for the northern
Protestants. During Reconstruction, representatives of the northern
denominations expressed mixed feelings about the initiative and
sacrifice accompanying the freedpeople's endeavors at "self-teaching."
The ideal of their benevolence had been to transform ex-slaves into
responsible citizens. Yet the realization of this ideal served to make the
white missionary's dominant role increasingly superfluous, even undesirable to men and women who equated duties of citizenship with
collective efforts of racial self-reliance.[22] By the 1880s, the Protestant
denominations sidestepped conflicts over common school education
by abdicating responsibility for mass instruction to the South's faltering
public school system. But with Reconstruction ended and white "home
rule" redeemed, public education fell into the hands of white administrators and teachers with little regard for black intellectual development. In the 1880s and 1890s southern cities witnessed challenges by

black residents who led protests and petitions for black teachers, equitable salaries, and adequate public school facilities.[23]

Private schools became imperative with the loss of black voting rights. Disfranchisement silenced the voice of the African American population concerning the allocation of funds in southern states. In 1890 the Blair Bill, which promised federal aid to public education, went down in final defeat after a protracted struggle in Congress. Thus black communities double-taxed themselves in order to support private schools. While southern education left much to be desired for whites as well, the trend for whites, rural and urban, at the turn of the century was toward reform rather than retrogression. James Anderson observes that between 1905 and 1914 white communities gained 186 new public high schools in Virginia; more than 200 in Georgia; in South Carolina and Arkansas, each in excess of 100; in Tennessee, 74; in Alabama, 60; and more than 30 in Mississippi.[24] As late as 1910 no southern black community could claim a single public school offering two years of high school. In some places, such as Augusta, black education fared worse than it had in the early 1880s.[25] It was the existence of private institutions that made black secondary education possible at all.

The Talented Tenth: Black Baptist Perspectives

Against this backdrop of conflict, schools of higher education proved an ineluctable, albeit ironic, catalyst for black Baptist separatism. The American Baptist Home Mission Society had never opposed black communities' efforts for a greater voice in elementary and secondary-level education. On the contrary, its policies facilitated this outcome by providing for the collegiate training of black schoolmarms, ministers, and educated parents throughout the rural and urban South. White Baptists such as Henry Morehouse envisioned the ABHMS's "vast expenditure" of money and effort for black higher education as a way of indirectly Americanizing the masses. The Talented Tenth was to teach them manners and morals, lessons of punctuality and thrift, and most of all a Yankee work ethic that would serve to discipline a generation of people who were considered as foreign to the dominant values of the American social order as the eastern and southern European immigrants who flooded the northern cities. Equally important to white Baptists, the black educated elite served a mediating function between a potentially uncontrollable mass and the interests of white Anglo-Saxon Protestant America.

Yet the ABHMS colleges had spawned race-conscious men and women whose commitment to self-help was informed by a collective rather than an individualistic ethos. Their acculturation notwithstanding, college-bred blacks retained the "long memory" of shared oppression and patterns of mutual support that served their forebears in slavery. In the struggle for survival and advancement, so the Talented Tenth reasoned, African Americans had initially found a strong ally in the American Baptist Home Mission Society, but the conflict over schools served as a lesson in continued racial inequality.[26] Reminders of blacks' inferior status vis-à-vis whites within the larger denomination only encouraged ideas about the unification of black Baptists into a separate and powerful force. The educated elite increasingly perceived the church as a public realm through which blacks as a people would counter social and political forces arrayed against them.

From the perspective of the Talented Tenth itself, the goal of higher education was not to produce a buffer group as much as to produce the representative and authoritative voice of the race. Reflecting upon African American needs in the face of declining political rights, the Reverend Walter H. Brooks typified this attitude on the part of black Baptist leaders: "It becomes our duty to speak out upon all questions that affect our people socially, economically, as well as religiously."[27] Continued white control of schools, publishing houses, and philanthropy failed to address black empowerment. As far as the separatists were concerned, the entire realm of white philanthropy had become little more than a euphemization for the existing racial hierarchy.

The Talented Tenth depended upon its own people for allegiance and financial support—in short, for legitimation as a leadership class. Linked inextricably to the masses by both the negative consequences of Jim Crow and positive feelings of racial pride, male and female leaders understood their individual status and well-being in American society to rest ultimately with the status and well-being of the larger black population. Black Baptist leaders sought to articulate their people's collective will through churches and denominational conventions, schools, and publishing facilities.

The quest for black denominational hegemony led to the establishment of schools of higher education by black Baptists themselves. Tensions heightened in states where the ABHMS expected black communities to strengthen already existing schools rather than divert funds into new and competing institutions. On behalf of the ABHMS, Henry Morehouse pleaded with blacks to little avail: "Let the American spirit be dominant over the race spirit."[28] The separatists were unwilling to heed this advice. An acrimonious exchange occurred in 1898–1899 over black Baptists' plans to establish Central City College in Macon, Georgia. Blacks resented their subordinate representation on the Atlanta Baptist College and Spelman trustee boards. Exasperated with limited job mobility and white control of black education in general, separatists determined to establish their own institution.

Relations were also strained by a speech made by Malcolm MacVicar to a meeting of black Baptists in 1894. MacVicar, the ABHMS superintendent of education, declared that it would take blacks a century to acquire the capability to manage their own churches and schools.[29] Likewise, the ABHMS officer T. J. Morgan offended the separatists in November 1899 by his repetitive use of the term "your people" in a published response to the Macon school's supporters. A letter from J. D. Gordon of Madison, Georgia, to the Reverend Emmanuel K. Love, a black nationalist and newspaper editor in Savannah, exemplifies the separatists' feelings. Gordon's letter to the editor rejected Morgan's argument that a black-run school would detract from existing schools: "Long live the Baptist college! Long live dear old Spelman! But if I am untrue to you simply by desiring a Baptist 'Negro College,' with all sadness of heart, I must say 'Adieu!'" Gordon stressed black role models as teachers and administrators, black ideals rather than the pejorative "your people," and exaltation of "the beauty in the black."[30]

The rivalry between black and white colleges existed in Texas and Virginia as well. Guadalupe College, founded in 1884 by the black Baptists in Texas, was a source of racial conflict for the remainder of the decade. The ABHMS had established Bishop College in Marshall, Texas, in 1881, but the black convention, desirous of educational facilities in other parts of the state, established Guadalupe College in Seguin. Controversy arose when the ABHMS refused to support more than one college per state. The society's sole support of Bishop was an affront to blacks, since they supported both schools.[31]

Virginia Baptist Theological Seminary in Lynchburg evolved out of the same spirit of racial self-determination. Organized in 1887 by the Virginia Baptist State Convention, the seminary was perceived as a counterpoint to the Home Mission Society's Virginia Union University. The sociologist St. Clair Drake, whose father had graduated from Virginia Seminary as a preacher (A.M.E.) and his mother as a teacher, contrasted Virginia Union with the black-owned seminary: "Union University was the white Baptists' gift to Negroes. Seminary was *theirs*."[32]

Building Women's State Conventions

The rising prominence of black church women and the flurry of organizational activity on their part occurred squarely within the racial struggle for denominational hegemony. However, women were not content to operate merely within the boundaries of individual churches, or silently within the larger ministerial-led state conventions. Beginning in the early 1880s and into the next decade, they struck out on a new and separate course by forging their own sphere of influence at the state level. All of the black women's state conventions promoted schools and black-controlled educational work. In Kentucky and Alabama the women's conventions organized for the purpose of supporting black Baptist-owned universities in their respective states. Arkansas women directed much of their attention to the support of Arkansas Baptist College in Little Rock—another black-owned school. In 1890 the first annual meeting of the convention of black Baptist women in Louisiana proclaimed support of education and missionary work as its twofold purpose. Missouri women led the movement to support the black Baptist–owned and controlled Western College in Macon, Missouri. In 1894 black Baptist women in West Virginia organized a missionary and educational convention. Several state organizations carried the title "educational" as part of their missionary identity: for example, the Baptist Women's Educational Convention of Kentucky; the Women's Baptist Educational and Missionary

Convention of South Carolina; and the Woman's Baptist Missionary and Educational Association of Virginia.

An examination of women's state conventions draws attention to the ways in which the black church acquired resources for the maintenance of its numerous institutions. Black Baptist women's societies generated funds at the local level. In some cases, women's fund raising served as the catalyst for securing matching funds from northern white Baptists. The examples of Kentucky and Alabama reveal the importance of women's societies to the support of black Baptist-owned colleges. Unlike the schools founded by the ABHMS, the black-controlled schools depended, in the final analysis, upon the support of their own people. For the most part, money was solicited from people who were largely without land or capital.

The first statewide convention of black Baptist women was organized in Kentucky in 1883 specifically around the issue of black higher education. Calling themselves the Baptist Women's Educational Convention of the State of Kentucky, black Baptist women marshaled their members from churches throughout the state in order to generate funds for the State University at Louisville (renamed Simmons University in 1918).[33] Despite its name, the university was not a public institution but rather a private school, owned and controlled by the black Baptists of Kentucky. As early as August 1865 black ministers led their churches into a statewide association and set the establishment of a school among their most immediate priorities. The ministers requested a monthly contribution of five cents from each member of their respective congregations; churches were further taxed according to size. Slow in starting and delayed by the transfer of its site from Frankfort to Louisville, the school, then named Kentucky Normal and Theological Institute, finally opened in 1879 with 25 students.[34] In the following year enrollment in the financially strapped school dropped to 11, but by 1890 the student body hovered at over 200.

One reason for the dynamic growth of the school during the 1880s was the school's president, the Reverend William J. Simmons. A Howard University graduate and pastor of the First Baptist Church in Lexington, Simmons was appointed to the presidency of the Louisville school in August 1880. In 1882 the school added a college department to its secondary school curriculum, and two years later officially changed its name from Normal and Theological Institute to State University at Louisville.[35] Simmons developed its curriculum along the classical liberal arts model prevalent at Howard University and the schools of the American Baptist Home Mission Society.[36]

The second reason for the school's impressive growth was the formation of a separate women's convention in 1883. At that time the ministerial-led convention, the General Association of Kentucky, had failed to raise sufficient funds to meet the school's growing debts. When this convention refused to admit women into its meetings for discussion of the university's support, the women formed a separate organization.[37] Women's societies already existed in many individual churches, and they were eager to create a statewide network. Simmons gave the women his support, providing his church for their initial meeting.

Simmons recognized the potential power of organized women. He had traveled to the annual conferences of northern white Baptists and studied the operation of the ABHMS and its auxiliary women's societies.[38] Mary V. Cook, a professor at State University at Louisville and a participant in the inception of the Kentucky women's educational convention, acknowledged Simmons's influential role in advocating a separate women's society along the model of northern Baptist women. Cook noted that he became "determined to institute such a movement among the colored women of the state of Kentucky, believing that more good could be accomplished by putting the women to work to assist the brethren in the educational enterprises they had undertaken."[39]

Presiding over the initial meeting on 18 September 1883, Simmons thereafter relinquished his authority and left the women to elect officers from among themselves and decide upon their own agenda. The constitution drafted by the Kentucky women spelled out their threefold objective: first, to encourage the attendance of youth at State University; second, to pay off the school's property debts and to build a girls' dormitory; and third, to develop missionary spirit. Women delegates representing nineteen societies attended the meeting in 1883. An educational committee, which had been established at the first meeting, urged all students at the university to make personal sacrifices for their education, to join local Baptist societies, and to contribute systematically to the liquidation of the school's debt.[40] In

1887 the executive board of the Kentucky women's convention identified the need to erect more buildings, support more teachers, and educate a greater number of young women.[41]

The Kentucky women took pride in distinguishing their university from those of the white northern Baptists. The constant struggle to maintain financial solvency was offset, as Louisville teacher Elizabeth Seeley indicated, by knowing that State University was "owned and controlled by the black Baptists, having a black president and except for one white teacher, a black faculty."[42] By 1890 the women's convention had proved itself a great success. Women met in churches and homes throughout the state and called their individual branches University Societies. The Kentucky women's convention claimed representatives from almost every black Baptist church in the state and publicized its activities, fund-raising goals, and meetings in the black Baptist–owned newspaper *American Baptist*, which was published out of Louisville.[43] Between 1883 and 1900 the women's convention contributed over $12,000 to the school. It achieved its goal of erecting a girls' dormitory—thereby permitting women students, although packed five or six to a room, to live on campus. In 1901 State University retired its floating debt largely as a result of the work of Kentucky black Baptist women and a matching contribution from the American Baptist Home Mission Society.[44]

Inspired by the Kentucky example, the Reverend Edward M. Brawley began to solicit support for the formation of an Alabama women's society that would promote the work of his school, Selma University (also known as Alabama Baptist University). A graduate of Bucknell, Brawley was the president of Selma, which was owned and supported by the black Baptists of Alabama. Brawley welcomed the role of women's church societies and encouraged their union. Meeting in the Tabernacle Baptist Church in Selma on 27 January 1886, the women launched a separate state convention.[45] Three years later they noted the importance of "preparing skilled workers in our religious organizations" and maintained that education would solve the race problem in America. The committee on education recommended that the women's convention endeavor to expand student enrollment at Selma University and, like their Kentucky sisters, introduced a motion to earmark contributions for the construction of a girls' dormitory. The Alabama women hailed the school as an example of racial self-help.[46] By 1890 the Baptist Women's State Convention represented 10,000 black women in sixty church societies.[47]

Black Baptist women in Alabama led a campaign to spread knowledge of their state convention by resolving that ministers annually designate a church service as Women's Day (also called "Sisters' Day"). In his history of the black Baptists of Alabama, the Reverend Charles Octavius Boothe recounted the public exhortations of women on this day, as they attempted to inspire church congregations to follow their own examples of giving. On Women's Day, the president of a women's mission band told her congregation that each member of her band had taxed herself a nickel monthly. A woman poultry-raiser testified that she set aside one of her hens and donated to her society all the money that was received from the sale of the hen's eggs and chickens. Another woman described the sacrificial devotion of her family when illness made it difficult to respond to her society's call for periodic contributions. Determined to meet the call, family members denied themselves sugar for a fixed amount of time.[48]

Throughout the 1880s and 1890s black Baptist women in other states fell in line with the Kentucky and Alabama examples. Organized for the support of black-owned educational institutions, black women's state conventions sprang up in Arkansas, South Carolina, Virginia, Louisiana, Mississippi, Missouri, Tennessee, Texas, and West Virginia. The leaders of the women's conventions were young—in their twenties and thirties during the 1880s and 1890s—and were educated in the schools of the American Baptist Home Mission Society and in the black-controlled schools.[49] Women leaders, typically teachers and the wives of prominent ministers, represented the black elite of their communities. In Alabama and Kentucky, officers of the women's conventions were either teachers or former students of Selma University and State University at Louisville, respectively. Within the Kentucky women's convention, three of the most vocal and prominent officers, Mary Cook, Lucy Wilmot Smith, and Mamie Steward, were on the faculty of State University. In February 1887 the university's president, William J. Simmons, described the women teachers "as strong as Hercules," and he added that they worked "like Trojans."[50]

Of the four presidents elected to office in the Alabama women's convention between 1886 and 1904, two were teachers and all were wives of outstanding ministers in the state. Eliza Pollard, a schoolteacher and also president of the Alabama women from 1894 to 1904, was one of the first graduates of Selma University. She was married to the Reverend Robert T. Pollard, a leader among Alabama Baptists and fourth president of the university.[51] Other officers of the women's conventions were married to faculty or trustees of the black-controlled universities. Lavinia Sneed of Kentucky was married to Charles Sneed, a professor at State University. In 1898 Mary Cook married the Reverend Charles H. Parrish, a teacher with her at State University and a leader of national stature among black Baptists. Mamie Steward, an influential force among Kentucky women, taught at State University and was the wife of the newspaper editor William Steward, the most powerful trustee of the school. Not a clergyman, Steward nonetheless held office in the ministerial-led state convention, the General Association of Kentucky. Mrs. Charles Dinkins, Mrs. Edward Brawley, Mrs. Charles Purce, and Mrs. A. A. Bowie, members of the board of managers of the women's state convention of Alabama, were married to ministers associated with both Selma University and the male-led state convention. Amanda Tyler, third president of the Alabama women, was married to the Reverend Manfield Tyler, chairman of Selma's board of trustees during its first twenty-seven years.[52] The social status of these women in their communities derived in part from their husbands. At the same time, by leading and broadening a network of numerous local educational support societies, the women enhanced their own prestige and also the prestige and actual power of their husbands in the denomination and the state.

The black Baptist women's conventions insisted that upward mobility for individuals and for African Americans as a group depended primarily upon education. Their fund-raising drives, children's bands, self-denial days, and even temperance crusades all reinforced this message and influenced many poor, uneducated blacks to divert money from personal consumption into the building of schools. For example, the *Baptist Woman's Era*, the monthly news organ of the Alabama women, kept Selma University before the public.[53] It presented the school's curriculum and fees, told of fund-raising activities and campus events, and solicited support from people of all ages.[54] In 1901 the *Baptist Woman's Era* editorialized: "That parent robs his own child who fails to educate him when it is in his power to do so. The most that a parent can give his child is a good education, with all that word means. This we ought to do even if we have to make a great sacrifice. Our hope as a race lies in a good Christian education."[55]

Toward a National Community

The educated ministry inaugurated the movement for national denom-inational hegemony during the 1880s, but women were certainly vocal participants and, in some cases, in positions of visible authority. In 1880 black Baptists from various states convened in Montgomery, Alabama, to form the Baptist Foreign Mission Convention for con-ducting missionary work in Africa.[56] In 1886 black Baptists from across the nation but mostly from the South met in St. Louis and launched the American National Baptist Convention. Under the presidency of William J. Simmons, this convention focused its energies on blacks in the United States and sought, in addition to the spiritual ends of the church, knowledge of one another, the writing and publication of literature by black intellectuals, and a forum for discussion of all issues of interest to their race.[57] In 1892 the National Baptist Educational Convention was founded in Savannah for facilitating the growth of black educational institutions, encouraging dialogue among black edu-cators, furnishing scholarships to students, and promoting employment for black graduates.[58]

Although women delegates attended the meetings of all three na-tional conventions, they numbered far fewer than men. Some women, nonetheless, held conspicuous positions.[59] In 1893 when the Reverend J. J. Coles died soon after his election to field secretary of the National Baptist Foreign Mission Convention, the executive board appointed his wife to fill the position until the next election a year later. Mary V. Cook, professor of Latin and philosophy at State University at Louisville, was elected recording secretary of the National Baptist Educational Convention (NBEC). At the first meeting of this conven-tion, two women, Mary Cook of Kentucky and Elizabeth A. Garland of Virginia, sat on the NBEC's executive board with twenty men.[60]

Of the three conventions, women were most prominent in the American National Baptist Convention (ANBC). They sat together on a separate women's committee and were also integrated throughout other committees. A few held office. Mary Cook was elected to the executive committee of the ANBC. In 1887 Lucy Wilmot Smith, also a professor at State University, held the position of historian of the ANBC. Amanda V. Nelson, president of the Kentucky women's state convention, served as a statistical secretary. Julia Mason, soon to be

Julia Mason Layton, of Washington, D.C. sat on the executive board of the ANBC's bureau of education. In 1888 women constituted three of the twenty members of the educational bureau. In fact, they served on all committees and delivered papers before the entire group. In 1892 Alice A. Bowie of Alabama was elected educational secretary of the ANBC.[61]

In 1895 the Baptist Foreign Mission Convention, American National Baptist Convention, and National Baptist Educational Convention merged to form the National Baptist Convention, U.S.A. (NBC).[62] The predominant mood of black Baptists had shifted steadily, though not without debate and some internal dissension, in the direction of an autonomous denominational community.[63] In 1896 Richard H. Boyd, head of the publishing board of the one-year-old convention, captured this bold, race-conscious spirit when he characterized the NBC as "simply a determination on the part of the Negroes to assume control of their race life and evolve along such lines and such ways as their spirit and genius may dictate . . . and not as the Anglo Saxon may outline."[64] Leaders such as the Reverends Elias C. Morris of Arkansas, Emmanuel K. Love of Georgia, Richard H. Boyd and Sutton Griggs of Texas, and Walter H. Brooks of Washington, D.C. welcomed the formation of the National Baptist Convention in 1895 as the fruition of black denominational hegemony. It marked the victory over those who had attempted to keep blacks subservient to whites. In 1896 E. K. Love applauded the economic and social opportunities created by the new convention, and he equated self-respect with black independence from white control:

> There is not as bright and glorious a future before a Negro in a white institution as there is for him in his own. It cannot be denied that we can better marshal our forces and develop our people in enterprises manned by us. We can more thoroughly fill our people with race pride, denominational enthusiasm and activity, by presenting to them for their support enterprises that are wholly ours.[65]

In 1900 the NBC stood at a total membership of 1,864,000. Between 1899 and 1900 black Baptists had contributed $174,418.57 for education, $35,580.95 for Sunday school expenses, $7,069.64 for foreign missions, $10,421.98 for home mission work, and $2,715,595.39 for church expenses. In 1902 black Baptists supported and contributed to eighty schools in addition to contributing to schools owned by white northern Baptists.[66] Organized black Baptist womanhood played a central role in these accomplishments. Indeed, women's support factored significantly into the movement for national denominational autonomy. As teachers, wives, students, missionary workers, and financial contributors, women shared in the impassioned racial consciousness of the late nineteenth century and helped to engineer the struggle for institutional control.

Women's voices resounded within the rising nationalist crescendo. In the *National Baptist Magazine*, the organ of the National Baptist Convention, Amelia Johnson contended that America comprised two distinct groups, blacks and whites, who "do not have the same interests nor the same pursuits; and all does not go well." Black women championed racial pride and dignity, and called upon blacks to patronize their own institutions. Spelman graduate Selena Sloan Butler wrote in the *Spelman Messenger* in 1898:

> Hang upon the walls of your homes pictures of the men and women of your own race who have given a chapter that deserves to be recorded in the history of the civilized world . . . We should appreciate everything that represents the achievement of our people, whether modern or ancient. Then, fill your libraries with books that are the product of the Negro brain. Do these things, and I prophesy that almost every child of the succeeding generation will speak with as much pride of his race and the Negro blood in his veins as does the Anglo-Saxon of his race.[67]

Some black women adopted the discourse of a strident black nationalism. For example, Amelia Johnson, novelist and wife of black separatist the Reverend Harvey Johnson of Baltimore, did not let her association with the American Baptist Publication Society mitigate against her scathing condemnation of white paternalism. Johnson had published two novels, *Clarence and Corinne* (1890) and *The Hazeley Family* (1894), with the society. Although her novels concerned issues of temperance and family life and made no reference to race, her racial identification and loyalties were clearly demarcated in black journals, such as *Joy*, a short-lived monthly women's journal edited by Johnson herself, and the *National Baptist Magazine*.[68] In 1899 Johnson captured the conflation of egalitarianism, guilt, and self-interest that character-ized the work of white northern Baptists. She mimicked and critiqued them:

"We cannot allow this host of people [blacks] to roam the country, untaught and unchecked, or our lives will not be safe. It is our fault that they are ignorant and untrained, and it is but just that we do what we can to remedy the evil we have wrought, although we cannot rub out all traces of it." And, so, they put forth efforts to help the already eager people to fit themselves for the exigen-cies of life. They founded schools to teach them to teach them-selves, and things began to look bright. . . . A strange phase of the matter is, that, while all along, the understanding has been that the colored people were, as soon as prepared, to help in the educating, uplifting and upbuilding of their own people, and to do generally for themselves what had been done for them, the white portion of the nation is inclined to refuse them the right to do this, and only allows them to work under protest.[69]

Johnson traced the rise of great nations and challenged her own people to rise similarly and to look to their own leaders for admiration and inspiration rather than "trying to prove to the world that we were born into it for the sole purpose of admiring the white people of the United States, and this is all we will ever be fit for." She urged black control of educational, financial, and religious institutions—insisting that "if our white brethren close their avenues to us because of this determination, we must create avenues for ourselves."[70]

Gender Self-Determination

While the separatist leanings of black men reflected interracial ten-sions and racial consciousness, the separatist leanings of black Baptist women reflected this and something more. The formation of black women's conventions derived also from gender consciousness, which served to reinterpret the philosophy of self-help beyond the singular discourse of race. Black women and men agreed neither upon "woman's place" in the larger racial struggle, nor upon the relations of power between themselves. In 1892 Anna J. Cooper alluded to this problem across denominations in her criticism of the black men of the Protestant Episcopal church: "While our men seem thoroughly abreast of the times on almost every other subject, when they strike the woman question they drop back into sixteenth century logic."[71] For black Baptist women, the double consciousness of race and gender led to the perception of a dual struggle.

Despite the support of outstanding individual men, black Baptist women encountered varying degrees of opposition in their early efforts to carve out their own separate space. In Kentucky, where William J. Simmons proved a powerful friend of the women's cause, they nonetheless met with hostility at the individual church level. Some women were denied the opportunity to speak publicly. "Others have been rebuked and abused," wrote Mary Cook of her Kentucky sisters' experiences, "but they held on and say they are determined to work till the last dollar [on the university] is paid." Helen Whipple, a white missionary in Charleston, observed that black women's state conventions faced opposition from some ministers and support from others.

Willis Anthony Holmes, historian of Arkansas Baptists, recounted the controversy over women's right to form separate missionary societies at the local and district level during much of the 1880s. According to Holmes, the men expressed a variety of reasons for their opposition. Some believed that a separate organization under the control of women would give them a sense of power and a desire to "rule the men." Others contended that women's financial contributions would cease to be under the men's control; others demanded male officers over women's societies, in the event they were permitted to form.[72] The women of Arkansas rebutted these arguments. They insisted that they could better accomplish the work of "religiously training the world" by uniting into their own organization. The women claimed their right to an independent voice in the church on the assumption that they were "equally responsible, in proportion to their ability, as the other sex."[73]

The self-determination of the women's state conventions sometimes translated into aggressive behavior and even protest against the actions of ministers and male-led conventions. The history of the Alabama women's convention records the positive role of men in its founding, but this male influence never deterred the Alabama women from expressing a gendered viewpoint. In 1889 an unidentified speaker presented a paper, "Woman's Part in the General Work of the State and her Relation to the State Convention," in which she complained that the male-run state convention of Alabama did not feel duty-bound to help the women's convention, although it always expected the women's assistance. Asserting first that "it is no more our duty to help them than it is theirs to help us," the speaker then enjoined the Alabama women to rise above this way of thinking and assume an unselfish posture toward the men.[74]

The work of Virginia Broughton and black Baptist women in Tennessee illustrates the curious combination of opposition from men and cooperation between women, black and white. Virginia Broughton, foremost leader of black Baptist women in Tennessee until her death in 1934, was a member of Fisk University's first graduating class. After her graduation in 1875, Broughton worked as a teacher in the public schools of Memphis.[75] It was during her years as a schoolteacher in the early 1880s that she met Joanna P. Moore, a white missionary for many years among southern blacks. Moore aroused Broughton's interest in missionary work by inviting her to a meeting exclusively for women. Having admittedly attended the meeting out of curiosity, Broughton found herself a participant in the formation of a Bible Band—a black women's society organized for the daily study of the Bible. According to Broughton, "the work began in one of our intelligent progressive churches, in which the pastor was a strong, intellectual, devout man, well prepared to encourage and defend this new feature in the church life of our people."

Within a short time the Bible Band grew immensely popular among the black women of Memphis. Joanna Moore encouraged the black women to petition the Women's Baptist Home Mission Society (WBHMS), the Midwestern women's auxiliary of the ABHMS, for a permanent mission station.[76] Heeding the request, the northern women established a station in Memphis in 1887 and soon sought Broughton's leadership skills. For several years Broughton taught school five days a week and on weekends engaged in missionary work in rural districts as much as fifty miles away from her home. As a missionary she traveled throughout the state, often on perilous journeys up the Mississippi River in leaky skiffs. She traveled in an open ox-drawn wagon and rode horseback to Cooter, Missouri, "a place where few Negro men dared to go to preach, and a woman missionary of no race had ever gone."[77]

In 1888 the trustees of black Baptist–owned Bible and Normal Institute (later Howe Institute) in Memphis commissioned Broughton and Emma King Jones to organize women into a district association in order to raise money for the school. The local societies or Bible Bands donated money and sent students to the school. However, their efforts to unite women into a separate association sparked a controversy that continued for more than a decade. In September 1888 black Baptist women from diverse parts of the state convened at the Mt. Zion Baptist Church in Stanton, Tennessee, and held their first organizational meeting. The first meeting did not address the right of women to organize separately, but rather emphasized noncontroversial issues related to women's domestic lives: simplicity, cleanliness, and neatness in dress and home furnishing; wholesome, well-prepared food; temperate use of all good things and total abstinence from tobacco and liquor; education of the head, heart, and hand; and daily study of the Bible.[78] White women missionaries warmly supported the black women's meetings, which occurred annually for the next decade. In 1891 Joanna Moore and other white women of the WBHMS attended the annual meeting in Trenton, Tennessee. In 1892 the WBHMS appointed Broughton as one of its black missionaries. Two years later Broughton called attention to the fruits of her labor: Bible Bands operated in fifty-seven places in Tennessee and conducted twenty industrial schools.

In the face of tremendous growth, the Tennessee women's movement also met with strong opposition. Broughton wrote: "Ministers and laymen, who looked with disdain upon a criticism that came from a woman, and all those who were jealous of the growing popularity of the woman's work, as if there was some cause of alarm for the safety of their own positions of power and honor, all rose up in their churches, with all the influence and power of speech they could summon to oppose the woman's work and break it up if possible."[79] Ministers carefully studied the Bible, Broughton further observed, to learn if aggressive missionary roles for women were sanctioned. Male hostility became especially strong after the ninth annual meeting in Durhamville. Broughton attributed the cause of the hostility to the powerful spiritual manifestations that some of the women revealed to the crowd: "Several sisters came with revelations, visions, and prophecies that made indelible impressions."[80]

The movement challenged male hegemony on several levels. The "general awakening" in the study of the Bible on the part of women proved threatening to ministers who feared the intellectual development of the women and assumed that their claims to prophecy and revelation portended the demand to preach in the near future. The women's efforts to establish separate women's societies did not include the demand for ordination to the clergy; rather the women attempted to exert power by insisting upon literacy and theological training for men who would preach to them.[81] The women used these criteria in asserting their right to judge ministerial candidates. The Bible Bands simultaneously drew attention to women's literacy and talent, and consequently to their rejection of an exclusively male right to theological interpretation. Their advocacy of reforming the church threatened male control, since women inserted their voices in areas where they had previously been silent and unwelcome—in the business and governance of the church, in disciplining church members, and in teaching and interpreting the gospel.

Undoubtedly, Broughton's popularity intimidated some men. Her picture hung on the walls of her followers' homes. Her aggressive, self-confident style won her the label "mannish woman."[82] Her speeches bore the stamp of her self-assured style, which she presented as indication of divinely inspired power over her adversaries. Broughton, referring to herself in the third person, recalled: "In concluding her address she said: 'If any one present is not convinced of the Divine authority of the woman's work, ask any question and as far as I am able I'll gladly give the Bible teaching related to it.' No one asked a single question, although the brother was present that had given the sisters of that church so much annoyance."[83]

Although some ministers remained loyal and kept their churches open to the women's meetings, male opposition grew so virulent during the following year that many Bible Bands were forced to discontinue. Ministers locked the doors of their churches and refused to accommodate them.[84] In the autobiographical account of her life as a missionary, Broughton recalled rumors of violence. On one occasion she noted that "dear Sister Nancy C. said, had not Sister Susan S. come to her rescue, she would have been badly beaten for attempting to hold a woman's meeting in her own church." On another occasion, a man drew a gun on his wife and threatened to kill her if she attended the

Bible Band meeting. The women felt vindicated, however, when the man died shortly after the incident. "He was not permitted," proclaimed Broughton, "to live long enough to prohibit that good woman a second time from going when her missionary sisters called a meeting." His death served to reinforce perceptions of the divine sanction of their work and helped diminish further persecution in the area.[85] As rumors of male hostility spread, the women acquired the image of martyrs for their cause and began to gain a greater following among both men and women.

Virginia Broughton contributed a great deal to the advancement of a separate women's convention in Tennessee. Undaunted by her enemies, she rallied support from sympathetic ministers who offered their churches as meeting places. During the 1890s Broughton taught at the Bible and Normal Institute in Memphis. In 1890 she taught a women's missionary training course, which ran concurrently with the ministers' training course. The Institute's courses, ranging from primary level instruction to theological study, stressed the importance of formal training as opposed to emotionalism with little biblical knowledge.[86] Each succeeding year attracted larger numbers of women. A report from the Bible and Normal Institute to the American Baptist Home Mission Society hailed the Bible Band program in 1892 for "bringing forth excellent fruit" and for contributing nearly $1,000 to the Christian Home and Training School for Women. The home was under Broughton's supervision and housed women students coming in from rural areas.[87] Broughton's missionary students and the Bible Bands signaled the demand for an educated ministry and laity.[88]

Through lectures and writing, Broughton began to appeal to the growing number of educated ministers in the state. She defended her case by drawing upon biblical precedent. Her scriptural justification of organized evangelical womanhood slowly transformed disbelieving ministers, who found it impossible to counter her arguments, into supporters of the women's cause. Broughton relished these conversions—as in the case of the unidentified Reverend H., a minister who had initially denounced women's missionary societies. On this occasion women had packed the church to hear her, and Reverend H. had come to build a case against her and to convey his disdain. As Broughton stood before the crowd and spoke, the minister sat conspicuously with his back to her, "as if warming himself near the stove." His hostile convictions were no match for Broughton's self-acknowledged eloquence and persuasive arguments. The following account of his remarks testifies to his conversion to the women's cause:

> When she [Broughton] concluded her remarks and asked those who wished to speak to express themselves, this Rev. H. arose and made a marvelous confession. He told his purpose in coming to that meeting, as already stated, and then said that he was regarded by his church as a fluent speaker, but he was then unable to speak and only rose to make a confession. The following are his words: "I have been washed, rinsed, starched, hung up, dried, sprinkled and ironed, and am now ready for service; not to destroy, but to do all in my power to forward this branch of God's work as zealously as I had determined to oppose it."[89]

The women's conventions found their greatest support in the cities and towns of the South, although a number of urban-based black and white missionaries worked also in the southern backwoods and countryside. Virginia Broughton carried the message of organized womanhood throughout Tennessee and found her strongest opposition in the rural, uneducated ministry. Broughton's movement undermined leadership by those who lacked formal education, for it set a standard of literacy, especially the ability to read and interpret the Bible, upon men seeking church pastorates.[90] The urban churches, with a larger concentration of educated ministers and laypersons, had participated in the formation of black Baptist ministerial conventions in every southern state and had organized regional conventions in the North and West.[91] Thus churches in the more urbanized areas provided fertile ground for the growth of the black women's convention movement.

Separatist Strategies

A state convention represented the banding together of women's associations within individual churches, and in some instances the banding together of larger subdivisions, known as district associations. Mississippi, for example, was divided into eleven districts, each of which included many individual church societies.[92] The organizational structure of black women's state conventions followed that of the ministerial-dominated state conventions. Each annually elected a pres-

ident and other officers and appointed, or in some cases hired, a field
missionary to canvass the state and organize local societies. Conventions elected, on a staggered basis, an executive board, also called a
board of managers, for the overall supervision of work.

Conventions sought to represent women in every black Baptist
church in a state, and thus the annual membership dues, usually one
dollar per person, provided the organization's financial base. Each
women's state convention met annually and, usually, on the same date
and in the same vicinity as the annual meeting of the male-led state
convention. Meeting places rotated within a state. Individual churches
selected delegates, who attended the annual meetings. Each state
convention executed its work through committees on education, nom-
inations, new societies, greetings, temperance, social service, obituary,
finance, and children's groups.[93] Women's conventions controlled their
own budgets and determined the allocation of funds. They explicitly
denied male participation in any role other than "honorary member."
The constitution drafted by the Baptist women of Alabama typified
most others in stipulating that "no society shall send a male member
to the convention; none but women shall be allowed to vote or hold
office."[94]

The president of the Kentucky women told a predominantly male
Baptist audience that the women had learned to delegate roles of
authority, to raise points of order, and to "transact business as well as
their brethren."[95] Sophia Shanks, president of the Arkansas women,
credited her state association with building ordinary women's self-
confidence as to their skills and abilities. "The State Association is the
inspiration of the local Associations throughout the State, as they all
look to the State Association as the head. . . . The Association has
also brought to the public eye women who were never heard of, some
in the cities and others in the rural districts, and so to be great factors
in helping to carry on our work." Shanks made explicit mention of
women's financial contribution. "From a financial standpoint," she
informed the men of her state, "we are prepared to prove that we have
given thousands that you would not have, had it not been for the
untiring and loyal women in the State." Similarly, in 1900 the women
of Missouri initiated a campaign to raise $2500 for the construction
of a girls' dormitory at the Baptist College in Macon, Missouri. In an

article entitled "Appeal to the Baptist Sisterhood of Missouri," the women described their goal as a "monument for the Lord and ourselves."[96]

Black women were aware of their crucial role in building the denomination. Mamie Steward of the Kentucky women's convention argued for a broader conception of church work than that performed by the ordained ministry. In an article written in 1898 she urged greater respect for women's work while citing the small participation of men in critical aspects of church life:

> It is safe to say that nine-tenths of the teachers in our Sunday schools are women. The Sunday school, being a part of the church work, makes the woman an important factor, not only in engaging in the work of the church as it is commonly understood, but also places her where she can even make the future church what she desires it to be. . . . The missionary work of the church has an ardent friend and a special advocate among women. You can often hear of a "Woman's Missionary Society," but seldom, if ever a "Men's Missionary Society." The men are often associated in the work, but by common consent or some other cause, missionary enterprises are encouraged to look to woman as its most ardent friend and advocate.[97]

Women's conventions grew in membership because of enthusiasm as well as systematic recruitment. At its first annual meeting in 1887, the Mississippi convention represented twenty-six women's societies; in 1888 it represented forty-two. The programs for meetings in 1888 and 1889 give an indication of the Mississippi convention's focus on organizational growth. In 1888 women read papers on such topics as "The Duty of Sisters to Engage in Mission Work" and "How to Induce the Sisters to Join the Society." In 1889 the Mississippi women's convention directed each of its eleven district associations to appoint an agent with the responsibility of organizing more societies in the local churches of her district. The state convention also appointed a field worker to supervise the formation of all new societies.[98] In a similar effort, Kentucky women selected Mrs. M. B. Wallace to serve as their field agent. The minutes of their meeting in 1885 recorded that Wallace had traveled throughout the state, organized thirty-three new societies, and delivered thirty-eight lectures during the previous year. Eliza W. Pollard, president of the Alabama women's convention, developed a booklet for missionary work. It was distributed throughout the state and provided a guide for the establishment and operation of women's missionary societies at the local church level.[99]

The black press served an important function in fostering an "imagined" racial community and women's community. In 1887 black Baptists published forty newspapers and magazines in various parts of the country—the great majority being in the South. The denominational press reported both religious and secular events at the local, state, and national levels. Articles covered such topics as the relation between religion and business, black history, upcoming political events, protests against lynching and disfranchisement, announcements and coverage of meetings, reprints from white newspapers, theological essays, foreign mission news, and reviews of women's subjects.[100] Through black Baptist–owned newspapers women affirmed their bond with one another, informed readers of their goals and periodic meetings, and featured news of general interest to their sex. The agenda for an upcoming meeting appeared a week or two before its scheduled date, while detailed coverage of a meeting usually appeared afterward. For instance, news coverage of the annual gathering of Kansas Baptists in 1894 reported that on one day of the gathering, "the rules were suspended and the Convention listened attentively for some time to the presentation of the Woman Suffrage question by a representative of the Women's Christian Temperance Union of Lawrence."[101]

A "woman's column" appeared in many black Baptist newspapers. The column featured articles on etiquette, marriage, home management, recipes, and the spiritual elevation of the black family. At a meeting of black Baptists in 1887, the *Baptist Tribune* of South Carolina, the *American Baptist* of Louisville, and the *Baptist Journal* of St. Louis were especially commended for their women's column. The *National Baptist World* of Wichita, Kansas, carried the column "Women and Home," which included articles on hairstyles, recipes, tests of good breeding, and physical exercise for back ailments.[102]

Yet writings in these newspapers ranged considerably outside home-related topics and even adopted iconoclastic tones. In 1893 the *Baptist*

Headlight of Topeka, Kansas, presented the following sketch: "A woman in New Hampshire is a street railway magnate, a good house-keeper and cook, a fine shot with the revolver, a first class swimmer, an excellent business woman, and worker in the church." A reprint from *Harper's Bazaar* appeared in the Wichita paper *National Baptist World* on 23 November 1894: "'No, George,' she said, 'I can never be yours.' 'Then I am rejected,' he moaned. 'No, dearest, not that; but I am a woman's suffragist and cannot be any man's. You, however, may be mine if you will.'"[103] Reporting the suicide of a woman in Chicago, an article in the *Baptist Headlight* added that her husband overworked her and treated her like a slave. "Even in the days of the 'institution' in the South human chattels were not worked to death. They were too valuable. But a wife costs nothing. If she dies another may be had for the asking. It is this fact that makes such bondage possible."[104] In an article appearing in Arkansas's *Baptist Vanguard*, Harriet Morris counterposed women's housework against child rearing and religious duties. Concerned that thousands of her sisters were overly preoccu-pied with cleanliness and housework, Morris drew upon the imagery of Judgment Day when all would be called to answer for their deeds on earth. She sadly concluded that most women would have little to show for their life's work except "polishing furnature [*sic*] and ruffling dresses . . . the best starching and ironing in all the neighborhood."[105]

In some states Baptist women's conventions elected an officer with the specific duty of editing a column on women's missionary news. In 1892 the Alabama women's convention appointed Eliza W. Pollard editor of such a column in the *Baptist Leader*. Issued out of Selma, Alabama, the *Baptist Leader* served as an important instrument in furthering the work of the women's state convention. Alice E. McEwen, a graduate of Spelman and an active member of the Alabama women's convention, became an associate editor to her father, the Reverend A. N. McEwen, editor of the *Baptist Leader*. The black Baptist women in Alabama used the paper to promote pride for Selma University and to advertise their fund-raising plans. During a fund-raiser in 1891, the Alabama Baptist women's convention assisted in the weekly circulation and distribution of 10,000 issues of the paper, in order to reach a considerably larger than usual readership.[106] By 1900 the Alabama women's convention published its own monthly news organ, the *Baptist Woman's Era*. The paper, edited by Eliza Pollard, carried the byline: "Let us convince the world that women can run a newspaper without debt. Read and Know for Yourself."[107]

The black Baptist press employed women as both agents and journalists. Ida B. Wells, the great journalist and crusader against lynching, began her newspaper career with the aid and encouragement of William J. Simmons.[108] As editor of the *American Baptist* and founding editor of *Our Women and Children* in 1886, Simmons gave several outstanding women journalists their start. Advertised as a "lively, spicy monthly magazine," *Our Women and Children* contained short stories, poetry, and articles on marriage, housework, children, women's religious activities, and racial concerns.

In the *Afro-American Press and Its Editors* (1891), I. Garland Penn devoted biographical sketches to nineteen women journalists, fourteen having contributed to black Baptist journals. Twelve of them worked as editors or correspondents for *Our Women and Children*. Several officers of the Kentucky women's state convention worked on the staff of the magazine. Ione Wood, Simmons's niece and a member of the board of managers of the Kentucky women's convention, edited the temperance column. Lavinia Sneed, an alumna of State University at Louisville and professor there upon graduation, regularly contributed to the magazine.[109] Lucy Wilmot Smith, a professor at State University, edited the children's column in *Our Women and Children*. Smith also chaired the children's committee within the Women's Baptist Educational and Missionary Convention in Kentucky. Mary Cook edited the woman's column in the *American Baptist* and headed the educational department of *Our Women and Children*. Penn quoted one of her editorials:

> White faces seem to think it their heaven-born right to practice civil war on negroes [sic], to the extent of blood-shed and death. They look upon the life of their brother in black as a bubble to be blown away at their pleasure. The same spirit that existed in the South twenty-four years ago, is still recognized in its posterity. The negro is still clothed in swarthy skin, and he is still robbed of his rights as a citizen, made dear and fairly won to him by the death of those who fell in the late Rebellion. This outrage cannot endure.[110]

With the formation of the National Baptist Convention, U.S.A., in 1895, women promoted their interests before a wider public. In the pages of the *National Baptist Magazine*, first organ of the NBC, women appeared regularly and wrote from a gender-conscious perspective. In the article "How the Church Can Best Help the Condition of the Masses," Hardie Martin of Montgomery, Alabama, reinforced the image of male and female leaders. She stressed the importance of ministers, journalists, and women missionaries who visited the homes of the common people. In an article in the *National Baptist Magazine*, Mary Cook credited the organized work of black Baptist women in the South with the acquisition of land, the construction of schools, and the establishment of homes for the aged and infirm. She called attention to the material progress of growing numbers of black women, who as journalists and educators "have overcome prejudice and made futile the arguments as to their proper sphere." Cook condemned the materialistic values of the age and told black women to "rally round our men and prove, by their culture and dignified bearing, that human rights are . . . more worthy of protection than American industry."[111] She enjoined her sisters to make race consciousness integral to church work.

Some women leaders even portrayed their role as ultimately more decisive than men's. Virginia Broughton contended that women held the key to the material and spiritual progress of the entire race. She maintained that women's efforts had already caused a considerable change in the domestic and public lives of blacks: "Now that the secret has been discovered by which our people may be reached and properly taught to live lives of purity by consecrated Christian women teaching in their homes, schools, and churches, we can all hope to see in the next twenty-five years, marked improvement among the colored people."[112]

Broughton's bias notwithstanding, organized women played a crucial role in building black denominational power, but their racial consciousness was mediated through gendered experiences. Thus the attainment of denominational power reflected the combined results of racial solidarity and women's solidarity. The success of the overall movement depended, in no small measure, upon what Estelle Freedman calls the "separatist strategy of female institution building." Moreover, the existence of a female community and its mobilization into a separate organizational base commanded greater authority and respect for women. Black women found themselves in the unique position of being at once separate and allied with black men in the struggle for racial advancement while separate and allied with white women in the struggle for gender equality.

Graduates of the Missionary Training Department of Spelman Seminary, 1893. Emma De Lamotta (*first row center*) became head of this department after graduation. The Spelman-trained missionaries traveled to black communities throughout Georgia imparting religious and moral instruction. Courtesy of Spelman College Archives.

Teachers' Professional Class, Spelman Seminary, 1898. Black women's preparation for careers in teaching formed the basis for the emergence of the "Female Talented Tenth." Courtesy of Spelman College Archives.

Interior of Union Hall. Spelman's growing student body held its classes in Union Hall after the school moved from the basement of Friendship Baptist Church to the site of an army barracks in 1883. Standing at the podium is Sophia Packard, and to her left is Harriet Giles. Courtesy of Spelman College Archives.

Nannie Helen Burroughs, dynamic leader of the
Woman's Convention and founder and head of the
National Training School for Women and Girls,
1909. Courtesy of the Library of Congress.

The officers of the Woman's Convention, ca. 1907: (*front row, left to right*): Nannie Helen Burroughs, S. Willie Layten, Sylvia C. J. Bryant; (*second row, left to right*): Mary V. [Cook] Parrish, Virginia W. Broughton, Mary E. Goins, [Mrs.] E. Arlington Wilson. Smithsonian Institution Photo No. 84-8867.

Missionary Training Class, National Training School, ca. 1911. The Reverend Walter H. Brooks (*first row center*) and the northern white Baptist missionary Jennie Peck (*third row center*) incorporated urban social service into the school's missionary training curriculum. Courtesy of the Library of Congress.

The "model house" on the campus of the National Training School. The house provided a setting for practical lessons in domestic service and housekeeping. It was built by funds donated by the Women's American Baptist Home Mission Society. The house was named in memory of WABHMS leader Mary G. Burdette (1842–1907). Courtesy of the Library of Congress.

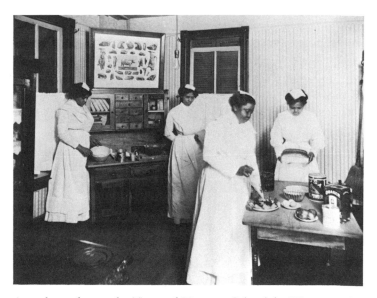

A cooking class at the National Training School for Women and Girls. Students were taught to look upon cooking as a "profession." Smithsonian Institution Photo No. 90-3355.

Basketball team, National Training School for Women and Girls. Physical education and competitive sports accompanied the industrial focus of the school's curriculum. Courtesy of the Library of Congress.

4

Unlikely Sisterhood

We are coming to help you, sisters,
   With "hearts that are loyal and true,"
To help you gather the harvest,
   And bind up the sheaves with you.

From a poem, by B.P.J. of Deep River,
Connecticut, *Home Mission Echo* (1885)

In January 1885 a young black woman in Kentucky, Mary Cook, penned a letter of gratitude to young white women in Maine for their support of her educational and professional aspirations. Cook was able to pursue her college degree because of their financial assistance. Her intellectual aptitude had been evident at an early age, but the poverty of both her family and the black schools in her home district made it extremely difficult to advance academically. As a teenager, she worked as a seamstress in order to clothe herself and go to school. White Baptist women, interested in furthering the education of black women, had learned of her need and paid her tuition at a school owned and controlled by black Baptists, the State University at Louisville. Cook's record as a student more than upheld their confidence. She served as president of both the school's literary society and its Young Men's and Women's Christian Association, and in 1883 she managed to graduate as valedictorian of her class. Afterward she joined the permanent faculty of her alma mater—her salary being underwritten by the same northern Baptist women who had come to know and admire her abilities.[1]

Cook's gratitude extended equally to Kentucky's black community, especially to Dr. William J. Simmons, black Baptist minister, newspaper editor, and president of the State University at Louisville.[2] It had been Simmons who introduced the northern white women to Cook's promise and need. While a student and for decades thereafter, she joined with the black Baptist women of Kentucky in an organized effort to promote women's higher education as well as secure funds for the maintenance and growth of the Louisville university.[3] In another letter to the New England women, Cook boasted of the black women's endeavors: "They organized at their several homes what is known as the 'Home University Society,' holding all offices and managing all business. There were seventeen societies represented the first year, with money to the amount of $715;—the second year twenty-six societies and $1000.10, and this year thirty-nine societies and $1,207.70."[4]

Mary Cook's letters, both of them written in 1885, capture two different but interrelated themes in the history of black women during the last two decades of the nineteenth century. The theme of racial self-help during a time of disfranchisement, segregation, and pervasive violence is readily apparent.[5] A second, less familiar theme is that of interracial cooperation. In the last two decades of the nineteenth century, the collective work of southern black Baptist women and northern white Baptist women challenged the representations and assumptions articulated by a racist society. Interracial cooperation, which is the focus of this chapter, does not negate or minimize the importance of black self-help in developing attitudinal and institutional counterweights to the oppressive and debilitating racial climate of the late nineteenth and early twentieth centuries. But the perspective of this "unlikely sisterhood" admits that self-help was not singularly capable, as it is not today capable, of combating tremendous inequality. This was and is particularly relevant to the massive costs of black education.

Despite the federal government's abandonment of black civil rights and the southern states' refusal to allocate tax dollars equitably between black and white schooling, black literacy as well as the number of black students at the secondary, college, and professional levels grew notably during the post-Reconstruction years because of the combined role of black self-help and white philanthropy.[6] The interrelation of self-help and philanthropy finds its most outstanding example in Booker T. Washington and his connections with the giants of big business, Andrew Carnegie, John D. Rockefeller, and Julius Rosenwald.[7] What tends to be overlooked, however, are connections between average people—like the communities of northern white women in contact with communities of southern black women—working in support of black education and the relief of poverty. This black-white coalition of sorts did not represent a unity of motives and interests on the part of black and white women. Rather, their coalition suggests that divergent motives did not preclude mutual goals. For southern black and northern white women, multiple allegiances and interests overlapped sufficiently to create common ground on which to counter the effects of racial oppression. Just as the last decades of the nineteenth century can be characterized as the nadir of race relations and the era of self-help, they can also be characterized as an age of women's missions and some interracial cooperation. At the same time that black women joined in concerted efforts with black men, they embarked upon a relationship with white women that had no precedent, and perhaps no sequel.

The Era of Women's Missions

During the last two decades of the nineteenth century black and white women came to be linked in evangelical work, begun by Protestant denominational societies during the 1860s but given new life and meaning in the post-Reconstruction years. James McPherson has persuasively argued for the continued important role of northern missionary societies in advancing black education during the decades following Reconstruction. Although some freedmen's education societies waned and in fact dissolved during and soon after Reconstruction, the larger societies, namely the American Missionary Association (Congregationalist), American Baptist Home Mission Society, Freedmen's Aid Society of the Methodist Episcopal Church, and the Board of Missions to the Freedmen of the Presbyterian Church witnessed a resurgence in income after suffering a decline during much of the 1870s. By 1878 these societies experienced renewed vitality, and they continued to grow although experiencing brief setbacks during the depression of 1893 and the recession of 1907–1908. McPherson observes that "in 1891 the amount these four societies spent for black education was double their former high of 1870, and in 1906 their combined budget was more than four times as large as in 1876." As a result, the number of missionary colleges and secondary schools for blacks tripled between 1880 and 1915.[8]

If freedmen's education societies continued to grow because of missionary zeal "rooted," as McPherson posits, "in the institutional structure of American Protestantism," they experienced renewed vigor, in no small measure, because of tremendous activity on the part of their predominantly female memberships.[9] By the 1870s a vibrant, separate voice, amplified in an age of growing demands on the part of women for equality in education, the workplace, government, and society in general, began to resonate within evangelical Protestantism. In the postbellum period women's missionary activities transcended local community activity to become large national operations—each with tens of thousands of members linked together through news organs, educational literature, missionary training schools, and sophisticated organizational structures and administrative skills.

Beginning in the 1870s all of the Protestant denominations witnessed the emergence of powerful national women's societies in an auxiliary relationship with the older male-run groups. These societies reached their peak in membership in the 1880s and 1890s, but their autonomous influence began to wane during the early 1900s partly as a result of subsequent merger with the male-run groups and also as a result of the popularity of women's clubs and the general trend toward secularization of reform activities at the dawn of the new century.[10] During the heyday of women's religious organizations, however, northern white Baptist women, like the women of the other Protestant denominations, had addressed issues of immigration, race, labor, temperance—all from the perspective of "woman's work for woman."[11] Rather than forsake the "abolitionist legacy," northern Baptist women in the post–Civil War period championed it with renewed fervor and commitment—even at a time when most white Americans expressed indifference or hostility to the "Negro question." Their neo-abolitionist rhetoric stressed the importance, centrality, even primacy of woman's role in solving the nation's race problem. As such, "woman's work for woman" served to connect women who would otherwise have never met at all, much less forged a sisterhood that traversed regional, class, and racial boundaries.

The formation of large associations of northern white Baptist women in the late 1870s can be traced to the influence of the male-run American Baptist Home Mission Society and its work for the religious

and secular education of the freedpeople during the Civil War and
Reconstruction years. Acknowledging the frequent requests of the
ABHMS for financial support, women's societies in individual Baptist
churches in Michigan formed a state association in 1873 to help
sustain the "feeble and newly organized churches" in their own state
and also to support a female teacher and students in the Home Mission
school for blacks in Nashville, Tennessee. On 1 February 1877 a second
organization, the Women's Baptist Home Mission Society, united
white women in the Midwest. With headquarters in Chicago, the
WBHMS reached eastward to New York and Pennsylvania, although
the strength of its constituency remained in mid-America. The group
concentrated its efforts on black family life and sent missionaries into
the South to work within homes, churches, and industrial schools. On
14 November 1877 a third group, the Woman's American Baptist
Home Mission Society, formed in Boston and united the women of
New England primarily in support of collegiate education for the
freedwomen. In 1879 Sophia B. Packard, then corresponding secretary
of the WABHMS, reported a membership of 102 churches. In 1880,
just one year before her move to Atlanta, Packard pleaded the cause
of organized Baptist womanhood in 123 public meetings throughout
New England.[12] White Baptist women greatly contributed to the
financial support of the American Baptist Home Mission Society and
its overall educational work in the South, but they focused their
attention on opportunities for women. For example, the various New
England state districts of the WABHMS raised money for the founding
and maintenance of schools for southern black women, for underwriting the salaries of female teachers, for supporting female student
beneficiaries, and for donating clothing, furniture, and other needed
items to the various schools.[13]

"Woman's work for woman," however, could and did translate into
racist paternalism and cultural imperialism on the part of white
women. Pious white missionary-educators, sent South by their denominational societies to teach the Gospel and academic or industrial
skills, felt compelled, all too often, to instruct blacks as to their
subordinate place within the racial hierarchy of the South and nation.
Yet to characterize whites' efforts exclusively in these terms obscures
their own complexity, as well as the will and agency on the part of

black community leaders who interacted with the white missionaries. Northern white women, such as Spelman's founder and first president Sophia Packard, who journeyed South to establish schools or mission stations in the years after 1880, found strong black churches, especially in the urban areas.

Unlike the Civil War years, when blacks had just begun to separate from the churches of their slavemasters and to form their own congregations independent of white control, the later decades witnessed tremendous growth and collective organization. In 1890 black Baptist church membership stood at an impressive 1,349,000 and would nearly double during the next decade.[14] As black Baptist women organized separate women's associations at the local and state levels throughout the 1880s and 1890s, white women missionaries became keenly aware of the power and influence of local black leaders. The masses of black women validated a leadership that arose primarily from their own ranks rather than from the black male or white female leadership.[15] Thus the northern white women came to link their own success to their ability to work with and through local black churches, black ministers, and most of all the black female community.

Joanna Moore, legendary white missionary among southern blacks since 1863, wrote to the Women's Baptist Home Mission Society of black women's work in Louisiana during the 1880s: "I wish you could know the great number of women who are doing real mission work within the bounds of their own home and their own church . . . holding mothers' and children's meetings, caring for the poor, reading the Bible in the homes of their neighbors."[16] Moore regularly attended and participated in the conferences sponsored by blacks throughout the South.

Northern missionary Anna Barkley wrote from Memphis that women's Bible Bands existed in all the black Baptist churches, which in turn held joint quarterly meetings of the bands. Barkley extolled these women, who, although burdened with home duties of their own, committed their time and energy to aiding the sick and destitute—visiting them and offering spiritual guidance, cleaning their homes and doing their washing. These same black women organized classes at the Bible and Normal Institute in Memphis and secured training from the city's best doctors in order to care for the sick.[17] Attending a leaders' meeting in October of 1890, Barkley met the presidents and secretaries of the black women's societies, and they "laid plans for the enlargement of the work, and the way in which it could best be accomplished."

Another white missionary, Helen Jackson, wrote to the WBHMS that during her illness black women in Richmond conducted the schools and meetings under her charge—leaving her "comforted by the way my dear sisters have gone on without me."[18] In 1885 white missionary Nora Bennett expressed similar sentiments in her praise of the organizational acumen of black women Sabbath school teachers in Wilmington, North Carolina. She noted that twelve black women, who had organized and met in one another's homes, had so enlarged their numbers during the year that they had become a powerful city-wide union.[19]

The WBHMS sent northern white women into the South, but it also employed southern black women for mission work within homes and churches. The WBHMS also paid the salaries of black and white teachers, later called preceptresses or matrons, in the domestic science and missionary departments of the Home Mission colleges (white-controlled) as well as the schools owned and controlled by black Baptists. In 1881 the WBHMS began to rely increasingly upon black women, who were often women with natural leadership skills but with little formal education. Identifying leaders among the black women with whom they came in contact in Sabbath schools, industrial classes, and other organized societies, the northern white women first appointed black women under the title "Bible women." Many Bible women performed the same duties as the white missionaries, although the title "missionary" was reserved for whites alone. In 1887 the northern white women employed black women under the title "colored assistant," a more racially charged and explicitly subordinate label than the more neutral "Bible woman." In 1891, however, the WBHMS abandoned racial distinctions and adopted the title "missionary" for both blacks and whites. The more egalitarian policy was a direct outgrowth of collegiate education and missionary training programs for black women, coupled with blacks' growing assertiveness against white paternalism. By 1900 the WBHMS operated sixty-one mission stations in southern towns and cities and employed fifty-seven missionaries, of whom twenty-four were black. Twenty-one of these black women were graduates of missionary training programs in the ABHMS schools.[20]

Nor were black women merely the recipients of white support. Black women's organizations contributed money to the societies of northern white Baptist women. At its ninth annual meeting the Arkansas women's convention sent contributions to the women of New England and the Midwest in appreciation for their paying the salaries of two teachers at Arkansas Baptist College and two at the Mothers' Training School in Little Rock.[21] The Women's Baptist Home and Foreign Missionary Convention of North Carolina, founded in 1884 to assist the state ministerial-led convention in programs of racial self-help, sent regular contributions to the Chicago headquarters of the WBHMS. In 1899 the North Carolina women collected $300 from its 150 delegates. Of this amount, $125 went to the treasury of the Women's Baptist Home Mission Society.[22] Black women in Memphis made a quilt "handsomely worked throughout with various designs and fancy stitches" and sent it to the northern white women as a donation to missions. At the annual meeting of black women in Tennessee, black missionary Virginia Broughton noted the resolution of her sisters to send forty dollars to the WBHMS. The contributions of black women led WBHMS leader Mary Burdette to acknowledge that such donations represented "more self-denial than double, quadruple and even ten times the amount in many [white] women's missionary societies which we can name."[23]

The Accomplishments of Sisterhood

That black and white women found common cause around which to work and communicate during an era of severely restricted racial contact testifies to the possibility of cooperation that evangelical religion and women's missions created. Interracial contact not only occurred inside schools of higher learning but also took place throughout the South in churches, homes, and other organizational settings. Indeed interracial cooperation was premised upon shared values, which social scientists label variously as Yankee, neo-Puritan, Victorian, or middle-class. Together these values represented normative standards for gender roles and conventions—which meant sexual purity and other "ladylike" or "gentlemanly" manners—and they also prescribed the dominant society's ethic of hard work, frugality, temperance, punctuality, neatness, and piety. Collective efforts of black and white women facilitated the role of the black church in promoting these values, which were accepted and disseminated not merely by the Talented Tenth, but by those who had very meager economic resources and never attended college or high school. The latter group constituted the largest segment of Baptist church members and remained the groundswell of support for the religious, educational, and social reform programs of the leadership.

The role of black churches, their educational institutions, and missionaries in disseminating bourgeois values underscores the bicultural reality of black existence in America. Starting in the days of slavery, but particularly in the decades thereafter, black men and women lived within spatial and ideological communities whose collective behavior developed not in a cultural vacuum, but in contexts continuously though unevenly informed by the social, political, and economic values and behavior of the dominant American society. Home missions and other self-help activities of black women served to inculcate within the masses of poor and uneducated blacks psychological allegiance to certain mainstream values and behavior. Such values and behavior, especially as related to motherhood and domestic duties, were deemed proper and correct, even if difficult to sustain in practice.

Adherence to middle-class values, while problematic for people with extremely limited income, tended to reinforce the philosophy of racial self-help and its implicit promise of upward mobility for individuals and the race. Black women missionaries zealously preached abstention from the use of tobacco, alcoholic beverages, and snuff, but, more important, they consciously strove to channel money that had once supported these habits into the long-term educational and other needed programs of the black community. The black church established a great many institutions during the late nineteenth century—schools, publishing houses, old folks' homes, and orphanages—which testified to the power of the church in transforming individual consciousness into the collective ethos of racial self-help. Black women played the critical role in the formation of this public sentiment.[24] The fund-raising capacity of black church women rested on the very ability to influence many poor people to make financial sacrifices, limit personal consumption, and divert their meager resources away from themselves and their own immediate gratification.[25] Their efforts were not premised on an acceptance of black inferiority or the racial status quo.

On the contrary, their efforts validated, according to black Baptist women, full inclusion and equal justice in American society. Their allegiance to middle-class values, if evidence of white cultural domination, was no less evidence of their commitment to transcend oppression.

Black southern women and white northern women missionaries worked together in imparting moral and cultural lessons, which they believed would enhance personal and group respect.[26] To women missionaries, black and white, these lessons formed the very core of black education and were not limited to the collegiate curriculum. Outside the college setting, in rural backwoods areas and cities, missionaries established "mothers' training schools" to prepare black women for child rearing and other domestic duties. They instructed their listeners in nutrition, sanitary rules, and care of the sick. Through house-to-house visitation and through training schools, women of both races sought to impose Victorian standards of domesticity.

Poverty made it impossible for the masses to duplicate northern tastes in home decorating, but they were told to approximate this standard as best they could. In her study of social work among immigrant and white working-class homes, Lizabeth Cohen describes the assimilationist goal of late nineteenth-century women reformers to organize domestic space along middle-class lines.[27] Black and white missionaries engaged in similar assimilating efforts to transform the tastes and habits of southern blacks, many of whom lived barely at subsistence level. The unkempt, dirty homes of the "unsaved" contrasted strikingly with homes receptive to the missionaries. The latter case is exemplified by the household of Priscilla, a young black woman and student in a Sabbath school in Vicksburg, Mississippi. According to a northern white missionary's report, Priscilla assumed housekeeping duties at an early age after her mother's death. She and her father lived together in a one-room cabin, which she kept immaculate. Newspapers sufficed for wall covering, while a few "inexpensive but chaste pictures" hung about. Her beds were well made and "dressed in spotless white." A small vase of chrysanthemums sat on a table, giving "evidence of an innate refinement which made the most of its opportunities for expression."[28]

Joanna P. Moore's work among the freedpeople represents the most outstanding illustration of women's interracial cooperation. Clearly not all northern white missionaries shared Moore's egalitarian racial views, but her example was genuinely respected, even lionized by blacks and whites alike.[29] Born in Clarion County, Pennsylvania, in 1832, Moore began her life's work among the freedpeople as a missionary for the American Baptist Home Mission Society during the Civil War. On 31 December 1863 Moore, the first woman ever to be appointed by the ABHMS, was sent to Island No. 10 in the Mississippi River near Memphis, Tennessee. On the island Moore worked with 1,100 women and children who had flocked to the Union Army camp for protection, food, and clothing. In 1864 she moved to Helena, Arkansas, and between 1868 and 1877 worked in the New Orleans area. Until her death in 1916, she labored in black communities throughout the South, as she recalled, in "loving fellowship in their churches, schools, social gatherings, weddings, funerals."[30]

Moore's close relationship with blacks did not permit her to accept notions of racial inferiority or the validity of segregation laws; she praised attitudes of racial self-help among blacks. Her exceptional case, and to some extent that of other well-liked white women missionaries such as Helen Jackson in Richmond and Jennie Peck in Dallas, did not reflect the same tensions and power struggles as were exhibited between the black ministerial-led conventions and the men of the ABHMS. Moore's daily contact with blacks and her humble personal style did not suggest issues of control or racial hierarchy. While not always in complete agreement with black ministers, Moore wrote of them in her autobiography: "We never argued or fussed about race or sex, we understood each other and each tried to help the other. It is true that there was a quiet understanding that we all belonged to the same family."[31]

It was blacks' endurance and triumph over hardship and discouragement that won Moore's admiration. She commended efforts of racial self-help in the face of limited civil and political rights, and she urged black leaders not to become immobilized by bitterness: "You have gained this strength to help your weak brother. If you dwell too much on injustice the weak will give up in despair."[32] Moore was the first missionary to be commissioned by the Chicago-based Women's Baptist Home Mission Society when it was organized in 1877. Stationed in Louisiana between 1877 and 1878, she submitted to the WBHMS her report of having made 5,000 visits as well as 300 Bible readings and teachers' meetings. She conducted four sewing schools and children's meetings on a weekly basis and formed seventy-five Sunday schools.[33] Part of Moore's success stemmed from her respect for and utilization of talented black leaders. Her efforts to organize societies among black women were responsible for the development of missionary leaders such as Virginia Broughton of Tennessee.

Moore advanced the idea of "mothers' training schools" in 1883, and the idea gained wide support in all of the southern black women's conventions. Moore's training school in Little Rock, Arkansas, consisted of a house with a dining room, parlor, and classroom on the first floor, and bedrooms on the second floor. Eight black women lived at the house while attending her training program. The house/school functioned as a "model home" for instruction in literacy and in homemaking skills for motherhood and wifehood. Emphasizing order in the household, Moore taught: "There are not many things that a husband values more than a clean, orderly fireside, adorned by a wife whose dress is clean, and well mended, if necessary." She advised: "Just because it is wash day is no reason why you should go with slipshod shoes, dirty dress and uncombed hair. No, no, fix yourself up nice and neat, then roll up your sleeves and put a large apron on, then wash away with all your might." But Moore also taught about establishing honesty in children and trust between husbands and wives. She considered marriage a partnership and urged husbands to assume greater responsibility in parenting.[34]

In 1885 in Plaquemine, Louisiana, she published *Hope*, a monthly magazine, as a lesson plan for mothers' training. She continued its publication as she moved to various mission stations in the South. Advertised as a nondenominational magazine, *Hope* included Sunday school lessons, guides for Bible Bands, and stories on family devotion. Through *Hope*, Moore preached the message of self-denial in stories of families who had forgone Christmas presents or other items of personal consumption in order to give money to missionary causes.[35] Black women and ministers wrote regularly to Moore, who in turn published their letters. The letters recounted temperance work, convention activities, and family life. Black Baptist leaders, such as Mary Cook of Kentucky and Virginia Broughton of Tennessee, appeared frequently in the pages of the magazine, which became an important network of information among the various black women's state conventions. Likewise, advertisements for *Hope* appeared in black Baptist newspapers, and their endorsement increased its readership.[36]

Through training schools and *Hope*, Moore worked with and through black churches and women's organizations in a program that emphasized a woman's duties to her family. Black women's state conventions sponsored mothers' institutes—giving certificates to women who successfully completed their programs. They encouraged ministers to preach monthly sermons on parenting. Mothers' training schools emphasized subjects such as housekeeping tips, care of the sick, hygiene, marital responsibilities and child rearing, and literature for parents and children.[37] While such emphasis tended to promote and reinforce the dominance of the father and the patriarchal family, black women's societies viewed "mothers' training" as important to family stability and to perceptions of black female respectability at a time when white society viewed black women as innately promiscuous and undeserving of protection from insult and even rape.[38]

During the 1890s the idea of training women for parenthood was not perceived as contradictory to the emphasis on black higher education or equal rights. Such training was espoused by two uncompromising civil rights advocates, W. E. B. Du Bois and Frances Ellen Watkins Harper. "Home uplift" was deemed essential to "race uplift" and was addressed in newspapers, novels, and other forms of popular literature.[39] Du Bois, a formidable spokesman for African Americans' and women's rights, stressed the duties of motherhood in the *Spelman Messenger*. Commenting on high birth rates for blacks, Du Bois insisted upon quality rather than quantity and impressed upon his readers: "If any one of you . . . thinks that learning to cook or sew or build houses alone is sufficient to make you home-makers, you are sadly mistaken. To interpret life and the world to the little group about you, until they in turn can give back to the world a soul and a purpose—this is the function of the home-maker and nothing less."[40] Harper's novel *Iola Leroy* (1893) conveys a similar message. Lucille Delaney, the novel's college-trained heroine and a woman of "suavity and dignity," proved her commitment to her people by establishing a southern school to train future wives and mothers. Yet also in the novel was the illiterate ex-slave Aunt Linda, who expressed her feelings in the language of the folk. She, too, perceived the need for mothers' training and for someone "who'll larn dese people how to bring up dere chillen, to keep our gals straight, an' our boys from runnin' in de saloons and gamblin' dens."[41]

Despite the moralistic and prosaic image of mothers' training, some white southerners went to violent lengths to prevent black women from being taught the domestic ideals of whites. Moore's dictums on housekeeping, maternal, and wifely duties carried a message of black dignity and equality that did not rest well with white supremacists. Such was the case when the "White League" threatened Joanna Moore and the black women students of her school in Baton Rouge. The students were the first to see the White League's note pinned to the gate of the school on the morning of 20 November 1890. The note, embellished with a drawing of a skull and crossbones, demanded that the school close. It charged: "You are educating the nigger up to think they are the equals of the white folks." On the following day, the League brutalized a black minister who lived nearby and supported Moore's work. The minister told her that a group of white men wearing "hideous masks" came to his house in the night. They beat him in front of his wife and children, who stood helplessly with pistols to their heads. Other blacks were similarly victimized. One was shot to death. After a week of violence, many blacks fled for safety and, in so doing, created a labor shortage. This prompted the "good white people of the community" to demand an end to the violence. Moore was forced to close her training school and suspend work in Baton Rouge.[42]

To avoid future attacks, she developed a new program, the Fireside School, as a plan of study for individual families within their own home settings. Virginia Broughton worked on the staff of the Fireside School and spoke as its representative at a conference of black Baptists in Decatur, Alabama, in 1900. Mary Flowers, another leader among black Baptist women in Tennessee, worked as the business manager of *Hope*, official organ of the Fireside School program.[43] Joanna Moore, like several other white missionaries of the Women's Baptist Home Mission Society, attended black Baptist meetings and participated in their proceedings. Moore delivered papers at the annual conferences of the American National Baptist Convention, and in 1888 held a position on its bureau of education. Moore's dedication to the advancement of black people continued until her death in 1916. At her death, she was eulogized in the *Crisis*, the magazine of the National Association of Colored People (NAACP): "Miss Moore was a careful reader of *The Crisis* and I think gave it a place next to . . . her Bible. She always wanted it sent to her wherever she went."[44]

Despite Moore's example and that of other northern white missionaries committed to cooperative efforts in southern black communities and schools, interracial contact did not occur solely on southern terrain, as is often assumed, with the introduction of the white missionary. If one looks at the white missionary in the South as the only point of contact, a range of other contact points is overlooked, and it is this broader, more representative picture that was truly exceptional for its time. Women's missions created structured avenues along which black and white women traveled together, heard each other's voices, and learned of each other's struggles and values. The white missionary, journeying South to teach the freedpeople, is but one component of a complex network that took black women into the North as well.

Northern white women from small communities in Maine, Vermont, Michigan, and in fact throughout most of New England and the Midwest would have had little if any opportunity to meet and talk to blacks had it not been for the mediating influence of women's missions. In 1890 more than 90 percent of the black population lived in the South. The rest had settled in large urban centers such as New York and Philadelphia, and to a lesser extent in the western territories. Boston's black population grew from 1.8 to 2 percent of the city's total population between 1890 and 1900, while Chicago's black population hovered slightly above 1 percent in 1890 and did not reach the 2 percent mark until 1910. Midwestern cities such as Cleveland and Detroit would not begin to gain significant numbers of blacks until the Great Migration during World War I, when a half-million blacks abandoned the South.[45] It is quite remarkable, then, that hundreds of white women came into direct contact with southern black women on northern soil. They did so when numerous black women, in their roles as missionaries, students, and teachers, traveled North at the invitation of white churches, schools, and northern women's branch and regional missionary societies. These black women articulated eloquently through their words and example the merit of "woman's work for woman."

In towns throughout the North southern black women told of the progress of their people, conditions at the schools, and their activities within their own southern communities. This interaction served as a catalyst enlisting further interest and support. For example, when Alabama black Baptist women relayed their success in erecting a girls' dormitory at Selma University, white Baptist women's societies in Elgin, Illinois, Logansport, Indiana, and Agawam, Massachusetts furnished several of its rooms.[46] The growing interest in the black schools led Anna Hunt, WABHMS vice-president from Maine and also editor of the society's *Home Mission Echo*, to systematize activities throughout the New England states so that speakers from the southern mission field could address as many women as possible. During the two-day period 6–7 October 1886, meetings of six associations, one state conference, and an individual church mission band all requested representatives from the southern schools. The demand had grown so large that Hunt endeavored to create a pool of six to eight speakers to accommodate each area.[47]

Black women's visits north, with their informative and inspiring speeches, challenged popular stereotypes of an immoral and childlike race. In 1888 at the joint meeting of the New England and Midwestern women, Annie Howard, a black teacher at Wayland Seminary in Washington, D.C., read, according to the white women, "an excellent paper" on her people's progress at the school. During the summer of 1888 Lulu Osborne, a black teacher at the State University at Louisville, spoke to the Maine associations in Portland and Fairfield. Mary Cook's visit to New England two years later afforded yet another opportunity to learn of the Louisville school, while in July 1892 Emma De Lamotta of Spelman Seminary spoke on fifteen occasions to large groups of women in Maine and Massachusetts and "reached the hearts of all her hearers."[48] Virginia Broughton of Tennessee attended the annual meeting of the Women's Baptist Home Mission Society at Saratoga in 1895 and from there visited Vassar, Wellesley, and other schools on behalf of black women's education. Broughton's speaking tour took her to Massachusetts, New York, New Jersey, Ohio, Pennsylvania, and Illinois. She was heartened by the large audiences, applause, and hospitality that greeted her at each point. Her visit to Rochester, New York, was particularly memorable, with a reception committee extending her "queenly entertainment, several young women vying with each other to see that she was well supplied with the delicacies of the feast."[49]

In addition, white teachers in the black schools took advantage of the summer months to return home to friends and relatives in the North. The summertime offered only partial relaxation for these teachers; of equal if not greater importance was the opportunity to present their work and rally support from women who would probably never step on southern soil. During her summer vacation in 1895 Emma Adams, formerly from New Hampshire but now a teacher at the black Baptist–owned University at Louisville, visited a large number of churches in her home state and also in Maine. Adams was so enthusiastically received that the WABHMS executive board noted: "This work of women for women in our own country commended itself to our sisters, and in many of our churches societies formed."[50] Addressing women in Connecticut, the secretary of the Merrimac River Association, L. G. Barrett, reminisced about her years as a teacher at Shaw University in North Carolina before returning north. Carrie Dyer shared her experiences as teacher at Hartshorn College in Richmond with the Worcester Association in Massachusetts.[51]

White northern Baptist women's organizations encouraged growing interest in southern mission work by effecting a variety of methods for the dissemination of information. Churches in each state were clustered into associations, led by directors responsible for reporting their activities to the state's vice-president. A director from an association in Massachusetts was typical of others when she reported that her job "was to put myself in communication with the sisters of each church as far as possible by writing, thereby endeavoring to ascertain just who they were, how situated, the state of church and Sabbath schools, and the interest in Missions; in short, everything that could assist me in reaching their hearts and purses."[52] After retrieving this information, she visited individuals and distributed circulars, leaflets, and reports. At association meetings, women from churches in a particular area gathered together for devotional services, singing, poetry, the reading of letters, and often a visit by a representative from one of the black schools.

Letters of black and white missionaries went back and forth across the Mason-Dixon line and served to keep northern whites intimately involved in the lives of many women yet unseen. Letter writing took on a publicist character, since letters were never written as private correspondence between individual women but rather to be shared in open forums and published in magazines. The exchange and reading of letters became focal points of the northern women's meetings, as exemplified in the report from Maine women who "found these letters from the schools invaluable as helps to our women in conducting their meetings."[53] The Madison Avenue Baptist Church in New York City contributed to the salary of the black missionary Emma De Lamotta, whose letters were read aloud at the meetings of its women's society. De Lamotta, a former slave, had come to Spelman to learn to read and write when she was well into middle age. By 1890 she served the school as missionary to the southwestern areas of Georgia and distinguished herself in this capacity. Paid a monthly sum of $25 by the New York church, Emma De Lamotta wrote to the church praising Spelman founders Sophia Packard and Harriet Giles for their impact upon her life: "I had never been to school a day in my life before they came but had the promise that I should read his [God's] word and tell it to others." Through correspondence the New York church members heard in vivid detail De Lamotta's missionary exploits as she visited churches and hundreds of homes. Her success can be gleaned, too, from Packard's letters, which assured the Madison Avenue church members of their worthy investment in De Lamotta—"a woman of excellent judgement and remarkable influence among her people." Packard continued, "We depend upon her advice and help in many things."[54]

Before the era of the telephone or mass media such as radio and television, print communication proved most effective in fostering a sense of women's common cause and mutual understanding. The northern white Baptist women formed a reading public that sought knowledge of the southern mission field and used print material to publicize their goals and programs. Such material played a central role in coordinating organizational planning, goals, and activities at the local level. In 1894 the WABHMS Bureau of Information advertised a hefty list of pamphlets and articles related to African American life for discussion at associational meetings. Under the direction of Hattie E. Genung of Shuffield, Connecticut, the Bureau afforded women a circulating library with information specifically on black Americans.

Representative items from the Bureau's literature included: "Negro Education"; "The New Negro"; "A Conference of Negro Women of the South"; "Present Condition of Negroes in the United States"; "Twenty-seven Years for the Afro-American"; "The Colored People in Oklahoma."[55]

The greatest source of publicity on southern black life came through the *Home Mission Echo* and *Tidings*, monthly magazines published by the New England and the Midwest women's societies, respectively. For tens of thousands of women in small northern towns and rural communities, the magazines generated an abundance of facts and correspondence and served as the chief medium of communication connecting women of the various organizational branches with one another, the national leadership, and southern black communities. *Tidings* enjoyed a circulation of 11,000 issues monthly in 1892, rising to 13,000 by 1900. Equally impressive was *Home Mission Echo*, which had grown from a subscription list of 2,700 in 1885, its first year of issuance, to 15,500 by 1899.[56] The magazines introduced various activities, often under the column "Questions for Mission Bands," in order to provoke study and discussion. Again, subject matter reflected a racial outlook atypical for the period. Between 1885 and 1887 the column revealed both the abolitionist heritage of northern women and a thirst for greater knowledge of African American history. A sample of the questions culled from these columns during the two-year period includes the following.

1. In what part of this country was slavery located?

2. When did strong opposition to slavery manifest itself in the North?

3. Mention the names of leading anti-slavery men who labored for years to suppress it.

4. What people engaged in the slave trade, and for what purposes?

5. Where is the slave trade still carried on, and what people are concerned about it?

6. Give some account of the condition of negroes in the South; what were the disabilities under which they labored, and what treatment did they receive from the whites?

7. Which was the first colored Baptist church at the South, and when was it organized?

8. Were there any ministers of marked ability among the colored race?

9. Describe the condition of thousands of refugees and contraband at the time of the Emancipation Proclamation.

10. Give some general facts about the schools and seminaries in the South, the courses of instruction, and the chief aim of the teachers.[57]

Although the immediate objective of the questions was to enhance discussion and appreciation of present educational work, thus keeping the women well informed and updated concerning the schools and curriculum receiving their support, they spurred deeper understanding of the historical legacy of race relations and also challenged the women to investigate the long tradition of autonomous black churches and outstanding black ministers—a tradition dating back to the late eighteenth century with the founding of black Baptist churches in both Petersburg, Virginia, and Savannah, Georgia.[58]

Tidings and *Home Mission Echo* brought northern women into an intimate acquaintanceship with the white and black personalities in the field and with the triumphs and hardships of black communities. Through the pages of both magazines, white northern women traveled in their imaginations across the distant and strange Southland to cities such as Atlanta and Richmond, with their colleges, middle-class blacks, and splendid church edifices. One article reported that the total value of black Baptist church buildings in 1890 exceeded nine million dollars, of which 99 percent had been raised by blacks themselves. Some of the urban black churches were described as elegant multifaceted buildings with pipe organs, carpeted floors, lecture rooms, infant departments, and ladies' parlors.[59]

The magazines, too, vividly portrayed the hard conditions of the urban and rural poor—black families huddled together in overcrowded, dilapidated shanties and victimized by dishonest landlords and merchants. Religion was no less important to these poor families, but their churches, particularly in the rural areas, were shockingly different from the edifices familiar to most northern white women. Rural southern blacks gathered together in one-room log churches. Joanna Moore, who often worshipped and held missionary meetings with blacks in these areas, described the stark conditions to her sisters in the North: "Oftentimes we meet in old sheds or cabins, in the sides of which there are holes large enough to put the fist. Of course in cold rainy weather this is not very comfortable. Again, we hold meetings in houses where there can be no fire, so a large log fire is built just outside the door. We stay in the house until we get so cold that we must go out and get warm, then we come in and go on with our meeting."[60]

The northern white women were also introduced to a folk culture markedly different from their own, and while the overwhelming majority equated much in black culture with superstition and emotionalism in need of reform, a few managed to transcend their racial and cultural chauvinism and to understand black folkways and mannerisms on their own terms. A telling account of the visit of Mary Reynolds, president of the New England women, to Hartshorn College in Richmond illustrates one such exceptional case. Reynolds recounted her conversation with Carrie Dyer, a white missionary teacher at Hartshorn: "I said to Miss Dyer, that noble Christian woman, who is doing so much in aiding girls in their spiritual lives, 'Are not these people very emotional?' She answered, 'Are not we very cold? When should we rejoice if not when we find peace to our souls.'"[61]

The Home Mission schools served as favorite focal points in these vicarious sojourns through the South. Spelman Seminary in Atlanta and Hartshorn College in Richmond, the only two schools exclusively for black women, received the widest attention and support from the northern Baptist women. In a two-part series of articles published in 1887, Mrs. A. E. Gray led her readers on a tour of the Spelman campus—describing its buildings, classes, and students, and identifying rooms by the donors from various northern states.[62] In the June 1887 issue, she guided her readers through the school's library and its Hovey collection, books given by Mrs. Hovey of Goston Highlands in memory of her son to whom they had belonged. Gray identified rooms named in honor of the various northern churches responsible for furnishing them. The magazine's readers also were told about two large recitation rooms connected by folding doors on which was engraved, "Wheat St. Baptist Church, Atlanta, Ga., W. H. Tilman, pastor." Gray observed that "the 'Deborah Society' in that church (colored) contributed largely toward the furnishing," and thus called attention to blacks' contribution to their own educational expenses. Moving next to the Wellesley Room, Gray expressed appreciation to Wellesley College students and reflected: "Dear girls, I often wish that they could know some of their darker sisters in this sunny south land, striving for similar attainments."[63] Wellesley administrators and students appeared to share Gray's sympathies. At the annual meeting of the WABHMS in 1886, Wellesley president Alice Freeman underscored the importance of women's missions in the South. In her paper and also in the paper by Wellesley student Lizzie White, northern women were admonished not to discourage their daughters from becoming missionary teachers in southern black schools.[64]

Excerpts from the school newspaper, the *Spelman Messenger*, were periodically reprinted in the northern women's magazines, giving information about campus events, student viewpoints, and conditions within the larger Atlanta community.[65] The pages of the white Baptist women's magazines featured as well campus life at the Home Mission Society's coeducational schools, such as Shaw University in Raleigh or Benedict in South Carolina. At the same time, the magazines carried reports of schools owned by black Baptists. These reports covered many of the same points of interest: a school's history; Thanksgiving and Christmas activities on campus; physical alterations or additions to school buildings; crowded dormitory conditions; the steady intellectual and religious growth of the students; the great financial sacrifice on the part of many to attend school; work of students during the summer months; deaths and illnesses of teachers and students; and the persistent plea for more teachers and buildings.[66] A common theme presented throughout all the school reports was that of black sacrifice to attend school. Jessie Rice, recently arrived as a teacher at Spelman, was typical of northern whites who had learned to change preconceived notions concerning the role of blacks in the educational expenses they bore. Rice learned to extol the virtue of the sacrifice of black mothers who made tremendous sacrifices to defray tuition costs. One poor mother, Rice related, received four dollars a month as wages, and yet she gave it all to Spelman for her daughter's education. Rice counseled her northern sisters to refrain from negative stereotypes:

> It is the impression of some in the North, that the colored people are indolent, and do not help themselves as much as they might. How many of our white people in the North, earning four dollars a month, would give the entire sum to educate a child? How many of our white students in the North, would work hard at school for eight months in the year, and spend the other four months in

the cotton field, out at service, or teaching a country school to earn sufficient money to attend school the next year?[67]

Black southern women communicated regularly with broad communities of northern women, since their letters and reports were printed monthly in *Tidings* and *Home Mission Echo*. Their letters conveyed racial pride and intimate thoughts as they documented the organizational achievements of black Baptists, related themes heard in a black minister's sermon, mourned the death of a black leader, or told of their own separate religious and teachers' conferences and other events of interest in black communities.[68] At other times, the letters of black women served as painful reminders of raw injustice and inhumanity. In 1892, when lynching reached a record high in the nation, Mary Cook wrote to the Kennebec Association in Maine expressing both despondency and outrage. As the year's death toll mounted to a recorded figure of 155 black victims of lynch law, Cook questioned both the possibility of true black progress and the tenacity with which blacks clung to Christianity given the repression aimed at them. She concluded her letter by describing the protest march that she and 200 other black Kentuckians had made on the state capitol.[69] The lynching in 1892 of Thomas Moss, who ran a successful store in Memphis, found a voice of condemnation not only from Ida B. Wells but also from women writing in the pages of *Tidings*. Powerful images were rendered of deserted churches and people desirous of migrating westward. One writer noted that church members went to the store where they used to buy corn and stood "leaning against the fence that surrounded the silent building, looking mournfully at the closed doors."[70]

Letters such as Cook's and those of black and white missionaries in such places as Mississippi, Tennessee, and Louisiana throughout the 1890s eventually led to an official position being taken by the New England women against lynch law. In 1899 the Woman's American Baptist Home Mission Society passed a resolution in condemnation of rising violence and urged petitions to go out on this matter. Although there is no record that they sent their protest to Congress, they did not smother the burning issue with the silence of most white Americans. Nor did they temper their words in the language of gentility or compromise, but candidly expressed their views on the atrocity of lynching, their commitment to jury trial, and their recognition of the different meaning lynching held for white versus black womanhood. In 1899 the minutes of their executive board read:

> *The terrible conditions which exist in the South* make us cry out in bitterness of soul, "How long, O Lord, how long!" Human beings of a darker hue than we are lynched without trial. A man made in the image of God, destined for eternal life or eternal death, is mutilated, partly burned at the stake, then cut up, and pieces of flesh and bones sold for souvenirs, while a part of the heart is sent in triumph to the Governor of the State. Is this better than barbarism? The cry of the white man, that all this is necessary to protect white women, provokes another question, Who protects negro [sic] women?[71]

The magazines served as barometers of northern Baptist women's attitudes on other racial issues. In their trip from Washington, D.C. to Hartshorn Memorial College in Richmond, WABHMS officers Mary Reynolds and Anna Sargent Hunt not only described the grass-covered earthworks and war-torn walls of Fredericksburg along their route, but also revealed their own racial sensibilities. "We were glad to see there was no color line on cars," Reynolds said in reference to railroad facilities, where "blacks shared like privileges with the whites."[72]

Mixed Motives

At the heart of the northern Baptist women's progressive humanitarian attitudes lay complex, even ambivalent motives. James McPherson's characterization of the "abolitionist legacy" clearly captures an essential factor motivating their work. The women spoke repeatedly of the "righteous indemnity" due blacks for centuries of unrequited toil under slavery. In 1887 Rachel Mather, the northern Baptist founder of a school for orphaned black children in Beaufort, South Carolina, expressed the combined sense of guilt and duty that characterized the WABHMS's neo-abolitionist critique: "The freedmen are natives of *our* land and citizens of *our* Republic; their fathers were brought from the mother country in *our* ships, by *our* merchants, and bought by *our* planters; and the nefarious traffic and subsequent bondage were sanctioned by *our* laws; and furthermore because they have been emancipated and enfranchised by *our* government"[73] (original emphasis).

Yet the humanitarian motives of the northern women were offset by a host of fears, veiled in language of patriotism, self-interest, and cultural chauvinism. Acknowledgment of self-interest resonates in the passage quoted above—in the emphasis on "our" laws, "our" land, "our" government. Underlying the women's missionary work was fear of tumultuous change in their own society. Like the men of the ABHMS and other Protestant evangelicals, they viewed the African American population simultaneously as a vast and fertile mission field and as a threat to national stability.[74] They alluded explicitly to both images as they promoted the cause of the freedpeople. In their efforts to generate financial and other material contributions from their sisters, they raised the specter of black population growth in sobering images. Rachel Mather's article exemplifies the duality of guilt and fear. While stirring the consciences of her sisters concerning their debt to the ex-slaves, she also heightened their awareness of the magnitude of the "Negro problem": "Let us for a moment consider and realize how many they are—more than all the population of New England, West Virginia, Delaware and Florida, with that of Oregon, Colorado, Nevada, and the ten territories all combined—ten times as many as all the Indians, Chinese, Mormons and Alaskans, within all our country's borders—more than twice as many as our whole nation numbered after the war of the Revolution, when she organized the Federal Government with thirteen States."[75]

In addition to fears of potential race warfare in the distant South were fears of upheaval from immigrant groups at their own doorstep. Replete in the writings, minutes, and speeches of northern white Baptist women in the late nineteenth century was anxiety over demographic changes in the North itself, and specifically over the increasing number of immigrants from southern and eastern Europe who, instead of moving to the Far West, "linger in the sea board or more eastern cities, adding to the idle and more dangerous classes."[76]

The New England women found the growing numbers and influence of Roman Catholics in Boston particularly disturbing. They expressed "something of the feeling of almost terror which has from our childhood enveloped the words Roman Catholic." For those present at the

Peoples' Church in Boston on 10 February 1894, the anti-Catholic bias was unmistakable in the sermon of ABHMS corresponding secretary T. J. Morgan, who called for the preservation of American democratic institutions, separation of church and state, and immigration restriction. The northern Baptist women posited no challenge to Morgan's strong pronouncement that "every honorable means and all upright methods should be employed by us of to-day, to resist the steady approaches of this insidious foe [Roman Catholics], and to preserve our constitution, our free schools, our free states, our free church, and hand them down to the next generation." Rather they reconfirmed Morgan's sentiments, linked the Catholic presence with the "liquor traffic," and waged an obsessive campaign against the prospect of Catholics' demanding the allocation of tax dollars for parochial schools. They labeled the activities of Catholics, who had called for censoring certain public school textbooks in Boston and who had removed their children from the public school system, as menacing to principles of free education—the hallmark of American democracy.[77]

The northern women's anxiety over their social location in late nineteenth-century America was not entirely unfounded. Unprecedented urbanization and industrialization spawned labor unrest along with the breakdown of familiar and traditional social patterns.[78] As immigration soared to new heights during the last quarter of the nineteenth century, a growing diversity of cultures and colors crowded the urban North and challenged the numerical hegemony of those Americans of northern European Protestant stock. The northern white women waged "peaceful Gospel warfare" against a multitude of foes who, in ever-increasing flanks, advanced against a retreating Protestantism. Their xenophobic and culturally elitist world view evoked the belief that only the assimilation of middle-class, Protestant values safeguarded America from peril. Without such assimilation, their nation stood defenseless against the impending reign of alien cultures—of immigrants prone to political agitation and anarchism; the un-Christian Chinese in the West; the polygamous Mormons in Utah; Roman Catholics with their allegiance to the Pope and parochial schools; Native Americans with heathen tribal practices; and blacks, whom slavery and illiteracy left prey to superstition and other degraded cultural practices.[79] Convinced of a national emergency, the northern Baptist women in the Midwest and New England consecrated themselves to the causes of spiritual regeneration and societal reform, for in their view both "eternal interests, and temporal good" were at stake. Such an emergency, as they perceived it, entangled their own destinies with those alien and opposing, but they frequently portrayed blacks, unlike the other groups, as potentially loyal and needed allies.

The mixed motives of the northern Baptist women did not preclude interracial cooperation. While different from those of black women, the white women's motives were not incompatible with blacks' desire for racial dignity and self-help. The northern white women exhibited their neo-abolitionist outlook in the fervor with which they committed themselves to aiding black education, working with black women's societies, and providing means to the needy. They did so while making parallels between the Civil War and what they feared would be a second Civil War in the 1880s.

Northern white women missionaries became acutely aware of the contribution of black soldiers in upholding the Union once they set up mission stations in the South. Rachel Mather wrote from South Carolina to her sisters in the North: "We have needed them in the history of our country; we may need them yet again. Two hundred thousand colored soldiers, it is estimated, served faithfully in the war of the Rebellion. Unlike other foreigners among us, they are a loyal people, and may be counted upon as true to the government that enfranchised them. Policy and papacy cannot shake their allegiance."[80]

In 1892 *Tidings* carried the report of the black missionary Amelia Scott, who called attention once again to the role of black soldiers. Noting the importance of May 30th to black Mississippians, Scott had joined with several hundred of her people in their quiet trek to the cemetery in observance of those lost in the Civil War. Her poignant story relayed to the northern women an explicit recognition of black loyalty to the Union cause. Scott confessed the "feeling of reverence" that came over her as she stood in the "city of the dead" and saw American flags at the head of sixteen thousand graves—"the flag they died to save."[81] It was this legacy of black patriotism that prompted northern Baptists to perceive a continued though double-edged black role, either aiding in the restoration of national harmony or abetting in its destruction.

Missionary work among blacks therefore sought to ensure the direction in which the black pendulum would swing. Patriotism and pragmatism dictated that the freedpeople be made an intelligent part of the body politic. Mary Burdette's sometime usage of the term "Anglo Africans" for blacks signified the assimilationist goal of her society.[82] Assimilation was to be based upon a single American prototype—the white middle-class northern Protestant. At the root of her organization and that of her sisters in New England rested the presumption that assimilation could be effected only through schools and families, and specifically through the medium of women either as mothers or as teachers. The northern white women rejected the idea that laws and prisons would hasten black conformity to Yankee values. In the case of black America, the white Baptists concluded that their patriotic duty was to send forth "a great army of colored women . . . qualified to labor in the black belt of the South and accomplish a work which white people cannot do."[83]

Baptist women's work for women, though filled with paradox, assumed a breadth unlimited by the racial and class boundaries of most late nineteenth-century Americans. At a time when Social Darwinist ideas held sway over the mass of white Americans and convinced them of the innate mental inferiority of blacks as compared to whites, the message put forward in the pages of Baptist women's magazines defied such assumptions. In many ways, their views countered the apathy or, worse yet, consent on the part of most Americans to the South's racist retrenchment policies during the late nineteenth century. This is not to say that negative, indeed racist pronouncements about black culture were absent from their writings. Northern Baptist women clearly believed in the civilizing influence of their home mission work and condemned black people to immediate ruin and barbarism if left to themselves. Most rejected the emotionalism in the black style of worship. Their own cultural chauvinism had little tolerance for diversity, as can be seen in their repeated references to the need for upgrading black preaching so as to appeal more to the intellect. Joanna Moore, though highly esteemed among black Baptists, revealed her cultural bias when she escorted four black ministers to the white Baptist church in New Orleans so that they could learn to emulate new preaching models, namely a less emotional style. However, her visit to the white church defied southern racial etiquette as well, for

Moore had no qualms about introducing her black colleagues with the expectation that they would be welcomed and treated as respectfully as any other visitors to the church.[84]

Duty and Privilege

Despite the paradox, the mixed motives of northern Baptist women produced a liberal response, which they interpreted as both "duty and privilege" in their endeavor to combat black poverty, degradation, and illiteracy. This response sought to develop within their own communities "the feeling of *individual responsibility*, to induce each sister, youth and child to experience for themselves the blessedness of cheerful giving."[85] The ability to aid in the home mission cause varied according to socioeconomic status and also by the state of the economy, but despite marginal resources on the part of some women and periodic economic recession, northern Baptist women continued to increase their financial support of the southern mission field throughout the last two decades of the nineteenth century. During the hard times of 1885 Maine's missionary leader observed much poverty in her travels throughout sections of her state. In a particular association there were only two large churches, and the poverty of many of the people caused her to feel guilty for even asking the financially weak churches to take part in the southern drive. She solicited their assistance nevertheless, believing that mission work ultimately stimulated and strengthened overall growth in women's organizations and churches. Even the poorest churches responded to the call for a Sunday collection for the support of Mary Cook's educational expenses. Other reports from Maine referred to poor churches without pastors who proved to be "noble examples of self-denial and consecration." In 1885 the report from Rhode Island observed the "all absorbing theme" of the depression, and yet the branch had gone forward with its support of Hartshorn Memorial College, named in memory of Rachel Hartshorn, WABHMS vice-president from Rhode Island.[86]

Gifts of material resources other than money were equally striking for the comfort and support they carried to the poor. Minutes of associations throughout New England and the Midwest reported that women met together, cut and basted garments, and sent boxes and barrels laden with Bibles, Sunday school literature, sewing materials, bedding, table-linen, groceries, and clothing.[87] Women from North Uxbridge, Massachusetts, noted in their report of 8 December 1887 the popularity of the barrel packing projects by which secondhand clothing and reading materials were sent to the southern states. In one New England town, where women were too poor to raise funds for the black schools, they gathered to make a quilt instead.[88]

Northern Baptist women, in effect, articulated a set of values that ran counter to social trends in the 1890s—first, in their perceived sense of interracial cooperation at a time of heightened Jim Crow and, second, in their emphasis on self-denial during an age of heightened materialism.[89] These alternate values not only underlay their percep- tion of women's spiritual responsibility in the advancement of race and gender interests, but formed the basis for integrating youth, along with ideas regarding youth socialization, into the religious culture of women's missions. This socialization process came to be realized through organized and systematic missionary activity, not merely from mothers' teaching within the home. Girls and boys at an early age were indoctrinated with the spirit of interracial cooperation and the "duty and privilege" of self-denial, although the women admitted difficulty in maintaining the interest of boys once they reached their teens.[90]

As northern Baptist women established children's groups, they once again found the missionary magazine to be their most effective me- dium— in this case linking children of different races and cultures in common cause and instilling in them an appreciation and zeal for organized work. Children of all ages were brought systematically into the larger program of women's missions and were urged to find "be- tween your tasks and your pleasures . . . time for sad thoughts upon those less fortunate than you, and longing to help them." White children were certainly taught to respect the same cultural elitism of their elders, but they were also urged to recognize the social responsi- bility mandated by their advantaged status. The didactic use of short stories allowed missionary women to preach to young and old alike about the virtue of sacrificial giving. The stories illustrate the effort to solicit a broad sympathy among young people for black education. For example, in "A True Incident" Fannie Allen tells the story of little six-year-old Jessie, who felt her heart "stirred to its very depths as she heard the sad story of four homeless little children, whose father was dead, mother dying, and who would be left without anyone to care for them, without food to eat, or clothes to wear, unless some kind friends took pity on them."[91] Through the children's missionary band Jessie made a pledge to collect pennies. Carrying her basket in which she was to save her pennies, she declared: "Mamma I mustn't buy any more peanuts" (peanuts had been her chief extravagance). Although her mother admonished that "if you save your money for them you won't have any for peanuts," the child rejected the parental advice and assured her mother that saving her pennies for the needy was more important. "'Why Jessie,' said papa, 'if you send your money to those children they will spend it for peanuts, then they will have peanuts and you will have to do without,'" but Jessie affirmed: "I don't care, pap. I've had them all my life and they never had any." Jessie's influence proved an incentive to other members of her band, whose "busy fingers flew faster as they worked on basted patchwork for the Industrial schools of the missionaries," and at the end of three months they had amassed $53.00.

In *Tidings* and *Home Mission Echo* columns with such titles as "My Precious Jewels," "Children's Corner," and "Our Young Folks" reproduced letters and short stories for children. Familial designations accompanied the names of the columns' authors, with "aunt" preceding the name of whites and "cousin" preceding that of blacks.[92] "Cousin Carrie," Spelman student Carrie Walls, and "Cousin Lulu," black Louisville teacher Lulu Osborne, appeared periodically in the magazines. Northern white children read the *Spelman Messenger*, in which "Cousin Carrie" featured their letters in her column "Children's Exchange." Letters came to her from cities as distant as New Haven, Connecticut, and Ann Arbor, Michigan. "Dear Little Cousin," Carrie Walls began words of gratitude to a child in Hoosick Falls, New York, who had sent 96 illustrated Bible cards. "One of the New Haven cousins wants to know if we would not like to have snow once in a while," she also reported, and then assured the child that snow came almost every winter, albeit nothing like the snowfall in the North.[93] Children's columns, whether appearing in southern black women's newspapers or northern white women's, were designed to instill a sense of civic responsibility and common cause in young children. Black Baptist children in Selma, Alabama, organized a page in the *Baptist Woman's Era*, published by the black women of the state, to encourage racial self-help by donating pennies to Selma University. Likewise a children's mission band in St. Albans, Vermont, ranging in age from 4 to 13, sponsored a fair in order to aid Minnie Robinson, a student at the black-controlled State University at Louisville.[94]

The role of women's missions proved a noteworthy exception to the betrayal of blacks' hopes for equality and justice during the late nineteenth century. As the white South structured a segregated society and sanctioned, either explicitly or implicitly, the violence perpetrated upon black communities, evangelical religion in the form of organized women's missions fostered bonds of interracial cooperation in an effort to uplift the quality of black life in the South. Notwithstanding its imperfections, interracial cooperation between black and white Baptist women did find concrete ways to offer hope and opportunity. For most black women, such a sisterhood promised too little to nullify the oppressive effects of racial caste. For a few, like Mary Cook, it indeed made upward mobility possible and instilled a new and gendered vision of self, inspiring dreams of racial justice and women's rights. This unlikely sisterhood, having been forged in the crucible of racial oppression, could deliver no panacea, but it could and did convey to many nameless black women greater optimism and sense of strength.

As critical historical actors in racial self-help and women's missions, black women, therefore, served as the node for two seemingly opposing trends in American race relations, and by so doing illustrate the convergence rather than the separation of racial and gender interests. They characterized their struggle for education, like their larger struggle for social and economic advancement, in the discourse of both race and gender. Black Baptist women, while experiencing racial identity through gendered lives and expressing their own contribution to the struggle of their people in a distinctly female voice, simultaneously perceived womanhood in American society through the lens of race. Black educator Anna J. Cooper stated in 1892: "When and where I enter in the quiet, undisputed dignity of my womanhood without violence and without suing or special patronage, then and there the whole Negro race enters with me."[95] To the degree that white women sympathized with and facilitated this quest of black women for full equality and respect, the fruits of interracial cooperation made America, even during the "nadir," better than it otherwise would have been.

5

Feminist Theology, 1880–1900

What if I am a woman; is not the God of ancient times the God of these modern days: Did he not raise up Deborah, to be a mother and a judge in Israel [Judges 4:4]? Did not queen Esther save the lives of the Jews? And Mary Magdalene first declare the resurrection of Christ from the dead?

Maria Stewart, "Farewell Address," 21 September 1833

Boston black minister Peter Randolph cited gender proscriptions among the "strange customs" that he confronted when he returned to his Virginia birthplace soon after the Civil War to assume the pastorate of Richmond's Ebenezer Baptist Church. Randolph noted the segregated seating for men and women and the men's refusal to permit women at the business meetings of the church. Charles Octavius Boothe, a black Baptist minister in Alabama, recalled that in the early years of freedom women were not accustomed to the right to pray publicly.[1] Even as late as the 1880s in Tennessee and in Arkansas, black women met with virulent hostility in their efforts to establish separate societies.

During the last two decades of the nineteenth century black Baptist women increasingly challenged such examples of gender inequality. Working within the orthodoxy of the church, they turned to the Bible to argue for their rights—thus holding men accountable to the same text that authenticated their arguments for racial equality. In drawing upon the Bible—the most respected source within their community—they found scriptural precedents for expanding women's rights. Black women expressed their discontent with popular conceptions regarding "woman's place" in the church and society at large. They challenged the "silent helpmate" image of women's church work and set out to convince the men that women were equally obliged to advance not only their race and denomination, but themselves. Thus the black Baptist women developed a theology inclusive of equal gender participation. They articulated this viewpoint before groups of men and women in churches, convention anniversaries, and denominational schools, and in newspapers and other forms of literature.

The religious posture of black Baptist women was contextualized within a racial tradition that conflated private/eschatological witness and public/political stand. Saving souls and proselytizing the unconverted were integral to black women's missions, but their work was not limited to the private sphere of spiritual experience. The public discourse of church leaders and members, both male and female, had historically linked social regeneration, in the specific form of racial advancement, to spiritual regeneration. According to the ethicist Peter Paris, the principle of human freedom and equality under God constituted the "social teaching" of the black churches. This social teaching survived as a "nonracist appropriation of the Christian faith" and as a critique of American racism. The social teaching of human equality distinguished black churches from their white counterparts and represented a liberating principle "justifying and motivating all endeavors by blacks for survival and transformation."[2]

While the "nonracist" principle called attention to a common tradition shared by black churches, it masked the sexism that black churches shared with the dominant white society. Black women reinterpreted the church's social teaching so that human equality embraced gender as well. In the process, they came to assert their own voice through separate women's societies and through their recognition of an evangelical sisterhood that crossed racial lines. Within a female-centered context, they accentuated the image of woman as saving force, rather than woman as victim. They rejected a model of womanhood that was fragile and passive, just as they deplored a type preoccupied with fashion, gossip, or self-indulgence. They argued that women held the key to social transformation, and thus America offered them a vast mission field in which to solicit as never before the active participation of self-disciplined, self-sacrificing workers.[3] Through the convention movement, black Baptist women established a deliberative arena for addressing their own concerns. Indeed, one could say that the black Baptist church represented a sphere for public deliberation and debate precisely because of women.

Orthodoxy's Gendered Vision

The feminist theology in the black Baptist church during the late nineteenth century conforms to Rosemary Ruether's and Eleanor McLaughlin's concept of a "stance of 'radical obedience.'" Referring to female leadership in Christianity, Ruether and McLaughlin distinguished women's positions of "loyal dissent" that arose within the mainline churches from women's positions of heresy that completely rejected the doctrines of the traditional denominations. They argued for the wider influence of women inside rather than outside the denominations, since women in the "stance of 'radical obedience'" seized orthodox theology in defense of sexual equality.[4]

If black Baptist women did not break from orthodoxy, they clearly restated it in progressive, indeed liberating language for women. In many respects their gendered vision of orthodoxy was analogous to the progressive racial theology already espoused by black ministers. In the Jim Crow America of the late nineteenth century, the Reverend Rufus Perry's *The Cushites, or the Descendants of Ham as Found in the Sacred Scriptures* (1893) dared to interpret the Bible as a source of ancient black history—as the root upon which race pride should grow.[5] Nor was a progressive, liberating theology new to blacks. For generations under slavery, African Americans rejected scriptural texts in defense of human bondage. Despite the reluctance of the slavemaster to quote the biblical passage "neither bond nor free in Christ Jesus," the slaves expressed its meaning in their spirituals and prayers. However, in the black Baptist church of the late nineteenth century, the women in the leadership called attention to the verse in its more complete form: "Neither bond nor free, neither male nor female in Christ Jesus."

By expounding biblical precedents, black women presented the intellectual and theological justification for their rights. But they expressed, too, a gendered interpretation of the Bible. The multivalent religious symbols within the Bible had obviously caused slavemasters and slaves, whites and blacks to invoke "orthodoxy" with meanings quite different from one another. It is perhaps less obvious that the Bible served dually to constrain and liberate women's position vis-à-vis men's in society. Caroline Bynum acknowledges gender differences in the way people appropriate and interpret religion in its symbolic and practical forms, inasmuch as people are gendered beings, not humans in the abstract. Bynum calls attention to the radical potential in this acknowledgment: "For if symbols can invert as well as reinforce social values . . . if traditional rituals can evolve to meet the needs of new participants . . . then old symbols can acquire new meanings, and these new meanings might suggest a new society."[6]

Even more important than the multivalent character of biblical symbolism are the very acts of reappropriation and reinterpretation of the Bible by black women themselves. As interpreters of the Bible, black women mediated its effect in relation to their own interests. Rita Felski asserts this point in her discussion of the social function of textual interpretation: "Radical impulses are not inherent in the formal properties of texts; they can be realized only through interactions between texts and readers, so that it becomes necessary to situate the . . . text in relation to the interests and expectations of potential audiences."[7]

The black Baptist women's advocacy of a new social order combined a progressive gendered and racialized representation of orthodoxy. However, their biblically based arguments were neither new nor unique. During the first half of the nineteenth century, black women such as Maria Stewart, Jarena Lee, and Sojourner Truth were precursors in adopting a scriptural defense of women's rights. In 1832 Maria Stewart, a free black in Massachusetts, was the first woman—black or white—to stand before an audience of men and women and offer biblical precedents in denunciation of sexism, slavery, the denial of adequate education to blacks, and other forms of oppression. Her social consciousness was molded by private religious conviction, which figured centrally in her public pronouncements. Marilyn Richardson has observed: "Resistance to oppression was, for Stewart, the highest form of obedience to God."[8] In her farewell address to the people in Boston in 1833, Stewart called forth names of biblical women who, with divine sanction, led the ancient Hebrew people. She then posed to the women of her own time: "What if such women as are here described should rise among our sable race?"[9]

During the 1880s and 1890s black women in the Baptist and Methodist churches, and such Protestant Episcopal women as Anna J.

Cooper, posed a similar question. It is conceivable that all were influenced by Stewart's speeches, since she lived to publish her collected works in 1879. Stewart's influence notwithstanding, the public discourse of black women formed part of a broader trend in liberal theology, which sought to bring the Bible into greater harmony with values and assumptions related to women's changing status and a variety of other social and scientific developments.

Women's Theologizing

Women members of the male-dominated American National Baptist Convention, forerunner of the National Baptist Convention, U.S.A., were the first to question the illusory unity of the convention as the voice of all its people. Within this national body, Virginia Broughton of Tennessee and Mary Cook and Lucy Wilmot Smith of Kentucky were the most vocal in defense of women's rights. Broughton, Cook, and Smith were active in organizing separate Baptist women's conventions in the face of varying levels of male support and hostility. They spoke for an expanding public of women who stood in opposition to exclusive male power and dominance.

All three women were born in the South during the last years of slavery, but Broughton's background was the most privileged. She described her father as an "industrious man" who hired out his time from his master and subsequently bought his wife's and his own freedom. Raised as a free black, Broughton enrolled in a private school taught by a Professor Daniel Watkins during her adolescent years. She graduated from Fisk University in 1875—claiming to be the first woman of any race to gain a collegiate degree from a southern school. She was married to John Broughton, a lawyer active in Republican Party politics in Memphis, although she continued to work as a teacher and full-time missionary throughout her married life. In 1885, Broughton's feminist attitude surfaced when she challenged the appointment of a less experienced, black male teacher over herself. Supported by her husband, she eventually won her case as head teacher in the Kortrecht school—the only black public school in Memphis to have one year of high school instruction.[10]

After working for twelve years as a teacher in the public school system and as a part-time missionary for at least five of those years,

Broughton left the school system to become a full-time missionary. She was immensely popular among southern black and northern white Baptist women. Her stature as a national figure among black Baptists continued to rise in the upcoming century.[11] Broughton's gendered appropriation of biblical symbols shaped her understanding of the women of her own day; she traced the Baptist women's movement and its providential evolution to Eve in the Garden of Eden. In *Women's Work, as Gleaned from the Women of the Bible* (1904), Broughton summed up the ideas that had marked her public lectures, correspondence, and house-to-house visitations since the 1880s, and she sought to inspire the church women of her day "to assume their several callings."[12]

Mary Cook was born a slave in Kentucky in 1862. Raised in a very humble environment, she was able to acquire a college education partly through the philanthropy of white Baptist women in New England and partly through the support of the Reverend William J. Simmons, black Baptist minister and president of the State University at Louisville. Cook graduated from the Normal Department of the State University at Louisville in 1883 and subsequently taught Latin and literature at her alma mater.[13] Like Broughton, Cook worked closely with the black Baptist women of her state and enjoyed communication with northern white Baptist women. In 1898 she married the Reverend Charles H. Parrish, a leader among black Baptists in Kentucky. She was active in the national convention of black Baptist women, which was founded in 1900, and also in secular black women's clubs, especially the National Association of Colored Women.

Cook, the most scholarly of the three women, expressed her views in the black press, in an edited anthology, and in speeches before various groups, including the American National Baptist Convention. She served on the executive board of the ANBC and was honored by being selected to speak on women's behalf in the classic statement of black Baptist doctrine, *The Negro Baptist Pulpit* (1890). In often militant language, Cook strove to enlarge women's power in the church. She termed the Bible an "iconoclastic weapon" that would destroy negative images of her sex and overcome the popular misconceptions of woman's place in the church and society. Like Broughton, Cook derived her position from the "array of heroic and saintly women whose virtues have made the world more tolerable."[14]

Although it is not clear whether Lucy Wilmot Smith was born a slave, she is reported to have grown up in a very poor household. Born in 1861, Smith was raised by her mother, who as sole provider struggled to give her daughter an education. Smith graduated from the normal department of the State University at Louisville, taught at her alma mater, and also worked as a journalist. She never married. At the time of her premature death in 1890, she was principal of the Model School at the State University at Louisville. A leader in the Baptist Woman's Educational Convention of Kentucky, she sat on its Board of Managers and served as the secretary of its children's division. Like Cook, she was one of very few women to hold an office in the male-dominated American National Baptist Convention. She served as Historian of the ANBC, wrote extensively in the black press, and delivered strong feminist statements at the annual meetings of the ANBC.[15] She ardently supported woman's suffrage. Her death in 1890 prevented her from joining Broughton and Cook in the later movement to organize a national women's convention. Cook eulogized her: "She was connected with all the leading interests of her race and denomination. Her pen and voice always designated her position so clearly that no one need mistake her motive."[16]

None of the women was a theologian in any strict or formal sense, and yet their theocentric view of the world in which they lived justifies calling them theologians in the broad spirit that Gordon Kaufman describes:

> Obviously, Christians are involved in theologizing at every turn. Every attempt to discover and reflect upon the real meaning of the Gospel, of a passage in the Bible, of Jesus Christ, is theologizing; every effort to discover the bearing of the Christian faith or the Christian ethic on the problems of personal and social life is theological. For Christian theology is the critical analysis and creative development of the language utilized in apprehending, understanding, and interpreting God's acts, facilitating their communication in word and deed.[17]

As Kaufman implies, the act of theologizing was not limited to the formally trained male clergy. Nor did it extend only to college-educated women such as Broughton, Cook, and Smith. Scriptural interpretation figured significantly in the meetings of ordinary black women's local and state organizations. Virginia Broughton noted a tremendous groundswell of black women engaged in biblical explication in their homes, churches, and associational meetings.[18] In 1884 Lizzie Crittenden, chairman of the board of managers of the women's convention in Kentucky, identified the women's gendered interpretation of orthodoxy as revelation of their continued organizational growth: "It has really been marvelous how much has been found in the sacred word to encourage us that before had been left unsaid and seemed unheeded."[19] The reports of northern white missionaries in southern black communities confirmed these observations. Mary O'Keefe, a white missionary in Tennessee, wrote to her Chicago headquarters that black women in Bible Bands recited and interpreted passages of Scripture at their meetings. O'Keefe was fascinated by their black expressive culture. One elderly black woman, interpreting a scriptural text, became louder and louder in her delivery. "The last word came out with a whoop," O'Keefe recounted, "which was echoed and re-echoed by the others until it was quite evident that her view was accepted."[20] Mary Burdette, a leader of white Baptist women in the Midwest, also found black Baptist women engaged in biblical study during her tour of Tennessee. The women discussed ancient role models in justification of current demands for participatory parity within the denomination. Burdette described their round-table discussion: "Six sisters added to the interest by brief essays and addresses relating to women's place and work in the church as illustrated by the women of the Bible. Mrs. Broughton spoke of Eve, the mother of us all and the wife given to Adam for a help-meet, and following her we heard of Deborah, and that from her history we could learn that while men might be called to deliver Israel, they could not do it without the presence and assistance of Christian women."[21]

The enthusiasm with which black women of all educational backgrounds claimed their right to theological interpretation was characterized by Virginia Broughton as part of the "general awakening and rallying together of Christian women" of all races. There were other black women who joined Broughton, Cook, and Smith in voicing gender concerns. Black women interpreters of the Bible perceived themselves as part of the vanguard of the movement to present the theological discussion of woman's place.[22] They used the Bible to sanction both domestic and public roles for women. While each of the feminist theologians had her own unique style and emphasis, a textual analysis of their writings reveals their common concern for women's empowerment in the home, the church, social reform, and the labor force. The Baptist women invoked biblical passages that portrayed positive images of women and reinforced their claim to the public realm. This realm, according to the literary critic Sue E. Houchins, provided black religious women like Broughton and others an arena in which they could transcend culturally proscribed gender roles and "could 'function as person[s] of authority,' could resist the pressures of family and society . . . and could achieve legal and structural support from the church for their work as spiritual advisors, teachers, and occasional preachers."[23]

The Gospel according to Woman

The feminist theologians of the black Baptist church did not characterize woman as having a fragile, impressionable nature, but rather as having a capacity to influence man. They described woman's power of persuasion over the opposite sex as historically positive, for the most part, although they also mentioned a few instances of woman's negative influence, notably, the biblical stories of Delilah and Jezebel. But even this discussion emphasized man's vulnerability to woman's strength, albeit sometimes pernicious, and never recognized an innate feminine weakness to fall to temptation. Mary Cook asserted that woman "may send forth healthy, purifying streams which will enlighten the heart and nourish the seeds of virtue; or cast a dim shadow, which will enshroud those upon whom it falls in moral darkness."[24]

According to the feminist theologians, while the Bible depicted women in a dual image, it also portrayed good and evil men, and thus only affirmed woman's likeness to man and her oneness with him in the joint quest for salvation. Virginia Broughton insisted that the Genesis story explicitly denied any right of man to oppress woman. Her interpretation of woman's creation stressed God's not having formed Eve out of the "crude clay" from which he had molded Adam. She reminded her readers that God purposely sprang Eve from a bone, located in Adam's side and under his heart, for woman to be man's companion and helpmate, and she noted that God took the bone neither from Adam's head for woman to reign over him, nor from his foot for man to stand over her. Broughton observed that if woman had been Satan's tool in man's downfall, she was also God's instrument for human regeneration, since God entrusted the germ for human redemption to Eve alone. By commanding that "the seed of woman shall bruise the serpent's head," God had linked redemption inseparably with motherhood and woman's role in the physical deliverance of the Redeemer.[25]

Feminist theologians praised and took pride in the mothers of Isaac, Moses, Samson, and other greater or lesser heroes of the Old Testament. They described the women of the Old Testament as providing far more than the bodily receptacles through which great men were born into the world. They were responsible for rearing and molding the sons who would deliver Israel from its oppressors. The mother's determining hand could extend as far back as the child's prenatal stage—or so concluded Virginia Broughton in a reference to Samson's mother: "An angel appeared to Manoah's wife, told her she should have a son and instructed her how to deport herself after the conception, that Samson might be such a one as God would have him be, to deliver Israel from the oppression of the Philistines."[26]

Since motherhood was regarded as the greatest sanctity, Mary the mother of Jesus personified the highest expression of womanhood. Of all biblical mothers, she assumed the position of the "last and sublimest illustration in this relation."[27] Hers was motherhood in its purest, most emphatically female form, for it was virginal and thus without the intercession of a man. To the feminist theologians of the black Baptist church, Jesus, conceived from the union of woman and the Angel of God, became the fruition of God's commandment in Genesis. Mary Cook used her knowledge of ancient history and the Latin classics to add further insight concerning the virgin mother theme: she revealed its roots in antiquity by calling attention to the concept of virgin mother as a literary motif. Citing parallels with the story of the twins, Remus and Romulus, the mythical founders of Rome, Mary Cook posited, "Silvia became their mother by the God Mars, even as Christ was the son of the Holy Ghost."[28]

Although motherhood remained the salient image in their writings and speeches, Broughton, Cook, and Smith did not find their own personal lives consumed with maternal responsibilities. Lucy Wilmot Smith never had a husband or child, nor did Mary Cook during the period when she wrote her feminist theological texts. Broughton, on the other hand, was married with five children, and even lectured on the subject of "the ideal mother." Yet she spent little time in the actual role of mothering. She admitted taking her son periodically with her on missionary trips, but more often the care of the younger children fell to older siblings, other family members, and a number of "good women secured from time to time." In fact Broughton noted that all her children were taught domestic duties at an early age. The eldest daughter, Elizabeth, fixed suppers for the family and "was always solic- itous about her mother's comfort."[29] Although she wrote lovingly of her children in her autobiography, Broughton undoubtedly valued her missionary work above every other responsibility. This is clearly re- vealed in the case of her daughter's illness. Broughton canceled a missionary engagement to join her sick daughter Selena, who died a few days after her mother's return home. She never again canceled a missionary engagement, for her daughter's death had taught her that "she could stay home and sit by the bedside of her children and have all the assistance that medical skill could render, and yet God could take her children to himself if he so willed it."[30] What may seem callous by today's standards was not viewed as such by Broughton's household. Broughton describes her last hours with her daughter as loving spiritual moments that influenced all of the family members to "think seriously of heavenly things." Her single-minded devotion to missions did not result in censure or condemnation by her community. Broughton commanded the respect of the women in her community and black Baptist women across the nation.

In addition to motherhood, the feminist theologians referred to the roles of wife, sister, and daughter in order to complete the larger picture of woman's participation in the home. They frequently attributed a man's conversion or a minister's righteous lifestyle to a mother's influence, a sister's guidance, or to the tender persuasion of a devoted wife or daughter. Marriage was presented as "a holy estate." Speaking before the American National Baptist Convention in 1888 on the subject "Women in the Home," Mrs. G. D. Oldham of Tennessee asserted: "The home is the first institution God established on earth. Not the church, or the state, but the home." To Oldham, woman's domestic role was of supreme importance and represented her "true sphere," since within the home, woman exercised her greatest influence of all; there she reigned "queen of all she surveys, her sway there is none can dispute, her power there is none can battle." Although Oldham acknowledged that exceptional women would seek work outside the home and indicated her hope that they not be excluded from careers in government and the natural sciences, she firmly believed that most women would confine their activities to domestic duties. She exhorted women to be the ministers, not the slaves of their homes. Woman as homemaker should provide her husband with an atmosphere of comfort and bliss. Oldham's image of marriage and home life romanticized woman's ability to create a refuge from worldly pressures and problems. Home life was to resemble the "center of a cyclone where not even a feather is moved by the hurricane that roars around it."[31]

For feminist theologians such as Cook and Broughton, the image of woman as loyal, comforting spouse transcended the husband-wife relationship to embrace that of Jesus and woman. They were quick to point out that no woman betrayed Jesus and noted that a woman had bathed his feet with her tears and wiped them with her hair, while Mary and Martha had soothed him in their home after his long, tiring journey. Biblical women had expressed their faith through acts of succor and kindness much more than had men. Yet Cook and Broughton coupled woman's domestic image as comforter with the public responsibility of prophesying and spreading the gospel. Cook remarked that in Samaria, Jesus engaged in conversation with the woman at the well, "which was unlawful for a man of respect to do," and by so doing set a new standard for encouraging woman's intellect and permitting "her to do good for mankind and the advancement of His cause."[32]

Their emphasis on woman's relationship with Jesus ironically, albeit subtly, shifted women's duties outside the home, since woman's primary obligation was interpreted to be to God rather than husband. This was evident in Virginia Broughton's own marriage. Broughton resisted pressures of family and society by proclaiming her allegiance to God above family. She boldly alluded to her work as independent of her husband's wishes. Not yet converted when she began mission work, Broughton's husband demanded that she cease this endeavor, since it took her away from home and family for several days at a time. When he asked, "When is this business going to stop?" Broughton replied with what she termed a divinely inspired answer. "I don't know," she hurled at him, "I belong to God first, and you next; so you two must settle it." According to Broughton, her husband eventually came around to her way of thinking, "after a desperate struggle with the world, the flesh, and the devil." Broughton was able to convince her husband that she was called by God for missionary work and that "to hinder her would mean death to him."[33]

During the late nineteenth century feminist theology turned to the example of women leaders in the Old and New Testaments as sanction for more aggressive church work. Both Cook and Broughton reinterpreted biblical passages that had traditionally restricted woman's role—particularly Paul's dictum in the book of Corinthians that women remain silent in church. For Cook, an analysis of the historical context of Paul's statement revealed that his words were addressed specifically "to a few Grecian and Asiatic women who were wholly given up to idolatry and to the fashion of the day." Her exegesis denied the passage universal applicability. Its adoption in the late nineteenth century served as merely a rationalization to overlook and minimize the important contribution and growing force of woman's work in the church. Both Cook and Broughton argued that Paul praised the work of various women and, at times, depended upon them. The feminist theologians particularly enjoyed citing Paul's respect for Phoebe, the deaconess of the church at Cenchrea. Having entrusted Phoebe with an important letter to Rome, Paul demanded that everyone along her route lend assistance if needed. The Baptist women added the names of others who aided Paul, for example, Priscilla, Mary, Lydia, and "quite a number of women who had been co-workers with the apostle."[34]

In a speech before the male-dominated American National Baptist Convention in 1887, Mary Cook praised ministers such as William J. Simmons, who took a progressive stand toward women and included them in the convention's programs. She acknowledged the traditional roles of assisting pastors and working in Sunday Schools, but noted the increasing interest of women in business meetings and other church affairs. Alerting the men that this was only the beginning of women's denominational activity, Cook expressed the rising expectations of black Baptist women for organizational work when she declared that women would play a vital role in the work of the Baptist church in the future. This would require many changes, which Cook interpreted as a holy mandate from God: "God is shaking up the church—He is going to bring it up to something better and that too, greatly through the work of the women."[35]

From a perspective slightly different from Cook's, Virginia Broughton also rejected a literal interpretation of Paul's injunction to silence women in church. As she had done in her own home life, Broughton insisted that a woman's allegiance to God transcended her more conventional and earthbound responsibilities. Paul, Broughton argued, was well aware that mankind was both carnal and spiritual. But Christians distinguished themselves by their spirituality; they served not Mammon but God through the spirit. Paul's meaning was clear to Broughton: "Woman according to the flesh is made for the glory of man; but when recreated in Christ or born of the Spirit, she is recreated for such spiritual service as God may appoint through the examples given in his Word." She added that Peter had affirmed Joel's prediction that both sons and daughters would prophesy. Despite the broad number of roles that Broughton believed the Bible authorized and her rather unusual autonomy within her own household, she explicitly warned women against the danger of aspiring to roles that had no female precedents in the Bible. She denied that women should have access to the clergy or perform the clergy's role of establishing new churches, baptizing converts, and administering the Eucharist. Notwithstanding these proscriptions, Broughton argued for the presence of women on the executive boards of both state and national conventions of the denomination.[36]

The black feminist theologians also found biblical precedent for leadership outside the church in charitable philanthropic work. Olive Bird Clanton, wife of the Reverend Solomon T. Clanton of New Orleans, addressed the American National Baptist Convention in 1887 and maintained that Christian doctrine "has placed the wife by the side of her husband, the daughter by the side of her father, the sister by the side of her brother at the table of the Lord, in the congregation of the sanctuary, male and female met together at the cross and will meet in the realms of glory." Unlike Broughton and Cook, Olive Clanton's northern upbringing made her sensitive to the plight of foreign immigrants and to the squalid conditions in urban tenements. She had little faith in ameliorative legislation if unaccompanied by the activity of women in social reform, especially female education, the care of children, and the cause of social purity. Clanton advocated an aggressive, outgoing Christianity to reach the oppressed and needy class of women and children who did not go to church and thus remained outside the purview of the minister. These types could be helped by women, whose kindness and compassion uniquely qualified them for uplift work. In Clanton's opinion, "the wearied wife, and anxious mother, the lonely woman, often feeling that she is forgotten by the world and neglected by the church will open her heart and life to the gentle Christian woman that has taken the trouble to visit her." She encouraged women to organize social purity societies, sewing schools, and other types of unions in order to uplift the downtrodden.[37] The tireless work of Dorcas, who sewed garments for the needy, became a standard biblical reference for women's charitable work.

Mary Cook proclaimed the unique capability of women to cleanse immorality, indecency, and crime "in the face of the government which is either too corrupt to care, or too timid to oppose." For Cook, Baptist women represented much more than the hope of the church. They represented the hope of the world, inasmuch as their influence would have greater moral than political sway. Since Cook perceived social ills as primarily a moral issue, she did not trust their eradication to legislation alone. Mary Cook pictured the ideal wife of a minister as a good homemaker, an intellectual, and at the forefront of social reform causes. She encouraged women to engage actively in charitable work in orphanages, hospitals, and prisons.[38]

Proponents of a feminist theology endeavored to broaden employment opportunities for women. Lucy Wilmot Smith, Historian of the American National Baptist Convention, put the issue squarely before her predominantly male audience in 1886 when she decried the difference in training between boys and girls. She noted that the nineteenth-century woman was dependent as never before upon her own resources for economic survival. Smith believed that girls, like boys, must be taught to value the dignity of labor. She rejected views that considered work for women disdainful, or temporarily necessary at best—views that conceded to women only the ultimate goal of dependency on men. "It is," she wrote, "one of the evils of the day that from babyhood girls are taught to look forward to the time when they will be supported by a father, a brother, or somebody else's brother." She encouraged black women to enter fields other than domestic service and suggested that enterprising women try their hand at poultry raising, small fruit gardening, dairying, bee culture, lecturing, newspaper work, photography, and nursing.[39]

Mary Cook suggested that women seek out employment as editors of newspapers or as news correspondents in order to promote women's causes and to reach other mothers, daughters, and sisters. She advocated teaching youths through the development of juvenile literature and urged women in the denomination's schools to move beyond subordinate jobs by training and applying for positions as teachers and administrators. Cook praised women with careers as writers, linguists, and physicians, and she told the gathering of the American National Baptist Convention in 1887 that women must "come from all the professions, from the humble Christian to the expounder of His word; from the obedient citizen to the ruler of the land."[40]

Again, the Baptist women found biblical precedents to bolster their convictions and to inspire the women of their own day. Cook and Broughton pointed to the biblical woman Huldah, wife of Shallum. Huldah studied the law and interpreted the Word of God to priests and others who sought her knowledge. In the Book of Judges another married woman, Deborah, became a judge, prophet, and warrior whom God appointed to lead Israel against its enemies. Depicting Deborah as a woman with a spirit independent of her husband, Cook asserted: "Her work was distinct from her husband who, it seems, took no part whatever in the work of God while Deborah was inspired by the Eternal expressly to do His will and to testify to her countrymen that He recognizes in His followers neither male nor female, heeding neither the 'weakness' of one, nor the strength of the other, but strictly calling those who are perfect at heart and willing to do his bidding."[41]

Biblical examples had revealed that God used women in every capacity and thus proved that there could be no issue of propriety, despite the reluctance of men. Mary Cook urged the spread of women's influence in every cause, place, and institution that respected Christian values, and she admonished her audience that no profession should be recognized by either men or women if it lacked such values. She concluded her argument with an assertion of women's "legal right" to all honest labor, as she challenged her sisters in the following verse:

> Go, and toil in any vineyard
> Do not fear to do and dare;
> If you want a field of labor
> You can find it anywhere.[42]

An Age of Liberal Theology

The feminist theology of the black Baptist church reflected several intellectual trends of the late nineteenth century. Like other Americans, the Baptist thinkers accepted a priori the notion of certain intrinsic differences between the male and female identity. The dominant thought of the age embraced an essentialist understanding of gender; it ascribed to womanhood a feminine essence that was virtuous, patient, gentle, and compassionate, while it described manhood as rational, aggressive, forceful, and just. Unlike man, woman was considered naturally religious, bound by greater emotionalism, and with a greater capacity to sympathize and forgive. Since the manifestation of the feminine essence became most readily apparent in the act of raising children in the home, feminine virtues were easily equated with maternal qualities.[43] It appeared axiomatic that God and nature had ordained woman's station in life by providing her with a job and workplace incontestably her own.

At the same time, the Baptist feminist theologians were influenced by the secular woman's movement, which rejected the bifurcation of the private sphere of home and family from the public sphere of business and politics. The goals of organizations such as the National American Woman Suffrage Association and other secular clubs gained momentum during the latter decades of the century among white and black women. These organizations sought to steer women's entrance into the public domain by such routes as voting rights and equal educational and employment opportunities. Yet even though their agenda questioned gender-prescribed roles, most adherents of nineteenth-century feminism remained bridled in a gender-specific, "do-

mesticating" politics.[44] They continued to adhere to essentialist conceptions of gender—defining woman's "nature" as separate and distinct
from man's. They translated the preeminence of the maternal responsibility for molding the future character of youth into woman's superior
ability to shape the destiny of society. Frances Willard, the suffragist
and temperance leader, asserted her belief in "social housekeeping"
when she maintained that woman carried her "mother-heart" into the
public realm and lost none of her femininity in the process. On the
contrary, woman's "gentle touch" refined and softened political institutions, professions, indeed every arena it entered.[45]

Even more directly, the writings and speeches of black Baptists
formed part of a feminist-theological literary tradition that spanned
the entire nineteenth century. Feminist theological literature especially proliferated in the century's latter decades—the years that the
historian Sydney Ahlstrom termed the "golden age of liberal theology."
Liberal theology emerged in response to Darwinist biological theories
of evolution, Social Darwinism, and a host of geological discoveries
and historical studies that challenged what had previously appeared to
be the timeless infallibility of the Bible. A radical tendency to deny
any sacred authority to the Scriptures found advocates among
"infidels" such as Robert Ingersoll and the suffragist Elizabeth Cady
Stanton. At the other end of the spectrum stood the fundamentalists,
many of whom were southern Protestants, holding tenaciously to the
literal truth of each biblical statement despite disclosures of particular
inaccuracies and contradictions.[46]

Between these extremes were liberals who came from the pulpits
and seminaries of northern Protestant denominations—in fact, some
of the same groups responsible for establishing institutions of higher
learning for black people in the South. The great majority of these
liberals attempted to reconcile their traditional religious beliefs with
the new social and scientific theories. By articulating a resilient and
vibrant orthodoxy, evangelical liberalism, led by such ministers as
Henry Ward Beecher, Newman Smyth, William Newton Clarke, and
Washington Gladden, effected the survival of traditional Protestantism
in an age of questioning and positivistic devotion to accuracy. Discussing the largely "conservative intent" of this liberalizing influence,
Winthrop Hudson argued that the primary interest of the evangelical

liberals was not to destroy Christian doctrines, but to restate them "in terms that would be intelligible and convincing and thus to establish them on a more secure foundation."[47]

This exact intent may be attributed to the writings of feminist theologians. Frances Willard, also a contributor to feminist theology, reconciled gender equality with the vital spirit of the Bible. She noted that the insistence on "real facts" had changed not only views toward science and medicine but also those toward theology, causing theology to become more flexible and to see the Bible as an expansive work that "grows in breadth and accuracy with the general growth of humanity." Willard advocated the "scientific interpretation of the Holy Scriptures" and urged women to lend a gendered perspective to the modern exegesis of the Bible.[48]

Other women and even a few men employed a feminist hermeneutic in biblical criticism. Anna Howard Shaw, a medical doctor and ordained Methodist Protestant minister, presented her views in 1891 in the speech "God's Women" before the annual meeting of the National Council of Women. Lille Devereaux Blake, novelist and author of Woman's Place Today (1883), wrote a series of four essays that challenged the sexist Lenten lectures of the Reverend Morgan J. Dix. Men such as Benjamin T. Roberts, Free Methodist minister and author of Ordaining Women (1891), and T. DeWitt Talmage, minister of Central Presbyterian Church in New York, espoused a feminist theological perspective. Talmage's sermons were syndicated in the black and white press across the country.[49]

Feminist theologians who emerged in the mainline denominations argued for women's rights from the standpoint of liberal orthodoxy. They stood in dramatic opposition to Elizabeth Cady Stanton's elaborate condemnation of the Bible in The Woman's Bible (1895). Stanton rejected orthodoxy, liberal or conservative. A compilation of interpretive essays from many contributors, The Woman's Bible critically questioned the Bible as the divinely inspired authority on women's position in society. Although some of the essays called attention to heroines and positive female images, The Woman's Bible pointed overwhelmingly to biblical images that were negative. The Bible, according to Stanton, had served historically as a patriarchal instrument for women's oppression. She condemned it for inspiring women only with the goals of obedience to husbands, subordination to men in general, and self-sacrifice at the expense of their own self-development. *The Woman's Bible* challenged women to reject Christian teachings as set forth in the Bible and to assert full equality with men.[50]

Feminist theology within the mainstream Protestant churches differed significantly from that of Stanton. Its goal was to make religion less sexist, not to make women any less religious. While feminist theology did not make converts of all who professed Protestant liberalism, it represented a significant movement within liberal evangelicalism's effort to relate theology to social issues. During the age of liberal theology, religious education and critical theological scholarship grew with unprecedented dynamism. Referring to the term "Christology" as a coinage of his day, Augustus Strong noted in 1884 that the study of Christ had become a science in its own right.[51] As biblical scholars investigated and debated the human and divine nature of Jesus, some of them also drew attention to his masculine and feminine qualities. In doing so they drew upon Protestant discourses that had their origin early in the nineteenth century and indeed can be traced to the eighteenth century's rooting of morality in the sentiments. The historians Ann Douglas and Barbara Welter, for example, have disclosed a wealth of early nineteenth-century religious and literary materials that identified the church and Christ himself with feminine attributes—representing Christ, that is, as soft, gentle, emotional, and passive.[52] The feminization of Christianity, needless to say, did not go unchallenged either before or after the Civil War. In fact, the debate concerning the association of the church and Savior with feminine virtues lost none of its vibrancy after 1875, as feminist theologians and women generally used a feminine image of Christ to justify their struggle for social justice in general and for women's rights in particular.

Popular ministers such as T. DeWitt Talmage referred to the "motherhood of God"; Laurence Oliphant urged the necessity of recognizing the "divine feminine principle in God"; and Frances Willard spoke of the "mother-heart" of God. Some of this discussion filtered into black communities. For example, *The Baptist Headlight*, a black newspaper in Topeka, Kansas, printed the Reverend Talmage's sermons in a syndicated column. In his sermon published on 25 January 1894, Talmage did not employ the phrase "motherhood of God," but he made an explicit analogy between God and mother: "All others may cast you off. Your wife may seek divorce and have no patience with you. Your father may disinherit you and say, 'Let him never again darken the door of our house.' But there are two persons who do not give you up—God and mother."[53]

Popular and scholarly literature addressed the "feminine nature" of Christ. In July and August, 1898, *The Biblical World*, journal of the Baptist-founded University of Chicago Divinity School, featured a two-part series on the subject of Christ as a feminine power. Written by George Matheson of Edinburgh, the articles contended that the Bible chronicled the centuries-old struggle between the masculine and feminine ideals. The book of Revelation was said to be the climax of Christ's victory over sin and, with this victory, the final triumph of feminine values. Matheson described feminine power as a passive force, equal in strength to the muscular power of men, but with a completely different nature. He derived his conception of a triumphant feminine ideal from the Beatitudes of Christ's Sermon on the Mount, in which Jesus not only blessed the virtues of meekness, tenderness, and forgiveness, but championed them as the new heroism for both men and women to respect. Matheson contrasted the feminine "force to bear up" against the masculine "force to bear down," and he distinguished feminine power from the neuter "inability to exert any power." He identified feelings of resignation and impotence as neuter, not feminine. Matheson praised women's charitable work on behalf of the neglected in society. He regarded women's work in hospitals, asylums, and orphanages to be representative of feminine ideals and indicative of a commitment to transform the world into a place that valued the worth of the individual over that of the state or a particular class. According to Matheson, this spirit would gradually bring about a social revolution in government, labor, and society at large.[54]

This metaphorical counterposing of feminine and masculine traits to reflect oppressed and oppressor groups throughout history in effect equated masculinity with negative social behavior. Like Matheson, Frances Willard adopted this tactic in *Woman in the Pulpit* (1888), a feminist polemic that advocated the ordination of women. Citing the testimony of numerous male and female supporters, she favored woman's right to the clergy not because of an androgynous personhood, but precisely because of womanhood, of feminine essence. Willard's concept of the "mother-heart," characterized as sympathetic, intuitive, and morally pure, became the instinctive, immutable trait that equipped women especially for religious work. In Willard's opinion the mother-heart was godlike, while religion was, above all, an "affair of the heart," a source of inner comfort and spiritual regeneration. She defined masculine qualities as market characteristics, that is, acquisitiveness and force, and then concluded that they had led to the pursuit of world dominion and the attendant reality of "the white male dynasty reigning undisputed until our own day." She castigated men for their historical inability to interpret the spiritual content of religion in any meaningful way: "It is men who have taken the simple, loving tender Gospel of the New Testament, so suited to be the proclamation of a woman's lips, and translated it in terms of sacerdotalism, dogma, and martyrdom. It is men who have given us the dead letter rather than a living Gospel. The mother-heart of God will never be known to the world until translated into terms of speech by mother-hearted women."[55]

Opponents of the feminine version of religion often conceded the feminine attributes in Christ but reaffirmed the predominance of the masculine. Gail Bederman argues that movements such as the Men and Religion Forward Movement and other advocates of a "muscular Christianity" adopted cultural constructions of gender in order to reconcile religion to the modern "corporate, consumer-oriented order" of the twentieth century.[56] The masculinist perspective countered efforts to subsume Christ's manliness in the glorification of the feminine by contending that his feminine virtues, namely, tenderness, sympathy, and forgiveness, were subordinate to his masculine attributes of assertive leadership, strong intellect, and business acumen. Defenders of the masculine orientation evoked the image of the "church militant" in the religious conquest of the world, and they offered a "tough Christianity" with stern, uncompromising features as a counterpoint to the softness and emotionalism of a feminized church.[57]

Carl Delos Case's *The Masculine in Religion* (1906) exemplifies this trend among white Baptist ministers in Brooklyn, New York. Case identified the "overfeminization of religious life" as both cause and effect of the preponderance of female church members. He blamed the feminizing process for creating a modern church predisposed to self-sacrifice, meekness, and self-abnegation. He charged that women's pervasive influence too narrowly defined Christian life as synonymous with feminine behavior and consequently made the church unattractive to men by denying them a continuity between the church and the male personality. Bemoaning the feminization of religious art, Case noted that portraits of Christ transmitted an effeminate male image with long brown hair, dreamy eyes, and a meek and resigned demeanor. By abolishing the notion of the church as woman's domain, Case and other spokesmen for virile sermons, martial hymns, and a rugged Christianity hoped to restore the church's appeal to men and to render it as legitimate an outlet for male expression as business, the factory, or the lodge.[58]

Double Gender Consciousness

Black Baptist men and women did not debate Christ's feminine versus masculine nature, but the duality captured the complexity of images surrounding their own racial and gender identities. A dialogic imagery of Christ as simultaneously feminine and masculine, passive and aggressive, meek and conquering informed African Americans' self-perceptions and self-motivations. This was true for them as individuals and as a group. Black Baptist women continually shifted back and forth from feminine to masculine metaphors as they positioned themselves simultaneously within racial and gendered social space. Whether united with black men, or working separately in their own conventions or cooperatively with white Baptist women, black Baptist women expressed a dual gender consciousness—defining themselves as both homemakers and soldiers. Their multiple consciousness represented a shifting dialogic exchange in which both race and gender were ultimately destabilized and blurred in meaning.

On the one hand, black Baptist women spoke in unambiguous gendered symbols. Virginia Broughton called attention to the feminine symbolism in the Bible (for example, the designation of the church as the "bride" of Christ), and she regarded such metaphors as conveying biblical esteem for women.[59] The black feminist theologians also contextualized women's gains in society within an evolutionary framework that repeatedly referred to the degraded status of women in ancient civilizations and in contemporary non-Christian cultures, and they argued that the standard of womanhood evolved to a higher plane with the spread of Christianity. This view undergirded their emphasis on motherhood and domesticity. Since mothers were considered to be the transmitters of culture, woman's virtue and intelligence within the home measured the progress of African Americans and all of civilization.[60]

Black Baptist women shared common bonds with white Baptist women who worked in similar societies. They were familiar with the history of white Baptist women's societies and praised their work for the freedpeople at the end of the Civil War. The white Baptist missionary Joanna P. Moore played an influential role in the lives of a number of southern black women. Moore cited biblical precedents for women as teachers and church leaders, although her conviction that women should engage in teaching, house-to-house visitation, and temperance work never minimized for her the singular importance of woman's domestic role. Her views coincided with the views of the black feminist theologians whose image of women's religious duties posited them within the traditional home setting, at the same time as they beckoned women into the world to spread the faith.[61]

The feminist theologians of the black Baptist church considered the combined efforts of black and white women critical to the progress of black people and to harmonious race relations. By Christianizing the home and educating the masses, women provided the key to solving the race problem in America. Black women likened their role to that of the biblical queen Esther, who had acted as an intermediary between the king and her people. They envisioned themselves as intermediaries between white America and their own people. Expressing the biblical analogy, Mrs. H. Davis compared Ida B. Wells to queen Esther and praised her crusade against lynching on the front page of the *National Baptist World*: "We have found in our race a queen Esther, a woman of high talent, that has sounded the bugle for a defenceless race."[62]

Frequently, citing black and white "apostles of modern missions," the feminist theologians pointed to well-known black leaders in the women's movement such as Sojourner Truth and Frances Ellen Watkins Harper, and white women such as Frances Willard and Joanna Moore. Lucy Smith alluded to two European luminaries, Harriet Martineau and Madame de Staël, when bolstering her arguments for women's right to equal employment and educational opportunities.[63]

Women such as Virginia Broughton, Mary Cook, and Lucy Wilmot Smith epitomized the high quality of woman's rational powers. Widely read, this educated female elite implicitly and explicitly challenged the conviction that assigned intellect to men and emotionalism to women. Mary Cook explained the cultivation of the female intellect as Christ's special mission to women and blamed sexism, not Christianity, for hindering women's intellectual development. "Emancipate woman," she demanded, "from the chains that now restrain her and who can estimate the part she will play in the work of the denomination."[64]

Yet the feminist sentiments articulated by these black Baptist theologians were neither uniform nor rigid. At times Virginia Broughton appeared to soften her demands for women's presence within the highest denominational councils and to adopt a more conciliatory attitude toward men. She urged, if sometimes with tongue in cheek, complementary work with a deeper sensitivity to what she called man's "long cherished position of being ruler of all he surveys." She referred to the "womanly exercise" of talent, and at a time when woman's role was emergent but not clearly defined, she tended to assure men that women would not seek unauthorized office.[65]

Lucy Wilmot Smith spoke less circumspectly. In strong feminist language, she insisted upon new expectations of women. Smith revealed her outspoken belief in the need for women to adopt attitudes identified as male in outlook: "Even in our own America, in this last quarter of the Nineteenth Century ablaze with the electric light of intelligence, if she [woman] leaves the paths made straight and level by centuries of steady tramp of her sex, she is denominated strong-minded or masculine by those who forget that 'new occasions make new duties.'"[66]

However, Lucy Smith could subordinate easily, almost imperceptibly, her feminist consciousness to that of race. On one such occasion she stated that educated black women held certain advantages over white women. She believed that the identical labor reality for male and female slaves created a solidarity not found in the white race, and she praised the black man of her day for continuing to keep his woman by his side as he moved into new types of work. Smith noted that the white woman "has had to contest with her brother every inch of the ground for recognition."[67] Mary Cook spoke of the freedom women exercised within the Baptist denomination and told the men of the American National Baptist Convention: "I am not unmindful of the kindness you noble brethren have exhibited in not barring us from your platforms and deliberations. All honor I say to such men."[68] Thus racial consciousness equally informed their identity and their understanding of gender.

Racial consciousness placed black women squarely beside black men in a movement for racial self-determination, specifically in the quest for national black Baptist hegemony. From the perspective of racial self-help, this movement so blurred values and behavior exclusively associated with either the masculine or the feminine identity that it implicitly undermined the validity of gender dichotomies. Despite nineteenth-century essentialist assumptions about woman's moral superiority, the black Baptist women's preoccupation with "respectability," as the cornerstone for racial uplift, never tolerated a double standard of behavior on the part of men and women.[69] In the same vein, concepts such as self-sacrifice and patience lost their traditionally feminine connotations and became sources of strength endorsed by men, not only women. Black ministers championed self-denial as a prerequisite for race development, while they hailed patience as the self-control necessary to build a strong black denominational force.

The writings of black Baptist ministers admitted no contradiction in encouraging humility and self-sacrifice while at the same time applauding "Christian manhood." In the anthology *The Negro Baptist Pulpit*, Edward McKnight Brawley praised the sacrificial attitude of missionaries to the South in the same breath as he shouted: "Contend for the faith!" In the 1890s Charles Octavius Boothe of Alabama commended the present wave of "charitable and self abasing" men over the older style of arrogant, boastful leaders. Anthony Binga, of Manchester, Virginia, described the ideal deacon as wise, grave, and lofty, but also long-suffering, gentle, and meek.[70]

For nineteenth-century African Americans, distinctions between the feminine and masculine identity were complicated by a racial system that superimposed "male" characteristics upon all whites (male and female) and "feminine characteristics" upon all blacks (male and female). Theories of racial essence, what George Fredrickson termed "romantic racialism," paralleled and overlapped essentialist gender assumptions. During the nineteenth century and into the twentieth, both blacks and whites subscribed to theories of innate characteristics and behaviorism that captured the soul of each race. Within the human family, so romantic racialists theorized, black people embodied an essence that was musical, emotional, meek, and religious. In contrast, the white race was perceived to be intellectual, pragmatic, competitive, and with a disposition to dominate. The counterposing of the two races paralleled the feminine-masculine dichotomy. During the Civil War, the white abolitionist Theodore Tilton described blacks as the "feminine race of the world." In the early twentieth century, Robert Park, the white sociologist, similarly described the Negro as an "artist, loving life for its own sake. . . . He is, so to speak, the lady of the races."[71]

Although blacks usually rejected the explicit analogy between their "soul qualities" and the feminine essence, they invariably re-presented and re-constructed a group identity with qualities reminiscent of those ascribed to women. Harvard-trained W. E. B. Du Bois championed theories of racial distinctiveness. In his article "The Conservation of Races," published in 1897, Du Bois disclosed his recognition and admiration for what he believed to be the "spiritual, psychical" uniqueness of his people—their "special gift" to humanity.[72] In *The Gift of Black Folk* (1924) he opined that the meekness and "sweet spirit" of black people "has breathed the soul of humility and forgiveness into the formalism and cant of American religion."[73] For blacks, the idealization of race served to negate notions of white superiority and, in turn, the legitimacy of white male power and racist institutions. Like the feminine ideal, the racial ideal valorized a more equitable, inclusive society.[74]

Perceiving themselves to be joined in a struggle for the economic, educational, and moral advancement of their people, black Baptist men as well as women employed masculine symbols when characterizing black women's efforts to combat the legacy of slavery and the continued rise of racism at the turn of the twentieth century. By so doing, black women and men once again confounded interpretations of race and gender essentialism that had their origins in white discourses. The black women in the Baptist church fused the rhetoric of war with that of domesticity. They represented themselves as the "home force" while at the same time exhorting one another to assume the role of valiant "soldier"—to go out into the "highways and hedges" and forge the "link between the church militant and the church triumphant."[75] Virginia Broughton looked to both the Bible and history for validation: "But what about man going alone to war? We answer by asking who was it that drove the nail into Sisera's temple? And what of the heroism of Joan of Arc? War is one of man's inventions; it is not good in itself, neither is it good for man to go to war alone, most especially in the Lord's work."[76]

This aggressive attitude, commonly identified with male subjectivity, underlay the black women's determination to insert their voices boldly into the deliberative arena of the convention movement. The Old Testament figures Deborah and Huldah became the recurrent reference points illustrating woman's capacity to combine humility and grace with aggressive zeal and strong intellect. The examples of Deborah and Huldah were also cited by the black Baptist women to prove that marriage need not negate public leadership for women.

The feminist theology of the black Baptist church never altered the hierarchical structure of the church by revolutionizing power relations between the sexes, nor did it inhibit ministers from assuming men's intellectual and physical superiority over women.[77] To the ire of black women, the black newspaper *Virginia Baptist* in 1894 presented a two-part series that adopted biblical arguments for restricting women's church work to singing and praying. The newspaper claimed divine authority in denying women the right to teach, preach, and vote.[78] Although the black feminist theologians opposed this line of thought, they did not challenge the basis for male monopoly of the clergy, nor did they demand equal representation in conventions in which both men and women participated. But feminist theology stirred women to find their own voice and create their own sphere of influence.

Throughout the last two decades of the nineteenth century, black women doubtless encouraged greater male appreciation for their potential contribution to the race and the denomination. Within the American National Baptist Convention, black feminist theology won outstanding male converts. It gained the respect of such ardent race leaders as William J. Simmons and Charles H. Parrish of Kentucky, Walter H. Brooks of Washington, D.C., and Harvey Johnson of Maryland.[79] In 1899 *The National Baptist Magazine*, the official organ of the National Baptist Convention, indicated women's growing influence. In the lead article of the magazine, the Reverend J. Francis Robinson supported "human rights for every individual of every race, of every condition, regardless of sex." Introducing biblical texts to illustrate the historical importance of women's church work and charitable activity,

Robinson concluded that women should be allowed to reign not only in the home, but in the political world as well. He endorsed woman's suffrage and admitted his preference for the ballots of women as opposed to those of saloon-keepers and ward bosses. He urged women's equality in the name of progress and enlightened thought by stating:

> The slaves have been emancipated; now let us emancipate women! The unconditional and universal and immediate emancipation of womanhood is the demand of the age in which we live; it is the demand of the spirit of our institutions; it is the demand of the teachings of Christianity; it is her right, and, in the name of God, let us start a wave of influence in this country that shall be felt in every State, every county, every community, every home and every heart.[80]

The progressive aspects of feminist theology, as part of the liberal theological impulse of the age, appear most clearly when counterposed to the image of women and the church presented in Ann Douglas's *The Feminization of American Culture* (1977). Douglas portrays the disestablished, non-evangelical clergy of the Northeast as anti-intellectual and misogynist. The clergy, like the predominantly female laity, occupied a position marginal to government and to an increasingly industrialized and urbanized America. According to Douglas, the clergy and the female laity worked together to feminize religion and to produce an ever-growing number of ministers who preferred to read fiction and poetry rather than think and develop theological scholarship. Worse yet, Douglas found women in these northeastern churches unable and also disinclined to provide a polemical theology to counter the sentimentalism and consumerism that finally engulfed them all.[81]

Late nineteenth-century feminist theological writings call into question generalizations of an insipid, anti-intellectual religious tradition. The contribution of black Baptist women is especially noteworthy, for they were farthest removed from the American political-economic structure. Yet it was through the church, and specifically the black Baptist convention movement, that they established an arena for discussion, debate, and implementation of their social, economic, and political agenda vis-à-vis white America.[82] If the National Baptist Convention symbolized a deliberative arena for people denied access to electoral and other strong secular institutions, black women were most responsible for expanding the true meaning of its "representative" character.

Feminist theology had significant implications for black Baptist women's future work. It buttressed their demand for more vocal participation and infused their growing ranks with optimism about the dawning twentieth century. It also encouraged women to establish and control their own separate conventions at the state and national levels. Black Baptist women did not, in the end, demand a radical break with all the sexist limitations of their church, but they were surely ingenious in fashioning the Bible as an "iconoclastic weapon" for their particular cause. The feminist theologians had operated "from a stance of 'radical obedience.'" And indeed it was this vantage of orthodoxy that compelled the brethren to listen.

6

The Coming of Age of the Black Baptist Sisterhood

> For a number of years there has been a righteous discontent, a burning zeal to go forward in His [Christ's] name among the Baptist women of our churches and it will be the dynamic force in the religious campaign at the opening of the 20th century.
>
> Nannie Helen Burroughs, 1900

Perhaps it was youthful brashness, perhaps age-old logic that led twenty-one-year-old Nannie Helen Burroughs to entitle her speech "How the Sisters are Hindered from Helping." She had traveled all the way from Louisville, Kentucky, to Richmond, Virginia, to deliver the speech, her first of many celebrated ones to the National Baptist Convention. Burroughs did not mince words on that September day in 1900. She boldly denounced the impediments to women's equal participation in the church. She proclaimed a long-standing "righteous discontent" on the part of black Baptist women and prophesied their dynamic role in the years ahead. "How the Sisters are Hindered from Helping" marked not only the beginning of Nannie Burroughs's long, illustrious career but the beginning of the Woman's Convention, Auxiliary to the National Baptist Convention.[1] By the close of the Richmond meeting, Burroughs and the other women present had succeeded in establishing the largest collectivity of black women in America.

The Woman's Convention (WC) stood squarely within the larger realm of the National Baptist Convention. Its membership belonged to the NBC, and its annual meetings were always held together with those of the NBC. Yet, while the Woman's Convention formed part and parcel of the National Baptist Convention, it did not claim the latter's universality. The proceedings and public pronouncements of leaders of the ministerial-led NBC represented the officially sanctioned voice of both men and women in the denomination. The records and pronouncements of the Woman's Convention, on the other hand, did not purport to speak for men. Through the Woman's Convention, the female membership of the NBC articulated its own values and concerns. The WC constituted a new discursive realm in which women's voices were neither silent nor subordinate to men's.

The Baptist women's convention legitimated a new form of representative politics. The convention afforded black women, though denied participation in the electoral procedures of the official public culture because of race and gender, the opportunity to learn about and participate in the rudiments of self-government within the separatist alternative world of black women's organizations.[2] It constituted a black women's congress, so to speak, where women as delegates from local churches, district associations, and state conventions assembled as a national body, discussed and debated issues of common concern, disseminated information outward to broader female constituencies, and implemented nationally supported programs. Far from isolating black women in a separate and marginal domain, the convention accentuated their presence within the denomination and, equally important, thrust issues of race and gender into the broad discursive arena of American social reform.

The formation of the Woman's Convention in 1900 followed five years after the formation of the National Baptist Convention. The later date for women reflected not an afterthought but a hard-fought struggle for gender self-determination that began before 1895 and continued throughout the first two decades of the twentieth century. The black Baptist women's quest for national identity and voice draws attention to gender relations as relations of power in black communities, for their efforts, like earlier ones at the state level, incurred male resistance.

The Baptist women's movement for self-representation and self-determination recounts a story that is similar to and yet significantly different from the parallel movement of middle-class club women. At the dawn of the 1890s black club women and church women both operated in the belief that they stood firmly on the "threshold of the woman's era."[3] Both spoke of organized womanhood as the vital force for change. In pursuit of social reform, black club women and church women alike felt the need to transcend local and regional boundaries by uniting into national organizations. Their reform activities embraced the same goals: an end to racial discrimination and violence; women's suffrage; mothers' training; equality of education and employment opportunities; better working conditions and wages; child care for working mothers; and numerous other reforms.[4]

However, the two movements evolved from different social contexts. The pull of sisterhood notwithstanding, it had been white racism more than the sexism of black men that sparked club women's awareness of the need for national organization. The precipitating factor of racism was acknowledged in the statement of Josephine St. Pierre Ruffin, who convened the first national conference of black club women in Boston in July 1895: "Year after year, Southern [white] women have protested against the admission of colored women into any organization on the ground of the immorality of our women and because our reputation has only been tried by individual work, the charge has never been crushed."[5] Slanderous remarks in the white press and the exclusionary policies of white women's clubs prompted the call that led to the eventual formation of the National Association of Colored Women (NACW) in 1896. Middle-class black women came together self-admittedly to vindicate their own respectability and uplift the downtrodden of their race.[6]

Unlike the call of Josephine St. Pierre Ruffin, Nannie Burroughs's call for a national Baptist sisterhood in 1900 summoned the need for collective self-criticism, in order to eradicate inequalities and exclusions within the black community itself. As the title of her speech suggests, "How the Sisters are Hindered from Helping" addressed at once familial bonds of race and gender divisions within the "household of faith." More than a decade before the founding of the NACW in 1896 or its regional forerunners (the Colored Woman's League of Washington, D.C. in 1892, the Women's Era Club of Boston in 1893, and the National Federation of Afro-American Women in 1895), black Baptist women struggled for self-articulation and self-representation within a racial movement that spawned its own internal divisions.

The race consciousness that forged a national black Baptist identity and hegemony during the 1880s proved catalytic to the emergence of a women's movement in the church. The black Baptist convention movement had served a critical mediating function—uniting women with men in the struggle for racial self-determination, while simultaneously creating a separate gender-based community reflective and supportive of women's equality. The denominational movement to control apparatuses of racial identity and agency, namely, conventions, schools, newspapers, and other community service institutions, proved successful largely because women contested female images and roles imposed upon them. Throughout the 1880s and 1890s Baptist women challenged gender proscriptions that thwarted the full utilization of their talents. Women of the middle class and laboring poor united in statewide organizational activities; and some even deployed the Bible as a weapon against gender subordination.

Black Baptist women became increasingly convinced that a national arena of their own would best advance both themselves and their people. This arena was perceived always within the context of a larger male-female community, namely, within a black denomination. Thus women's demands for participatory equality remained dependent upon the approval of men. On two occasions, once in 1890 and again in 1895, black Baptist women succeeded in winning such approval only to see it rescinded. The black church, the preeminent site of racial solidarity and self-determination, proved, as well, a site of gender division and conflict.

A National Women's Convention

The precursor organizations to the National Baptist Convention—the Baptist Foreign Mission Convention, American National Baptist Convention, and National Baptist Educational Convention—nurtured women's desire for national self-articulation. Of the three precursor conventions, women were most visible in the American National Baptist Convention, whose first president was the Reverend William J. Simmons of Kentucky. Women of the ANBC held more offices, delivered more papers at annual meetings, and sat on larger numbers of committees than women in the other two conventions. Through the ANBC's committee on women's work, state leaders assembled regularly, established a network of communication and cooperation, and created a forum for the discussion of gender-related topics such as family issues, women's education, organizational methods, and the expansion of rights within the church and larger society.[7]

The annual meetings of the National Baptist Foreign Mission Convention, the American National Baptist Convention, and the National Baptist Educational Convention served to instill a sense of national community among women. At these meetings, black Baptist women discussed and debated their need to institutionalize a national identity within the larger black Baptist convention movement. The annual meetings also provided the occasion for women to engage in critical discussion with men on the subject of women's rights and to present formal motions for an organization of their own. Women members of the American National Baptist Convention petitioned for a national organization at the annual meeting in 1890—the last meeting presided over by William J. Simmons. Simmons had long supported women's right to higher education and to professional careers, but he opposed their desire for a separate sphere of national power. Instead, he continued to advocate women's integration into the offices and committees of the ANBC. Women themselves were divided over the issue. The Kentucky women, some of whom held office in the ANBC, remained loyal to the wishes of Simmons, and thus the motion for a separate organization went down in defeat.[8]

Women also sought a separate organization at the annual meeting of the National Baptist Foreign Mission Convention in 1890. Unlike the ANBC, the Foreign Mission Convention voted to form a committee with the responsibility of drafting plans for a woman's auxiliary. However, within two years the ministerial-led convention reversed its position. Lewis G. Jordan, a historian of black Baptists and a member of the Foreign Mission Convention, recorded, without comment, that in 1892 the convention blocked the implementation of a woman's auxiliary, although it allotted women special time at annual meetings to present reports of their work.[9]

As race consciousness heightened during the first half of the 1890s and reached its apogee with the formation of the National Baptist Convention, U.S.A., gender consciousness heightened with equal intensity. In 1895 black women championed the transition to the all-powerful new convention, but they expressed discontent with their growing subordination within the denomination. The death of William J. Simmons in 1890 had silenced any support he might have given toward women's equality.[10] Indeed, no woman held office in any of the three male-led conventions on the eve of their merger.

At the founding meeting of the National Baptist Convention, U.S.A., in 1895, women appropriated the historic moment for advocating a separate, auxiliary convention. Their separatist vision appeared to fall upon a receptive audience. Assembled in Atlanta's Friendship Baptist Church, where Spelman Seminary had held its first classes fourteen years earlier, the delegates to the National Baptist Convention endorsed the women's call for sisterhood. The following month, the *National Baptist Magazine* reported the formation of the Woman's National Baptist Convention. The article applauded the action as recognition of a new era for women. Proclaiming the times as "preeminently a woman's age," it observed that women were due equality within the denomination as a matter of justice, not sentiment. The officers of the new women's convention were leaders at the state level. Mrs. Alice A. Bowie of Alabama was elected president; Mrs. Virginia Broughton of Tennessee, recording secretary; and Mrs. C. J. Robinson of Arkansas, corresponding secretary. The *National Baptist Magazine* pledged its cooperation.[11]

The magazine's endorsement proved premature and hardly indicative of the dominant mood of the male-led convention. Virginia Broughton recorded in her autobiography that when the NBC met the following year in St. Louis, "by the Counsel of the brethren, the woman's auxiliary national convention was disbanded and women were placed on the various boards of the NBC." Broughton failed to explain the men's reluctance or the women's reaction; she simply stated that women continued to attend the annual meetings of the NBC and reinforce one another.[12] Through the sharing of ideas and information, women continued their drive to institutionalize a national platform of their own.[13]

Women's mounting demands for greater participation in the denomination reached a high point in September 1900, when the convention met in Richmond. Inspired by the eloquence of Nannie Helen Burroughs and convinced of the moral justness of their cause, forty women caucused secretly at the Third Street A.M.E. Church in order to plan a strategy and a structure for their still-to-be-sanctioned organization.[14] Virginia Broughton was elected one of four women commissioned by the women's caucus to solicit ministerial support.[15] Among the brethren, the women found their closest allies in the leaders of the Foreign Mission Board of the National Baptist Convention—Lewis G. Jordan, corresponding secretary of the board, and Charles H. Parrish, board treasurer. Powerful figures within the leadership hierarchy of the National Baptist Convention, the two proved critical in fostering favorable sentiment among the men. At the Richmond meeting, Jordan officially recommended the formation of a Baptist Women's Missionary League. Parrish seconded his motion, and the convention voted affirmatively.[16]

The support from the leadership of the Foreign Mission Board was hardly serendipitous. Lewis G. Jordan and Charles Parrish were linked directly to outspoken advocates of the women's cause. Lewis G. Jordan was most likely familiar with the general tone, if not the actual text, of Nannie Burroughs's speech before its delivery, since at the time she was employed as Jordan's secretary in Louisville. Jordan's sympathies were unmistakable. After the establishment of the Baptist women's convention he continued his support, lending the fledgling organization office space and giving them a column in his newspaper, the *Mission Herald*.[17] Charles H. Parrish first became acquainted with women's rights issues as a student and teacher at State University at Louisville during the early 1880s. At the university and also within the American National Baptist Convention, forerunner of the NBC, Parrish worked closely with Mary V. Cook and Lucy Wilmot Smith. In 1898 Parrish married Mary Cook—having for more than a decade supported her feminist outlook. The birth of her son prevented her from attending the founding meeting of the Woman's Convention, but her wishes were clearly reflected in her husband's actions.[18]

It was no coincidence, then, that the first project of the Woman's Convention enabled the work of the Foreign Mission Board. In 1901 the women supported the board's effort to send Spelman graduate Emma Delaney to Africa; they sent money to Delaney for her work in Chiradzulo in Blantyre, British Central Africa (now Malawi). In 1902 the women supplied funds to build a brick mission house for her. In 1910 they contributed to the NBC's mission station in Capetown, South Africa. During its first ten years, the WC shipped boxes of food and clothing to missionaries on foreign fields, and between 1900 and 1920 underwrote the educational expenses of African students in the

United States. Throughout the years the WC stood loyally by the Foreign Mission Board and gave liberally to its work.[19]

While supportive of the programs of the NBC's boards, the Woman's Convention held tight control over its own finances, programs, and leaders. This control often caused tension between the men and women, but the precedent for women's self-determination was established in the WC's institutional structure and national officers: Sarah Willie Layten of Philadelphia, president; Sylvia C. J. Bryant of Atlanta, vice-president-at-large; Nannie H. Burroughs of Washington, D.C. and Louisville, corresponding secretary; Virginia Broughton of Nashville, recording secretary; and Susie C. Foster of Montgomery, Alabama, treasurer.[20]

The minutes for 1900 listed twenty-six state representatives, also called state vice-presidents, including representatives from Indian Territory, Oklahoma Territory, and Washington, D.C. The women described their mission as coming to the rescue of the world, and they adopted the motto: "The world for Christ. Women arise. He calleth for thee."[21] The constitution, which designated the group's official title, the Woman's Convention, Auxiliary to the National Baptist Convention, stated that its objectives were to disseminate knowledge; facilitate the growth and activities of existing women's societies at the church, district, and state levels; work through these societies and organize new ones; and enlist the assistance of women and children in fund raising for educational and missionary purposes.[22]

Neither Sarah Willie Layten (called S. Willie Layten) nor Nannie Helen Burroughs derived their leadership status in the WC from their marriage to officials in the National Baptist Convention.[23] Their election to the highest offices within the convention related primarily to their advocacy of women's rights within the denomination. By her own testimony, Layten had championed rights for blacks and women when she was a young girl. Her background well acquainted her with the racial and gender concerns of black Baptist women during the closing decades of the nineteenth century. She was born in 1863 in Memphis and grew up in a household that preached the philosophy of racial self-determination. Her father, William H. Phillips, staunchly advocated a trained ministry and participated in the movement for black denominational hegemony.

Layten graduated from LeMoyne College in Memphis in 1881 and soon moved along with her parents to Fort Smith, Arkansas. Her father had assumed a church pastorate in Fort Smith, and she taught in the public schools there. Upon marriage in 1882, she moved from Arkansas to Los Angeles. Layten's activism as a leader of religious and secular women's organizations began during her residency on the West Coast. She served as president of the Western Baptist Association of California. In 1890 she participated in the unsuccessful drive to organize a national woman's foreign mission convention. Layten was also among the founders of black women's clubs in California.

In 1894 Layten established residence in Philadelphia, where her father and mother had moved not long before. Her father had assumed the pastorate of Shiloh Baptist Church in the city, and she relocated there in order to join her parents. Layten remained in Philadelphia for the duration of her life.[24] No mention is ever made of Layten's husband in her own speeches and writings, in her father's writings, or in biographical treatments of her. Layten moved to Philadelphia as a single parent with a young daughter, and she rose to national stature without the presence of a husband. Her involvement in secular club work continued with her presidency of the Woman's Convention. During the first decade of the twentieth century, Layten was active in the National Association of Colored Women and was a leader in the National Urban League and the Association for the Protection of Colored Women.[25]

Nannie Helen Burroughs was never married and was not related in a familial way to any of the men in the National Baptist Convention. An eloquent speaker and organizational genius, she was the corresponding secretary and dynamic force behind the Woman's Convention. During her first year in office, she reported having labored 365 days, traveled 22,125 miles, delivered 215 speeches, organized 12 societies, written 9,235 letters, and received 4,820 letters.[26] Burroughs was born in Culpepper, Virginia, in 1879. She moved to Washington, D.C. with her mother at the age of five and remained there until after her graduation from the city's colored high school. In 1896 she wrote to Booker T. Washington in hope of finding employment as a typist and stenographer at his school.[27] Although she failed to secure a job at Tuskegee, she obtained clerical work in Philadelphia and later in Louisville. She was employed as bookkeeper and editorial secretary for

Lewis Jordan and the Foreign Mission Board until 1909, when she returned to Washington, D.C. to head the National Training School for Women and Girls. While in Louisville, Burroughs participated in Baptist women's societies and established a city-wide industrial club with classes in bookkeeping, shorthand, typing, sewing, cooking, child care, and handicrafts.[28]

Burroughs, more than anyone else, embodied the Baptist women's independent spirit. Determined to maintain women's autonomy, she led the convention over a number of symbolic and real obstacles during the first two decades of its existence. Her long leadership of the convention (from 1900 until her death in 1961) was fraught with tension around the issue of women's recognition and power within the denomination. Burroughs exhibited her feminist consciousness on innumerable occasions. Perhaps the earliest example of her strong commitment to women's interests occurred one year after the birth of the Woman's Convention. On the WC's official stationery, she wrote to Booker T. Washington in 1901 inviting him to address the Woman's Convention and National Baptist Convention at their next annual meeting in Birmingham. Receiving his acceptance in early 1902, she reveled in delight that the women, rather than the men, had first extended the invitation: "There may be an effort later on by our brethren to secure you, but I beg that you bear in mind that the Baptist women gave the first invitation, even before they [men] thought of it."[29] Washington's speech went down in the annals of history, not so much for the source of the invitation or for its content, but rather for the tragedy that ensued during its delivery. A shout of "fight" was interpreted mistakenly for "fire," and the audience stampeded out of the church, causing the loss of more than 100 lives. A few weeks later, an apologetic Burroughs wrote to Washington in hope that he would not refuse future invitations from her.[30] Washington continued to present an annual address to the National Baptist Convention and Woman's Convention until his death in 1915.

Burroughs's demand for recognition of women's independent identity mirrored the overall determination of the Baptist women's movement to sustain itself as an autonomous power base. Not only Burroughs but the broad female membership of her convention did not hesitate to contest arguments and efforts to subordinate the Woman's Convention—whether put forward by male or by female high-ranking officials. Just one year after the WC's founding, for instance, Elias Camp Morris, president of the National Baptist Convention, expressed his reservation concerning the desirability of the women's autonomy and national influence. Morris suggested that the women abdicate their growing power to the men by operating as a board of the National Baptist Convention and centralizing their activities under the aegis of the larger male "parent body," as the NBC referred to itself. A Woman's Home and Foreign Mission Board, he posited, should be established according to the same criteria as the other boards of the NBC; it should, like the other boards, have a distinct headquarters; and should, also like the other boards, report annually to the male-controlled convention.[31] Even S. Willie Layten, a more accommodating personality than Burroughs, acquiesced to Morris's suggestion and recommended in her second presidential address that the "name of our organization be changed from Convention to Board, in order that we become perfectly harmonious to the policy of the National Baptist Convention." The women of the convention, however, refused to surrender their hard-won recognition and identity. They countered Layten's recommendation by passing resolutions to retain both the title "convention" and the existing format of the constitution. Virginia Broughton, recording secretary of the WC and veteran leader of the Baptist women's movement, observed that the "women took a decided stand to hold their organization intact."[32]

Powerful male allies pronounced their support for the Woman's Convention at this time. In addition to Lewis G. Jordan was Richard H. Boyd, leader of the NBC's Home Mission Board and also head of its publishing board. Second in influence only to Morris, Boyd noted the reluctance of the women to relinquish their autonomy and expressed his willingness to yield to their stubbornness. Robert Mitchell, auditor of the NBC, also defended the women's separate status. His report for 1902 called for the men's "unqualified support and endorsement" of the Woman's Convention. Mitchell applauded Burroughs's efficiency in fund raising and urged the NBC to permit the women to work unfettered by specific requests and dictates.[33]

Throughout the first decade of the twentieth century, the Woman's Convention extended its influence. Visits by WC officers to communities across the nation facilitated discussion and coordination of local and national objectives. In addition to Layten and Burroughs, one of the most active officers was WC field secretary Ella E. Whitfield. Described as a "super-woman" and a person of "untiring zeal and commanding appearance," Whitfield reported annual visits to virtually every state in the nation on behalf of the Woman's Convention.[34] The convention also developed an extensive literature and communications network in order to publicize the ideas and activities of its growing constituency. The proceedings of the women's meetings and other issues of concern to the WC were regularly featured in the "Woman's Column" in the NBC's weekly newspaper, the *National Baptist Union,* and also in the monthly newspaper of the NBC's Foreign Mission Board, *The Mission Herald.* Proceedings of the WC were not restricted to the religious press, however, but were accessible to the broad readership of the secular black press as well.[35]

In 1903 corresponding secretary Nannie Burroughs reported that the WC represented nearly a million black Baptist women. By 1907 she reported one and a half million.[36] She sought to systematize the work of women's societies by publishing the handbook *What To Do and How To Do It.* The WC distributed record books and bookkeeping advice to local and state societies along with the reminder that mission work included both business and spiritual aspects. Burroughs filled annually hundreds of orders for guides, pictures, buttons, and leaflets, and she received thousands of letters and postcards.[37] In 1908 she sought to publicize the Baptist women's activities by designating "National Woman's Day." Local churches and state societies promoted its annual celebration. Scheduled for the last Sunday in July, the day was conceived as an expression of sisterhood and a means of financial support for the WC.[38]

Women's state and local missionary societies constituted the financial backbone of the national convention. Not a wealthy constituency, the Woman's Convention depended upon the talents and resources of women with very little income. Yet the sacrificial and other fund-raising contributions of such women constituted the primary mainstay of individual churches, of local and state educational and charitable-relief projects, and of the projects of their national convention. The fund-raising activities of the Woman's Convention united black women of all ages, classes, and geographic regions at new levels of collective self-help. These activities served to valorize the resourcefulness and skills of poor women. Such was the case when the

WC sponsored a needlework exhibit during its annual meeting in Chicago in 1905. Inspired by needlework displays in the large department stores, the WC's exhibit became a biennial event—impressive for its beauty as well as for the sacrificial labor that went into it. Burroughs proudly observed that the fine needlework represented the talent of "daily toilers, who find but an hour or two each week to call their own." The proceeds from the sale went to the convention's mission fund.[39]

The commemoration of "Stamp Day" illustrates the resourcefulness and cooperation of thousands of ordinary women in defraying the huge mailing costs necessary for the maintenance of a national communication and information network. The meager budget of the Woman's Convention could not adequately reimburse its leaders, who more often than not sacrificed personal income to pay for convention expenses. "Stamp Day" solved the problem of mass mailing by rallying women in state and local societies in an annual drive to save postage stamps. Throughout each year church women from the various states raced against one another and on the allotted day presented their yield to the Woman's Convention.[40] Missionary societies also donated a dollar annually for the distribution of free literature on street corners, in schools and other public places, and in homes. In 1915, 5,000 volunteers went monthly into homes in every section of the country with tract literature.[41] They circulated leaflets in black neighborhoods and on thoroughfares heavily trafficked by black people. Burroughs's annual reports noted a huge response to the literature. She received numerous messages each week from readers who wanted to join both local societies and the national convention.[42]

Nannie Burroughs asserted in 1907 that through their "national organization, women from the North, South, East and West know each other by name, and are in sympathy with the work that is being carried on in the respective sections."[43] The Woman's Convention enabled women throughout the nation to establish links with one another, plan programs of mutual interest, and define their own priorities. The convention established its own educational institution, the National Training School for Women and Girls, and it also established a settlement house in Washington, D.C. under the direction of a trained social worker.[44] The black Baptist women also supported secular institutions and organizations that worked for racial and gender advancement, such as the National Association for the Advancement of Colored People (NAACP), the National Association of Colored Women (NACW), and the National League for the Protection of Colored Women.

The success of black Baptist women in building their own national convention was accompanied by growing pains, however. Jealousies, the generation gap, and differences in leadership style existed among the women and had to be reconciled. For example, in late 1902 and throughout most of 1903 tensions between the youthful Nannie Burroughs and the veteran missionary Virginia Broughton received widespread attention in the Baptist press. The two women vied with each other over the editorship of the "Woman's Column" in the *National Baptist Union*. Burroughs asserted that the column rightfully belonged to her, since it functioned as a medium of communication to women across the nation. Burroughs acknowledged that Broughton had been a leader among Baptist women before she was born, but argued forcefully: "If I am incompetent to edit the Woman's Column of our Convention, which column should give information on the work throughout the country, reports from time to time of visits made and the condition of the field as we go over it, then Mrs. Broughton cannot until she is made Corresponding Secretary, for she cannot get these facts unless she is doing work, and the Convention must go all the way by giving her the job."[45] Broughton's use of the column was primarily for religious instruction and personal reflections.

The Reverend I. W. D. Isaac, editor of the *National Baptist Union*, divided the women further by his negative public coverage of the controversy. His goal was to place the women under the control of the male-dominated National Baptist Convention by revealing them to be too internally divided for self-government. Although WC president S. Willie Layten sided with Broughton, the convention's executive board and membership rallied around Burroughs. By August 1903 Burroughs, Broughton, Layten, and the convention in general put the controversy behind them and, with a call for "higher ground," conveyed an impressive show of solidarity in the black Baptist press.[46] In retreat, the newspaper editor acknowledged to the NBC in October 1903: "Since they have removed all previous differences and become thoroughly united in the prosecution of their work, they [should] be given the 'right of way,' undisturbed and unmolested to the intent that they may develop the highest and noblest within them."[47]

Ironically, it was the male leadership that suffered an irreconcilable division. In 1915, a controversy surrounding the National Baptist Publishing Board left black Baptists split into two separate conventions. The larger convention, under the presidency of E. C. Morris, incorporated and adopted the official title the National Baptist Convention, U.S.A., Inc., while the unincorporated convention, under Richard H. Boyd, became the National Baptist Convention of America. The unincorporated convention never achieved the size and power of the incorporated one.[48] The strong sense of autonomy engendered by fifteen years of the Woman's Convention precluded the extension of this schism among women Baptists. The WC's minutes for 1915 differ radically in tone from the men's, with the women themselves noting their regret that "so much had been said about the men's disturbance and nothing about the harmonious, inspiring sessions of our women's convention."[49]

The Annual Session

It is difficult to overstate the importance of the annual sessions of the National Baptist Convention and Woman's Convention to African Americans during the early twentieth century. Most of the men and women attending them had very limited resources. They were the "common people," as Nannie Burroughs fondly called them—men and women "of whom God has made more than of the other kind."[50] Despite low income and the transportation and housing difficulties posed by segregation laws, thousands traveled to the annual gatherings to share experiences and friendships. They also went there to establish an agenda for racial progress and to renew their strength for the struggle against the debilitating intent and effects of Jim Crow. The conferences entailed tremendous planning. Throughout the year individual churches and missionary societies at the local and state levels saved money to send their delegates to the annual meetings. The meeting signaled the high point of the year not only for those who attended, but for the host city as well. Virginia Broughton described in her autobiography "truly immense" crowds of African Americans, when the NBC met in Austin, Texas, in 1904. Broughton remarked that the orderly behavior of the convention's delegates made a positive impact, and elicited praise from streetcar conductors, who were usually "uncouth and unkind" to black riders.[51]

Since blacks were denied accommodations in white hotels and restaurants, the churches took up the responsibility of housing the meetings, feeding thousands of delegates, arranging travel between meeting places, and coordinating an extensive housing network so that travelers could stay at homes in and near the conference city. For example, Union Baptist Church of Cincinnati, Ohio, hosted the one-year-old Woman's Convention when the NBC met in the city in 1901. The church proved to be multifaceted in its ability to accommodate the large number of women present. In a black Baptist women's newspaper as far away as Alabama, a delegate to the conference praised the Ohio church's facilities—describing them for the benefit of those who were unable to attend: "A kitchen, pantry and all necessary to make an excellent restaurant were there. Hot meals were served and the tables were beautifully arranged. It was no small matter to serve 500 or 600 people each day."[52]

When churches could not adequately accommodate the size of a gathering, alternative arrangements were made. This was the case when the convention met in Memphis in 1906. A large cotton shed held the combined crowd of men and women, although the women convened their separate meetings in a church.[53] Philadelphia's largest conference center, Convention Hall with its several-thousand seating capacity, was the site of the annual session in September 1914. In that year 8,000 black Baptist men and women from all over the United States converged on the city's downtown area.[54] In the following year, when the NBC met in Chicago, a minimum of 15,000 delegates attended.[55]

The annual session of the Woman's Convention, held always in conjunction with that of the National Baptist Convention, climaxed each year's work. Meetings were structured with overlapping panels and with special events for everyone. The annual message of the president of the NBC represented the state of the union address and was attended by men and women alike. The annual message of the officers of the Woman's Convention was considered no less important to the women, and was overwhelmingly attended by them. Daily meetings also included those specifically organized and run by the women. The yearly gatherings afforded an opportunity to travel to new cities, to renew acquaintances and make new friends, and most of all to gain information and experiences to share back home. The gatherings also reinforced blacks' appreciation of their cultural traditions. For example, music figured prominently in the evening programs. In Philadelphia in 1914, a chorus of nearly a thousand voices led the massive congregation in the singing of slave spirituals. The *Philadelphia Tribune* noted that the "plantation songs" were "dear to the hearts of the people and they responded with a will that made the huge building echo and re-echo."[56]

The annual sessions evoked a group identity that racialized denominational affiliation. To be a "National Baptist" affirmed black collective strength and encouraged a sense of confidence vis-à-vis whites. The sheer size of the convention served as a source of pride. In 1906 the National Baptist Convention comprised 2,354,789 people—representing 61.4 percent of all black church members in the United States. By 1916 its numbers had risen to 2,938,579. The convention was not only larger than any other black religious group, it was larger than either of the two major white Baptist groups, namely, the Northern Baptist Convention with 1,232,135 and the Southern Baptist Convention with 2,708,870.[57] The NBC's race consciousness found expression in various forms—in its organ of publicity, *The National Baptist Magazine*, and its other newspapers; its schools and central publishing house; its requirement for the use of black history textbooks; and its formation of a doll factory. In the last case, the National Baptist Convention advertised in the pages of the NAACP's *Crisis* and other black newspapers: "Your child would be happy if it had a Negro doll. . . . The Negro doll is calculated to help in the Christian development of our race."[58]

The National Baptist Convention infused a similar consciousness in women, who formed more than 60 percent of the NBC's membership.[59] But their interpretation of racial self-determination included a gender dimension. For women, race consciousness did not subsume or negate their empowerment as women, but rather encouraged it. This attitude is captured in a letter from Rebecca Pitts to her sisters in Alabama. Pitts traveled to Richmond in 1900 as a delegate from her women's society in Uniontown, Alabama. Published in the state convention newspaper, the *Baptist Woman's Era*, upon her return home, Pitts's letter described the "beneficial, instructive, and inspiring" experiences that she had on her way to the Richmond conference in 1900. She departed from Selma with twenty other members of the Alabama delegation on a train described as "one of the finest cars that ever came to Selma." Traveling to Birmingham and Anniston, the Alabama group was reinforced by thirty more members. When the train stopped in Atlanta, Pitts remarked on the many additional conventioneers on their way to Richmond. Boarding the train in Atlanta was a group from East Alabama, and also delegations from the states of Mississippi, Tennessee, and Georgia. "We had a solid Baptist train," she exclaimed. Once arriving in Richmond, Pitts looked in awe at the two thousand delegates present. She marveled at the lectures and sermons that she heard. The address of Elias Camp Morris, president of the National Baptist Convention, related the mission of the church to social and political questions confronting black Americans. But Pitts was most ecstatic about witnessing the formation of the Woman's Convention. She asserted that it "will give our sisters an opportunity to prove their ability to control great forces and to do mission work in a practical and systematic way."[60]

For women disadvantaged by race, gender, and low income at the turn of the twentieth century, the convention's annual sessions afforded an opportunity to transcend narrow social and intellectual confines and become exposed to new personalities and ideas that negated racist and sexist stereotypes and limitations. For women, many of whom were domestic servants, the communally paid travel to the yearly conferences presented their only opportunity to venture outside their state. Women from cities such as Atlanta and Birmingham and women from small towns such as Rebecca Pitts's home of Uniontown traveled to new and different cities, heard thought-provoking speeches, met leaders of national prominence, and networked with one another. The annual conferences nurtured women's intellectual growth and self-esteem, since reports and speeches were delivered by women delegates and convention officers as well as by guest speakers. Armed with new ideas and perspectives, delegates returned to their homes eager to convey what they had heard.

The schedule of the Woman's Convention program for 1907 is typical in format and illustrative of the breadth of issues discussed by the delegates themselves. For Thursday afternoon on 13 September 1907, the schedule read as follows:

2:00   Devotionals led by Mrs. L. W. Landrum, Reevesville, Indian Territory

2:30   Address, "State of the Country"—Mrs. M. E. Fowler, Tampa, Florida

2:45   Address, "Some Essential Reforms"—Mrs. M. E. Clarke, Cincinnati, Ohio

3:00   Address, "Lessons on the Race Problem from Magazines and Daily Papers"—Mrs. Florence Cook, Quincy, Illinois

3:15   Address, "The Trend of Race Sentiment"—Mrs. E. E. Whitfield [Field Secretary of the Woman's Convention]

3:30   Address, "Recent Educational Gifts, and What They Mean to the Masses"—Miss Cecilia B. Garey, Columbia, South Carolina

3:45   Address, "The Labor Question and the Negro's Relation to It"—Miss M. M. Kimball, Texas

4:00   Address, "The Immigration Question and the Negro's Relation to It"—Mrs. M. E. Addison, Baltimore, Maryland

Discussion—(Persons desiring to speak on either of the above questions may send their card to the President, stating upon which subject they desire to talk. Three minutes will be allowed each speaker.)

5:00   Collection. Announcements. Adjournment.[61]

The annual sessions served to disseminate useful knowledge related to the operation of state and local societies. Delegates discussed strategies for broadening their appeal and organizational base. In 1910, for instance, R. T. Frye addressed the audience on "How To Increase the Attendance at Each Meeting" and included the following among her tips for successful work: extending public invitations; discussing current news events; holding missionary rallies; celebrating women's day; being represented in the national convention; and getting coverage in the press.[62]

The annual conferences offered important opportunities to learn of activities occurring in all the states, since each state leader presented the work of women's missionary societies. The state reports, which were presented orally and also printed in the proceedings of each year's meeting, were accessible to everyone. During the WC's first decade state reports reveal a continuation of nineteenth-century charity work: visiting homes and reading the Bible; counseling prisoners; comforting the sick; conducting mothers' training classes; donating clothes to the needy; establishing and supporting orphanages and old folks' homes; crusading for temperance; establishing day nurseries and kindergartens; and establishing and/or financing educational institutions. The minutes for the meeting in 1905 record that a woman from Arkansas solicited the convention's aid in maintaining an orphan's home in Helena. At the same meeting Mary Flowers of Tennessee discussed the work of the Fireside School and requested all to subscribe to the magazine *Hope*. At the meeting in 1910 the vice-president from Kansas noted that the women of her state supported an old folks' home and other charities. Mary V. (Cook) Parrish, also elected treasurer of the Woman's Convention in 1908, proudly reported that Kentucky women had distributed 558 garments to the needy and had provided relief to 608 poor people. The vice-president from Missouri referred to the work of her sisters in erecting a girls' dormitory, while the vice-president from Texas reported on the schools and old folks' home supported by the Baptist women of her state.[63]

The Woman's Convention invited prominent people from all walks of life to address the annual gatherings. Although the majority of invited speakers were black, the program always included representatives from white Baptist women's organizations, as well as white reform activists and government officials.[64] The presence of black male and female leaders, however, introduced a repertoire of talent and expertise from which the women undoubtedly derived racial pride. In sharing their work and vision, the black speakers refuted Social Darwinist claims of racial inferiority. Black women speakers, such as entrepreneur C. J. Walker and bank president Maggie Lena Walker, inspired their listeners with their personal stories of success against the odds. All of the black speakers presented to their female listeners otherwise inaccessible information and awakened the aspirations of many.

In 1905 J. Max Barber, editor of the magazine *Voice of the Negro*, presented a lecture on the black press. Madame C. J. Walker, manufacturer of black women's hair products and thought to be the first black woman millionaire, addressed the convention in 1912 and 1916 on the subject "From the Kitchen to the Mansion." When the convention met in Chicago in 1915, anti-lynching crusader and clubwoman Ida Wells-Barnett spoke to the women, along with National Urban League director George Edmund Haynes. In 1918 Haynes returned to the annual meeting—this time as director of Negro economics for the U.S. Department of Labor. He praised the Baptist women, and especially their president, S. W. Layten, for work in social reform. The annual conference in 1919 witnessed another cast of impressive black speakers: Emmett J. Scott, secretary-treasurer of Howard University; James Weldon Johnson, field secretary for the National Association for the Advancement of Colored People; Mary Talbert, president of the National Association of Colored Women; John Hope, president of Morehouse College; Alice Dunbar Nelson, noted writer and widow of Paul Lawrence Dunbar; and Eugene Kinkle Jones, president of the Urban League. In 1920 the black Baptist women received financial advice from Maggie Lena Walker, black woman president of the Penny Savings Bank in Richmond, Virginia.[65]

If the Woman's Convention inspired black women with a sense of agency instead of victimization, it also created avenues of rare and unprecedented opportunity. By the standards of most Americans, white or black, some of these opportunities would be exceptional. More exceptional, however, was the fact that daughters of slaves, by welding a powerful national constituency, had engineered the mechanism by which they came to enjoy unimaginable recognition. For example, convention officers Nannie Burroughs and Ella E. Whitfield were among thirty-five delegates to represent the National Baptist Convention at the World Baptist Congress held in London during 11–19 July 1905. Burroughs won international acclaim for her oratorical abilities when she delivered two speeches—"Woman's Work" on 13 July at Exeter Hall and the "Triumph of Truth" on 16 July in Hyde Park. When the WC convened for its annual meeting the following September, Burroughs eloquently conveyed her appreciation to the WC for underwriting the financial expenses of the trip. Her exhilaration was vicariously enjoyed as she described the representatives from the many countries, the racial justice message of black Baptist speakers, and the overall impact of the National Baptist Convention upon the 5,000 people present: "When we reported in the World Baptist Congress 2,110,269 members, with over 16,000 churches, the people marveled at our strength. . . . The delegates to that congress had no idea that we represented so much numerically, financially and spiritually. It was indeed a revelation to the English people, and they never tired of hearing us tell of the struggles and achievements of the American Negro in church work."[66]

For the black women who gathered together at the annual meetings of the Woman's Convention, exciting and unusual events were not left solely to the realm of vicarious enjoyment. During the NBC's annual conference in Philadelphia in 1914, John Wanamaker, the department store tycoon, hosted a reception in honor of the black Baptists. On the Saturday of the conference, black Baptist men and women from northern cities and southern hamlets toured Wanamaker's department store and afterward converged on Egyptian Hall, where elaborate hors d'oeuvres and an orchestra awaited them. Late in the festivities, Wanamaker himself welcomed his guests. The event caused the women to note in their minutes: "This was the rarest feast of the Convention. We have never had such an experience before."[67]

The Black Church and Progressive-Era Reform

After 1910 the Woman's Convention increasingly focused upon new challenges, particularly that of black urbanization. Between 1900 and 1910 the black population grew significantly in southern cities as blacks forsook agriculture for better economic opportunity. The most dramatic increases occurred in Birmingham, which tripled its black population from 16,575 to 52,305; Atlanta, which grew from 35,727 to 51,902; Richmond, which rose from 32,230 to 46,733; and Jacksonville, Florida, which increased from 16,236 to 29,293.[68] After the turn of the century, economic factors together with pervasive racial restrictions and violence in the South accentuated the relative attractiveness of northern cities. World War I accelerated the migration already under way. The cessation of foreign immigration and wartime demands for labor pulled waves upon waves of black migrants northward.[69]

Carole Marks describes northern businesses' extensive labor recruitment. War-related industries "did not hesitate to promise the moon to those who qualified, though they managed to pay low wages nonetheless." The Pennsylvania Railroad and the Illinois Central "imported" several thousands of blacks for unskilled work in the north.[70] In the decade between 1910 and 1920 the black population soared upward in such cities as Chicago (from 44,103 to 109,458), Detroit (from 5,741 to 40,878), Cleveland (from 8,448 to 34,451), New York (from 91,709 to 152,467), and Philadelphia (from 84,459 to 134,229).[71] The North's unskilled and semi-skilled jobs offered wage rates considerably higher than the South's. Florette Henri observes that "to farm workers in the South who made perhaps $.75 a day, to urban female domestics who might earn from $1.50 to $3.00 a week, the North during the war years beckoned with factory wages as high as $3.00 to $4.00 a day, and domestic pay of $2.50 a day." For most migrants, however, progress was undermined at nearly every turn. Their pay fell on the lowest rung of the northern economic ladder, and they learned only too quickly the meaning of "last hired, first fired." Restricted to overcrowded black ghettos, the migrants suffered from poor quality housing, exploitive housing costs, disease, high rates of infant mortality, and other hardships of poverty.[72]

In responding to the demographic and socioeconomic changes that were under way, organized black Baptist women came increasingly to employ the language and methods of secular reformers. With the birth of the Baptist women's national organization, the mediating role of women's church work served to connect local and state activities with more sophisticated and changing reform trends. Indeed the general direction of reform activities endorsed by the leadership of the Woman's Convention reflected the interest in sociology that was characteristic of the Progressive era.[73] This influence marked a significant departure from nineteenth-century patterns of women's church work.

By 1912 the Woman's Convention embraced the sociological emphasis of the Social Gospel Movement and secular progressivism. Although the Woman's Convention continued the charity work begun in the nineteenth century and worked to provide rural black women with schools and recreational facilities, it increasingly devoted its principal attention to urban conditions.[74] In its effort to make the Baptist church responsive to urbanization and industrialization, the WC joined the mainstream of "social Christianity," which was drawing adherents among both black and white Protestants. The Social Gospel movement, which inextricably linked individual salvation with the salvation of society, turned its attention to such secular issues as labor, race, immigration, and housing conditions. Through the Social Gospel, white middle-class Protestants sought to bridge the gap between their churches and the working class. Convinced that society, not merely the individual soul, was at stake, churches involved themselves in the practical work of social salvation—establishing settlement houses, holding forums to discuss industrial problems, and creating social service commissions.[75]

Although usually presented as a white phenomenon, the Social Gospel movement flourished in black churches. Baptist and African Methodist Episcopal Churches, as well as black churches of other denominations, established a variety of social and economic programs, and some even adopted the title "institutional church" like their white counterparts. The concept of the institutional church operated in much the same way as the settlement house in addressing its programs to the plight of the urban poor. The programs of white institutional churches were usually funded by wealthy parishioners or sometimes by philanthropists, as in the case of John D. Rockefeller's support of Judson Memorial Church in New York city.[76] Such churches stressed a responsibility to the "total person" and offered a variety of activities including vocational training, athletics, sewing courses, and recreation.

Without adopting the title "institutional church," black churches had historically sought to address both the spiritual and the social condition of their people. Especially in the late nineteenth and early twentieth centuries, black churches generated extensive programs as part of the larger philosophy of racial self-help. In response to a hostile environment that denied so many opportunities and services to the black community, black churches nurtured schools, health clinics, publishing houses, libraries, recreation centers, and innumerable other organizations. In his commencement address to the class of 1898 of Fisk University, W. E. B. Du Bois stated that black churches were "for the most part, curiously composite institutions, which combine the work of churches, theaters, newspapers, homes, schools, and lodges." Fannie Barrier Williams arrived at the same conclusion in 1905. Commenting on twenty-five black churches in Chicago's black ghetto, she stated that the masses considered their churches to be much more than centers of preaching and Sunday Schools. The people viewed their churches as a "sort of tribune of all their social and civic affairs."[77]

In 1900 the A.M.E. minister and future bishop Reverend Reverdy Ransom launched the Institutional Church and Settlement House in

Chicago, which included a day care center, kindergarten, mothers' and children's clubs, sewing classes, cooking classes, an employment bureau, and a penny savings bank.[78] Similarly in 1901, the Baptist minister John Milton Waldron established Bethel Institutional Church in Jacksonville, Florida. The church operated a kindergarten, cooking school, and night school. In addition it launched the Afro-American Life Insurance Company, which began as a church society but eventually opened up to the entire black community on a nondenominational basis. Upon assuming the pastorate of Shiloh Church in Washington, D.C. in 1907, Waldron dubbed his new church "institutional," and under his tenure Shiloh proceeded to establish a wide variety of activities from day care for working mothers to programs for alley dwellers.[79] Also in Washington, D.C., the Nineteenth Street Baptist Church, a church of more than 2,000 members under the leadership of the Reverend Walter H. Brooks, sponsored a health clinic for the needy. The clinic was described by the *Colored American Magazine* in 1908 as operating a "free dispensary, under the care of a dozen physicians, pharmacists, trained nurses and dentists."[80]

The concept of social salvation was not new to blacks, but the Social Gospel movement carried radically different meanings for blacks than for whites. The struggle for racial self-help and self-determination in the last two decades of the nineteenth century had united the educated leaders and the uneducated laboring poor in mutual efforts. Black Baptists had historically operated from a social reality different from that of whites, inasmuch as support of educational institutions and charity work in the nineteenth century represented the cumulative efforts of many poor blacks rather than the philanthropic efforts of a well-to-do few. Before the rise of such secular organizations as the National Urban League in 1911, the black church and, to a lesser extent, black fraternal organizations and mutual aid societies enhanced the survival and socialization of urban blacks. Churches adopted such programs as vocational training, relief to the needy, kindergartens, day nurseries, industrial schools, job placement, and recreation for youth.[81]

The black church's involvement in social reform was not confined to the activities of the male ministry, however. Not merely followers, women initiated, funded, and executed many of the aforementioned programs. Black Baptist women perceived themselves as co-laborers with black ministers and white social reformers. In 1915, for instance, the annual report of the executive board of the Woman's Convention invoked Jane Addams and her work with immigrants in Chicago. The image of Addams established a perceived commonality between her work and that of the black Baptist women while it simultaneously accentuated the unique financial circumstances of black reform: "Do you wonder how Jane Addams built up that great Hull House? She has done it because her people have invested faith, money, and lives in it in response to her appeals. It is not large gifts that we need, but a large number of givers. We can do as much with small gifts from a large number of givers as Miss Jane Addams has done with large gifts from a small number of givers."[82]

The convention movement among black Baptist women during the late nineteenth and early twentieth centuries encouraged and, at times, demanded a progressive ministry which was sympathetic to social reform. The minutes of the Woman's Convention pronounced scathing critiques of the unprogressive and unprepared ministry. The women went on record in their denunciation of churches that refused to include social salvation in their program of saving souls. At the annual meeting of the Woman's Convention in 1912, Mrs. Lillie Smith, state representative from Colorado, delivered the paper, "A Need for a Larger Conception of Home Missions," in which she advocated greater social service and less emotionalism in churches. Nannie Burroughs repeatedly addressed the subject of the unprogressive clergy in her annual speeches and reports to her convention. Burroughs measured the quality of the clergy by its commitment to social service and criticized ministers who preached "too much Heaven and too little practical Christian living." Hurling unrestrained epithets, Burroughs denounced the uneducated and emotional as "sleek, lazy 'jack leg'" preachers who found a following among the poor and illiterate but did nothing to help them. According to Burroughs, such ministers preyed upon the poor and ignorant—exploiting their followers' sacrificial monetary contributions for selfish personal gain.

In a printed address to her sisters in 1915 Burroughs categorized three types of ministers. The first and most respected group comprised well-trained theologians who understood contemporary social issues and participated in community uplift work. The second and largest group comprised those men who were poorly educated, underfinanced, and yet conscientious and well-meaning. The third and totally unsatisfactory group formed the second largest number of ministers. This group consisted of intellectually inept men who exploited their congregations. Burroughs labeled them "grafters" and urged that "public sentiment be molded against men who go into the ministry to dodge hard work." Reminding ministers that women provided the greatest financial as well as numerical support to churches, Burroughs asserted the right of her sisters to endorse only well-trained clergymen.[83] In a report to the convention in 1914, she opined: "No church should be allowed to stay in a community that does not positively improve community life."[84] In her annual report for 1920 Burroughs insisted that the church should not substitute shouting for service.[85]

Women's organizational networks at the state and national levels facilitated a wide dissemination of ideas and expertise for utilization at the local level. Nannie Burroughs referred to the informative programs of the WC's annual meetings as "schools of methods" for local communities: "Women come up here, get new ideas, new material, new spirit, and go home and infuse and enthuse their sisters. The thousands of workers in local churches who have never been to one of our annual meetings have had the meetings brought to them. A month after we close our Convention, the speeches, reports, songs and suggestions are heard at every crossroad."[86] After 1910 the Woman's Convention increasingly depicted its role as an "institute" for the study of modern reform methods. Through the convention, a national network of communication and cooperation identified women with expertise, collected data, and introduced new methods. The annual meetings of the WC featured papers delivered by physicians, social workers, and civic-improvement activists. Calling for "practical religion," the Baptist women endeavored to bring "education closer to religion, [and] relate it to health needs, industrial life, character building, work in prisons, reform work."[87]

With the incorporation of sociological and scientific findings into its programs, the Woman's Convention consciously distinguished between "rescue" and "prevention."[88] Rescue constituted the older form of service, which relieved and aided people already in distress, while the updated and preferable form sought preventive remedies for social ills through (as Burroughs noted) a "larger sociological direction." "Efficiency is the watchword of the day," the WC's leaders declared, and they insisted upon the incorporation of modern sociological methods into the work of the church.[89] To be sure, they were motivated by moralistic and religious sensibilities, but their advocacy of social service borrowed increasingly from the language of scholarly research and trained social work. In 1912 the report of the committee on education of the Woman's Convention observed that "ethics and sociology are claiming the attention of men of learning as nothing else has done." The Woman's Convention, like other progressive reformers, engaged in settlement house work, campaigns for public health, and efforts to ameliorate the conditions in city slums.[90]

Emphasizing the "formation" of character, rather than its "reformation," the women argued that churches must provide recreation and job placement services as a deterrent to idleness and crime. Under the section "How to Employ Your Idle Churches and Your Idle Children," Burroughs's annual report for 1912 advocated the use of church buildings as recreational outlets for youth during the summer months. She pointed out that the overwhelming majority of children from poor, working-class black homes had no access to playgrounds, while thousands of churches stood vacant during the great part of each week. She also suggested that churches employ teachers in search of employment or college students in need of practical experience.[91]

On 15 October 1913 the WC opened a settlement house in a slum neighborhood in Washington, D.C. under the direction of M. Helen Adams, a trained social worker.[92] Called the Centre, the settlement operated in a cooperative relationship with the WC's National Training School for Women and Girls, Howard University, the Associated Charities, and the Juvenile Court of the District. Burroughs referred to the Centre as a "sociological experiment station" because of the diversity of programs it offered the poor. The settlement operated a program for clothing and feeding the poor. Its soup station, for instance, fed 1,200 people during the winter months of 1915. The Centre provided a medical clinic through the volunteer services of physicians. The Centre offered classes for adults and children, sponsored a baseball team and other recreational activities, and represented children in court.[93]

The influence of Progressivism on the Woman's Convention was reflected in its growing desire to rely upon trained specialists. In response to the recommendation in 1912 for a system of community education, the convention instituted a social service committee responsible for acquainting conference delegates with the findings of social workers, sociologists, and other social scientists. In 1914 the Woman's Convention launched its social service committee under the chairmanship of Helen Adams, director of the Centre. In that year the committee scheduled two days of the annual conference for discussing the theme "Reaching the People Where They Are." Helen Adams read a paper entitled "What Is Social Service?" while Dr. Charlotte Abbey of Pennsylvania addressed the topic of "Child Welfare."[94] The annual meetings of the Woman's Convention provided a forum for social workers, state representatives, and others engaged in social reform activities to discuss implementation of their work at the local level and to keep abreast of the latest research methods. In 1915 the WC laid plans for a series of three-day regional institutes and workshops for reassessing charity and social service work. Advocating the need for expertise, Burroughs advised her sisters in state and local societies to become "specialists" by reading the literature of social reform organizations. She called attention to the need for black women to write such literature, for she considered most white women incapable of writing objectively on black social conditions.[95]

The WC's interest in the findings of social scientists encouraged the introduction of two new committees—child welfare and vital statistics. The first report of the committee on vital statistics compared mortality rates for blacks and whites in relation to nutrition. In 1920, the committee produced an informative report that identified diseases prevalent among blacks, made correlations between life expectancy and overcrowded housing, and assessed the nutritional benefits of foods commonly found in the diets of blacks. The report also urged the importance of sex education for boys and girls and concluded that the safest foundation "for a healthy sex life is an individual and social morality combined with full knowledge of sexual realities." The report called for knowledge of both reproduction and venereal disease. It also suggested that church societies sponsor annual health programs.[96]

The WC's open and objective discussion of venereal disease was an important departure from the attitude of many Americans, including the medical profession. Elizabeth Fee's study of venereal disease in

Baltimore during the early decades of the twentieth century finds that venereal diseases remained "blanketed in silence." Their prevalence during World War I forced the subject into the public eye, but even then the American Social Hygiene Association spoke of venereal disease as a moral issue of vice and prostitution. In the postwar years, the medical profession linked race to moralistic interpretations of veneral disease. The health establishment did not speak in the dispassionate tone of germ theory, nor did it make any effort to correlate the incidence of venereal disease with socioeconomic conditions. Fee observes that it was not until syphilis had reached epidemic proportions in the white community that Baltimore's health officials began to redefine it as a disease that struck "innocent" victims, namely "the educated, respectable white population."[97]

Thus the black Baptist women's discussion of sexually transmitted disease was progressive for the times, inasmuch as it did not rely solely on moralistic language but drew upon sociological data as well. Discussion of child welfare, too, figured into the WC's progressive agenda—reflecting the new influence of sociology. Although state reports indicated a continuation of the nineteenth-century tradition of mothers' training schools, the black Baptist women urged research and data collection for the "study of youth" by the second decade of the twentieth century. For example, in 1912 Adella Crawford of Missouri addressed the convention on "Proper Amusements for Children." Unlike earlier reports, which spoke in the moralistic and sentimental tones of Victorian domestic ideals, Crawford's paper analyzed stages of child development and associated various types of play activity with a child's mental and physical development.[98]

In 1914 Mary V. (Cook) Parrish chaired the newly formed committee on child welfare and juvenile delinquency. In a comprehensive synthesis of modern social reform work, Parrish provided a wealth of statistical information on infant mortality, common diseases, prenatal care, and diet. She discussed the role of the private and public sectors in providing medical services, dental clinics, school lunches, open-air schools, and assistance to the physically and mentally handicapped. Parrish linked juvenile delinquency to such causes as poor housing, lack of home discipline, failure of public education, urban dislocation, and inadequate recreational facilities.[99] The minutes for the women's

annual gathering in 1918 referred to motherhood as a "science as exact
as mathematics." In 1920 the education committee devoted its report
to modern kindergarten methods.[100]

Ties That Bind

The convention's interest in Progressive-era reform was directly attributable to its leaders. Although the officers of the Woman's Convention
had grown to maturity in the "great preparatory schools" of women's
church societies, they had branched out into secular reform activity,
which complemented and gave meaning to their church-related activity. The reciprocal relationship between church and secular organizations positioned black women reformers in a variety of contexts.
Leaders of the black Baptist women's movement represented the educated elite of their communities, and they held membership and
leadership positions in a variety of secular organizations.

S. W. Layten, president of the Woman's Convention, worked closely
with the white social worker Frances Kellor in the National League
for the Protection of Colored Women. In 1905 Kellor founded protective associations in New York and Philadelphia with a corps of white
and black workers in employment agencies, lodging houses, churches,
and working girls' homes. Northern and southern churches functioned
as intermediaries between Layten and future migrants. Church workers
informed Layten of women who wanted to move North, and she, in
turn, provided them with directions and other pertinent information.[101] Churches also aided her work by discouraging the migration
of the ill-prepared, by sending women to ship docks and train stations
to meet new arrivals, and by assisting migrants in locating lodging and
employment.[102]

In 1906 the Philadelphia and New York branches of the association
officially launched the National League for the Protection of Colored
Women, and between 1906 and 1910 the organization added local
branch associations in Boston, Memphis, Baltimore, and Norfolk, in
order to protect women at both departure and arrival points. In 1910
Layten replaced Frances Kellor as general secretary of the NLPCW. In
1911 her organization merged with the Committee on Urban Conditions and the Committee for Improving the Industrial Conditions of
Negroes in New York to form the National Urban League. George

Haynes, the first African American to receive a Ph.D. in sociology from Columbia University, became director of the Urban League, while S. Willie Layten joined Victor Flinn and Eugene Kinkle Jones as its first field secretaries.[103]

As president of the Woman's Convention, Auxiliary to the National Baptist Convention, Layten integrated her secular social work with the social service work of the church. She pursued graduate courses in sociology at Temple University and took extension courses in social work from the University of Pennsylvania.[104] Her annual speeches advocated "practical Christianity"—church work that spoke to the social and economic needs of black people. In her annual address in 1905, Layten informed her Baptist sisters about her then two-month-old protective association, its rescue home, and the study on black labor conditions conducted by Frances Kellor and the Inter-Municipal Committee on Household Research. From May through September in 1905 the Philadelphia Association for the Protection of Colored Women assisted more than 450 black women and girls and 16 whites. Layten and the agents of her association met women traveling by boat to Philadelphia from the Carolinas, Virginia, Maryland, and Delaware.[105] Arriving at Ericson Pier in Philadelphia, the migrants were often destitute and vulnerable to "wharf sharks"—Layten's term for exploitive labor agents and other unscrupulous people.[106]

In her presidential addresses in 1909 and 1910 Layten again discussed the work of her protective association with the Woman's Convention. The WC committee on recommendations praised Layten's organization and thanked her for "placing our Baptist women in charge of a work that is destined to reach, rescue, and save girls as no other agency now operating." The Woman's Convention pledged its financial assistance. In 1912 Layten proudly announced her affiliation with the National Urban League, and in her annual speech in 1915 she devoted considerable attention to female urban migration. She advised women's missionary societies to participate in protective work by acquainting themselves with young working women in their respective areas, investigating their places of employment, monitoring their housing situation, and learning how and where these young women found amusement.[107]

The Woman's Convention endorsed the work of secular organizations whose objectives complemented their own. The minutes for 1912 alluded to the growing ties between black women's church work and other community reform efforts: "The first striking effect observed in the review of the field in each State is that women are not doing less work in and for their churches directly, but that they are entering more into the work of transforming their communities and in co-operating with those agencies that have been inaugurated to reach a larger number of people."[108] This was particularly true of the WC's relationship with the National Association of Colored Women, which held its founding meeting in 1896 at the Nineteenth Street Baptist Church in Washington, D.C. The church's pastor, Walter H. Brooks, had vigorously supported both the movement for black Baptist hegemony and women's higher education during the 1880s and 1890s.[109] Nineteenth Street Baptist Church was also the church where Nannie Burroughs held membership. Yet stronger ties bound NACW members to the black Baptist women's national convention: several of the Baptist women's leaders also held membership and office in the NACW. It was not uncommon for delegates at the annual conferences of the Woman's Convention to repeat the NACW motto, "Lifting as we climb." In 1914 three veteran black Baptist leaders, Mary Parrish and Mamie Steward of Kentucky and Mary McDowell of Missouri, held national office within the NACW as statistician, first recording secretary, and auditor, respectively. In 1916 Burroughs headed the NACW's young people's department. In that same year Layten delivered a paper on black women migrants at the tenth biennial meeting of the NACW, and in 1918, during the First World War, she urged Baptist women to cooperate with the NACW in its study of black women's contributions to the nation's war effort.[110]

Representatives from the National Association of Colored Women reported on clubwomen's programs and activities at annual meetings of the Woman's Convention. At the meeting in Houston in 1912, Mrs. H. E. Frierson extended greetings from the Women's Federation of Clubs and also noted her presence at the founding of the Woman's Convention in 1900. In 1920 Mary V. Parrish referred to the recent NACW conference in Tuskegee and specifically to the role of black Baptist women at the conference. She commended Layten to the black Baptist sisterhood along with recognizing other outstanding state leaders who held dual membership in the WC and NACW. As Parrish reported on the states represented at the NACW conference, she was received with a "storm of applause, state after state vying with each other in their cheering."[111]

Conversely, the NACW included church-related work despite its nondenominational character. The purpose and identity of the National Association of Colored Women were not strictly secular, as is often presumed. Outlining women's clubwork for one of W. E. B. Du Bois's Atlanta University studies, NACW leader Josephine Silon Yates disclosed the ties that bound black women's church and secular work within her organization. In 1908 the NACW was structured into nineteen departments. Along with such departments as social science, temperance, domestic science, and literature appeared the following three: church clubs, evangelistic work, and religious work.[112] The role of church-related clubs within the NACW remains overlooked, but their presence was quite visible among the affiliated clubs of the NACW. Moreover, titles such as Art Club and Book Club often camouflaged church-related goals. The Minnesota federation of clubs exemplified this pattern. In presenting its work for Du Bois's study, the Minnesota federation provided the most detailed breakdown of clubs by activities. Of the eighteen NACW clubs from Duluth, Minneapolis, and St. Paul, nine were explicitly identified as church-related in purpose and affiliation. Some clubs bore titles that indicated a church affiliation, such as the Florida Grant Missionary Society and the Dorcas Society, which listed among its objectives "to pay the insurance money on the church property." However, secular-sounding titles often masked church-related activity. Within the Minnesota federation, the Book Club aided St. Marks A.M.E. Church, and the Literary Club and Social Club were both church-related. In the latter case the proceeds from the group's weekly activities "aided the church [unnamed] in many ways." One of the Minnesota clubs noted among its purposes raising money for the National Training School for Women and Girls—the school established and controlled by the Woman's Convention.[113]

Commitment to progressive reform and improvement in race relations led to the black Baptist women's endorsement of certain white secular organizations as well. In 1913 the Woman's Convention passed a resolution in support of the Southern Sociological Congress.[114] Funded by the philanthropist Anna Russell Cole and led by James E. McCulloch, a Methodist minister from Virginia, and W. D. Weatherford, a leader of the YMCA movement in the South, the Southern Sociological Congress represented the liberal element of the white South. At the call of Governor Ben Hooper of Tennessee, the Congress held its first annual conference in Nashville on 7–10 May 1912 and attracted 700 participants from twenty-eight states, Washington, D.C., Canada, and Africa. In its annual conferences the Southern Sociological Congress focused on social, civic, and moral conditions in the South. To the Woman's Convention, the Congress exemplified the best in southern white Progressivism. The Congress's annual meetings covered topics of specific concern to the black women—industrial problems, alcoholism, sanitary conditions, public health, race relations, and mob violence.[115]

The women's movement of the black Baptist church grew to maturity under the influence of Progressivism during the early twentieth century. Reflecting upon her convention's advancement during its first two decades, president S. Willie Layten remarked: "The growth of our work is indeed remarkable—we have extended its membership to every State and territory in the Union, we have found quiet and obscure women, who knew not their talents, and we have brought them forth, given them inspiration and work, developed them into some of the strongest and most resourceful women of the age, if known only among their own people."[116]

Otherwise unheralded women worked together in quotidian fashion in fund-raising drives, organizational meetings, and community programs. Though known only among themselves and within their communities, these nameless historical actors established protective homes, training centers, settlement work, kindergartens, and child care in the urban north and south. They supported public health programs, protective labor laws, and better municipal services. Their story enriches the history of American social reform.

7

The Politics of Respectability

The American people need help. They need missionaries to go to them and warn them of the awful sin that they are committing by allowing these lines of color, of race, of blood and of birth, to stand in the way of the onward march of religion and civilization. The greatest service that could be rendered to this country at this time would be to rid it of its prejudice that stands more formidable than the walls of Jericho.

Woman's Convention, 1905

The women's movement in the black Baptist church came of age between 1900 and 1920, during the best and worst of times for African American women. In the very years when support for women's rights grew in intensity and sympathy, racial prejudice became acceptable, even fashionable, in America. Ironically, this contradiction spun a creative tension that both motivated and empowered black women to speak out. It was in the church, more than in any other institution, where black women of all ages and classes found a site for "signifying practice"—for coming into their own voice.[1] And theirs was a dissonant voice in a society equally dissonant and in flux. Massive black migration and urbanization, employment patterns, the heightened materialism of consumer culture, the growing dominance of industrial education, the suffragist movement, and world war—all evoked responses from black women.

The formation of the Woman's Convention, Auxiliary to the National Baptist Convention, in 1900 brought into existence an arena for discussing these myriad, often competing concerns. More than this, it afforded black women what Patricia Hill Collins calls a "safe space" for self-definition.[2] The vast crowds who flocked to the WC's annual assemblies stirred feelings of freedom and security. In these assemblies black Baptist women expressed themselves openly and without fear of reprisal. In so doing, a national constituency of black women asserted agency in the construction and representation of themselves as new subjectivities—as Americans as well as blacks and women. They contested racist discourses and rejected white America's depiction of black women as immoral, childlike, and unworthy of respect or protection. The texts of their speeches and writings reveal the power of language in resisting self-perceptions as hapless, impotent victims of racism and sexism.[3] The rhetoric employed by the black Baptist women at once reflected and facilitated the acceptance and internalization of their own representations. The discursive effort of self-representation, of re-figuring themselves individually and collectively, was an immense one—stretching well beyond the limited context of their relationship with black Baptist men and white Baptists. Members of the Woman's Convention certainly continued to advance themes of racial self-determination and women's rights within the denomination, but they also positioned race and gender themes within the context of an American identity.

Between 1900 and 1920 the women's movement in the black Baptist church contested the racial-exclusivist image of America as it was understood and promoted by the dominant white society. In fact, black Baptist women envisioned themselves as sorely needed missionaries to America. For the sake of America's soul, they reasoned, the nation must put an end to "lines of color, of race, of blood and of birth."[4] Their religious-political message was drawn from biblical teachings, the philosophy of racial self-help, Victorian ideology, and the democratic principles of the Constitution of the United States. Black Baptist women appropriated all these discourses as they infused concepts such as equality, self-respect, professionalism, and American identity with their own intentions and interpretations. In the dialogic sense of multiple and conflicting meanings, these concepts became new, resistant pronouncements against white public opinion.[5]

The black Baptist women's opposition to the social structures and symbolic representations of white supremacy may be characterized by the concept of the "politics of respectability." For the Baptist women, respectability assumed a political dimension and may be likened to the variant of politics described by Nancy Fraser as follows: "There is the discourse sense, in which something is 'political' if it is contested across a range of different discursive arenas and among a range of different publics."[6] While adherence to respectability enabled black women to counter racist images and structures, their discursive contestation was not directed solely at white Americans; the black Baptist women condemned what they perceived to be negative practices and attitudes among their own people. Their assimilationist leanings led to their insistence upon blacks' conformity to the dominant society's norms of manners and morals. Thus the discourse of respectability disclosed class and status differentiation. The Woman's Convention identified with the black working poor and opposed lower-class idleness and vice on the one hand and high society's hedonism and materialism on the other. The convention's class sympathies, especially with regard to domestic servants, found concrete expression in the National Training School for Women and Girls, which the WC established in 1909 to win respect for black women in menial employment.

The politics of respectability emphasized reform of individual behavior and attitudes both as a goal in itself and as a strategy for reform of the entire structural system of American race relations. With regard to the black Baptist women's movement, such a politics did not reduce to an accommodationist stance toward racism, or a compensatory ideology in the face of powerlessness. Nor did it reduce to a mindless mimicry of white behavior or a "front" without substance or content.[7] Instead, the politics of respectability assumed a fluid and shifting position along a continuum of African American resistance. Through the discourse of respectability, the Baptist women emphasized manners and morals while simultaneously asserting traditional forms of protest, such as petitions, boycotts, and verbal appeals to justice. Ultimately, the rhetoric of the Woman's Convention combined both a conservative and a radical impulse. Although the black church offered women an oppositional space in which to protest vigorously social injustice, this space remained, nonetheless, situated within the larger structural framework of America and its attendant social norms. Black church women, therefore, did not escape the influence of the dominant society. The women's movement in the black Baptist church reflected and reinforced the hegemonic values of white America, as it simultaneously subverted and transformed the logic of race and gender subordination.

Contested Discourses

In an era when crude stereotypes of blacks permeated popular culture and when "scientific" racism in the form of Social Darwinism prevailed among professional scholars and other thinking people, African Americans' claims to respectability invariably held subversive implications. The Baptist women's emphasis on respectable behavior found expression in the writings of most black leaders of the time, male and female alike, and was perceived as essential to racial self-help and dignity.[8] From the perspective of the Baptist women and others who espoused the importance of "manners and morals," the concept of respectability signified self-esteem, racial pride, and something more. It also signified the search for common ground on which to live as Americans with Americans of other racial and ethnic backgrounds. This search for common ground—to be both black and American— occurred as the nation worked assiduously to deny this possibility by isolating the "Negro's place" within physical and symbolic spaces of inferiority. For many, the search for common ground portended too pyrrhic a victory, if attainable at all. W. E. B. Du Bois poignantly acknowledged the problem as he bemoaned the fate of those who succumbed to disrespect and mockery. Du Bois insisted that black self-doubt and self-hatred were born of "ridicule and systematic humiliation, the distortion of fact and wanton license of fancy, the cynical ignoring of the better and the boisterous welcoming of the worse, the all-pervading desire to inculcate disdain for everything black."[9]

Nor were blacks the only group to feel the sting of prejudice. Racist xenophobia permeated such books as Madison Grant's *The Passing of the Great Race* (1916), which presented a hierarchical ranking of European ethnic groups and affirmed nativist demands for restricting "undesirable" immigrants, namely, Jews and Catholics from eastern and southern Europe.[10] Asian immigrants, largely from China and Japan, suffered no less demeaning caricatures. During the spring of 1905, for instance, the San Francisco *Chronicle* carried such headlines as "Crime and Poverty Go Hand in Hand with Asiatic Labor" and "Japanese a Menace to American Women."[11]

Unlike the recent immigrant groups, however, black Americans endured a deeply rooted history of stigmatization that had begun centuries earlier in slavery and survived long after slavery's abolition. When hundreds of thousands of blacks abandoned the Jim Crow South between 1900 and 1920, they found little respite from the institutions and symbols of white supremacy. Their Great Migration to the urban North met with riots as well as discriminatory housing and employment practices. A virtual epidemic of violence pervaded the nation's cities as whites responded to black urbanization with fear and anger. Random attacks on black neighborhoods and full-scale rioting ravaged urban communities in both the North and the South: New Orleans in 1900; New York in 1900; Springfield, Ohio, in 1904; Greensburg, Indiana, and Atlanta in 1906; and Springfield, Illinois, in 1908. In 1917 riots erupted in Philadelphia and Chester, Pennsylvania, and in East St. Louis, Illinois. Racial violence reached a peak in the summer of 1919. During the "Red Summer," so labeled for the bloodbath that occurred, riots exploded in dozens of cities, large and small—including Chicago; Washington, D.C.; Omaha, Nebraska; Longview, Texas; and Knoxville, Tennessee.[12]

Moreover, "technologies of power" at the everyday level—films, school textbooks, art, newspapers—produced and disseminated a "rhetoric of violence" (to borrow from Teresa de Lauretis) in the form of negative caricaturing and stereotyping.[13] For example, the film epic *Birth of a Nation*, which was inspired by Thomas Dixon's novel *The Clansman*, demonized blacks by juxtaposing images of rapacious, brutish black men alongside delicate, chaste white women. With unseemly vividness the newly burgeoning film industry incited and perpetuated popular myths that equated black men with rapists. Michael Rogin persuasively argues that the mass appeal of *Birth of a Nation* was reflected in the tremendous accolades it inspired from then-President Woodrow Wilson, Supreme Court justices, and the general public across class, ethnic, and sectional lines. Rogin states: "The opposition between North and South in the film, as well as that between immigrant and native in the history outside it, had been replaced by the opposition between white and black."[14]

The "rhetoric of violence" was not confined to black men, however. Equally negative representations of black women's sexuality figured in popular and academic discourses. Indeed, the disjunction between images of white and black women was more glaring than that between white and black men. Black manhood was represented as male sexuality run rampant. Black womanhood and white womanhood were represented with diametrically opposed sexualities. This viewpoint was typified by a white woman who was quoted in a newspaper in 1904: "Negro women evidence more nearly the popular idea of total depravity than the men do. . . . When a man's mother, wife and daughters are all immoral women, there is no room in his fallen nature for the aspiration of honor and virtue . . . I cannot imagine such a creation as a virtuous black woman."[15]

Artistic imagery added compelling realism to such presumptions. Portraits in art galleries, pictures in books, photographs, and drawings constituted not a mirror of human heterogeneity, but an icon that generalized upon all black people. Their effect was to ascribe pathological uniformity onto black women as a group, such that every black woman regardless of her income, occupation, or education became the embodiment of deviance. The black woman came to symbolize, according to Sander Gilman, an "icon for black sexuality in general."[16] The issue of rape epitomized the breadth of the racial divide. From the days of slavery well into the twentieth century, widespread assumptions of the black woman's innate promiscuity prevented legal redress in the case of her victimization by rape.[17] Neil McMillen's study of Jim Crow Mississippi observes that courts did not convict white men for the rape of black females beyond the age of puberty.[18]

The historians Beverly Guy-Sheftall and Patricia Morton both discuss the construction and representation of black women in popular and academic discourses during the age of Jim Crow. Guy-Sheftall notes the prevalence of the following racist themes: the immoral black female teacher as cause for the weakness of black schools; the immoral black mother as responsible for the degeneracy of the black family; the acquiescence of the black husband to his wife's infidelity; and the widespread belief that black women were unclean.[19] Patricia Morton, in her explication of the "disfigured images" of black women, discloses that the professionalization of history and sociology, with its shift from the amateur scholar to the university-trained Ph.D., provided an authoritative, seemingly "objective" basis for such generalizations. Morton reveals that well-respected historians of the time, such as James

Ford Rhodes, Frances Butler Simkins, and Ulrich B. Phillips, portrayed slave women not as victims but as lazy, promiscuous, and brutish figures.[20]

The Baptist women's emphasis on respectable behavior contested the plethora of negative stereotypes by introducing alternate images of black women. The annual meetings of the Woman's Convention were themselves the product and process of black women's collective self-construction and self-representation. The high quality of their programs implicitly contradicted the lazy, immoral, and inept images portrayed in racist literature. Speeches and reports bestowed dignity upon the convention's members—commending the sacrifice of "daily toilers," the faithfulness of "everyday women," as well as the impressive achievements of members such as banker Maggie Lena Walker of Richmond, Virginia, and lawyer Gertrude Rush of Des Moines, Iowa.[21] By privileging respectability, and particularly the capacity and worthiness of poor, working-class black women for respect, the WC's public discourse emphasized a critical message to its members, namely, that self-esteem and self-determination were independent of contexts of race and income.

The politics of respectability tapped into Christian teachings that exalted the poor and the oppressed over the rich and powerful. Christianity had historically advocated political submission to the laws of governments, while it simultaneously demanded the autonomy and transformative power of the individual will.[22] This seeming contradiction stood at the core of respectability's meaning to African Americans. Submission to Jim Crow laws, it was reasoned, abrogated the civil rights of blacks, but it could not abrogate the power of self-definition. Nannie Burroughs, corresponding secretary of the Woman's Convention, emphasized this important tenet of the politics of respectability when she affirmed: "Men and women are not made on trains and on streetcars. If in our homes there is implanted in the hearts of our children, of our young men and of our young women the thought they are what they are, not by environment, but of themselves, this effort to teach a lesson of inferiority will be futile."[23]

The rhetoric of the WC's leaders rejected income or social status as definitive of one's worth. Burroughs wrote in the "woman's column" of the *National Baptist Union*, the weekly newspaper of the National

Baptist Convention: "Every mother can become a benefactor to the race. It matters not how poor the mother if she possesses a character in which sobriety, honor and integrity, and every other wholesome virtue hold sway . . . Many of the most noted women and men of the ages have been those of the persevering poor."[24] The Woman's Convention identified its constituency as women of the working poor and insisted that "the poor washer-woman, cook and toiler has built up nine-tenths of all our institutions and churches."[25] While locked in menial employment, black women found in the church theological and concrete affirmation of their talent and leadership. In choirs, missionary conventions, deaconess boards, and other church-related organizations, they internalized subjectivities deemed worthy of respect.

By claiming respectability through their manners and morals, poor black women boldly asserted the will and agency to define themselves outside the parameters of prevailing racist discourses. Notwithstanding the sincerity of the Baptist women's appeals to respectable behavior, such appeals were also explicit rejections of Social Darwinist explanations of blacks' biological inferiority to whites. Respectability was perceived as a weapon against such assumptions, since it was used to expose race relations as socially constructed rather than derived by evolutionary law or divine judgment.

From the perspective of the Woman's Convention, polite behavior on Jim Crow streetcars and trains did not constitute supine deference to white power. Nor did politeness constitute *unconscious* acts of political concession, as Pierre Bourdieu's oft-quoted analysis would otherwise have us believe. Bourdieu writes of politeness:

If all societies . . . that seek to produce a new man through a process of 'deculturation' and 'reculturation' set such store on the seemingly most insignificant details of *dress, bearing,* physical and verbal *manners,* the reason is that, treating the body as a memory, they entrust to it in abbreviated and practical, i.e. mnemonic, form the fundamental principles of the arbitrary content of the culture. The principles em-bodied in this way are placed beyond the grasp of consciousness, and hence cannot be touched by voluntary, deliberate transformation . . . The whole trick of pedagogic reason lies precisely in the way it extorts the essential while seeming to demand the insignificant . . . The concessions of politeness always contain political concessions.[26]

On the contrary, the politics of respectability constituted a deliberate, highly self-conscious concession to hegemonic values. While deferring to segregation in practice, adherents of respectability never deferred to it in principle. The Baptist women's emphasis on manners and morals served to reinforce their sense of moral superiority over whites. For instance, the minutes of the WC for 1910 contained the section "Conduct in Public Places," which admonished blacks to maintain "proper conduct" on streetcars:

A certain class of whites have set a poor example for the Negro in many sections, by making it a point to rush in and spread out, so that we cannot get seats . . . We have seen our people provoked to act very rudely and to demand seats, or squeeze in, and almost sit in the laps of the "spreaders." Here is an opportunity for us to show our superiority by not squeezing in . . . Let us at all times and on all occasions, remember that the quiet, dignified individual who is respectful to others is after all the superior individual, be he black or white.[27]

Likewise, the Baptist women's adherence to temperance, cleanliness of person and property, thrift, polite manners, and sexual purity served to refute the logic behind their social subordination. The politics of respectability, as conceived by the black Baptist women, formed an integral part of the larger resistance that would eventually nullify unjust laws. In 1915 the executive board of the Woman's Convention conveyed this understanding: "Fight segregation through the courts as an unlawful act? Yes. But fight it with soap and water, hoes, spades, shovels and paint, to remove any reasonable excuse for it, is the fight that will win."[28]

Respectability, too, offered the black Baptist women a perceived weapon in defense of their sexual identities. In 1916 the minutes of the Woman's Convention noted that "since she [the black woman] is liable to these insults and encroachments . . . she must become a tower of moral strength and by her reserve and dignified bearing, defy and cower her aggressors."[29] The historian Darlene Clark Hine, in calling attention to black women's fear of rape by white and black men in the

early twentieth century, argues that black women adopted a "culture
of dissemblance"—a self-imposed secrecy and invisibility—in order to
shield themselves emotionally and physically.[30] While this "culture of
dissemblance" was illustrative of the everyday resistance of black
women, it formed part of a larger discourse that often explicitly deployed manners and morals to challenge charges of black immorality.
Such manners and morals, as deployed by black women, were perceived as protection from sexual insult and assault. They were also
perceived by some as tools for winning sympathetic white allies.

It was the positive image of respectable African Americans that the
Baptist women sought to promote by means of "distinctive" literature,
their term for literature written by black authors. Virginia Broughton,
recording secretary of the Woman's Convention, explained the need
for "distinctive literature" in 1902 when she declared that blacks must
publish their side of history in order to contest racist discourses and
instill pride in their people.[31] Similarly, the WC's formation of "Negro
Doll Clubs" in 1914 was an attempt to instill in young black girls pride
in their skin color. The Negro dolls were manufactured by the National
Negro Doll Company, which was under the management of National
Baptist officer Richard H. Boyd. Boyd's doll company received the
endorsement of the National Baptist Convention in September 1908
and by January 1909 had sold some 3,000 of the dolls. The dolls were
advertised as exhibiting the grace and beauty of a "refined American
Negro woman." Attempting to portray the "real American Negro
woman" and the "representative American Negro," the dolls' features
and clothing were constructed in such a way as to refute unflattering
images of black women, along with the idea that beauty was "flaxen-
haired, blue-eyed, rosy-cheeked."[32]

Assimilationist Leanings

The public discourse of the Woman's Convention betrayed yet another, even opposite understanding of blacks' position vis-à-vis white
Americans. The WC's enormous concern for whites' perceptions of
black behavior regularly prompted scathing critiques against nonconformity to "proper" values. In its denunciation of those blacks who
rejected hard work, piety, cleanliness, sexual purity, and temperance,

the WC unwittingly reinforced prevalent stereotypical images of blacks. Through leaflets, newspaper columns, neighborhood campaigns, lectures, and door-to-door visits, an army of black Baptist women waged war against gum chewing, loud talking, gaudy colors, the nickelodeon, jazz, littered yards, and a host of other perceived improprieties.[33] The production and dissemination of tract literature constituted a favorite method for conveying their values. The tracts, which offered practical talks on daily conduct, caught the eye and interest of their readers by their straightforward titles: "Take a Bath First," "How To Dress," "How to Get Rid of Bed Bugs," "Ten Things the Negro Needs," "Anti-Hanging Out Committee," and "Traveler's Friend."[34] The popularity of "Traveler's Friend" led W. E. B. Du Bois to include it in his study *Efforts for Social Betterment* (1909). Written by Burroughs, the tract urged blacks to make "respectful" complaints against unequal treatment on railroads, but it paid more attention to behavioral advice: "Don't stick your head out of the window at every station . . . don't talk so loud to your friends who may be on the platform that a person a block away may hear you."[35]

Brian Harrison, in his discussion of traditions of respectability among the British working class in the late nineteenth and early twentieth centuries, asserted that "respectability was always a process, a dialogue with oneself and with one's fellows, never a fixed position."[36] For the Woman's Convention, the politics of respectability constituted a counter-discourse to the politics of prejudice, but it was aimed dually at white and black Americans. Respectability held an identifiable and central place in the philosophy of racial self-help. It entrusted to blacks themselves responsibility for constructing the "Public Negro Self" (to borrow from Henry Louis Gates, Jr.), a self presented to the world as worthy of respect.[37] When early twentieth-century black educators, clubwomen, and leaders from diverse backgrounds referred to the "New Negro," they linked respectability with proof of the race's uplift from the degradation of slavery and from the disparaging images of Sambo and blackface minstrelsy.[38]

Uplift, however, encoded the church women's assimilationist leanings. Organized black church women disseminated throughout the black community the assimilationist message implicit in respectability, and they endeavored to implant middle-class values and behavioral patterns among the masses of urban blacks who retained rural folkways of speech, dress, worship, and other distinct cultural patterns. With evangelical fervor, they strove to win converts from the ranks of the poor and "unassimilated." Leaders of the Woman's Convention declared: "Despite charges to the contrary, the submerged, abandoned, neglected people of ours as well as other races, have in them latent powers of moral recovery, and we must join hands in giving them an opportunity for honest living and self-improvement."[39] This evangelical message, like the historic work of Home Missions among other ethnic and racial groups, sought to bring black America in line with both the religious and class values of the dominant society.

Respectability demanded that every individual in the black community assume responsibility for behavioral self-regulation and self-improvement along moral, educational, and economic lines. The goal was to distance oneself as far as possible from images perpetuated by racist stereotypes. Individual behavior, the black Baptist women contended, determined the collective fate of African Americans. It was particularly public behavior that they perceived to wield the power either to refute or confirm stereotypical representations and discriminatory practices. The Baptist women spoke as if ever-cognizant of the gaze of white America, which in panoptic fashion focused perpetually upon each and every black person and recorded his or her transgressions in an overall accounting of black inferiority. There could be no laxity as far as sexual conduct, cleanliness, temperance, hard work, and politeness were concerned. There could be no transgression of society's norms. From the public spaces of trains and streets to the private spaces of their individual homes, the behavior of blacks was perceived as ever visible to the white gaze. The black Baptist women imagined constant surveillance by whites, in much the way that Michel Foucault analyzed panopticism. Foucault wrote: "He [or she] is seen, but . . . does not see; he [or she] is the object of information, never a subject in communication."[40]

Through the discourse of respectability, black church women initiated the process of dialogue. They perceived respectability to be the first step in their communication with white America. Given the pervasiveness of racist stereotypes, this first step took on daunting proportions. Even progressive-reformers were not particularly progressive on the question of race. Although white women reformers grew increasingly sensitive to the plight of the new immigrants, only an exceptional few exhibited the same interest in black Americans.[41] S. Willie Layten, president of the Woman's Convention, conveyed the Baptist women's recognition of the magnitude of the challenge before them: "The misfortune not to be judged as other people, behooves us to become more careful until we have gained a controlling influence to contradict the verdict already gone forth."[42] The WC's advocacy of "respectable" behavior attempted to bridge the emotional distance between blacks and potential white allies. The convention's leaders fully recognized that where interracial cooperation had proved most successful, its work generally focused on behavior modification or self-help strategies on the part of African Americans, not on demands for structural changes in American laws and institutions. Often to the dismay of the Woman's Convention, enlisting white women's support for educational, religious, and other assimilating programs proved far easier than gaining their support for the nullification of disfranchisement and Jim Crow laws.[43] Yet the black Baptist women never relinquished their belief in the role of shared manners and morals in the fight for equal rights.

Respectability functioned as a "bridge discourse" that mediated relations between black and white reformers.[44] Examples of cooperation included relations between WC leaders and white women reformers in the Association for the Protection of Colored Women, Travelers' Aid, and the Associated Charities.[45] Cooperation also existed between black and white Baptist women. For example, leaders among northern white Baptist women appeared on the programs of the WC's annual sessions and offered tangible support to the convention's National Training School for Women and Girls. The black Baptist women were perhaps most encouraged by the new spirit of cooperation that emanated from southern white church women. Annie Armstrong, corresponding secretary of the Woman's Missionary Union of the Southern Baptist Convention, attended and addressed the annual meeting of the Woman's Convention in 1901. Impressed with the one-year-old national organization of black Baptist women, she wrote to Layten in order to keep the lines of communication open. In 1902 the two groups devised a policy of cooperation, which entailed jointly contributing to the salary and expenses of two black women missionaries on the southern field. The field missionaries were under the sole charge of the Woman's Convention. They engaged in house-to-house visitation, distributed tracts and other literature, held conferences, and organized affiliate societies of the WC.[46]

At the invitation of the southern white women, Layten presented the work of the Woman's Convention to the Woman's Missionary Union when it convened its annual meeting in Nashville in 1904. While in Nashville, delegates from the southern white Baptist women's union attended a city-wide conference of black Baptist women. Layten commended the spirit of cooperation between black Baptist and southern white Baptist women and remarked that the annual meetings of both women's groups in 1904 constituted the greatest women's achievements for the year. While noting other gatherings held in 1904, namely, the International Congress of Women in Berlin, the National Association of Colored Women in St. Louis, and the upcoming meeting of the Women's Christian Temperance Union, Layten maintained that the meeting of the Woman's Missionary Union in May and that of the Woman's Convention in September together symbolized the most significant events because of the precedent set for interracial cooperation. She considered their efforts at dialogue a crucial step toward encouraging greater understanding between the races in the South.[47]

Jacquelyn Dowd Hall's work on southern women's opposition to lynching in the 1930s underscores S. W. Layten's views. Hall identifies cooperative efforts between black and white church women as the precursor to later forms of southern interracial cooperation. Hall reveals that in 1912 white Southern Methodist women contributed financially to a settlement founded by women of the Colored Methodist Church in Nashville. She concludes that "the biracial staffs, governing boards, and welfare leagues associated with these Methodist settlements set a precedent for the postwar [World War I] idea of interracial cooperation."[48]

Respectability provided a discursive common ground in its concern for sexual purity, child rearing, habits of cleanliness and order, and overall self-improvement. In the context of the progressives' assimilationist agenda for immigrant groups in the early twentieth century, the black Baptist women's moralistic language and their social reform goals appear to parallel closely those of white Progressive-era reformers. For example, a recurrent theme of the official records was the growing self-indulgence and independence of youth. In 1904 S. W. Layten remarked: "The tendency of the age is to relaxation and frivolity which will develop loose and morally weak character: our young people are inclining this way." The many attractions of urban life were presented as particularly destructive to family cohesion and character formation, since they lured and fascinated youth into idle preoccupations outside the home.[49] The minutes of the annual meetings expressed fears that mothers had lost control over their daughters and emphasized control of behavior. In 1909 the corresponding secretary's and executive board's report denounced the excessive freedom of young girls: "They go in pairs or in shoals, string themselves in a line across the sidewalk, making it almost impossible for others to pass, and are exceedingly boisterous in their conduct . . . and their mission seems to be to grin, chew gum and get company to patrol the streets until late in the night."[50] The Woman's Convention argued that by allowing their daughters such freedom at night, mothers undermined all positive influences.[51]

For the black Baptist women, the positive influence of the home and church counterbalanced the street with its dance halls and nickelodeons. The street became the metaphor for all that was unwholesome and dangerous—for the "demoralizing habit of hanging out," for "perpetual promenading," and for "gamblers and criminals." In the rhetoric of the Woman's Convention, the street, too, became a concrete, identifiable site of assembly—for the "crowds on Wylie Avenue in Pittsburgh, Lombard and South Streets in Philadelphia, Lenox and Seventh Avenues in New York, Central Avenue in Cleveland and Dearborn Street in Chicago."[52] Between 1910 and 1920 the Woman's Convention repeatedly advised churches to organize athletic programs, music activities, and other recreation as alternatives to the street's allurements. One Baptist leader claimed that "the poison generated by Jazz music and improper dancing will completely demoralize the womanhood of today. The sure way to ruin is by way of the public dance hall."[53]

The WC's perception of unwholesome youthful activities was consistent with the rhetoric of other Progressive-era reformers. For example, in *The Spirit of Youth* (1909), Jane Addams advocated organized recreation for youth in similarly moralistic tones. She bemoaned that "never before in civilization have such numbers of young girls been suddenly released from the protection of the home and permitted to walk unattended upon city streets." In language similar to that of the black Baptist women, Addams condemned the public places of amusement that lured youth: the "gin-palaces" where liquor was sold; the five-cent theaters that promoted "a debased form of dramatic art and a vulgar type of music"; and the "huge dance halls . . . to which hundreds of young people are attracted, many of whom stand wistfully outside a roped circle, for it requires five cents to procure within it for five minutes the sense of allurement and intoxication which is sold in lieu of innocent pleasure."[54]

Similar Victorian ideals and assimilationist goals informed the black Baptist women's negative critique of jazz music and dance halls. The black Baptist women could neither appreciate nor acknowledge the rich contribution of black secular music and dance to American culture. They could not perceive the creative genius or the legitimacy of black working-class cultural forms such as jazz and dance, much less their importance as expressions of resistance to social privation and despair.[55] In accordance with the way the black clubwoman Jane Edna Hunter described dance halls, the black Baptist women considered them destructive to moral virtue and racial uplift. Hunter, a friend of Burroughs and active in both the YWCA and the National Association of Colored Women, described dance halls as places of "unbridled animality," where blacks made "a voluntary return to the jungle."[56]

Women's fashions, too, fell under the harsh critique of the black Baptist leadership. Virginia Broughton warned black women to pay more careful attention to their dress and to discard "gaudy colors and conspicuous trimmings."[57] Bright colors and other culturally unique designs were characterized as dissipating the high ideals of young women. Denouncing the slashed skirt and décolleté dress of 1913, the executive board of the Woman's Convention perceived the more revealing styles as lowering man's respect for woman and opening her to sexual advances. The report admonished that women should be stylish, yet modest. Mothers should insist that their "daughters make their dresses wide enough, so that it will not be necessary to slit them; and that they call less attention to their physical charms and more attention to the intellectual, moral, and spiritual."[58] Although black

Baptist male and female leaders proudly used the term "distinctive," to denote their "distinctive literature" and "distinctive Baptist work," they did not use the term to applaud black cultural patterns that were distinctively different from white patterns. "Distinctive" as used by black Baptists signified control of their own institutions. Cultural patterns that deviated from those of white middle-class Americans were viewed as retrogressive.

The insistence on conformity was reinforced in the institutional structure of black churches. Values were imparted in sermons, Sunday school lessons, and home missions, but in addition churches in the early twentieth century commonly regulated behavior—what Foucault refers to as "disciplining the body"—by performing a judicial, even punitive function.[59] Peter Goldsmith's anthropological study of black denominationalism observes that "strict expectations on individual comportment *outside* of church" were prevalent in black Baptist churches on the Georgia coast. Goldsmith also notes, in the case of the First African Baptist Church on St. Simon's Island during the 1920s, that members who were "too noisy" in their worship style were asked to leave the church.[60] In 1914, the church minutes of Shiloh Baptist Church in Washington, D.C. reveal that individuals caught dancing, imbibing alcoholic beverages, or engaging in other "improper" behavior were literally delivered a summons to come before the church for censure. At this time Shiloh was a leading Social Gospel church in the city, and its minister, J. Milton Waldron, was a founding member and officer of the NAACP.[61] The theologian and former Morehouse president Benjamin Mays remembered the judicial role of the Baptist church in the South Carolina community of his boyhood. On the second Saturday in each month, members were brought before the church for misconduct. If unrepentant, they could suffer exclusion, and if repentant, they were brought back into the church fold with some admonishment. Mays recounted that sexual offenses came before the church membership for judgment, as witnessed in the case of a young unmarried couple whose sexual intimacy led to pregnancy. The couple confessed their transgression before the church, after which the minister demanded that the man marry the young woman, live with her, and perform the duties of husband and father. If the young man failed to obey, so the minister warned, "something unspeakably bad would happen to him."[62]

While issues of purity, order, and cleanliness figured prominently in the discourse of respectability, such issues called attention to perceptions of an inextricable connection between the physical bodies of black women and black-inhabited physical space. Racist representations of black women as unclean, disease-carrying, and promiscuous conjoined with representations of black households as dirty, pathological, and disorderly.[63] In response, the discourse of respectability tended to hold black women primarily accountable for the rise or fall of the black family, and by extension for the rise or fall of the entire race. In 1904 S. Willie Layten, president of the Woman's Convention, positioned women's gender roles within this deterministic framework: "Mothers be stern, be firm and yet you can be kind and sympathetic. As a race we cannot afford to contribute ONE single life to the bad, though the individuals force it upon us. We are impoverished, unfortunately the minority or bad Negroes have given the race a questionable reputation; these degenerates are responsible for every discrimination we suffer."[64]

As the caretaker of the home, ergo the caretaker of the race, black mothers were charged with the responsibility of maintaining disciplined and clean homes. The failure to do so, however, left black mothers ultimately accountable for *contributing* lives to the "bad" and for "every discrimination we suffer." Respectability's emphasis on individual behavior served inevitably to blame blacks for their victimization and, worse yet, to place an inordinate amount of blame on black women. In the article "Straight Talk to Mothers," Nannie Burroughs noted the following cause-and-effect relationship: "It is a mother's duty to try and give her children wholesome food and an attractive home. Many a bad habit has been acquired because the meals did not contain all the necessary nourishments for the system. Chewing, smoking, and ofttimes drinking can be traced back to a poor dinner. Many a young man has left home because it was minus of attractions that his intelligence called for."[65] Black women's house cleaning habits inevitably fell under the same deterministic framework: "As a practical part of our Home Mission work, we urge the women here to give more attention to civic improvement. . . . Clean out the rubbish; whitewash and put things in order. Clean out germ-breeding cellars and rubbish corners in our homes. This is the only practical way to show that education and Christianity are counting in the development of the race."[66] Repairing broken fences, clearing debris, and improving lawns became crucial to gaining the respect of whites and removing excuses for color prejudice. The Baptist women's hygienic fervor saw the "woman who keeps a dirty home and tolerates trifling shiftless inmates . . . as great *an enemy to the race as the man who devotes his life to persecuting and maligning the race*"[67] (emphasis added).

At times, the rhetoric of the black Baptist women sounded uncannily similar to the racist arguments they strove to refute. The black Baptist women asserted that "proper" and "respectable" behavior proved blacks worthy of equal civil and political rights and made it possible for them to "demand what they can not hope to demand if they are boisterous and unclean."[68] Conversely, the politics of respectability equated nonconformity with the cause of racial inequality and injustice. This conservative and moralistic dimension tended to privatize racial discrimination—thus rendering it outside the authority of government regulation. This tendency was reflected in Nannie Burroughs's speech on alley reform in 1913. The racist residential patterns that restricted blacks to alley dwellings did not escape Burroughs's criticism;[69] nor did she fail to condemn the role of urban government and slum landlords in perpetuating unsanitary and unsafe housing conditions. Yet Burroughs placed greater responsibility on her own people: "In Washington City there is much talk about getting the seventeen thousand Negroes out of the alleys. To the student of euthenics, who believes that the shortest cut to health is by creating a clean environment in which to live this plan is most feasible, but to do a work that will abide we must first 'get the alley' out of the seventeen thousand Negroes, and it will be an easy task to get them out of the alley."[70]

The Baptist women's repeated condemnation of nonconformity indicated the significance they attached to individual behavior in the collective imaging of black people. Their pronouncements indicated as well the great value they attached to cultural assimilation (Burroughs's term was "thoroughly socialized") in the struggle for racial equality. The public discourse of the Woman's Convention rebuked those blacks who transgressed the dominant society's norms. Peter Stallybrass and Allon White's analysis of the "politics of transgression" proves useful for understanding the role of respectability in the formation of the black Baptist women's collective identity. Their identity (to borrow from Stallybrass and White) "continuously defined and re-defined itself through the exclusion of what it marked out as 'low'— as dirty, repulsive, noisy, contaminating."[71] The repeated references to negative black Others became central to, indeed constitutive of, the social identity of the respectable black American.

Class and Status Differentiation

If respectability signified dialogue with oneself and with others, it also signified class and status differentiation between those who exhibited its definitional criteria and those who did not. The politics of respectability, especially as defined by proper gender roles for women, marked differences of social status within the working class itself. The black working class has never been monolithic in its values and cultural style. What Thomas Wright described in 1873 for the British working class—that it "was not a single-acting, single-idea'd body"—held equally true for the African American working class.[72] The church played the single most important role in influencing normative values and distinguishing respectable from non-respectable behavior among working-class blacks during the early twentieth century. Indeed, the competing images of the church and the street symbolized cultural divisions within the mass of the black working poor. As both physical and discursive space, the church and the street constituted opposing sites of assembly, with gender-laden and class-laden meanings. The street signified male turf, a public space of worldly dangers and forbidden pleasures. Churches and households, both rejecting the worldly attractions of male social space, signified female and also sacred space. Women who strolled the streets or attended dance halls and cheap theaters promiscuously blurred the boundaries of gender. In the minds of "respectable" church women of the working poor, a diminished social status befell working women who (as Hazel Carby describes) "had broken out of the boundaries of the home and taken their sensuality and sexuality out of the private and into the public sphere."[73]

Thus the church women's visible assimilation of the dominant society's sexual codes and other "ladylike" behavior conveyed class-laden meanings. Although white society perceived blacks as an undifferentiated mass and confined them together in segregated neighborhoods, blacks—including those of the working poor—relied upon values and behavior in distinguishing class and status differences among themselves. Indeed, social scientists as well as members of the black community invariably focused on adherence to bourgeois standards of respectability and morality in designating social status.[74] Because of the limited economic options available to all blacks and especially black women, early twentieth century leaders rarely alluded to income or occupation when referring, as they frequently did, to the "better class of Negroes." Domestic servants could be included, and some were cited in this category, for it comprised all who were hardworking, religious, clean, and, so far as sex was concerned, respectful of the dominant society's manners and morals.

For the Woman's Convention, the discourse of respectability was informed by unprecedented migration, which contributed to growing class cleavage in the black community. At one extreme emerged a black middle class of lawyers, educators, physicians, ministers, and entrepreneurs—a new male and female elite that was conscious of its higher class position and was, in many respects, culturally and psychologically alienated from the less "assimilated," unskilled masses of the working poor. At the other extreme was an unproductive lower class (in today's terminology the "underclass") of vagrants, criminals, prostitutes—men and women whose lifestyles blatantly transgressed American social norms. Between these two extremes stood the great mass of the black working poor.

Although the officers of the Woman's Convention were clubwomen and members of the black middle class, the WC's membership hailed largely from the working poor. Leaders of the WC maintained an organic relation to this constituency. Their lives and experiences had been intertwined with those of the working poor in the larger struggle for black Baptist hegemony, in the nineteenth-century movement for women's separate conventions at the state and national levels, and in a host of other segregated institutions in local black communities. More important, the WC's leadership interpreted its essential function as that of articulating the economic, social, and political interests of poor working women.

The voice of the working poor was expressed most cogently in the annual reports of the executive board and corresponding secretary. This joint report drew from information sent directly from the convention's membership and represented the goals and activities of church women throughout the nation. Corresponding secretary Nannie Burroughs clearly integrated her own values and vision into the writing of this report, but its form and content were determined by communication with the convention's broad constituency. It was compiled from reports sent to the national office by state and local organizations, from the letters of ordinary women, from accounts by national officers of their visits to organizations and churches throughout the country, from reports of special convention-sponsored projects, such as the WC's training school, and from records related to financial receipts and disbursements. At every annual assembly of the Woman's Convention, Burroughs read the report, which went under the signed imprimatur of herself and the executive board. After its delivery to the entire body, the report was affirmed by a resolution of the delegates, and state directors were charged with the responsibility of sharing its contents with their constituencies back home.

A textual analysis of the annual reports of the executive board and corresponding secretary reveals the construction and representation of a collective identity that differed significantly from that of the National Association of Colored Women. The annual reports make explicit distinctions between the WC's identity and that of elite clubwomen. The black Baptist women's identity was (as in Stallybrass and White's analysis of identity formation) "produced and reproduced through the process of denial and defiance."[75] The convention's public statements often accused the black middle class of being contemptuous of the poor. Clubwomen themselves were certainly aware of such accusations, as is evident in a speech by NACW president Mary Church Terrell. Terrell stated in her presidential address in 1904: "It must be patent to the most careless observer that the more intelligent and influential among us do not exert themselves as much as they should to uplift those beneath them." Her sincere concern for her less fortunate sisters nonetheless belied an elitist orientation:

It has been suggested, and very appropriately, I think, that this Association should take as its motto—*Lifting as we climb*. In no way could we live up to such a sentiment better than by coming into closer touch with the masses of our women, by whom, whether we will or not, the world will always judge the womanhood of the race. Even though we wish to shun them, and hold ourselves entirely aloof from them, we cannot escape the consequences of their acts. So, that, if the call of duty were disregarded altogether, policy and self-preservation would demand that we go down among the lowly, the illiterate, and even the vicious to whom we are bound by the ties of race and sex, and put forth every possible effort to uplift and reclaim them.[76]

Terrell's statement, like the motto "lifting as we climb," admitted the difference in class status between clubwomen and "lowly" black women. Moreover, the NACW did not define or represent itself as a collective body of "common toilers"; nor did the NACW actively recruit them into its ranks. As an elite, who otherwise "might wish to shun them and hold ourselves entirely aloof," clubwomen understood only too well that American racism lumped and judged all black women together. Thus a sense of duty as well as expedience ("policy and self-preservation") resonated in Terrell's appeal to her sisters. In contrast, the leadership of the Woman's Convention targeted its appeal to a vast constituency of poor working women, and explicitly characterized its membership as the "persevering poor," "daily toilers," "common everyday women," and the "common people of whom God made more of than the other kind." These images, which were attributed to working women and typically domestic servants, contrasted sharply with images of a hedonistic bourgeoisie and an unproductive lower class. In the executive board and corresponding secretary's report for 1905, Nannie Burroughs asserted that the working poor of the church were neither vain nor idle. In a metaphorical conflation of the images of domestic servant and queen, Burroughs spoke of the women in the black Baptist church:

> We do ourselves honor when we have associated with us in our religious life women who think it a disgrace not to toil rather than those who look down in disdain upon a woman because she has character enough to work for an honest living. It does not require very much character nor brains to scorn labor, but it requires a great deal of both in this day of false pride to earn your bread by sweating for it and holding up your head above public sentiment, feeling in your heart that though you are a servant, yet you are a queen.[77]

Convention reports frequently counterposed images of domestic servants against images of elites. The washerwoman and cook, whose productive labor and sacrifice had made possible needed institutions and services, stood arrayed against elite "parasites [who] make a social kingdom, and never consider the comfort of the humble who live on the rim of their realm." In 1915 the executive board of the Woman's Convention castigated those teachers, physicians, and others who refused to contribute to racial advancement. This self-centered group, the report maintained, valued ease, honor, and money and felt no obligation to the struggling masses, who had built the very religious and educational institutions responsible for black upward mobility.[78]

The WC fiercely attacked women who engaged in social service as a fad or for "social prestige." Burroughs, always candid in her criticism, denounced the social butterfly who "smoothes her well-gloved hand while she studies the 'wonderfully interesting slum' problem as a diversion."[79] She stressed living among the masses, and she advised social reform organizations to recruit ordinary women: "Go out of your way to get an ordinary, common-sense, spirit-filled everyday woman. There are thousands of them to be had, and you can do more work in one month with this type of a woman than you can do in one year with the 'would-be' Social Leader, who is entering these organizations devoted to uplift, for no other reason than to show her finery and to let her less fortunate sisters see how brilliantly she shines."[80] Mary Parrish, a convention leader and prominent clubwoman, reiterated the value of "ordinary women." In her report on Kentucky Baptist women's work in city slums, Parrish remarked that the most helpful workers were not highly educated women, but were "Christian women whose hearts God has touched."[81]

The convention's self-representation as the "common people" assumed perhaps its greatest power when articulated in the apocalyptic language of religion. Drawing upon Old Testament imagery, Nannie Burroughs compared the black Baptist women to the ancient Israelites during their wilderness journey to the Promised Land. She described their foes, the giant Anakite people (white America and the black elite) and the nomadic, marauding Amalekites (white and black idle and lawless classes). As Burroughs moved back and forth between the past and the present, she portrayed the women of her denomination as the "advance guard" of a mighty army. She proclaimed in her millennial vision of America:

> There is an army of them down in the bottoms that you have never seen, and never will see until you walk the streets of the New Jerusalem. . . . The women throughout this country are waking up. The ordinary, everyday, pure-hearted women who have not lifted their souls to vanity, nor sworn deceitfully, are lining up . . . The common people of whom God has made more than of the other kind, are shouting the tidings of salvation as they dig the trenches and throw up the breastwork for battle, and the children of Amalek will be routed and the giant sons of Anak driven back, and Satan's strongholds shall tumble before a blow is struck. God is going to line up the common people . . . and crush . . . all the avarice, the secular spirit, worldly schemes, ignorance, and practical indifference.[82]

The black Baptist women's tireless crusade against worldliness, ignorance, and indifference expressed their sense of evangelical mission in restoring the primacy of spiritual concerns in the lives of people. But their crusade also expressed anxiety over the church's declining status and their own diminished influence as church women within the context of twentieth-century urban America and its impersonal and secularized social relations. In the teeming cities of the North and, to a somewhat lesser extent, in southern cities the dominant position of the church as well as the organic link between church leaders and the masses appeared to be on the decline and to be unable to stem the tide of commercialism and materialism that swept all of American culture.[83]

The Baptist women were particularly fearful of commercialism's negative impact on the struggle for racial self-help and self-determination. Historically the black church had been able to establish needed social programs and educational institutions because of the willingness of many poor people to make financial sacrifices, limit personal consumption, and divert their meager resources away from themselves and their own immediate gratification. Moreover, the black educated elite of the nineteenth century had, at least in theory if not always in practice, formed part of this tradition. It had stressed an identity of service to the race, not an identity of affluence and aloofness from the masses. As far as the black Baptist women were concerned, the new era of materialism threatened to undermine the achievements of an earlier and nobler time. They looked doubtfully at the new crop of college-bred women: "Why haven't our great colleges given us women brave enough to throw themselves into the conflict? Why do they give us women from our schools who are not big enough to minister; but only big enough to look down with contempt or wonder upon the surging mass of neglected humanity?"[84] Their criticism of the ascending black middle class prefigured E. Franklin Frazier's *Black Bourgeoisie* (1957), which depicted a fully blossomed world of pretentiousness and conspicuous consumption. Frazier argued that, with the transition to the more affluent and secularized black middle class, "respectability became less a question of morals and manners and more a matter of the external marks of a high standard of living."[85]

With the rise of department stores, mass advertising, and installment buying, commercialism's impact was felt by all classes and races. Consuming passions and other materialistic values superseded older, nineteenth-century ideals of thrift and self-sacrifice. Stewart and Elizabeth Ewen argue that at the turn of the twentieth century "the promise of the 'melting pot' was inextricably tied to the consumption of American goods," which in turn shaped perceptions of one's self-worth and American identity.[86] The black Baptist women endeavored to resist commercialism's influence by advocating the older ideals. In their newspapers and meetings, they attacked installment buying as particularly detrimental to individual character and racial progress. Referring to the dress styles and spending patterns of domestic servants in northern cities, the executive board described the "pitiful state" of "poor working girls . . . dressed to death on the Installment plan." The convention admonished young women to save money and buy "sensible" clothes. The Baptist women were equally critical of furnishing homes with "fancy installment plan stuff." Rather than "carpets of flaming hues, fancy clocks, lace curtains, plush furniture, brass beds," homes needed "more of the old-fashioned comfort . . . clean walls, bare floors, a few rugs, and a good library with the best books and magazines."[87] In a speech entitled, "Don't Live on the Installment Plan," Anna Griffin raised the following questions at the annual meeting of the Woman's Convention in 1903: "Is it increasing the wealth of our people . . . or is it enriching the installment houses? Do you ever stop to think that the per cent on each dollar's worth you buy is a gain to them? You are keeping up with the forms and fashions of this world, but how are you being benefited?"[88] However, in the bustling streets of urban America, the nineteenth-century missionary homilies on piety, thrift, and self-sacrifice came to be increasingly contested by an ascendant commercial vernacular.

The National Training School for Women and Girls

By establishing their own educational institution, black Baptist women articulated Victorian ideals of self-help and respectability in twentieth-century discourses of professionalism and efficiency. In October 1909, after five years of planning and fund raising, the Woman's Convention opened the National Training School for Women and Girls under the presidency of Nannie Burroughs.[89] It was Burroughs who first introduced the idea for a school to the black Baptist women and inspired their enthusiasm: "This is going to be the 'national dream' realized [and] a million women in our churches will make us have it."[90] The convention's identification with the working poor and its concern for the employment options of black women led to the establishment of an industrial school rather than a liberal arts college. The school adopted for its motto: "Work. Support thyself. To thine own powers appeal."[91] The motto captured the convention's valorization of work—a central tenet in the discourse of respectability.

As far as the Woman's Convention was concerned, idleness or activity contrary to productive labor repudiated racial self-help. The rhetoric of the WC extolled all forms of honest labor, no matter how menial, and in the discourse of respectability admonished: "Don't be idle. Don't scorn labor nor look with contempt upon the laborer. Those who encourage Negro women to loaf, rather than work at service for a living are enemies to the race."[92] At one level the black Baptist women interpreted productive labor (as is evident in the school motto) to mean individual self-help and responsibility for one's own support and livelihood. At another level, however, the black Baptist women interpreted productive labor to mean "race work" or responsibility to the collective cause of African Americans. It was in the collective sense of productive labor that the Training School addressed the reality of low-status black women's work by attempting to "professionalize" it.

In 1910 more than 80 percent of all non-agricultural black working women were servants and laundresses.[93] From the WC's perspective, the preponderance of black women in domestic service dictated the need for a program of systematic and formal training in order to reduce drudgery and monotony for the individual worker, while simultaneously according greater respect to domestic service as a form of employment. The National Training School's emphasis on preparing women for domestic service, while not the only vocational emphasis of the school, was the most widely discussed and promoted in the minutes of the Woman's Convention.[94] The decision to locate the school in Washington, D.C. was determined in large part by the focus on domestic training and especially by perceptions of greater job opportunities for domestic servants in the Washington area. Competing for the school site, residents of Georgia, Mississippi, West Virginia, Kentucky, and Indiana had offered plots of land and monetary inducements. Yet the most persuasive inducement was the argument that black women migrated to Washington from the South and West because of job opportunities in the homes of government officials and other wealthy residents.[95]

Professionalizing domestic servants epitomized the Baptist women's politics of respectability, since it constituted an effort to re-define and re-present black women's work identities as skilled workers rather than incompetent menials. The pedagogic orientation of the school complemented the overall missionary work of the Woman's Convention. In 1913 the convention defined this work: "The Home Mission Work for the mass of our people, consists in giving them a true understanding of living and creating in them a desire to be something and to do something. We must not allow the people to get the mistaken idea that they cannot begin where they are to improve."[96] If the Training School's decision to train servants revealed a certain amount of pragmatism about the employment reality of most black women, it expressed as well idealism in improving upon reality. Nannie Burroughs conveyed the school's pragmatic idealism when she asserted: "Until we realize our ideal, we are going to idealize our real."[97] Burroughs endeavored to apply the philosophy of "idealizing the real" to every aspect of the National Training School. She assured her sisters in the

Woman's Convention that the school's limited budget did not preclude high standards: "We may have the poorest, but we are going to do the best that can be done with what we have. Our table linen will be as white as that used in the Executive Mansion. If we eat out of tin plates and drink from tin cups, they will be as clean and shining as the finest china and cut glass, and we will serve with as much grace as those who have the best."[98]

Unlike educators who challenged the Talented Tenth to aspire to high-status professions in spite of racism and economic hardship, Burroughs entreated women in low-status jobs to perform with skill and efficiency. The Training School taught women to do "ordinary things in an extraordinary way." Large numbers of Training School students worked as domestic servants in New York, New Jersey, Virginia, West Virginia, and Washington, D.C. during the summers in order to earn tuition for the next school session. In 1911 Burroughs noted that her students had won such a fine reputation for their work that the school received requests for more workers than it could supply. Along with her insistence upon student excellence went the insistence that her students be placed in respectful and comfortable living situations. Burroughs maintained that "first-class help must have first-class treatment."[99]

The attempt to command greater respect and dignity for vocations represented by the vast majority of black working women positioned the school and Burroughs on the side of industrial education in the debate over the primacy of industrial versus liberal arts schools for blacks.[100] Dubbed the "female Booker T. Washington" by her contemporaries, Burroughs, like Washington, stressed an educational curriculum more suited to the "hand training" of the unskilled masses than to the "mind training" of black professionals.[101] Burroughs never believed that industrial education alone would end blacks' racial subordination in America. Yet she maintained that the measure of black progress rested not upon the Talented Tenth, but upon the economic and moral status of the great mass of laboring people—especially black women. She stated on one occasion: "Teachers, preachers and 'leaders' cannot solve the problems of the race alone. The race needs an army of skilled workers, and the properly educated Negro woman is the most essential factor."[102] For Burroughs, mastery of the most ordinary trade taught students accuracy, thoroughness, self-reliance, and an appreciation of their own achievement and usefulness. As the school president, she voiced concern for the many young women who were ill-prepared to earn a living. In her opinion, an ideal education provided academic background and, more important, a trade so that students could enter a specific vocation upon graduation.

A comparison of the curriculum of Tuskegee Institute and that of the National Training School reveals little difference in women's instruction. In the article "What Girls are Taught and How," Margaret Murray Washington, wife of Booker T. Washington, noted in 1905 that the women of Tuskegee were taught academic preparatory work along with such trades as housekeeping, tailoring, printing, upholstering, sewing, millinery, and laundering. The Tuskegee program demanded proficiency in at least one trade, and there appear to have been no restrictions by sex. Burroughs's school also taught academic subjects and a range of trades.[103] A study undertaken by the U.S. Bureau of Education reported that her school enrolled 105 students from across the nation and from several African countries in the year 1915. The listing of courses included secondary-level academic instruction with emphasis on developing specializations in domestic science, gardening, missionary and social service, clerical skills, and printing.[104]

However, Burroughs distinguished her school from other black schools because of its strong identification with the training of domestics. When the training school was still in the planning stage, she told the Woman's Convention: "We need an institution that is going to make domestic and manual training a business and not a side issue in its educational scheme." The domestic science department became the school's most extensive and well-funded program. Courses in the department included homemaking, housekeeping, household administration, interior decorating, laundering, home nursing, and management for matrons and directors of school dining rooms and dormitories. Much of this work was implemented in the model house on the school grounds.[105]

Undoubtedly, the industrial focus of the National Training School affirmed the position of the Woman's Convention in the debate over black education, but this focus also affirmed the black Baptist women's consciousness of trends in women's education. The beginning of the twentieth century witnessed what Phyllis Palmer terms "the professionalization of home economics as a female-led scientific field."[106]

Domestic science courses began to appear in the curriculum of public schools, colleges, and technical institutes throughout the country. This trend, along with the influence of Frederick Taylor's ideas on scientific management, led to a proliferation of literature and practical programs related to household efficiency and management.[107] "Taylorized" techniques came to be applied to a variety of household roles—housewife without servants, household managers of servants, and household servants themselves. Classes funded by the federal government under the Smith-Hughes Act (1917) as well as collegiate-level certification programs and national organizations such as the American Home Economics Association facilitated the movement to "professionalize" housework. For both wage and non-wage housework, such an educational trend demanded knowledge of technological innovations, nutrition, and methods of efficiency. Proponents of domestic science advocated the use of a "model house" or "practical house" specifically for testing and implementing skills.[108]

The founders of the National Training School were explicit in identifying their goals within the larger context of professionalization. For example, Nannie Burroughs referred to women who worked as cooks: "Women will begin to look upon cooking as a profession and not as drudgery, for cooking is no more a drudge than school teaching."[109] Yet an obvious difference existed between white and black women's training. Domestic science in white schools was designed to train white women to become good homemakers or else good managers of household servants. At the collegiate level white women also prepared for jobs as dieticians or teachers of domestic science. White schools did not prepare their graduates for domestic service.[110] Conversely, in the model house of the National Training School, practical lessons emphasized the role of black women as both homemakers and servants. The catalog of the Training School described the model house as offering instruction in "the actual preparation and serving of food, cleaning of rooms and making beds. . . . Housemaids and office attendants [were] taught how to answer the door bell and telephone. . . . Day workers [were] taught the fundamental things which most employers expect them to know or to do. All applicants [were] instructed in the principles of good conduct, manners and dress."[111]

The Training School, as its name implies, entailed a disciplining function that served to regulate the manners and morals of the students as well as the utility and efficiency of their bodies.[112] This disciplining function was perceived by Burroughs as critical to "professionalizing" menial workers. In regard to domestic servants, the school endeavored to produce workers with skills and attitudes that ensured their smooth fit in the employer-employee relations of household service. Professionalism became synonymous with respectability, and training was portrayed as a weapon that would disprove the charges of incompetence, immorality, and unreliability that were leveled at black domestics. The black Baptist women argued that since employers had shown inadequate concern for the training of their servants, the school performed this needed function. Its goal was to solve the oft-lamented "servant problem" by filling the demand for workers who were efficient, hard working, moral, and neat and clean in appearance. The Training School, in addition, was envisioned by the black Baptist women as a vehicle for winning friends for the race and for fostering positive images of blacks in the minds of white employers.[113]

The disciplinary dimension of the school lay at the heart of the school's identity. The National Training School was otherwise called the "School of the 3 B's" for its emphasis on the Bible, bath, and broom as tools for race advancement.[114] The school rigorously enforced this image. Students were trained to exhibit hard work, cleanliness, piety, reliability, and morals. At six o'clock each morning students were inspected for personal cleanliness and neatness. They were ranked as critically on appearance and deportment as on course work, with attention being paid to body odor, hair, and clothing. In 1912 Burroughs noted that several girls failed to receive diplomas that year because of untidiness and carelessness in attire.[115]

Professionalizing domestic service, then, betrayed the contradictory character of the politics of respectability. The school's preoccupation with personal cleanliness and household order appeared naive in light of the societal imperatives that positioned white and black women in an unalterable relationship of inequality—a relationship constitutive of the social identities of white employer and black employee, of superior and inferior race, and of pure and impure women. Phyllis Palmer describes the interconnected identities of white and black women: "Bourgeois women could attain this preciousness because working-class domestics scrubbed floors and stoops on their knees, emptied chamber pots, cooked every meal, scoured pots and pans, and laundered the family's clothing weekly. The wife's cleanliness was made possible by the domestic's dirtiness. The class and race divisions between mistress and servant visibly heightened the emotional attributions of the division of household labor . . . and this work distribution confirmed the dominant beliefs that class and race differences were due to the moral superiority of middle-class white women and the moral degradation of working-class and black women."[116]

The public discourse of the Woman's Convention reverberated with naiveté and ambivalence with regard to training domestics. The black Baptist women expressed fears that a growing demand for servants would be filled by immigrant women if black women were not prepared. Yet employment statistics for the first two decades of the twentieth century defied that possibility. National trends in domestic service between 1900 and 1930 revealed a significant drop in native and immigrant white women workers; both groups of women abandoned this work for newly opened factory and clerical jobs.[117] Elizabeth Clark-Lewis's work on black domestic servants in Washington, D.C., the home of the National Training School, calls attention to the confinement of black women to jobs in domestic service. Clark-Lewis observes that the lack of other options resulted in a growing percentage of black women domestics between 1900 and 1930. In 1900 fifty-four percent of employed black women in Washington, D.C. worked as domestics, while in 1930 the percentage had risen to seventy-eight.[118]

No leader spoke as eloquently as did Nannie Burroughs in defense of the dignity of manual labor, especially domestic service; but she was the first to admit that many of her people found such work "offensive." Her personal story accentuates the contradictory meaning of domestic service. Burroughs's strong feelings about the value of work stemmed from her childhood and recollections of her parents. Her mother, Jennie Burroughs, worked as a domestic for white employers; and Burroughs described her as "independent, proud, sweet, industrious, a marvelous cook." She described her father, on the other hand, as personable but irresponsible as a breadwinner. Her father's parents and sister helped to supplement his income, since, according to Burroughs, "they seemed to think he was 'too smart' to do ordinary work and he concurred in their opinion." Educated at Virginia Union University, he worked as an itinerant preacher and, without a regular church of his own, failed to earn income on a steady basis. Burroughs's mother appears to have raised her, for the most part, without the presence of her father. Despite the comparison of her parents and the deep admiration for her mother, she rejected her mother's advice that she take up domestic service instead of secretarial work. Praising her own foresight, Burroughs recalled her mother's reiteration of her employer's words—"colored girls had no chance in the world to make a living as a stenographer and bookkeeper." Strong-willed and determined to prove both her mother's boss and her mother wrong, Burroughs moved to Philadelphia after her graduation from high school and found a job as a secretary for a black newspaper. Her mother's limited vision, Burroughs reminisced in later years, was based on the belief that "there was no future in business."[119]

It would be incorrect, however, to conclude that the school was simply an expression of false consciousness on the part of the Woman's Convention, or a tool for maintaining black women in servile employment. Burroughs clearly distinguished the interests of working-class black women from those of working-class white women. In her report to the Woman's Convention on the eve of the ratification of the Nineteenth Amendment, she advocated the unionization of black domestics precisely because of the opposing interests of black and white women:

> The women voters will be keen to see that laws are passed that will give eight hours a day and insure a square deal and human treatment to women in other industries, but they will oppose any movement that will, in the end, prevent them from keeping their cooks and house servants in the kitchen twelve or fifteen hours a day and storing them away in cellars, up over garages, or in attics. . . . The only possible way for the Domestic Workers to get what others will demand and finally get, is to organize their own unions.[120]

As early as 1910 the committee on recommendations of the Woman's Convention endorsed, at Burroughs's request, the idea of organizing domestic workers. Burroughs, at the meeting of the Woman's Convention in 1919, presented her plan to call a conference in December of that year in order to inaugurate a labor organization. In 1920 she launched the National Association of Wage Earners, which emphasized the need for "radical changes" in domestics' living and working conditions. The demands of the association proved hardly radical, but they did suggest self-esteem on the part of domestic workers and resistance to subordination. Black churches disseminated news of the association and helped to recruit members. The newspaper of Shiloh Baptist Church of Washington advertised: "The National Association of Wage Earners is making an effort to secure 10,000 members among the women of the Race. Their canvass for members began last week and will continue for a month or more. This organization is planning to operate a factory and practice house, that women may be prepared to earn better wages and be in line for promotion . . . We recommend 'The National Association of Wage Earners' to the careful consideration of the women of our church."[121]

In her report to the Woman's Convention in 1920, Nannie Burroughs noted that her union would demand shorter working hours, a "little corner, outside of the kitchen in which to eat and receive company," and satisfactory sleeping and bathing quarters.[122] The union's national board, over which Nannie Burroughs presided, included leaders in the Woman's Convention and in the National Association of Colored Women. The National Association of Wage Earners operated independently of the Woman's Convention and appears to have died by 1926. Its nine-point program reflected, nonetheless, the logical extension of the politics of respectability, which had been promoted by the National Training School for Women and Girls.

1. To develop and encourage efficient workers.
2. To assist women in finding the kind of work for which they seem best qualified.
3. To elevate the migrant classes of workers and incorporate them permanently in service of some kind.
4. To standardize living conditions.
5. To secure a wage that will enable women to live decently.
6. To assemble the multitude of grievances of employers and employees into a set of common demands and strive, mutually to adjust them.

7. To enlighten women as to the value of organization.

8. To make and supply appropriate uniforms for working women. This shall be done through a profit sharing enterprise operated by the Association.

9. To influence just legislation affecting women wage earners.[123]

The WC's politics of respectability deployed the image of the domestic servant in a rallying appeal to the race and gender consciousness of working-class black women. This was particularly true for fund raising. The report of the WC's executive board and corresponding secretary defended the vocational emphasis of the training school: "Why not help the women who work at service? They are the best friends the churches have. They give more and attend services better than any other class of laborers." Support from thousands of ordinary black women throughout the country attested to their belief in the school's goals and program. Without the assistance of large philanthropic donations, the school survived because of the cumulative power of countless small gifts. Burroughs wrote to Booker T. Washington in 1912: "You know of the poverty of our people and yet they have responded beautifully to our appeal for the establishment of work here."[124] The Woman's Convention consciously decided against soliciting money from whites for the purchase of the property in Washington. Only after the actual opening of the school and erection of the first buildings did the Training School solicit and receive funds from white donors. At no point did the school's existence depend upon white funding.[125]

Year after year black women, many without education themselves, regularly contributed small amounts of money enclosed in barely literate letters of support. By giving "pantry parties," collecting redeemable soap wrappers, and continually devising imaginative money-making ventures, black church women across the nation worked for the furtherance of their school. Ella Whitfield zealously canvassed the nation in her job as field secretary of the Woman's Convention and solicited funds for the school at every opportunity.[126] The financial reports of state contributions to the Woman's Convention between 1900 and 1920 revealed that no other project ranked as high as the National Training School for Women and Girls. The school accounted for 59 percent of all donations to the Woman's Convention.[127]

Black women's endorsement of the Training School and Burroughs's formation of the National Association of Wage Earners underscore the centrality of self-definition in the discourse of respectability. Moreover, the school's efforts to instill in domestic servants both self-esteem and a standard of excellence on the job resisted the tendency to accept and internalize externally imposed definitions of oneself as inferior. In fact, the school encouraged expectations for fair treatment. Such efforts complement other early twentieth-century strategies of black resistance, which are described by Tera Hunter for domestics in Atlanta and by Elizabeth Clark-Lewis for domestics in Washington, D.C.[128] The Training School's efforts also reinforce recent findings of sociologists. For example, the school's philosophy that "first-class help must have first-class treatment" was reechoed decades later in interviews with domestic servants in the 1970s and 1980s. A respondent told the sociologist Bonnie Thornton Dill: "When I went out to work . . . my mother told me, 'Don't let anybody take advantage of you. *Speak up for your rights, but do the work right.* If they don't give you your rights, you demand that they treat you right. And if they don't, then you quit'" (emphasis added).[129]

Speaking up for Rights

If Burroughs and the Woman's Convention sided with Booker T. Washington in regard to industrial education, they unequivocally sided with W. E. B. Du Bois and the NAACP in regard to civil rights. The politics of respectability, while emphasizing self-help strategies and intra-group reform, provided the platform from which black church women came to demand full equality with white America. Speaking up for rights constituted not the antithesis of respectability but its logical conclusion. James Scott's work on the politics of everyday resistance confirms the subversive role of the discourse of respectability. Scott convincingly argues that overt political protest often evolves from critiques originating within the hegemony of the dominant ideology—within the plasticity and dialogic character of ideological discourses.[130] Thus the reigning values in society are sufficiently multivalent to be appropriated and reinterpreted by subordinate groups for their own purposes, even for resistance against the power of the dominant group. The nexus between respectability and protest is captured in the seven-point manifesto adopted by the Woman's Convention in 1913. Entitling the manifesto, "What We Want and What We Must Have," the black Baptist women outlined what they perceived to be the pressing needs of their people:

1. Well-built, sanitary dwellings . . . and streets that are paved and kept just as clean as others in the town are kept.
2. Equal accommodation on common carriers.
3. Franchise for every Negro—North, South, East, and West—who is an intelligent and industrious citizen.
4. Equal treatment in the courts.
5. Equal division of school funds.
6. Lynching stopped.
7. Convict lease system broken up and better prisons and humane treatment of Negro prisoners.[131]

By invoking manners and morals ("sanitary dwellings" and "intelligent and industrious citizens"), the manifesto drew upon the politics of respectability in a demand for broad structural changes in society, for reform of the South's educational, electoral, judicial, and penal systems. Indeed the rhetoric of "sanitary dwellings," "clean streets," and "intelligent, industrious citizens," while illustrative of the behavioral emphasis of self-help, demanded of local governments a reformed public policy with regard to safe housing codes, proper sewerage and paved streets, and educational and employment opportunities for blacks. By insisting upon conformity to society's norms and established rules, black Baptist women subverted the cultural logic of white superiority and condemned white America for failing to live up to its own rhetoric of equality and justice as found in the Constitution.

The black Baptist women never accepted the legitimacy of segregation or its doctrine of "separate but equal." Their attack on Jim Crow laws exemplified the malleable and dialogic quality of this doctrine, when articulated as a discourse of resistance. The black Baptist women's early protest attempted to hold white America accountable for "equal," though separate, accommodations. Their later protest, however, openly acknowledged the doctrine as a euphemism and demanded the dismantlement of segregation altogether. In 1904, for instance, the report of the executive board and corresponding secretary called attention to the separate car policies of railroad companies. In this report Nannie Burroughs focused on unequal conditions and not on segregation in principle. The report called for united protest against unsanitary toilet facilities for black women and the failure to provide step boxes for the alightment of black passengers. Identifying racist railroad companies by name, Burroughs promised to continue to "annoy" the railroads until facilities were upgraded.[132]

At the WC meeting in 1908, Burroughs again demanded equal yet separate facilities: "The women of this Convention will never be reconciled to the toilet arrangements on the cars. Everybody else may get tired of talking about it, but we are at least going to say that we don't like it, because it is indecent. We want a separate toilet for colored women, just as they have a separate toilet for white women. We want basins, soap and towel. We pay the same fare and are entitled to the same treatment."[133] As a result of her speech a committee of three women was appointed to go to Washington and present a petition to the Interstate Commerce Commission. The failure of the government to respond positively prompted yet another petition for equal toilet facilities in 1910.

By 1918 the convention no longer called for "separate but equal" facilities, but rather argued for desegregation of railroad transportation: "Nothing short of a repeal of the separate laws is going to bring a permanent and satisfactory change in travel in those states where the law is in operation. The very fact that the railroads are allowed to operate separate cars for people who pay the same fares is a temptation to make a difference in accommodations for and treatment of those people. The very purpose of the 'Jim Crow' car law is to make such striking differences in accommodation and treatment as will suggest the inferiority of one race to the other and humiliate the race thus discriminated against."[134]

The Woman's Convention greatly respected the work of the NAACP. It supported the NAACP's civil rights agenda and invited representatives from the organization to appear at the Baptist women's annual meetings. In 1914 the Woman's Convention joined forces with the NAACP to end negative stereotyping of blacks in literature, film, school textbooks, newspapers, and on the stage. The minutes advocated boycotts and written protests to publishers and others who

practiced racial slurring.[135] Like the NAACP, the Woman's Convention perceived no issue of greater magnitude than the issue of lynching,
and the two organizations worked in concerted action for its elimina-
tion. In 1918 and 1919 the report of the convention went on record
in demanding congressional passage of anti-lynching legislation. In
1919, the report of the executive board enjoined every black American
to stand behind the NAACP in its fight against lynch law: "Let
15,000,000 Negroes line up with the National Association for the
Advancement of Colored People. Any man who is not a member of
that organization stands with the mob. There is no middle ground."[136]

In September 1919 the executive board of the Woman's Convention
recommended that Baptist churches and Sunday schools throughout
the nation dedicate the Sunday before Thanksgiving to fasting and
prayer in order to protest the "undemocratic and un-Christian spirit
of the United States as shown by its discriminating and barbarous
treatment of its colored people." The NAACP and the National
Association of Colored Women joined the black Baptist women in
advertising the day of protest. The December 1919 issue of the
NAACP's magazine *Crisis* reported the commemoration of the day on
30 November with a noontime prayer hour having been observed for
the denunciation of lynching and racial injustice.[137]

In 1920 the WC's executive board repeated its call for prayer. The
call, this time for a week of prayer including Thanksgiving day, revealed the black Baptist women's appropriation of prayer itself as a
discourse of resistance. Black Baptist women across the nation held
meetings in homes and churches to pray for the end to mob violence.
A white woman editor of the *Swarthmore News* printed the text of the
black Baptist women's call for prayer in her newspaper and implored
whites to pray in support. The Woman's Convention admitted the
resistant politics implicit in their observance of prayer. Nannie Burroughs was quick to agree with a Florida newspaper that labeled the
week of prayer against lynching a "clever and mischievous piece of
propaganda" that permitted blacks to speak up in ways they would not
otherwise dare to do openly. Burroughs explained: "How true! That is
why all Christians pray. Their neighbors can or will not help them.
God can and will. The Negro is praying because his case must go before
the highest court. A just judge presides over it."[138] As white America

celebrated Thanksgiving, black Baptist women lamented the nation's inhumanity and injustice.

In the "safe space" of the Woman's Convention, black Baptist women critiqued the nation's democratic rhetoric during World War I. Filled with patriotic fervor, S. Willie Layten's presidential address in September 1918 called upon black women to help win the war. Layten advised her sisters to conserve food and fuel, purchase Liberty Bonds and war stamps, and to cultivate liberty gardens, but she proclaimed no less ardently that patriots on the front line become "restless and discontent when their rights are abridged at home." In her report as corresponding secretary, Nannie Burroughs reminded her sisters at this same meeting of the convention that their fight against race prejudice in America could not take a back seat to their fight against autocracy abroad. Her report called for the passage of anti-lynching legislation and for the repeal of segregation. Burroughs told her sisters that since the federal government had assumed control of the railroads as a necessity of war, it had the power to suspend Jim Crow laws as another wartime necessity. And Burroughs did not soften her critique of President Woodrow Wilson and his war slogan, "Make the world safe for democracy": "He likes to write—he likes to say things. He has used up all the adverbs and adjectives trying to make clear what he means by democracy. He realizes and the country realizes that unless he begins to apply the doctrine, representatives of our nation would be hissed out of court when the world gets ready to make up the case against Germany and to try her for her sins."[139]

Protest continued to run throughout the annual conference the following year. As Woodrow Wilson cried loudly to the American people for a League of Nations, Burroughs once again denounced his silence on lynching and segregation. The Woman's Convention voted to send Burroughs's report for 1919 to Wilson, the U.S. Congress, and the governors of all the states. Also on the program of the convention in 1919 was a representative from the NAACP. At the conclusion of his speech, the convention choir sang "We've Fought Every Race's Battles but Our Own."[140] It is not surprising that the War Department targeted Burroughs for investigation. Between August and November 1917 the government monitored her activities and considered her a potentially dangerous radical. Collected by the military intelligence division, the file contains coverage of Burroughs's trips, a listing of all persons with whom she corresponded, and surveillance of individuals she visited.[141] It is unlikely that Burroughs was aware of the investigation. In any event, she did not silence her criticism of the government's racial policy.

The issue of voting rights further distinguished the politics of the Woman's Convention from Booker T. Washington's. At the very time when Booker T. Washington's influential voice failed to venture public criticism against black disfranchisement in the South, the Woman's Convention called for a united leadership that would "neither compromise nor sell out." Women's suffrage figured prominently in the protest politics of the Woman's Convention. In 1912 the minutes of the WC recorded: "If women cannot vote, they should make it very uncomfortable for the men who have the ballot but do not know its value."[142]

Leaders of the WC perceived women's suffrage as a weapon to right racial wrongs, but they also perceived suffrage as a weapon for protecting their own rights as women. In 1909 the Baptist women specified that their political input in state legislatures and the federal government would help improve the conditions under which black women lived and labored.[143] In 1912 the WC committee on the state of the country, headed by Mrs. L. D. Pruitt of Texas, asserted women's full capabilities in assisting men in social reform and affirmed that reform would occur only when women were included in the electoral process. In 1912 the same committee endorsed the presidential candidacy of Theodore Roosevelt and the Progressive Party platform, which included women's suffrage, prohibition, and child labor legislation.[144] In the *Crisis* in 1915 Nannie Burroughs candidly observed the importance of the vote in shielding black women from male dominance and abuse. Burroughs contended that the black woman's virtue was viewed with "amused contempt" in courts of law. Women's suffrage, she maintained, would enable black women "to reckon with men who place no value upon her virtue."[145] In 1919 Gertrude Rush, a prominent black lawyer and delegate from a Baptist church in Des Moines, posited that the vote would enable black women to fight for better working conditions, higher wages, and greater opportunities in business. With the suffrage, Rush continued, black women could better regulate moral and sanitary conditions, end discrimination and lynch law, obtain better educational opportunities, and secure greater legal justice.[146]

Leaders of the Woman's Convention insisted that women's suffrage, when coupled with black northward migration, held the key to black political power. Immediately after World War I, S. Willie Layten urged blacks to turn their Great Migration into a political advantage. Without racist voting restrictions, northern states afforded many southern migrants an opportunity to wield the ballot for the first time. Layten challenged her sisters, although disfranchised because of sex, to educate the male migrants concerning their political rights and the potential enlargement of the black electorate because of black women voters. She urged northern urban churches to assist in the political mobilization of the migrants. The church, Layten reasoned, remained the most logical institution to promote a voter education program.[147]

At the annual meeting of the convention in 1920, the black Baptist women celebrated the ratification of the Nineteenth Amendment. Burroughs commended by name such white suffragists as Susan B. Anthony, Anna Howard Shaw, Alice Paul, and Carrie Chapman Catt, although she cited the racism of white women as a cause for the limited participation of black women in the organized suffragist movement.[148] Reiterating that the ballot would aid women to fight for fair labor laws, she stated: "For industrial and economic reasons, the ballot will be a sure defense for women in industries who should demand equal pay for equal service." Like Layten, Burroughs advocated that the church politicize its members to exercise their right to vote, and she exhorted her sisters to organize suffrage clubs in their churches. Predicting a wave of protest by those who would separate religious from political issues, she continued to assure her sisters that practical Christianity included the exercise of the ballot.[149] During the 1920s Layten was appointed by the National Republican Committee of Pennsylvania to organize the black women in her state, and Burroughs became head of the National League of Republican Colored Women.[150]

The politics of respectability afforded black church women a powerful weapon of resistance to race and gender subordination. It provided the very groundwork for protest, voting, and other traditionally recognized forms of political activity. Thus the history of women in the black Baptist church not only challenges the historical validity of the accommodation versus protest dichotomy that has for too long dominated studies of the black church and the black community, it also challenges the authorial voice of such overarching figures as Booker T. Washington and W. E. B. Du Bois in the consciousness of ordinary black people. The black church and certainly church women played a tremendous and decisive role in the formation of a black collective will in the late nineteenth and early twentieth centuries. At the local and national levels, the church produced male and female leaders who maintained direct and ongoing communication with large constituencies of black women and men.

Few if any men surpassed Nannie Burroughs in popularity among her people. By all accounts, Burroughs was a charismatic leader with a tremendous following. She was acknowledged in newspapers and in other literature of her day as a powerful orator, who rivaled the best of male orators. In 1906 the *Colored American Magazine* praised her in an article devoted otherwise entirely to prominent black men: "No writer or speaker has more courageously and eloquently championed the cause of the race than has Miss Burroughs." The editor of the *National Baptist Union*, the weekly newspaper of the ministerial-dominated National Baptist Convention, captured her towering image as she spoke on a program that included ministers at a meeting of the Baptist state convention of Georgia:

> Miss N. H. Burroughs appeared before the Convention for the first time, and like Saul, towered head and shoulders, above the men in Israel for the magnetism of her speech, the earnestness of her appeal, the nobleness of her work, all of which combined called for such an ovation that has not been given in the annals of our *"Distinctive Baptist" work*. When she finished speaking tears flowed from some; applause was deafening from others; while young and old, white and black, cast money at her feet with an enthusiasm that has never been equaled in the history of our Convention.[151]

Leaders such as Burroughs, and also Virginia Broughton and Sarah Willie Layten, rose to prominence precisely because they articulated openly and eloquently the yearning and indignation, the joy and pain, the protest and accommodation of masses of unknown and unheard historical actors.[152] Most of all they captured their people's vision of

America—a vision that was simultaneously optimistic and critical, but ultimately hopeful. Nannie Burroughs referred futuristically to a new day and a "real American," who was more "spiritual and humanistic" than the American of the present:

> A new day is dawning for us. In spite of the fact that we are facing problems more grave and aggravating than any other race in the world and have less of material things to utilize in the solution of them, yet we are abundantly rich in faith and in physical powers to endure the hardships incident to foundation laying. The most hopeful sign is the awakening within to fundamental needs and a setting in motion of a new force to beat back fanatic race prejudice. We have just seen clearly enough to discover that in the real American is the making.[153]

This vision of a "new day dawning" and a "real American" would inspire later leaders—a Rosa Parks and a Martin Luther King, a Fannie Lou Hamer and a Medgar Evers—and countless women and men who, in the sacred space of black churches, held rallies in support of boycotts, sit-ins, and protest marches and who transformed the songs of the church into the freedom songs of the Civil Rights Movement. The women's movement in the black Baptist church between 1880 and 1920 contributed to "foundation laying" and to "setting in motion" future forces that would escalate the assault on race and gender discrimination. The Baptist women's struggle for self-definition tells the story of African American women in the making of the church, in the making of black communities, and in the remaking of America.

Notes

1. The Black Church: A Gender Perspective

1. See Jualynne Dodson, "Nineteenth Century A.M.E. Preaching Women: Cutting Edge of Women's Inclusion in Church Polity," in Hilah F. Thomas and Rosemary Skinner Keller, eds., *Women in New Worlds: Historical Perspectives on the Wesleyan Tradition*, vol. 1 (Nashville: Abingdon Press, 1981), 276–292; Jean McMahon Humez, ed., *Gifts of Power: The Writings of Rebecca Jackson, Black Visionary and Shaker Eldress* (Amherst: University of Massachusetts Press, 1981), 1–50; William L. Andrews, ed., *Sisters of the Spirit: Three Black Women's Autobiographies of the Nineteenth Century* (Bloomington: Indiana University Press, 1986), 25–234.

2. C. Eric Lincoln and Lawrence H. Mamiya, *The Black Church in the African American Experience* (Durham, N.C.: Duke University Press, 1990), 25–26; Leroy Fitts, *A History of Black Baptists* (Nashville: Broadman Press, 1985), 64–79; Joseph H. Jackson, *A Story of Christian Activism: The History of the National Baptist Convention, U.S.A., Inc.* (Nashville: Townsend Press, 1980), 23–27.

3. Winthrop S. Hudson, *Religion in America: An Historical Account of the Development of American Religious Life*, 2nd ed. (New York: Charles Scribner's Sons, 1973), 202–203; Sydney E. Ahlstrom, *A Religious History of the American People* (New Haven: Yale University Press, 1972), 719–725.

4. See James Melvin Washington, *Frustrated Fellowship: The Black Baptist Quest for Social Power* (Macon, Ga.: Mercer University Press, 1985), 22–45.

5. Sandy D. Martin draws some attention to women's organized involvement in foreign mission support during the formative years of the National Baptist Foreign Mission Convention, but his discussion is brief. Most scholarly works on the black Baptist church identify a few individual women by name, but they fail to discuss women as a group and as significant contributors to the church's historic role. See Sandy D. Martin, *Black Baptists and African Missions: The Origins of a Movement, 1880–1915* (Macon, Ga.: Mercer University Press, 1989), 129–134; Washington, *Frustrated Fellowship*, 139; Jackson, *Story of Christian Activism*, 87–90, 135–145; Fitts, *History of Black Baptists*, 121–134; Lewis G. Jordan, *Negro Baptist History* (Nashville: Sunday School Publishing Board, National Baptist Convention, 1930); Owen D. Pelt

and Ralph Lee Smith, *The Story of the National Baptists* (New York: Vantage Press, 1960).

6. The Baptist Foreign Mission Convention was founded in 1880. It was one of three organizations to merge in the formation of the National Baptist Convention, U.S.A. in 1895. Because of this, the NBC uses the 1880 date as its founding date. For a history of this convention, see Martin, *Black Baptists and African Missions*, 56–106.

7. Joel Williamson, *A Rage for Order: Black/White Relations in the American South since Emancipation* (New York: Oxford University Press, 1986), 171.

8. For a discussion of women during the Reconstruction and post-Reconstruction period, see Jacqueline Jones, *Labor of Love, Labor of Sorrow: Black Women, Work, and the Family from Slavery to the Present* (New York: Random House, 1985), chap. 2.

9. Rayford W. Logan, *The Negro in American Life and Thought: The Nadir, 1877–1901* (New York: Dial Press, 1954); Logan, *The Betrayal of the Negro: From Rutherford B. Hayes to Woodrow Wilson* (New York: Collier Books, 1965), 292–302; Neil R. McMillen, *Dark Journey: Black Mississippians in the Age of Jim Crow* (Urbana: University of Illinois Press, 1989), 197–253; Williamson, *Rage for Order*, 117–151.

10. In a series of cases between 1876 and 1896, the Supreme Court moved in a conservative direction, which culminated with the Plessy case and the euphemistic doctrine of "separate but equal." *United States v. Cruikshank*, 92 U.S. 542 (1876); *Civil Rights Cases*, 109 U.S. 3 (1883); *Plessy v. Ferguson*, 163 U.S. 537 (1896). See Derrick A. Bell, Jr., *Race, Racism, and American Law*, 2nd. ed. (Boston: Little, Brown, 1980), 34–38, 83–91.

11. Early scholars of black history called attention to the importance of the home mission and educational work of the black church during the decades that followed the demise of Reconstruction. They especially emphasized the church's racial self-help efforts in response to diminishing civil and political rights. See William Edward Burghardt Du Bois, ed., *The Negro Church* (Atlanta: Atlanta University Press, 1903), 111–152; Carter G. Woodson, *History of the Negro Church* (Washington, D.C.: Associated Publishers, 1921), chaps. 4, 5.

12. The most comprehensive studies of slave religion are Albert J. Raboteau, *Slave Religion: The "Invisible Institution" in the Antebellum South* (New York: Oxford University Press, 1978), and Mechal Sobel, *Trabelin' On: The Slave Journey to an Afro-Baptist Faith* (Westport, Conn.: Greenwood Press, 1979). See also Eugene D. Genovese, *Roll Jordan Roll: The World the Slaveholders Made* (New York: Random House, Pantheon Books, 1974), 232–284.

13. E. Franklin Frazier, *The Negro Church* (New York: Schocken Books, 1964), chap. 3.

14. Gary Nash, *Forging Freedom: The Formation of Philadelphia's Black Community, 1720–1840* (Cambridge, Mass.: Harvard University Press, 1989), 227–233, 259–267; Gayraud Wilmore, *Black Religion and Black Radicalism: An Interpretation of the Religious History of Afro-American People*, 2nd ed. (Maryknoll, N.Y.: Orbis Books, 1989), 78–89; Lincoln and Mamiya, *Black Church in the African American Experience*, 47–75.

15. The figure for black Baptists in 1906 represents the number of Baptists under the National Baptist Convention and does not reflect those black Baptists who are listed under the Northern Baptist Convention, or those found among the Primitive Baptists, Two Seed Baptists, and Freewill Baptists. When all these groups are

considered, black Baptists numbered 2,354,789 in 1906. I have also distinguished the A.M.E. church from such black Methodist groups as the A.M.E. Zion and the Colored Methodist Episcopal. The entire black Methodist population in 1906 was 1,182,131. See U.S. Department of Commerce and Labor, Bureau of the Census, *Special Reports: Religious Bodies, 1906*, vol. 1 (Washington, D.C.: Government Printing Office, 1910), 137–139; Sobel, *Trabelin' On*, 182.

16. For statistics of religious denominations, see Bureau of the Census, *Religious Bodies, 1906*, vol. 1, 137–139; Bureau of the Census, *Religious Bodies, 1916*, Part I (Washington, D.C.: Government Printing Office, 1919), 40.

17. For statistics on black Baptists, see Bureau of the Census, *Religious Bodies, 1916*, vol. 1, 121, 123–128. For a survey of the black population's predominantly rural and southern character during this period, see U.S. Department of Commerce, Bureau of the Census, *Negro Population, 1790–1915* (Washington, D.C.: Government Printing Office, 1918), 88–94.

18. Philip S. Foner, ed., *W. E. B. Du Bois Speaks, 1890–1919* (New York: Pathfinder Press, 1970), 97.

19. A wealth of materials related to the Woman's Convention, Auxiliary to the National Baptist Convention is found in the papers of Nannie Helen Burroughs, former corresponding secretary and president of the organization and also founder and president of the National Training School for Women and Girls. See Nannie Helen Burroughs Papers, Library of Congress.

20. Berger and Neuhaus are not concerned with historical perspective, nor do they see the church as the only such structure. Their concern is with mediating structures in the contemporary welfare state. They observe: "Not only are religious institutions significant 'players' in the public realm, but they are singularly important to the way people order their lives and values at the most local and concrete levels of their existence." They go on to note that the black community cannot be understood from a historical perspective without looking at the role of the black church. Peter L. Berger and Richard John Neuhaus, *To Empower People: The Role of Mediating Structures in Public Policy* (Washington, D.C.: American Enterprise Institute for Public Policy Research, 1977), 26–28.

21. For differing interpretations of "civil religion," see essays in Donald G. Jones and Russell E. Richey, eds., *American Civil Religion* (San Francisco: Harper and Row, 1974), especially chaps. 1, 2, 6, 7, 10; Robert N. Bellah and Phillip E. Hammond, *Varieties of Civil Religion* (San Francisco: Harper and Row, 1980), 3–23.

22. See the discussion of "mythic patterns of national mission" and the idea of national community in the form of covenant in John F. Wilson, *Public Religion in American Culture* (Philadelphia: Temple University Press, 1979), 34–39.

23. Frederick Douglass, "The Meaning of the Fourth of July to the Negro, 1852," in Philip E. Foner, ed., *The Life and Writings of Frederick Douglass*, vol. 2 (New York: International Publishers, 1950), 192; also see an analysis of Frederick Douglass's millennialist vision in David W. Blight, *Frederick Douglass' Civil War: Keeping Faith in Jubilee* (Baton Rouge: Louisiana State University Press, 1989), 101–121.

24. See Sidney E. Mead's usage of Gilbert Chesterton's phrase in his discussion of civil religion. Sidney E. Mead, "The 'Nation with the Soul of a Church,'" in Jones and Richey, eds., *American Civil Religion*, 45. However, the black scholar Charles Long

writes from the point of view of African Americans: "The distinction between civil religion and church religion is not one that would loom very large for us." See Charles H. Long, "Civil Rights—Civil Religion: Visible People and Invisible Religion," in ibid., 211–221, especially 216; and Washington, *Frustrated Fellowship*, 135–157.

25. Benedict Anderson defines nation as "an imagined political community—and imagined as both inherently limited and sovereign." For black Baptists, the "imagined community" was racially bounded and its sovereignty was perceived as free of white control—hence black denominational hegemony. See Benedict Anderson, *Imagined Communities: Reflections on the Origin and Spread of Nationalism* (London: Verso, 1983), 14–16.

26. Jürgen Habermas, "The Public Sphere: An Encyclopedia Article (1964)," *New German Critique*, 1 (Fall 1974): 49–55; Habermas, *The Structural Transformation of the Public Sphere: An Inquiry into a Category of Bourgeois Society*, trans. by Thomas Burger with the assistance of Frederick Lawrence (Cambridge, Mass.: MIT Press, 1989), especially chap. 2. For differing interpretations that draw upon Habermas in discussing the role of religion in the public sphere, see Robert Wuthnow, *The Restructuring of American Religion* (Princeton, N.J.: Princeton University Press, 1988), chap. 4; Wuthnow, *The Struggle for America's Soul: Evangelicals, Liberals, and Secularism* (Grand Rapids, Mich.: William B. Eerdmans, 1989), 10–15; and Jose Casanova, "Private and Public Religions," *Social Research*, 59 (Spring 1992): 17–57.

27. Critics of Habermas do not share his assessment of the breakdown and decline of the public sphere itself, nor do they agree with him when he attributes decline to the historical emergence of competing interest groups (the non-bourgeois strata) and the resultant diminution of the state's accountability to its citizenry. In contradistinction to Habermas, Nancy Fraser submits that "in stratified societies, arrangements that accommodate contestation among a plurality of competing publics better promote the ideal of participatory parity than does a single, comprehensive, overarching public." Nancy Fraser, "Rethinking the Public Sphere: A Contribution to the Critique of Actually Existing Democracy," *Social Text*, 25/26 (1990): 56–80.

28. They are responding to Habermas's discussion of the emergence of the public sphere as a distinct phase of bourgeois social formation in late seventeenth and eighteenth-century Europe. His critics note instead a multiplicity of competing publics, which existed then and continue to exist now based on racial, ethnic, class, and gender interests. For treatment of various types of counter-publics, see ibid., 61–68; John Keane, *Public Life and Late Capitalism: Toward a Socialist Theory of Democracy* (New York: Cambridge University Press, 1984), 92–94; Rita Felski, *Beyond Feminist Aesthetics: Feminist Literature and Social Change* (Cambridge, Mass.: Harvard University Press, 1989), 154–182.

29. *The Free Speech and Headlight* was published by the Reverend Taylor Nightingale, pastor of the Beale Street Baptist Church, although Ida Wells was its editor and chiefly responsible for voicing its social message. Wells does not figure as a participant of the women's movement of the black Baptist church, since she was a member of the A.M.E. Church and was active with the organized women's movement of that denomination. See Samuel Shannon, "Tennessee," in Henry Lewis Suggs, ed., *The Black Press in the South, 1865–1979* (Westport, Conn.: Greenwood Press, 1983), 325.

30. For example, black Baptist newspapers are discussed for the states of Alabama, Arkansas, Florida, and Missouri in Suggs, ed., *The Black Press in the South,* 30, 34, 38, 70–71, 103, 105, 212–214; also see National Baptist Convention, *Journal of the Twentieth Annual Session of the National Baptist Convention, Held in Richmond, Virginia, September 12–17, 1900* (Nashville: National Baptist Publishing Board, 1900), 191; Du Bois, ed., *Negro Church,* 121.

31. For discussion of the *National Baptist Magazine,* see Penelope L. Bullock, *The Afro-American Periodical Press, 1838–1909* (Baton Rouge: Louisiana State University Press, 1981), 73–76.

32. This statement can be found in the combined report for 1901 and 1902 of the National Baptist Convention, U.S.A., which is printed in Du Bois, ed., *Negro Church,* 115.

33. In 1917 the Department of War monitored the activities and mail of Nannie Helen Burroughs, corresponding secretary of the Woman's Convention, for remarks in condemnation of Woodrow Wilson. Records of the War Department, General and Special Staffs, Military Intelligence Division, "Black Radicals (Church of God)," from Record Group 165, National Archives.

34. Benjamin E. Mays and Joseph W. Nicholson, *The Negro's Church* (New York, 1933; rpt. New York: Arno Press and the *New York Times,* 1969), 9.

35. The most extensive holdings of northern white Baptist women are the records of the Woman's American Baptist Home Mission Society and the Women's Baptist Home Mission Society, which are located in the American Baptist Archives Center in Valley Forge, Pennsylvania, and the American Baptist—Samuel Colgate Historical Library, Rochester, New York. Materials are also housed at the Franklin Trask Library in Andover-Newton Theological Seminary in Massachusetts.

36. The women's movement in the black Baptist church reflected a trend found in all the denominations in the late nineteenth century. Studies of white women's societies include Lois A. Boyd and R. Douglas Brackenridge, *Presbyterian Women in America: Two Centuries of a Quest for Status* (Westport, Conn.: Greenwood Press, 1983); Virginia Lieson Brereton and Christa Ressmeyer Klein, "American Women in Ministry: A History of Protestant Beginning Points," in Rosemary Ruether and Eleanor McLaughlin, eds., *Women of Spirit: Female Leadership in the Jewish and Christian Traditions* (New York: Simon and Schuster, 1979), chap. 11; Ruether and Rosemary Skinner Keller, *Women and Religion in America: The Nineteenth Century* (San Francisco: Harper and Row, 1981), 243–293.

37. Suzanne Lebsock, "Women and American Politics, 1880–1920," in Louise A. Tilly and Patricia Gurin, eds., *Women, Politics, and Change* (New York: Russell Sage Foundation, 1990), 35–59.

38. Anna J. Cooper, *A Voice from the South* (Xenia, Ohio, 1892; rpt. New York: Negro Universities Press, 1969), 143.

39. For black women's educational and social reform activities, see Dorothy Salem, *To Better Her World: Black Women in Organized Reform, 1890–1920,* 7–103, vol. 14 in Darlene Clark Hine, ed., *Black Women in United States History: From Colonial Times to the Present* (Brooklyn: Carlson Press, 1990); Bettina Aptheker, "Black Women's Quest in the Professions," in Aptheker, *Woman's Legacy: Essays on Race, Sex, and Class in American History* (Amherst: University of Massachusetts Press, 1982), 89–110;

Cynthia Neverdon-Morton, *Afro-American Women of the South and the Advancement of the Race, 1895–1925* (Knoxville: University of Tennessee Press, 1989), 78–103; Jacqueline Rouse, *Lugenia Burns Hope: Black Southern Reformer* (Athens: University of Georgia Press), 41–85. Also see for white women, Lynn D. Gordon, *Gender and Higher Education in the Progressive Era* (New Haven: Yale University Press, 1990); Rosalind Rosenberg, *Beyond Separate Spheres: Intellectual Roots of Modern Feminism* (New Haven: Yale University Press, 1982); Robyn Muncy, *Creating a Female Dominion in American Reform, 1890–1935* (New York: Oxford University Press, 1991).

40. Hazel V. Carby, *Reconstructing Womanhood: The Emergence of the Afro-American Woman Novelist* (New York: Oxford University Press, 1987), 96–115; I. Garland Penn, *The Afro-American Press and Its Editors* (Springfield, Mass.: Willey, 1891), 366–427.

41. See E. Franklin Frazier's recognition of the middle-class orientation of the National Baptist Convention in Frazier, *Black Bourgeoisie* (New York: Macmillan, 1957), 89.

42. Houston Baker, in his discussion of the black vernacular, characterizes the "quotidian sounds of black every day life" as both a defiant and entrancing voice. Similarly, John Langston Gwaltney calls the "folk" culture of today's cities "core black culture," which is "more than ad hoc synchronic adaptive survival." Gwaltney links its values and epistemology to a long peasant tradition. See John Langston Gwaltney, *Drylongso: A Self-Portrait of Black America* (New York: Random House, 1980), xxv–xxvii; also Houston Baker, Jr., *Afro-American Poetics: Revisions of Harlem and the Black Aesthetic* (Madison: University of Wisconsin Press, 1988), 95–107; Baker, *Blues, Ideology, and Afro-American Literature: A Vernacular Theory* (Chicago: University of Chicago Press, 1984), 11–13.

43. Genovese, *Roll Jordan Roll*, 163.

44. Lincoln and Mamiya, *Black Church in the African American Experience*, 10–16.

45. The Russian linguist and critic Mikhail Bakhtin discusses "dialogism" and "heteroglossia" in specific regard to his theory of language: "Everything means, is understood, as part of a greater whole—there is a constant interaction between meanings, all of which have the potential of conditioning others." See M. M. Bakhtin, *The Dialogic Imagination: Four Essays*, ed. Michael Holquist and trans. Caryl Emerson and Michael Holquist (Austin: University of Texas Press, 1981), 293, 352, 426.

46. See Fannie Barrier Williams, "The Club Movement among Colored Women of America," in Booker T. Washington, N. B. Wood, and Fannie Barrier Williams, *A New Negro for a New Century* (Chicago: American Publishing House, 1900), 383.

47. For discussion of black and white women's church work as a forerunner to secular reform, see Ann Firor Scott, *The Southern Lady: From Pedestal to Politics, 1830–1930* (Chicago: University of Chicago Press, 1970), 141; Jean Friedman, *The Enclosed Garden: Women and Community in the Evangelical South, 1830–1900* (Chapel Hill: University of North Carolina Press, 1985), 111, 113, 115–126; Jacquelyn Dowd Hall, *Revolt against Chivalry: Jessie Daniel Ames and the Women's Campaign against Lynching* (New York: Columbia University Press, 1979), 70–77; Kathleen C. Berkeley, "'Colored Ladies also Contributed': Black Women's Activities from Benevolence to Social Welfare, 1866–1896," in Walter J. Fraser, Jr., R. Frank Saunders, Jr., and John L. Wakelyn, eds., *The Web of Southern Social Relations: Women, Family, and Education* (Athens: University of Georgia Press, 1985), 181–185.

48. Eric Hobsbawm, "Peasants and Politics," *Journal of Peasant Studies*, 1 (1973): 12, 16.

49. James Scott uses the phrase "prosaic and constant struggle" in his study of everyday forms of resistance in a Malaysian community. See James Scott, *Weapons of the Weak: Everyday Forms of Peasant Resistance* (New Haven: Yale University Press, 1985), 301.

50. Edward L. Wheeler, *Uplifting the Race: The Black Minister in the New South, 1865–1902* (Lanham, Md.: University Press of America, 1986), xvii.

51. W. E. Burghardt Du Bois, ed., *Efforts for Social Betterment among Negro Americans* (Atlanta: Atlanta University Press, 1909), 16, 22.

2. The Female Talented Tenth

1. W. E. Burghardt Du Bois, *The Souls of Black Folk* (New York: Fawcett Publications, 1967), 42–54.

2. Ibid., 74–87; Du Bois, "The Talented Tenth," in Booker T. Washington et al., *The Negro Problem: A Series of Articles by Representative Negroes of Today* (New York: James Pott, 1903), 33–75. For Booker T. Washington's defense of industrial education, see his essay "Industrial Education for the Negro," in ibid., 9–29.

3. During the 1880s and 1890s black leaders such as the Episcopal bishop Alexander Crummel, the editor Calvin Chase, the novelist and reformer Frances Ellen Watkins Harper, and the educator Anna J. Cooper preceded Du Bois in arguing for the greater merit of liberal arts education over that of industrial training. See recent discussion of early advocates of black liberal arts education in James D. Anderson, *The Education of Blacks in the South, 1860–1935* (Chapel Hill: University of North Carolina Press, 1988), 64–65; Hazel V. Carby, *Reconstructing Womanhood: The Emergence of the Afro-American Woman Novelist* (New York: Oxford University Press, 1987), 83–85, 99–101.

4. "Our Schools," *Baptist Home Mission Monthly*, 2 (hereafter BHMM) (August 1880): 158, 160–161; "Freedman Work," BHMM, 2 (July 1880): 141–142.

5. G. M. P. King, "Christian Education for the Colored Women," BHMM, 2 (August 1880): 152–153.

6. Quarles went north specifically to allay the doubts of the Woman's American Baptist Home Mission Society. Initially the women questioned the wisdom of committing their young organization to such a large financial undertaking. The women also doubted the ability of Packard and Giles, aged 57 and 48 respectively, for the challenging task ahead. See Beverly Guy-Sheftall, *Spelman: A Centennial Celebration, 1881–1981* (Atlanta: Spelman College, 1981), 13. For a discussion of the founding of Spelman, see also Florence Read, *The Story of Spelman College* (Atlanta: Spelman College, 1961), 1–59.

7. Henry Morehouse, "General Survey of Spelman's Twenty Years," *Spelman Messenger*, January 1902 (Supplement to *Spelman Messenger*), unpaginated; Guy-Sheftall, *Spelman, 1881–1981*, 13.

8. Anthony Binga, "The Social Condition of the Freedman of the South," BHMM, 2 (March 1880): 42.

9. Walter H. Brooks, "Wanted—A Baptist College for Colored Youth in Virginia," *BHMM*, 3 (January 1881): 8–9; "Our Schools," 157.

10. Woman's American Baptist Home Mission Society (hereafter WABHMS), *Fifth Annual Report of the Woman's American Baptist Home Mission Society with the Report of the Annual Meeting Held in Warren Avenue Church, Boston, May 9, 1883* (Boston: G. J. Stiles, 1883), 21.

11. American Baptist Home Mission Society (hereafter ABHMS), *Baptist Home Missions in North America, Jubilee Volume* (New York: Baptist Home Mission Rooms, 1883), 60–70.

12. WABHMS, *Tenth Annual Report of the Woman's American Baptist Home Mission Society Held in the First Baptist Church, Worcester, Massachusetts, May 2, 1888* (Boston: C. H. Simonds, 1888), 18.

13. Malcolm MacVicar, "Report of the Superintendent of Education," *BHMM*, 14 (July 1892): 250–251; ABHMS, *Forty-eighth Annual Report of the American Baptist Home Mission Society, Convened in the First Baptist Church, Saratoga Springs, N.Y., May 26, 1880* (New York: American Baptist Home Mission Society Rooms, 1880), 49; *Sixtieth Annual Report of the American Baptist Home Mission Society, Convened in Philadelphia, Pa., May 27–28, 1892* (New York: American Baptist Home Mission Society, 1892), 88.

14. ABHMS, *Baptist Home Missions in North America, Jubilee Volume*, 415; also see *Forty-sixth Annual Report of the American Baptist Home Mission Society, Convened in the First Baptist Church, Cleveland, Ohio, May 29, 1878* (New York: Baptist Home Mission Rooms, 1878), 49.

15. Henry Morehouse, "The Talented Tenth," *BHMM*, 18 (August 1896): 277. James McPherson has noted an earlier printing of the same article in the *Independent*, 13 April 1896; see James M. McPherson, *Abolitionist Legacy: From Reconstruction to the NAACP* (Princeton, N.J.: Princeton University Press, 1975), 222.

16. See, for example, the annual report for 1893 of Malcolm MacVicar, superintendent of education for the ABHMS. The report notes that the masses of blacks will gain an education no higher than the secondary school level, and thus the great contribution of black colleges will be to staff these segregated schools with the finest teachers. The report also states that many primary and secondary schools were managed and supported by blacks themselves, and this fact also strengthened the need for quality instruction. MacVicar, "Report of the Superintendent of Education," *BHMM*, 15 (July 1893): 229–231.

17. George Sale, "The Education of the Negro," *BHMM*, 20 (October 1898): 345–348.

18. Citing the several outstanding black colleges and universities, T. J. Morgan remarked that these institutions "have been for Negro education since the war what Harvard, Yale, Dartmouth, and other institutions were in the early history of education in the North." Edward C. Mitchell, the president of Leland University in New Orleans, attributed American progress to the tradition of her universities and colleges. Mitchell argued that blacks needed the same agencies that had enabled white Americans to become scholars, statesmen, and professionals. "Editorial," *BHMM*, 15 (May 1893): 116; T. J. Morgan, "Negro Preparation for Citizenship," *BHMM*, 22 (December 1900): 336; Morgan, "The Education of the Negroes," *BHMM*, 17 (October 1895): 370.

19. James B. Simmons, "A Cluster of Facts," *BHMM*, 4 (March 1882): 66.

20. Sale, "Education of the Negro," 347.

21. H. L. Morehouse, "The Negro Problem," *Home Mission Echo* (February 1891): 9–10.

22. Morgan, "Negro Preparation for Citizenship," 336. Black educators also argued that educated black leaders would lessen the possibility of race conflict between the masses of blacks and whites. See Du Bois, *Souls of Black Folk*, 84–87.

23. See, for example, the report of the committee on work among the freedmen: "We rejoice also in the efforts for broadened and elevated theological education. There must be Christian leaders in order that there may be real advance. At the same time, we cannot forget the equally urgent need of an intelligent laity of members who are wise enough to be willing to be led." "Extracts from Reports of Committees at Annual Meeting," *BHMM*, 4 (July 1882): 198. Also see R. Agnes Wilson, "Facts Concerning Mission Work in the South," *BHMM*, 3 (February 1881): 28; Samuel H. Greene, "Our Obligation to the Educational Work of the Home Mission Society," *BHMM*, 13 (August 1891): 217.

24. The missionary training program established in the black colleges was patterned after the white Missionary Training School in Chicago, founded and operated by the Women's Baptist Home Mission Society. The Women's Baptist Home Mission Society based in the Midwest opened the Missionary Training School on 5 September 1881 in Chicago. Women's Baptist Home Mission Society, "The Training School," *BHMM*, 3 (September 1881): 198–199.

25. Lyman B. Tefft, "Hartshorn Memorial College," *BHMM*, 20 (February 1898): 56; *BHMM*, 21 (August 1899): 315.

26. Morgan, "The Higher Education of Colored Women," *BHMM*, 18 (May 1896): 160–162.

27. Ibid., 163–164.

28. For example, the effort to expose blacks to the quality of instruction found in white schools was revealed when the ABHMS scheduled Dr. E. G. Robinson, former president of Brown University, to deliver a course of lectures at Richmond Theological Institute in February 1892 and at Shaw University in the following month. "News and Notes," *BHMM*, 14 (May 1892): 166; Morgan, "Negro Preparation for Citizenship," 336; Morgan, "The Education of the Negroes," 371–372; Greene, "Obligation to Educational Work of Home Mission Society," 217.

29. For example, Charles White's pamphlet on the history of the educational work of the American Baptist Home Mission Society admits: "We cannot handicap the Negro race and then ask it to equal us who are not handicapped." Charles L. White, *The Training of a Race: A Southern Problem of National Importance* (New York: ABHMS, 1912), 16.

30. Sheila M. Rothman, *Woman's Proper Place: A History of Changing Ideals and Practices, 1870 to the Present* (New York: Basic Books, 1978), 26–42, 46–47.

31. Jacqueline Jones, *Labor of Love, Labor of Sorrow: Black Women, Work, and the Family from Slavery to the Present* (New York: Random House, 1985), 58–68.

32. "An Unbiased Opinion of Spelman Seminary," *BHMM*, 14 (August 1892): 315; *BHMM*, 8 (August 1886): 192; *BHMM*, 3 (September 1881): 194; [Mrs.] James McWhinnie, *Historical Sketch of the Woman's Baptist Home Mission Society from*

November 14, 1877 to April 30, 1894 (Boston: Press of the S. G. Robinson, 1894), 21–22, 25.

33. In 1910 George Sale, by then superintendent of education for the American Baptist Home Mission Society, best explained the relationship of the head, heart, and hand in northern Baptist pedagogy: "Still the faith of our schools is that 'life is more than meat' and the measure of the man is not the hand, however skillful, but the mind and the heart, and so we put the spiritual and intellectual first." George Sale, "Our Part in the Solution of a Great Problem," in W. N. Hartshorn and George W. Penniman, eds., *An Era of Progress and Promise 1863–1910* (Boston: The Priscilla Publishing Company, 1910), 70.

34. "Report of the Committee on Work among the Freedmen," *BHMM*, 3 (May 1881): 170; "Schools," *BHMM*, 3 (May 1881): 103–104; Lyman B. Tefft, "Our Work in Nashville," *BHMM*, 3 (September 1881): 181–182.

35. A short history of the WABHMS from 1877 to 1894 states the following about Spelman: "If in this sketch we have spoken of one school more than another, it is because the Woman's American Baptist Home Mission Society and Spelman Seminary are identical. The history of one is the history of the other; and Spelman is a type of all the schools cared for by the Society." McWhinnie, *Historical Sketch*, 33–34; Read, *Story of Spelman*, 49–69; Morehouse, "General Survey of Spelman's Twenty Years," unpaginated.

36. Rabinowitz noted that in 1892 Friendship Baptist Church was the second largest black Baptist church in the state of Georgia. See Howard Rabinowitz, *Race Relations in the Urban South, 1865–1890* (Urbana: University of Illinois Press, 1980), 204.

37. Henry Morehouse, "History of Spelman Seminary," *Home Mission Echo* (February 1886): 4–5; "Memorial Services for Miss Packard," *Home Mission Echo* (October 1891): 4.

38. WABHMS, *Fifth Annual Report, 1883*, 13; WABHMS, *Eighteenth Annual Report of the Woman's American Baptist Home Mission Society, Held in the Second Baptist Church, Holyoke, Massachusetts, April 29, 1896* (Boston: C. H. Simonds, 1896), 78; McWhinnie, *Historical Sketch*, 9.

39. See letter from Packard and Giles in the *Home Mission Echo* (February 1886): 2.

40. See Spelman report in *Home Mission Echo* (January 1886): 2–3.

41. In 1924 the Booker T. Washington High School opened in Atlanta for black students. Martin Luther King, Jr., would be one of its most illustrious graduates. John Dittmer, *Black Georgia in the Progressive Era, 1900–1920* (Urbana: University of Illinois Press, 1977), 148; Louis R. Harlan, *Separate and Unequal: Public School Campaigns and Racism in the Southern Seaboard States, 1901–1915* (New York: Atheneum, 1969), 212–213.

42. Six women constituted the first class to receive the diploma for the higher normal course. The principal's report for 1887 stated that one planned to continue in the nurse training program, one or two would teach, and another would work with her husband as a missionary in Africa. The report for the following year noted that of the six students who graduated in May 1887, most were teachers, and two were principals of schools. WABHMS, *Ninth Annual Report of the Woman's American Baptist*

Home Mission Society, Held in the First Baptist Church, Providence, Rhode Island, May 4, 1887 (Boston: C. H. Simonds, 1887), 15; WABHMS, *Tenth Annual Report, 1888,* 18; WABHMS, *Seventeenth Annual Report of the Woman's American Baptist Home Mission Society, with the Report of the Annual Meeting Held in First Baptist Church, Malden, Massachusetts, May 1-2, 1895* (Boston: C. H. Simonds, 1895), 29; Harriet E. Giles, "Spelman Seminary, Atlanta, Georgia," BHMM, 20 (January 1898):15; Read, *Story of Spelman,* 140–141. See also the transcript of the recorded reminiscences of Claudia White Harreld, first graduate to receive the baccalaureate degree from Spelman in 1901; Claudia White Harreld, Interview, Winter 1952, Transcript, Schlesinger Library, Radcliffe College, Cambridge, Massachusetts.

43. This information is presented in White, *The Training of a Race,* 13.

44. Two decades after the school's founding, however, T. J. Morgan of the ABHMS opposed the idea of training students for domestic service: "I am slow to favor any scheme which will encourage the idea that Spelman exists for the purpose of providing domestic servants, and that the vast outlay of money made there by us is to accrue to the special benefit of Southern people whose highest opinion of the Negro is that of a faithful servant." See Thomas J. Morgan to Harriet Giles, 18 January 1901, Spelman College Archives; also WABHMS, *Fifth Annual Report, 1883,* 12–13; WABHMS, *Seventh Annual Report of the Woman's American Baptist Home Mission Society, Held in the Baptist Church, Old Cambridge, Massachusetts, May 7, 1885* (Boston: C. H. Simonds, 1885), 5; WABHMS, *Eighth Annual Report of the Woman's American Baptist Home Mission Society, Held in the Baptist Church, Newton, Massachusetts, May 5, 1886* (Boston: C. H. Simonds, 1886), 19; *Sixth Annual Catalogue of Spelman Seminary,* Spelman College Archives.

45. Spelman was a favorite of the Slater Fund. When the Fund cut back its donations to only a few schools in the South, Spelman was second only to Hampton Institute. Its general agent, Dr. Atticus G. Haygood, praised Packard and Giles for the successful payment of the property in Atlanta and stated in 1884: "My judgment is, no school in proportion to the investment of money in it is doing so much good work." WABHMS, *Sixth Annual Report of the Woman's Baptist Home Mission Society with the Report of the Annual Meeting Held in Baptist Church, Jamaica Plain, Massachusetts, May 7, 1884* (Boston: G. J. Stiles, 1884), 15.

46. Dr. Sophia Jones came to Atlanta through the influence of Atticus G. Haygood of the Slater Fund. In 1888 she was no longer in charge of the nurse training program, but she was listed in Spelman's annual report as the resident physician. Miss L. J. Bothwell, a graduate of the Massachusetts General Hospital in Boston, succeeded Jones in the supervision of nurse trainees. In 1905 Sophia Jones's name appeared in a listing of prominent black women. She was described as a successful doctor with a "splendid practice" in St. Louis, Missouri. WABHMS, *Eighth Annual Report, 1886,* 19–20; WABHMS, *Ninth Annual Report, 1887,* 15; WABHMS, *Tenth Annual Report, 1888,* 17; George F. Richings, *Evidences of Progress among Colored People,* 12th ed. (Philadelphia: Geo. S. Ferguson, 1905), 413; WABHMS, *Eighteenth Annual Report, 1896,* 81; "Spelman Seminary," *Home Mission Echo* (July 1889): 5.

47. Five years after its founding, Spelman reported between 400 and 500 conversions out of a total of 3,500 pupils connected with the school since its inception. WABHMS, *Fifth Annual Report, 1883,* 12; WABHMS, *Sixth Annual Report, 1884,* 15;

WABHMS, *Tenth Annual Report, 1888*, 14; James D. Tyms, *The Rise of Religious Education among Negro Baptists* (New York: Exposition Press, 1965), 127–153.

48. The Spelman annual report to the WABHMS in 1883 read: "We had no idea of the heathenism existing in our own country until we came to Atlanta." The wife of Thomas J. Morgan likewise noted in 1884 that the beneficiaries of the WABHMS promised to be teachers among their own people rather than go to Africa because "they realize, all too bitterly, from the depths of their own sad experiences that Africa lies all about them, and that the ignorance and superstitions of their own homes must be done away with first of all." WABHMS, *Fifth Annual Report, 1883*, 14; WABHMS, *Sixth Annual Report, 1884*, 10–12; "Woman's American Baptist Home Mission Society," *BHMM*, 5 (February 1883): 44; McPherson, *Abolitionist Legacy*, 62–64; Maria T. Richards, "Relation of the Freedmen's Work to Foreign Missions," *BHMM*, 4 (August 1882): 214.

49. WABHMS, *Fifth Annual Report, 1883*, 12; WABHMS, *Sixth Annual Report, 1884*, 14; WABHMS, *Eighth Annual Report, 1886*, 19–20; WABHMS, *Ninth Annual Report, 1887*, 16; WABHMS, *Tenth Annual Report, 1888*, 19; WABHMS, *Fourteenth Annual Report of the Woman's American Baptist Home Mission Society, with the Report of the Annual Meeting Held in Central Baptist Church, Newport, Rhode Island, May 4–5, 1892* (Boston: C. H. Simonds, 1892), 15–16; WABHMS, *Fifteenth Annual Report of the Woman's American Baptist Home Mission Society, with the Report of the Annual Meeting Held in Temple Church, Dorchester, Massachusetts, May 3–4, 1893* (Boston: C. H. Simonds, 1893), 27.

50. M. C. Reynolds, "The Work and the Workers," *Home Mission Echo* (November 1891): 4. See also WABHMS, *Fifteenth Annual Report, 1893*, 27; WABHMS, *Sixteenth Annual Report of the Woman's American Baptist Home Mission Society, with the Report of the Annual Meeting Held in Warren Avenue Baptist Church, Boston, Massachusetts, May 2–3, 1894* (Boston: C. H. Simonds, 1894), 30.

51. Giles stated in 1896: "When, as it is at this moment, the case in some counties in Georgia, schools are closed until the summer, because no teachers can be obtained who passed the January State examinations, and when those now teaching are trembling lest their licenses should not be renewed, then thorough preparation for teaching is appreciated." WABHMS, *Eighteenth Annual Report, 1896*, 84; WABHMS, *Fifth Annual Report, 1883*, 12, 60; WABHMS, *Seventh Annual Report, 1885*, 15; WABHMS, *Eighth Annual Report, 1886*, 18; WABHMS, *Fourteenth Annual Report, 1894*, 30; "Woman's American Baptist Home Mission Society," *BHMM*, 13 (June 1891): 157.

52. Proudly announcing the erection of the practice school, the report of the superintendent of education, Malcolm MacVicar, stated that Spelman offered "as good accommodations and appliances for the training of teachers as are to be found anywhere, North or South." The reorganization in 1893 permitted the men of Atlanta Baptist College to take courses in method on the Spelman campus and to practice-teach on their own. "The Normal Training School at Atlanta," *BHMM*, 15 (January 1893):23–24; *BHMM*, 15 (July 1893):230; WABHMS, *Sixteenth Annual Report, 1894*, 33–34; WABHMS, *Fifteenth Annual Report, 1893*, 26; WABHMS, *Eighteenth Annual Report, 1896*, 86; A. D. Mayo, *Southern Women in the Recent*

Educational Movement in the South, ed. Dan T. Carter and Amy Friedlander (Baton Rouge: Louisiana State University Press, 1978; reprint of 1892 edition), 200.

53. *Home Mission Echo* (July 1889): 6.

54. The article from the *Gazette* was reprinted in the *Home Mission Echo* (February 1888): 10.

55. A letter from Ellen Cook, a Spelman student teacher, admitted her preference for female teachers over male because the former placed far more emphasis on the importance of refinement. See "Spelman Seminary," *BHMM*, 13 (March 1891): 74–76; "Notes," *BHMM*, 24 (January 1902): 6; "Woman's American Baptist Home Mission Society," *BHMM*, 5 (July 1883): 160; WABHMS, *Seventh Annual Report, 1885*, 12; WABHMS, *Tenth Annual Report, 1888*, 19–21.

56. Nora Gordon to Sophia Packard, 1 July 1885, printed in the *Home Mission Echo* (September 1885): 4, and Gordon to Packard, 13 September 1886, printed in ibid. (October 1886): 4.

57. De Lamotta to Packard, n.d., attached with letter from S. B. Packard to Dear Brother, 21 October 1890, Emma De Lamotta Biography File, American Baptist Archives Center, Valley Forge, Pa.

58. "The Freed-people," *Tidings* (May 1883): 3; *Home Mission Echo* (May 1894): 10; Emma De Lamotta to Packard, attached to letter of Packard to Dear Brother, 21 October 1890, Emma De Lamotta Biography File, American Baptist Archives Center, Valley Forge, Pa.

59. WABHMS, *Sixth Annual Report, 1884*, 11.

60. WABHMS, *Eighth Annual Report, 1886*, 18; WABHMS, *Sixteenth Annual Report, 1894*, 30; *BHMM*, 15 (July 1883): 60.

61. See findings of 1906 survey in *Tidings* (July 1910): 22.

62. Lucy Upton, who became the third principal of Spelman after the death of Giles, made similar statements while a teacher in 1896: "We see in imagination, among the daughters of Spelman college graduates, physicians, poets, editors, artists. . . . Spelman ought to become the Wellesley of the South." See Lucy Upton, "The Needs of Spelman Seminary," *Spelman Messenger*, May 1896; also Giles, "Spelman Seminary," 16.

63. Sophia Packard also emphasized the Spelman students' important mediating influence between the races when she stated that they "go among their own people and help Christianize and educate them, doing what white people cannot do, going where white people cannot go, and reaching hearts that white people cannot reach." WABHMS, *Eighth Annual Report, 1886*, 18; also see Morgan, "What Spelman Seminary Stands For," *BHMM*, 24 (January 1902): 11–19; Morehouse, "General Survey of Spelman's Twenty Years," unpaginated.

64. U.S. Department of Commerce, Bureau of the Census, *Negro Population, 1790–1915* (Washington, D.C.: Government Printing Office, 1918), 526.

65. The number of male professionals rose by 51 percent between 1890 and 1910, while that of all male workers rose by the same percentage. Ibid.

66. Ibid.

67. Ibid.

68. Jacqueline Jones notes that black women's teaching salaries averaged 45 percent of those of whites. Jones, *Labor of Love, Labor of Sorrow*, 143–144, 146.

69. U.S. Department of Commerce and Labor, Bureau of the Census, *Statistics of Women at Work* (Washington, D.C.: Government Printing Office, 1907), 33, 109–118.

70. Ibid., 109.

71. Lawrence Levine argues that the greater "cultural self-containment" of the slave community gave way to cultural marginality in freedom. Lawrence Levine, *Black Culture and Black Consciousness: Afro-American Folk Thought from Slavery to Freedom* (New York: Oxford University Press, 1977), 138–143; E. Franklin Frazier, *Black Bourgeoisie* (New York: Macmillan, 1957), 112–129.

72. For the example of black leaders who distinguished themselves from "crude and undeveloped believers," see the speech of Elias Camp Morris, president of the National Baptist Convention, in National Baptist Convention, *Journal of the Nineteenth Annual Session of the National Baptist Convention, Held in Nashville, Tennessee, September 13–18, 1899* (Nashville: National Baptist Publishing Board, 1899), 20, 35–36. For a similar argument see Edward M. Brawley, ed., *The Negro Baptist Pulpit* (Philadelphia: American Baptist Publication Society, 1890), 7–10.

73. Rabinowitz, *Race Relations in the Urban South*, 215–217.

74. Ibid., 214. For a discussion of African American cultural practices and values in conflict with those of the dominant culture, see also John W. Roberts, *From Trickster to Badman: The Black Folk Hero in Slavery and Freedom* (Philadelphia: University of Pennsylvania Press, 1989), chap. 5.

75. See, for example, the letter from Mary Traver to the Women's Baptist Home Mission Society: "It seems strange to think of such a thing as opposition to education on the part of any of the colored people, but among some of the older ones, especially the more ignorant preachers, the opposition is very bitter, prompted by jealousy of the more educated young men. It is easy to see that there is a fight before them." *Home Mission Echo* (May 1894): 10.

76. For beliefs and practices under slavery, see Albert Raboteau, *Slave Religion: The "Invisible Institution" in the Antebellum South* (New York: Oxford University Press, 1978); Eugene D. Genovese, *Roll Jordan Roll: The World the Slaves Made* (New York: Random House, Pantheon Books, 1974), 211–219; Levine, *Black Culture and Black Consciousness*, 57–67, 140–142.

77. Sutton Griggs is quoted and discussed in Wilson Jeremiah Moses, *The Golden Age of Black Nationalism, 1850–1925* (New York: Oxford University Press, 1978), 170–193.

78. Brawley, ed., *Negro Baptist Pulpit*, 19.

79. Letter from Hartshorn teacher Carrie Dyer to the WABHMS, 12 February 1886, published in *Home Mission Echo* (March 1886): 3.

80. "What the Hartshorn Women Are Doing," *Home Mission Echo* (February 1888): 9; WABHMS, *Eleventh Annual Report of the Woman's American Baptist Home Mission Society, with the Report of the Annual Meeting Held in Perkins Street Baptist Church, Somerville, Massachusetts, May 8, 1889* (Boston: C. H. Simonds, 1889), 22–23; for similar activities in other locations in the South, see "A Year's Work among the Freed People," *Tidings* (May 1885): 1, 4.

81. "The Growing Need of Higher Schools for the Colored People," *Home Mission Echo* (December 1897): 13.

3. Separatist Leanings

1. Gramsci states: "Every social group coming into existence on the original terrain of an essential function in the world of economic production, creates together with itself, organically, one or more strata of intellectuals which give it homogeneity and an awareness of its own function not only in economic but also in the social and political fields." See David Forgacs, ed., *An Antonio Gramsci Reader: Selected Writings 1916–1935* (New York: Schocken Books, 1988), 301.

2. For studies devoted to the subject of nationalism, see Wilson Jeremiah Moses, *The Golden Age of Black Nationalism, 1850–1925* (New York: Oxford University Press, 1978); John Bracey, Jr., August Meier, and Elliott Rudwick, eds., *Black Nationalism in America* (Indianapolis: Bobbs-Merrill, 1970); Sterling Stuckey, *Slave Culture: Nationalist Theory and the Foundations of Black America* (New York: Oxford University Press, 1987); and Stuckey, *The Ideological Origins of Black Nationalism* (Boston: Beacon Press, 1972).

3. Moses, *Golden Age*, 23–30.

4. Benedict Anderson, *Imagined Communities: Reflections on the Origin and Spread of Nationalism* (London: Verso, 1983), 15–16.

5. For discussion of the role of print in the formation of nationalism as "imagined community," see ibid., 62–23, 74–75.

6. See Nancy Fraser's discussion of "intrapublic relations" in her feminist critique of Habermas's "bourgeois public sphere," and especially her discussion on the inability to bracket social inequalities, in Fraser, "Rethinking the Public Sphere: A Contribution to the Critique of Actually Existing Democracy," *Social Text*, 25/26 (1990): 63–64.

7. James McPherson has documented the black Baptist struggle along with that of blacks in other denominations for greater administrative and faculty representation in the missionary-founded colleges. James M. McPherson, *Abolitionist Legacy: From Reconstruction to the NAACP* (Princeton, N.J.: Princeton University Press, 1975), 262–295.

8. Ibid., 268–275.

9. For example, Georgia school commissioner G. R. Glenn was among several whites who admired the work of Spelman. Sending forth black teachers to staff segregated rural schools did not offend southern sensibilities, but Spelman's MacVicar Hospital excluded black doctors as part of its policy of appeasing the white South. Only black student nurses, working under the direction of white doctors, were permitted in the hospital. MacVicar's closed staff did not admit non-white doctors until 1928. In that year nurse training was discontinued and the hospital was used exclusively as a student infirmary for Spelman and Morehouse students. See Florence Read, *The Story of Spelman College* (Atlanta: Spelman College, 1961), 138–139; "Spelman Seminary," *Baptist Home Mission Monthly* (hereafter BHMM), 24 (January 1902): 6.

10. McPherson, *Abolitionist Legacy*, 285–286.

11. Ibid., 287–288.

12. Louis Harlan notes Washington's reticence in discussing his stay at Wayland, and suggests that the rural, pragmatic Washington felt ill at ease with city life and the scholarly atmosphere at the seminary. See Harlan, *Booker T. Washington: The Making of a Black Leader, 1856–1901* (New York: Oxford University Press, 1972), 86–98, 194. In his autobiography Washington does not specifically mention his time at Wayland, but says only that he spent eight months of study in Washington, D.C. Booker T. Washington, *Up from Slavery: An Autobiography* (New York: Association Press, 1901), 87.

13. The seven-page grievance was written by a committee with representatives from twenty-six churches on 15 June 1885 at Shiloh Baptist Church in Washington, D.C. See "The Grievances against Prof. G. M. P. King, Principal of Wayland Seminary, Washington, D.C. as Stated by the Colored Baptists of the District of Columbia, Alexandria, Va. and Vicinity," Shiloh Baptist Church Archives, Washington, D.C.

14. Ibid.

15. McPherson, *Abolitionist Legacy*, 285.

16. Ibid.

17. Leon F. Litwack, *Been in the Storm So Long: The Aftermath of Slavery* (New York: Vintage Books, 1979), 464–465.

18. For discussion of the influence of the concept "fatherhood of God and brotherhood of Man" on late nineteenth century black ministers, see Edward L. Wheeler, *Uplifting the Race: The Black Minister in the New South, 1865–1902* (Lanham, Md.: University Press of America, 1986), 46–48.

19. See Jacqueline Jones, *Soldiers of Light and Love: Northern Teachers and Georgia Blacks, 1865–1873* (Chapel Hill: University of North Carolina Press, 1980), 59.

20. Ibid., 63.

21. These Sabbath schools were found in all the cities and in many rural areas; they presented "thrilling spectacles . . . gathered upon the Sabbath day, sometimes of many hundreds, dressed in clean Sunday garments, with eyes intent upon elementary and Christian instruction." Quoting John W. Alvord is James D. Anderson, *The Education of Blacks in the South, 1860–1935* (Chapel Hill: University of North Carolina Press, 1988), 7–9, 12; see also the discussion of the importance of Sunday schools in education, especially in developing literacy in the nineteenth century, in Ann M. Boylan, *Sunday School: The Formation of an American Institution, 1790–1880* (New Haven: Yale University Press, 1988), 22–40.

22. Anderson, *Education of Blacks in the South*, 28–29; Vincent P. Franklin, *Black Self-Determination: A Cultural History of the Faith of the Fathers* (Westport, Conn.: Lawrence Hill, 1984), 161–169; Jones, *Soldiers of Light and Love*, 69–70; Ronald Butchart, *Northern Schools, Southern Blacks, and Reconstruction: Freedmen's Education, 1862–1875* (Westport, Conn.: Greenwood Press, 1980), 169–179; Robert C. Morris, *Reading, 'Riting, and Reconstruction: The Education of Freedmen in the South, 1861–1870* (Chicago: University of Chicago Press, 1981), 115–126.

23. Howard Rabinowitz, *Race Relations in the Urban South, 1865–1930* (Urbana: University of Illinois Press, 1980), 161–181; Kathleen C. Berkeley, "The Politics of

Black Education in Memphis, Tennessee, 1868–1891," in Rick Ginsberg and David N. Plank, eds., *Southern Cities, Southern Schools: Public Education in the Urban South* (Westport, Conn.: Greenwood Press, 1990), 199–236.

24. Anderson, *Education of Blacks in the South*, 193–196. For a comparison of the expenditures for white and black public education, see Robert A. Margo, *Race and Schooling in the South, 1880–1950* (Chicago: University of Chicago Press, 1990), chap. 2.

25. For a history of the struggle and defeat of blacks in Augusta to gain public education, see June O. Patton, "The Black Community of Augusta and the Struggle for Ware High School, 1880–1899," in Vincent P. Franklin and James D. Anderson, eds., *New Perspectives on Black Educational History* (Boston: G. K. Hall, 1978), 44–55. For a discussion of the lack of public schooling for blacks throughout the South at this time, see Henry Allen Bullock, *A History of Negro Education in the South: From 1619 to the Present* (Cambridge, Mass.: Harvard University Press, 1967), 123; Horace Mann Bond, *Negro Education in Alabama: A Study of Cotton and Steel* (Washington, D.C., 1939; rpt. New York: Octagon Books, 1969), 151–152; Louis Harlan, *Separate and Unequal: Public School Campaigns and Racism in the Southern Seaboard States* (New York: Atheneum, 1969), 9, 13, 23, 39–40; John Dittmer, *Black Georgia in the Progressive Era, 1900–1920* (Urbana: University of Illinois Press, 1977), 141–151.

26. Other reminders appeared to affirm their inferior status within the larger denomination. In addition to discriminatory hiring policies at ABHMS schools, the American Baptist Publication Society insulted black leaders when it refused to publish the work of black intellectuals in the 1890 issue of its periodical *The Baptist Teacher*. Not wishing to lose southern white support, the financially insecure American Baptist Publication Society reneged on its earlier acceptance of writings by the Reverends William J. Simmons, Emmanuel K. Love, and Walter H. Brooks and "erased" their names from the list of contributors. See James Melvin Washington, *Frustrated Fellowship: The Black Baptist Quest for Social Power* (Macon, Ga.: Mercer Press, 1982), 163–170.

27. American National Baptist Convention (hereafter ANBC), *Journal of the American National Baptist Convention: Three Sessions, 1889, Indianapolis; 1890, Louisville; 1891, Dallas* (Louisville: The Bradley and Gilbert Company Printers, 1892), 19.

28. Quoted in Edward M. Brawley, ed., *The Negro Baptist Pulpit* (Philadelphia: American Baptist Publication Society, 1890), 299.

29. See article reprinted from the *Christian Organizer* out of Lynchburg, Virginia, in *The Baptist Truth*, 26 October 1898.

30. Gordon wrote: "Each institution must bear the stamp of its founders. Our school will be one built, born in the tears of a struggling race, our own hands helping our own children. There is something so noble in this." See "Communicated," letter to the editor by J. D. Gordon of Madison, Georgia, in *The Baptist Truth*, 30 November 1899.

31. Michael R. Heintze, *Private Black Colleges in Texas, 1865–1954* (College Station, Tex.: Texas A & M University Press, 1985), 31–33; Leroy Fitts, *A History of Black Baptists* (Nashville, Tenn.: Broadman Press, 1985), 97–98.

32. See St. Clair Drake, "The Black University in the American Social Order," *Daedalus*, 100 (Winter 1971): 833; also Lester F. Russell, *Black Baptist Secondary Schools in Virginia, 1887–1957* (Metuchen, N.J.: The Scarecrow Press, 1981), 49–57, 140–148.

33. For a comprehensive history of the school, see Lawrence H. Williams, *Black Higher Education in Kentucky, 1879–1930* (Lewistown, N.Y.: The Edwin Mellen Press, 1987), 28.

34. Ibid., 20, 51, 80; "State University of Louisville," *Home Mission Echo* (March 1898): 6; also see the article by James L. Diggs, president of State University in the early 1900s. James L. Diggs, "State University, Louisville, Ky.," *Colored American Magazine* (May 1908): 312–314.

35. Williams, *Black Higher Education in Kentucky*, 36, 79–80.

36. In 1885 the school was organized into four departments: College, Normal, Preparatory, and Model School. Students took courses in cooking and printing, and they engaged in a variety of extracurricular activities, such as the literary society and the Young Men's and Women's Christian Association. The latter association conducted a large Sabbath School and sent missionary workers among the city's destitute. William J. Simmons, "History of the School at Louisville, Chap. I," *Home Mission Echo* (May 1885): 3.

37. Mary Cook relates the history of the Kentucky women's convention and the sacrifices of black women in support of the school in a letter printed in the *Home Mission Echo* (November 1885): 3.

38. See the introduction by Henry McNeil Turner, bishop in the A.M.E. church, in William J. Simmons, *Men of Mark: Eminent, Progressive and Rising* (Cleveland: Geo. M. Rewell, 1887), 43, 57; BHMM, 9 (August 1887): 207.

39. Mary V. Cook, "The Work for Baptist Women," in Brawley, ed., *Negro Baptist Pulpit*, 279–280.

40. In his report to the ABHMS in 1883, William J. Simmons referred to the formation of the women's convention in Kentucky: "They had a fine meeting. They visited the school in a body, and made able and cheering speeches. They promise big things next year." See "Schools," BHMM, 5 (November 1883): 247; Brawley, ed., *Negro Baptist Pulpit*, 279; *Minutes of the Baptist Women's Educational Convention of Kentucky, First, Second, Third, Fourth, and Fifth Sessions, 1883–1887* (Louisville: National Publishing Co.'s Print, 1887), 4.

41. Perhaps the Kentucky women encouraged black women's education for the same reason that Anna J. Cooper pleaded to black Protestant Episcopalians. Cooper argued for more financial assistance and scholarships for women's collegiate training, "to offset and balance the aid that can always be found for boys who will take theology." Anna J. Cooper, *A Voice from the South by a Black Woman of the South* (Xenia, Ohio, 1892; rpt. New York: Negro Universities Press, 1969), 79. Also see letter from Mary Cook published in *Home Mission Echo* (November 1885): 3; also *First through Fifth Sessions, Kentucky, 1883–1887*, 30.

42. See Seeley's report to the white northern Woman's American Baptist Home Mission Society (hereafter WABHMS) in WABHMS, *Twenty-first Annual Report of the Woman's American Baptist Home Mission Society with the Report of the Annual Meeting Held in the Free St. Baptist Church, Portland, Maine, May 3–4, 1899* (Boston: C. H. Simonds, 1899), 93–94.

43. See the letter to the Presidents of the University Societies, by Lizzie Crittenden and M. V. Cook, under "Women's Work," *American Baptist*, 22 July 1887.

44. Brawley, ed., *Negro Baptist Pulpit*, 279; ANBC, *Journal, Sermons, and Lectures of the Third Anniversary of the American National Baptist Convention, Held with the Spruce Street Baptist Church, Nashville, Tennessee, September 22–24, 1888*, 45; Charles H. Parrish, ed., *Golden Jubilee of the General Association of Colored Baptists in Kentucky* (Louisville: Mayes Printing, 1915), 144–145; BHMM, 14 (February 1892): 74.

45. Brawley, *Negro Baptist Pulpit*, 281–282; S. N. Reid, *History of Colored Baptists in Alabama* (n.p., 1949), 91–93.

46. At their ninth annual meeting, the women's convention depicted Selma as "child of the Baptists of Alabama" and praised the school for educating male and female leaders. *Minutes of the Sixth Annual Session of the Baptist State Women's Convention, Held with the Second Baptist Church of Eufaula, Alabama, June 25–June 28, 1891* (n.p., n.d.), 14, 22–23; *Minutes of the Seventh Annual Session of the Baptist Women's State Convention, Held with the New Morning Star Baptist Church of Demopolis, Alabama, June 23–26, 1892* (Montgomery: Baptist Leader Print, 1892), 13; *Minutes of the Baptist Women's State Convention, Ninth Annual Session, Held at the Sixteenth Street Baptist Church, Birmingham, Alabama, June 21–24, 1894* (Montgomery: State Normal School Press, 1895), 10.

47. *Minutes of the Fourth Annual Session of the Baptist Women's State Convention, Held with the First Baptist Church of Greenville* (Montgomery: Baptist Leader Print, 1889), 5, 15; Brawley, ed., *Negro Baptist Pulpit*, 282.

48. *Sixth Annual Session, Alabama, 1891*, 13; Charles Octavius Boothe, *The Cyclopedia of the Colored Baptists of Alabama* (Birmingham: Alabama Publishing Company, 1895), 256.

49. Outstanding ministers, who led the ministers' state conventions and also inspired women's organized work, were in their twenties and thirties in the 1880s. William J. Simmons was born in 1849 and Charles H. Parrish, also a leader in Kentucky, was born in 1859. Of Alabama leaders, Edward M. Brawley was born in 1851; Charles L. Purce, 1856; and Robert T. Pollard, 1860. Louisiana minister Solomon T. Clanton was born in 1857. Arkansas leaders Elias C. Morris and Joseph A. Booker were born in 1855 and 1859, respectively. See A. W. Pegues, *Our Baptist Ministers and Schools* (Springfield, Mass.: Willey, 1892), 61, 78, 122, 353, 357, 393, 399, 439.

50. Parrish, ed., *Golden Jubilee*, 162–167; Simmons, "State University," BHMM, 9 (February 1887): 67–68.

51. Pegues, *Our Baptist Ministers and Schools*, 398; BHMM, 9 (March 1887): 73; Reid, *History of Colored Baptists in Alabama*, 93–94.

52. Pauline Dinkins, wife of Charles Dinkins, was a graduate of the State University at Louisville. Both she and her husband taught there prior to coming to Selma University. Mrs. Purce was married to Charles Purce, president of Selma University after the resignation of Brawley in 1885. In 1894 Purce left Selma to become president of the State University at Louisville. See Parrish, ed., *Golden Jubilee*, 162–166, 172, 284–285; Reid, *Alabama Baptists*, 94; Pegues, *Baptist Ministers and Schools*, 399–404.

53. *Baptist Woman's Era*, 15 October 1900. Black Baptist–owned newspapers in other states featured the colleges of their conventions. The advertisement for Arkansas

Baptist College in Little Rock announced that the school had begun its eighth session on 3 October 1892. The school offered courses at three levels: Grammar School, Academic, and College. College courses reflected the classical curriculum, but included courses in moral and religious training as well as industrial training. *The Baptist Vanguard*, 14 October 1892.

54. See, for example, the advertisement for Alabama Baptist University, which opened October 2. Courses in operation were primary, preparatory, normal, college, and theological. General expenses included: board at $7.00; tuition, $1.00; instrumental music, $1.00; vocal music, free. See also the "Baby Department," which featured letters encouraging small children to give pennies in support of the school. *Baptist Woman's Era*, 15 October 1900.

55. See the advertisement/editorial for the university in ibid., 15 September 1901.

56. Sandy D. Martin, *Black Baptists and African Missions: The Origins of a Movement, 1880–1915* (Macon, Ga.: Mercer University Press, 1989), 43–72; Lewis G. Jordan, *Negro Baptist History, U.S.A.* (Nashville: Sunday School Publishing Board, National Baptist Convention, 1930), 260–263.

57. Jordan, *Negro Baptist History*, 260–263; ANBC, *Journal and Lectures of the Second Anniversary of the American National Baptist Convention, Held in Mobile, Alabama, August 25–28, 1887* (n.p., n.d.), 65.

58. *National Baptist Educational Convention, Held in the First African Baptist Church, Savannah, Georgia, September 20–21, 1892* (Washington, D.C.: Francis D. Smith, Printer, 1892), 5.

59. Relative to men, the numbers of women delegates to the annual meetings of the American National Baptist Convention were small. The minutes for 1892 report 213 delegates as present. Of the total, only 32 were women and the rest were ministers. Of the 32 women present, 53 percent indicated college training; 9 percent indicated night, public, or common schools; and 38 percent, no schooling. Nearly 38 percent of the women identified themselves as teachers, while 25 percent reported church-related work, such as organist, missionary, or matron in an old folks' home. Nearly 38 percent of the women indicated no occupation. ANBC, *Journal of the American National Baptist Convention, Seventh Annual Session, Held in the First African Baptist Church, Savannah, Georgia, September 15–18, 1892, and Eighth Annual Session, Held in the Vermont Avenue Baptist Church, Washington, D.C., September 16–19, 1893* (Louisville: Courier-Journal, Job Printing, 1894), 2, 6–11.

60. Jordan, *Negro Baptist History*, 238; *National Baptist Educational Convention, 1892*, 3.

61. ANBC, *Journal, 1892, 1893*, 2, 6–11; ANBC, *Journal and Lectures, 1887*, 1, 25; ANBC, *Journal, Sermons, and Lectures, 1888*, 1, 27–28, 50; ANBC, *Journal, 1889, 1890, 1891*, 24, 34, 47–48, 52, 61–64.

62. The National Baptist Convention, U.S.A., Inc. adopted the 1880 founding date of the oldest of the three conventions, to establish the chronology of its annual meetings. ANBC, *Journal and Lectures, 1892, 1893*, 47; National Baptist Convention (hereafter NBC), *Journal of the Nineteenth Annual Session of the National Baptist Convention, U.S.A., Held in Nashville, Tennessee, September 13–16, 1899* (Nashville: National Baptist Publishing Board, 1899), 41–42; Joseph A. Booker, "National

Federation of Negro Baptists," *National Baptist Magazine* (July 1896): 155–157; Fitts, *History of Black Baptists*, 73–84.

63. "Cooperationists," so called for their position with respect to the ABHMS, challenged the philosophy's more militant advocates. To cooperationists, demands for racial self-determination in the form of black control of schools portended the self-defeating consequence of total black financial responsibility. However, the titles "separatist" and "cooperationist" tend to mislead rather than clarify the different positions of black Baptist leaders. For example, some historians label as "cooperationist" both Edward M. Brawley and William J. Simmons—the respective presidents of Selma University and the State University at Louisville—since they questioned their people's ability to maintain institutions of higher learning without any aid from the ABHMS. But the title "cooperationist" fails to capture that Simmons and Brawley, amidst the school controversies of the 1880s, advanced the movement toward national black denominational hegemony through their presidency of the American National Baptist Convention. In actuality, the black Baptist convention movement was never anti-white, nor did advocates of black-controlled schools call for a rejection of white financial assistance. Separatists and so-called cooperationists both wanted whites' assistance without white control of black institutions. On the subject of "assistance without control," see Franklin, *Black Self-Determination*, 161–176; also see Williams, *Black Higher Education in Kentucky*, 131–137; McPherson, *Abolitionist Legacy*, 284–285; Washington, *Frustrated Fellowship*, 159–185; Fitts, *History of Black Baptists*, 73–84.

64. Boyd is quoted in McPherson, *Abolitionist Legacy*, 288–289.

65. E. K. Love, "The National Baptist Publishing House," *National Baptist Magazine* (October 1896–January 1897): 260–267.

66. NBC, *Journal of the Twentieth Annual Session of the National Baptist Convention, Held in Richmond, Virginia, September 12–17, 1900* (Nashville: National Baptist Publishing Board, 1900), 191. For a listing of the schools supported by black Baptists in 1902, see William Edward Burghardt Du Bois, ed., *The Negro Church* (Atlanta: Atlanta University Press, 1903), 117–119.

67. Selena Sloan Butler, "Heredity," *Spelman Messenger*, June 1897, quoted in Cynthia Neverdon-Morton, *Afro-American Women of the South and the Advancement of the Race, 1895–1925* (Knoxville: University of Tennessee Press, 1989), 4.

68. I. Garland Penn notes that Johnson launched *Joy* in 1887 as "a journal in which the writers among our people, especially females, could publish stories, poetry, and matter of a purely literary character, for the perusal of young people." I. Garland Penn, *The Afro-American Press and Its Editors* (Springfield, Mass.: Willey, 1891), 422.

69. A. E. Johnson, "Some Parallels of History," *National Baptist Magazine*, 7 (July 1899): 4.

70. Ibid., 5.

71. Cooper, *Voice from the South*, 75.

72. Mary Cook's letter appears in *Home Mission Echo* (November 1885): 3; Helen Whipple to Mary Burdette, 1 June 1891, Mary Burdette File, Correspondence, 1891–1898, WABHMS Archives, American Baptist Archives Center, Valley Forge, Pa.; Willis Anthony Holmes, *History, Anniversary, Celebration, and Financial Report of*

the Work of the Phillips, Lee, and Monroe County Missionary District Association (Helena, Ark.: Helena World Job Print, 1890), 90.

73. Brawley, ed., *Negro Baptist Pulpit*, 283.

74. *Fourth Annual Session, Alabama, 1889*, 16. Women in other states recorded similar impressions. In 1894 the women's convention of West Virginia resolved that ministers should devote two sermons per year to the specific interests of women's societies. At the annual gathering of Mississippi women in 1889, a delegate from Grenada, Mississippi, protested against male discouragement of women's church work. The speaker, citing biblical precedents for women's participation, criticized ministers who opposed women's societies but still expected their financial contributions. *Proceedings of the Sixteenth Annual Meeting of the West Virginia Baptist State Convention, Held with the First Baptist Church, Huntington, West Virginia, May 31–June 2, 1894* (n.p., n.d.), 10; *Minutes of the Third Annual Session of the Women's General Baptist Missionary Society of Mississippi, Held with the New Zion Baptist Church, Magnolia, Mississippi, October 21–25, 1889* (Starkville, Miss.: A. G. O'Brien and Son, 1890), 10–11.

75. Berkeley, "The Politics of Black Education in Memphis," 215–217.

76. Virginia W. Broughton, *Twenty Years' Experience of a Missionary* (Chicago: The Pony Press Publishers, 1907), 7–14; Thomas O. Fuller, *History of the Negro Baptists of Tennessee* (Memphis: Haskins Print–Roger Williams College, 1936), 147.

77. Broughton, *Twenty Years' Experience*, 13, 15–18.

78. Fuller, *Negro Baptists of Tennessee*, 119; Broughton, *Twenty Years' Experience*, 20–22; Wheeler, *Uplifting the Race*, 105.

79. Broughton, *Twenty Years' Experience*, 34–35.

80. Ibid., 31.

81. Fuller, *Negro Baptists of Tennessee*, 238.

82. Broughton, *Twenty Years' Experience*, 60, 63; also see Broughton's report to the WBHMS in BHMM, 14 (February 1892): 74.

83. Broughton emphasized that the women's movement was divinely inspired, and thus the opposition was inspired by the devil: "While men opposed and Satan strove our progress to retard, God was with us and was only permitting those trials our dross to consume and our gold to refine." Broughton, *Twenty Years' Experience*, 38–39.

84. Ibid., 35, 38.

85. Ibid., 31, 33–39.

86. Ibid., 24, 35; BHMM, 14 (February 1892): 74. WABHMS, *Fifteenth Annual Report of the Woman's American Baptist Home Mission Society with the Report of the Annual Meeting, Held in Temple Church, Dorchester, Massachusetts, May 3–4, 1893* (Boston: C. H. Simonds, 1893), 36–37; WABHMS, *Sixteenth Annual Report of the Woman's American Baptist Home Mission Society, with the Report of the Annual Meeting Held in Warren Avenue Baptist Church, Boston, Massachusetts, May 2–3, 1894* (Boston: C. H. Simonds, 1894), 46; WABHMS, *Seventeenth Annual Report of the Woman's American Baptist Home Mission Society, with the Report of the Annual Meeting Held in First Baptist Church, Malden, Massachusetts, May 1–2, 1895* (Boston: C. H. Simonds, 1895), 43.

87. See report from Mrs. V. W. Broughton of the Bible and Normal Institute, Memphis, in *Home Mission Echo* (May 1891), 5; also Mary Burdette, "Our Southern

Field," in *Tidings* (January 1894): 9; also see letter from Broughton and the report of Emily Vann, printed under "Bible and Normal Institute," *Home Mission Echo* (February 1894): 9.

88. Thomas Fuller, historian of Tennessee's black Baptists, described the Bible Bands of the late nineteenth century: "They were prompt in attendance and enthusiastic in the study of the lessons. Some pastors, noting this interest, became alarmed at seeing so many women with Bibles in their hands and asked them, 'What are you women doing with so many books? Are you going to preach?' The reply was, 'No, we are not going to preach, but we are going to learn so much about the Bible that nobody can preach to us but a real preacher.'" Fuller, *Negro Baptists of Tennessee*, 238.

89. Broughton, *Twenty Years' Experience*, 24, 35–38, 42.

90. Ibid., 41. See gleanings from Mary Burdette's trip to the South and her report of Broughton's work in "Our Southern Field," *Tidings* (January 1894): 9.

91. Jordan, *Negro Baptist History*, 87–88, 123–124.

92. See the constitution and by-laws of representative state conventions: *Seventh Annual Session, Alabama, 1892*, 1; *Minutes of the Seventh Session of the Baptist Women's Educational Convention Held with the Fifth Street Baptist Church, Louisville, Kentucky, October 10–14, 1889* (Louisville: American Baptist, 1890), 5; *Minutes of the New England Baptist Missionary Convention, Women's Missionary Bible Band, and the New England Baptist Sunday School Convention, June 17–22, 1896* (Washington, D.C.: Baptist Magazine Print, n.d.), 39; *The Seventeenth Annual Meeting of the West Virginia Baptist State Convention, and the Second Annual Meeting of Its Auxiliaries, the West Virginia Baptist State Sunday School Convention, and the West Virginia Baptist Women's Convention, Held at St. Albans, West Virginia, May 30–June 1 1895* (Charleston, W.Va.: Zion Watchman, 1895), 6–7; *Third Annual Session, Mississippi, 1889*, 21.

93. *Seventh Annual Session, Alabama, 1892*, 11–13; *First through Fifth Sessions, Kentucky, 1883–1887*, 13–20; *Eleventh Anniversary of the Baptist Educational, Missionary, and Sunday School Convention of South Carolina, Held with the Calvary Baptist Church, Columbia, May 4–8, 1887* (Greenville, S.C.: Hoyt and Keys, Book and Job Printers, 1888), 17.

94. *Seventh Annual Session, Alabama, 1892*, 1.

95. ANBC, *Journal, Sermons and Lectures, 1888*, 45.

96. Sophia Shanks, "The Woman's Association: What It is Doing," in the *Journal of the Thirty-seventh Annual Session of the Arkansas Missionary Baptist Convention, Held with the First Baptist Church, Little Rock, November 23–28, 1904*, 48–49; "Appeal to the Baptist Sisterhood of Missouri," *Missouri Messenger*, 26 January 1900.

97. Mamie E. Steward, "Woman in the Church," *National Baptist Magazine*, 6 (August-October 1898): 147–148.

98. *Minutes of the First Annual Session of the Women's General Baptist Missionary Society of Mississippi, Held with the Mt. Zion Baptist Church, Sardis, Mississippi, October 19–24, 1887* (Jackson: Sword and Shield Book Print, 1887), 5; *Minutes of the Second Annual Session of the Women's General Baptist Missionary Society of Mississippi, Held with the Kosciusko Baptist Church, Kosciusko, Mississippi, November 21–24, 1888* (Jackson: Baptist Messenger Print, 1880), 15–16; *Third Annual Session, Mississippi, 1889*, 6–7, 10.

99. *First through Fifth Sessions, Kentucky, 1883–1887*, 21–25; Reid, *History of Colored Baptists in Alabama*, 92.

100. See, for example, "Religion and Business," *National Baptist Headlight*, 19 October 1894; "Negro Development in History," *Christian Banner*, 12 January 1900; "Condition of the Negro South," *Baptist Headlight*, 18 July 1894; ANBC, *Journal and Lectures, 1887*, 65–66; ANBC, *Journal, Sermons, and Lectures, 1888*, 68–70.

101. "Programme," *Baptist Headlight*, 15 October 1893; *Baptist Headlight*, 1 August 1894; "Our State Meeting," *National Baptist World*, 26 October 1894.

102. ANBC, *Journal and Lectures, 1887*, 65–66; "Woman and Home," *National Baptist World*, 21 September 1894.

103. *Baptist Headlight*, 1 October 1893; *National Baptist World*, 23 November 1894; *National Baptist World*, 12 October 1894.

104. *Baptist Headlight*, 15 September 1893.

105. Harriet M. Morris, "Our Home Circle—Which Shall It Be," *Baptist Vanguard*, 14 October 1892.

106. *Sixth Annual Session, Alabama, 1891*, 23–24; *Seventh Annual Session, Alabama, 1892*, 10; Penn, *Afro-American Press*, 396–397.

107. See the *Baptist Woman's Era*, 15 July 1900.

108. Writing under the pen name "Iola," Ida B. Wells edited the column "Home" in Simmons's magazine *Our Women and Children*. See ANBC, *Journal and Lectures, 1887*, 65; Alfreda M. Duster, ed., *Crusade for Justice: The Autobiography of Ida B. Wells* (Chicago: University of Chicago Press, 1970), 32.

109. See the advertisement for *Our Women and Children* on the back cover of ANBC, *Journal and Lectures, 1887*; Simmons, *Men of Mark*, 46; Penn, *Afro-American Press*, 366–427.

110. Penn, *Afro-American Press*, 366–374, 376–381; *Seventh Session, Kentucky, 1889*, 16.

111. [Miss] Hardie Martin, "How the Church Can Best Help the Condition of the Masses," *National Baptist Magazine* (October 1896–January 1897): 279–281; Cook, "Our Women," *National Baptist Magazine* (July 1895): 137–139.

112. "Women's Baptist Home Mission Society," BHMM, 14 (February 1892): 74.

4. Unlikely Sisterhood

1. See "From Miss Cook, Louisville, Ky.," letter dated 29 January 1885, in *Home Mission Echo* (February 1885): 5; Woman's American Baptist Home Mission Society (hereafter, WABHMS), *Fifth Annual Report of the Woman's American Baptist Home Mission Society with the Report of the Annual Meeting, Held in Warren Avenue Church, Boston, May 9, 1883* (Boston: G. J. Stiles, 1883), 25; WABHMS, *Seventh Annual Report of the Woman's American Baptist Home Mission Society, Held in the Baptist Church, Old Cambridge, Massachusetts, May 7, 1885* (Boston: C. H. Simonds, 1885), 29; WABHMS, *Eighth Annual Report of the Woman's American Baptist Home Mission Society, Held in the Baptist Church, Newton, Massachusetts, May 5, 1886* (Boston: C. H. Simonds, 1886), 38; *Baptist Home Mission Monthly (BHMM)*, 5 (July 1883): 160.

2. See Henry McNeil Turner for biographical information on Simmons in Introduction to William J. Simmons, *Men of Mark: Eminent, Progressive and Rising* (Cleveland: Geo. M. Rewell, 1887), 40–63.

3. Mary Cook, "What the Colored Baptists are Doing," *Home Mission Echo* (November 1890): 3–4; Cook, "A Tribute to the Memory of Rev. William J. Simmons," *Home Mission Echo* (December 1890): 3; also see reports from the southern field in *Home Mission Echo* (January 1886): 6; *Home Mission Echo* (February 1888): 4.

4. Letter from Mary Cook published in *Home Mission Echo* (November 1885): 3.

5. Rayford W. Logan, *The Negro in American Life and Thought: The Nadir, 1877–1901* (New York: Dial Press, 1954); August Meier, *Negro Thought in America, 1880–1915: Racial Ideologies in the Age of Booker T. Washington* (Ann Arbor: University of Michigan Press, 1963); Louis Harlan, *Booker T. Washington: The Making of a Black Leader, 1856–1901* (New York: Oxford University Press, 1972).

6. Jacqueline Jones, *Labor of Love, Labor of Sorrow: Black Women, Work, and the Family from Slavery to the Present* (New York: Random House, 1985), 91; Jones, *Soldiers of Light and Love: Northern Teachers and Georgia Blacks, 1865–1873* (Chapel Hill: University of North Carolina Press, 1980), 191–208; James McPherson, *Abolitionist Legacy: From Reconstruction to the NAACP* (Princeton, N.J.: Princeton University Press, 1975), 146–148; Robert C. Morris, *Reading, 'Riting and Reconstruction: The Education of Freedmen in the South, 1861–1873* (Chicago: University of Chicago Press, 1981), 243–249; James D. Anderson, *The Education of Blacks in the South, 1860–1935* (Chapel Hill: University of North Carolina Press, 1988), 33–78.

7. Louis Harlan, *Booker T. Washington: Wizard of Tuskegee, 1901–1915* (New York: Oxford University Press, 1983), 130, 133–142, 197–199.

8. McPherson, *Abolitionist Legacy*, 143–145.

9. Although McPherson does not mention the role of women, the American Baptist Home Mission Society recognized their important role at the time. In 1878 the ABHMS observed women's numerical preponderance in the church and their essential role in the Society's work of evangelization, admitting that women "by their active spiritual sympathy, and by their facility for organization, are capable more than the other sex, of giving to the missionary cause the universality of cooperation which is so essential to the full vigor of its work." By 1882 the ABHMS surveyed its fifty-year history since its inception in 1832 and acknowledged that women constituted 375 of the 693 persons who made bequests to the treasury during the society's first forty-six years. See McPherson, *Abolitionist Legacy*, 148; also see American Baptist Home Mission Society (hereafter, ABHMS), *Forty-sixth Annual Report of the American Baptist Home Mission Society, Convened in the First Baptist Church, Cleveland, Ohio, May 29, 1878* (New York: Baptist Home Mission Rooms, 1878), 47.

10. See, for example, Virginia Lieson Brereton and Christa Ressmeyer Klein, "American Women in Ministry: A History of Protestant Beginning Points," in Rosemary Ruether and Eleanor McLaughlin, eds., *Women of Spirit: Female Leadership in the Jewish and Christian Traditions* (New York: Simon and Schuster, 1979), 301–332; Margaret Lamberts Bendroth, "The Social Dimension of Woman's Sphere: The Rise of Women's Organizations in Late Nineteenth Century Protestantism" (Ph.D. dissertation, Johns Hopkins University, 1985); Bendroth, "Women and Missions:

Conflict and Changing Roles in the Presbyterian Church in the United States of America, 1870–1935," *American Presbyterians*, 65 (Spring 1987): 49–59; Lois A. Boyd and R. Douglas Brackenridge, *Presbyterian Women in America: Two Centuries of a Quest for Status* (Westport, Conn.: Greenwood Press, 1983), 15–58; Mary S. Donovan, *A Different Call: Women's Ministries in the Episcopal Church, 1850–1920* (Wilton, Conn.: Morehouse–Barlow, 1986); Rosemary Skinner Keller, "Creating a Sphere for Women in the Church," *Methodist History*, 18 (January 1980): 83–94; John Patrick McDowell, *The Social Gospel in the South: The Women's Home Mission Movement in the Methodist Episcopal Church, South, 1886–1939* (Baton Rouge: Louisiana State University Press, 1982), 116–130.

11. See the concept of "woman's work for woman" in Jacqueline Dowd Hall, *Revolt against Chivalry: Jesse Daniel Ames and the Women's Campaign against Lynching* (New York: Columbia University Press, 1979), 67; Mary E. Frederickson, "Shaping a New Society: Methodist Women and Industrial Reform in the South, 1880–1940," in Hilah F. Thomas and Rosemary Skinner Keller, eds., *Women in New Worlds: Historical Perspectives on the Wesleyan Tradition* (Nashville: Abingdon Press, 1981), 345–361; also see Bertha Grinnell Judd, *Fifty Golden Years: The First Half-Century of the Women's Baptist Home Missionary Society, 1877–1927* (New York: WABHMS, 1927); Women's Baptist Home Mission Society (hereafter, WBHMS), *A Picture Gallery: Women's Baptist Home Mission Society* (Chicago: WBHMS, 1901), 45; also see Frances K. Davidson, "The Woman of Yesterday and Today," *Tidings* (August 1900): 12–16.

12. M. E. D. Trowbridge, *History of Baptists in Michigan* (n.p.: Michigan Baptist State Convention, 1909), 208; ABHMS, *Forty-seventh Annual Report of the American Baptist Home Mission Society, Convened in the First Baptist Church, Saratoga Springs, New York, May 29, 1879* (New York: Baptist Home Mission Rooms, 1879), 55–57; ABHMS, *Forty-eighth Annual Report of the American Baptist Home Mission Society, Convened in the First Baptist Church, Saratoga Springs, New York, May 26, 1880* (New York: Baptist Home Mission Rooms, 1880), 51; ABHMS, *Baptist Home Missions in North America, Jubilee Volume* (New York: Baptist Home Mission Rooms, 1883), 415, 518–522, 552.

13. Judd, *Fifty Golden Years*, 5–6, 238; Eleanor Hull, *Women Who Carried the Good News* (Valley Forge, Pa.: Judson Press, 1975), 11–12.

14. U.S. Census Office, Department of the Interior, *Census Bulletin, Statistics of Churches*, No. 376 (13 March 1893), 3–13; Charles Octavius Boothe, *The Cyclopedia of the Colored Baptists of Alabama* (Birmingham: Alabama Publishing Company, 1895), 250–251; Thomas O. Fuller, *History of the Negro Baptists of Tennessee* (Nashville: Haskins Print–Roger Williams College, 1936), 93–110; William Hicks, *History of Louisiana Negro Baptists* (Nashville: National Baptist Publication Board, n.d.), 31–33; Willis Anthony Holmes, *History, Anniversary Celebration, and Financial Report of the Work of the Phillips, Lee and Monroe County Missionary District Association* (Helena, Ark.: Helena World Job Print, 1890), 12–35; Charles H. Parrish, ed., *Golden Jubilee of the General Association of Colored Baptists in Kentucky* (Louisville: Mayes Printing Company, 1915), 89–125.

15. Mary V. Cook, "Work for Baptist Women," in Edward M. Brawley, ed., *The Negro Baptist Pulpit* (Philadelphia: American Baptist Publication Society, 1890),

279–280; Virginia W. Broughton, *Twenty Years' Experience of a Missionary* (Chicago: The Pony Press Publishers, 1907), 7–14.

16. See Joanna Moore to Miss Burdette, 2 September, n.d., Mary Burdette Files, Correspondence, 1891–1898, WABHMS Archives, American Baptist Archives Center, Valley Forge, Pa. (hereafter cited as "Mary Burdette Files, ABAC, VF"). While no date is given on the letter from Moore, all of the correspondence in this file is dated from the late 1880s to the early 1890s.

17. Report from Mrs. V. W. Broughton of Bible and Normal Institute, Memphis, in *Home Mission Echo* (May 1891), 5; Anna Barkley to Burdette, 1 April 1891, Mary Burdette Files, ABAC, VF; also see *Tidings* (April 1892): 9. For similar activities on the part of African Methodist Episcopal women see Kathleen C. Berkeley, "'Colored Ladies also Contributed': Black Women's Activities from Benevolence to Social Welfare, 1866–1896," in Walter J. Fraser, Jr., R. Frank Saunders, Jr., and John L. Wakelyn, eds., *The Web of Southern Social Relations: Women, Family and Education* (Athens: University of Georgia Press, 1985), 181–184, 188–189, 191–194.

18. Helen Jackson to Burdette, 2 April 1891; Helen Whipple to Burdette, 1 June 1891, Mary Burdette Letters, ABAC, VF.

19. "Voices from the Field," *Tidings* (May 1885): 1.

20. WBHMS, "Work among Afro-Americans," *Tidings* (October 1897): 4–25; WBHMS, *Woman's Work in Helping to Solve the Negro Problem* (Chicago: Women's Baptist Home Mission Society, 1906), 8–12, 65–68; ABHMS, *Baptist Home Missions in North America*, 552; "Plan of Cooperation for Bible and Industrial Education of Young Women in Freedmen Schools," BHMM, 4 (August 1882): 222; "Women's Baptist Home Mission Society," BHMM, 3 (November 1881): 248; BHMM, 4 (May 1882): 134–135.

21. *Minutes of the Arkansas Baptist Sunday School Convention and the Women's State Association, and the Union District Sunday School Convention, 1895* (Little Rock, Ark.: Vanguard Print, 1895), 9.

22. In a letter dated 21 October 1884, S. A. Mial and Lizzie Neily, respective secretary and president of the North Carolina women's convention, notified the ministerial-dominated state convention: "Dear Brethren—We, the Sisters of our denomination, have organized ourselves into what is known as the Woman's Baptist Home Mission Convention of the State of North Carolina for the purpose of aiding you in the work of Missions, especially among the women." *Minutes of the Eighteenth Annual Session of the Baptist State Convention of North Carolina, Held with the First Baptist Church, Goldsboro, October 22–27, 1884* (Raleigh: Baptist Standard Print, 1884); *Hope*, 13 (November 1899): 225; *Worker's Guide for the Woman's Baptist Home and Foreign Missionary Convention of North Carolina* (Raleigh: Capital Printing Company, 1939), 7–8.

23. *Hope*, 13 (November 1899): 225; "Colored People," *Tidings* (November 1892): 7; Broughton, *Twenty Years' Experience*, 41; "Our Southern Field," *Tidings* (January 1894): 12.

24. E. Franklin Frazier, *The Negro Church* (New York: Schocken Books, 1964), 36. See also Peter J. Paris, *The Social Teaching of the Black Churches* (Philadelphia: Fortress Press, 1985); W. E. Burghardt Du Bois, ed., *The Negro Church* (Atlanta: Atlanta

University Press, 1903); Carter G. Woodson, *History of the Negro Church* (Washington, D.C.: The Associated Publishers, 1921); James H. Cone, *God of the Oppressed* (New York: Seabury Press, 1975); Cornel West, *Prophesy Deliverance! An Afro-American Revolutionary Christianity* (Philadelphia: Westminster Press, 1982).

25. Mary Burdette, "Our Southern Field," in *Tidings* (January 1894): 5–6.

26. The "politics of respectability" will be analyzed in terms of its conservative and progressive intent in Chapter 7.

27. For a discussion of social reform efforts that attempted to transform the home furnishing tastes of the white working class into models that more closely resembled the middle class, see Lizabeth A. Cohen, "Embellishing a Life of Labor: An Interpretation of the Material Culture of American Working-Class Homes, 1885–1915," in Dell Upton and John Michael Vlach, eds., *Common Places: Readings in American Vernacular Architecture* (Athens: University of Georgia Press, 1986), 261–278.

28. Burdette, "Our Southern Field," 5.

29. Frances K. Davidson, "The Woman of Yesterday and Today," *Tidings* (August 1900): 14; Benjamin Brawley, *Women of Achievement* (Chicago: Woman's American Baptist Home Mission Society, 1919), 5–6.

30. See her autobiography: Joanna P. Moore, *In Christ's Stead* (Chicago: Women's Baptist Home Mission Society, 1902), 26–27; ABHMS, *Baptist Home Missions in North America*, 517; also see the sketch written by Moore and published at the time of her death, "Joanna P. Moore—1832–1916," *Crisis*, 12 (August 1916): 177.

31. Moore later noted that there were "differences of opinion" between the men and women: "I said to our women, 'We will take our place in the church as workers together with God,' and said to our brethren, 'You find your place and then you will know we are not far apart.'" This statement, she admits, did not settle the question. See Moore, *In Christ's Stead*, 105, 131.

32. Moore wrote, "I have never seen the need of special schools, churches, railroads and laws for the Negro. It is an insult to humanity to treat him thus." See "Joanna P. Moore," *Crisis*, 177; Moore, *In Christ's Stead*, 106; ABHMS, *Baptist Home Missions in North America*, 517.

33. See the report of the executive board for the year ending 30 April 1878, WBHMS, *The Women's Baptist Home Mission Society, 1877 to 1882* (Chicago: R. R. Donnelly and Sons, 1883), 29–31; "Plan of Cooperation for Bible and Industrial Education of Young Women in Freedmen Schools," *BHMM*, 4 (August 1882): 222.

34. The "Parents' Pledge" superseded the "Mothers' Pledge" that the WBHMS had introduced earlier in its training schools. Moore emphasized that the black father must assume greater parental responsibility, which she believed had diminished, to some extent, because of slavery. However, she stated: "I'm a little afraid that in all races fathers too often shirk their part in the training of their children, though they may provide for their temporal wants." Moore, *In Christ's Stead*, 107–109, 143, 153, 159–166, 192–193; Moore, *For Mother* (Chicago: Women's Baptist Home Mission Society, 1916, first printed in 1894), 8–22; *Hope*, 15 (January 1901): 259–260; Hull, *Women Who Carried the Good News*, 16; Judd, *Fifty Golden Years*, 14–15.

35. See lesson on self-denial in *Hope*, 13 (February 1899):24; *Hope*, 14 (December 1900): 235.

36. *Hope*, 13 (January 1899): 17–19; *Hope*, 15 (January 1901): 259; *Christian Herald*, 10 July 1890, in Benjamin G. Brawley Papers, Moorland-Spingarn Research Center, Howard University; Simmons, *Men of Mark*, 419–421.

37. See Moore, *In Christ's Stead*, 153. See also the report of Belle Pettigrew, who met with black women attending a training school three days per week. She praised their commitment, for "some of these women depended upon their daily toil not only for their own support, but for dependent relations, yet they arrange with their employers so they can regularly attend the class sessions." *BHMM*, 9 (March 1887): 76.

38. Mary Cook wrote in 1894 that violence against blacks dictated that "our safety and protection will be in the most vigilant use of every advantage and opportunity we have in the thorough training of every boy and girl." She especially warned women to be "exceeding cautious in their conduct." See Mary V. Cook, "Our Women," *National Baptist Magazine*, 2 (July 1895): 137–139.

39. For discussion of blacks' views on training women to be good wives and mothers, see Beverly Guy-Sheftall, *Daughters of Sorrow: Attitudes toward Black Women, 1880–1920*, vol. 11 of *Black Women in United States History: From Colonial Times to the Present*, ed. Darlene Clark Hine (Brooklyn: Carlson Publishing, 1990), 73–75, 142–143.

40. See W. E. Burghardt Du Bois, "The Work of Negro Women in Society," *Spelman Messenger*, February 1902.

41. Frances E. W. Harper, *Iola Leroy, or Shadows Uplifted* (Philadelphia, 1893; rpt. New York: AMS, 1971), 161, 199.

42. Joanna Moore, "The 'White League' at Baton Rouge," *Home Mission Echo* (February 1891): 10–11. The article was reprinted from the Chicago *Standard*.

43. "Tennessee Baptist Conventions and Associations," *Hope*, 14 (October 1900): 199; Fuller, *Negro Baptists in Tennessee*, 147.

44. See "Joanna Moore," *Crisis*, 12 (August 1916): 177–178; American National Baptist Convention, *Journal, Sermons, and Lectures of the Third Anniversary of the American National Baptist Convention, Held with the Spruce Street Baptist Church, Nashville, September 23–24, 1888* (n.p., n.d.), 1, 27–28.

45. James R. Grossman, *Land of Hope: Chicago, Black Southerners, and the Great Migration* (Chicago: University of Chicago Press, 1989), 3–4, 13–20; Allan H. Spear, *Black Chicago: The Making of a Negro Ghetto, 1890–1920* (Chicago: University of Chicago Press, 1967), 5–11, 16–17, 129–145; David M. Katzman, *Before the Ghetto: Black Detroit in the Nineteenth Century* (Urbana: University of Illinois Press, 1973), 61–64; John Daniels, *In Freedom's Birthplace: A Study of Boston Negroes* (New York, 1914; rpt. New York: Negro Universities Press, 1968), 136–141, 458; Elizabeth Hafkin Pleck, *Black Migration and Poverty, Boston, 1865–1900* (New York: Academic Press, 1979), 43–90; Florette Henri, *Black Migration: Movement North, 1900–1920* (Garden City, N.Y.: Anchor Press/Doubleday, 1975), 50–51, 83; Daniel M. Johnson and Rex R. Campbell, *Black Migration in America: A Social Demographic History* (Durham, N.C.: Duke University Press, 1981), 58, 65–73.

46. There were many examples of white women's support of black self-help. See the reports of William J. Simmons and Charles Purce, presidents of the State University at Louisville and Selma University, respectively, in *BHMM*, 5 (July 1883):

160; BHMM, 13 (September 1891): 266; Parrish, *Golden Jubilee*, 172–173; *Minutes of the Sixth Annual Session of the Baptist Women's Educational Convention of Kentucky, Held with the Green Street Church, Danville, Kentucky, September 14–17, 1888*, 8, 28; [Mrs.] James McWhinnie, *Historical Sketch of the Woman's American Baptist Home Mission Society from November 14, 1877 to April 30, 1894* (Boston: Press of S. G. Robinson, 1894), 21–22; WABHMS, *Thirteenth Annual Report of the Woman's American Baptist Home Mission Society, Held in the First Baptist Church, Cambridgeport, Massachusetts, May 6–7, 1891* (Boston: C. H. Simonds, 1891), 28.

47. See "Suggestions," *Home Mission Echo* (October 1886): 2–3.

48. "Joint Meeting of the Societies of the East and West at Washington," *Home Mission Echo* (June 1888): 2–3; "New England Echoes," in *Home Mission Echo* (August 1888): 4; also *Home Mission Echo* (January 1890): 4 and (July 1892): 4.

49. WBHMS, "Minutes of the Executive Board, March 5, 1895," in *Minutes 1881–1904*, 153; Broughton, *Twenty Years as a Missionary*, 40–41.

50. WABHMS, *Fifth Annual Report*, 1883, 26–29.

51. "New England Echoes," *Home Mission Echo* (August 1888).

52. WABHMS, *Seventh Annual Report*, 1885, 30.

53. Ibid., 29.

54. See Sophia B. Packard to A. J. Winterton, Madison Avenue Baptist Church, N.Y., 17 January 1890; Packard to Winterton, 27 February 1890; Packard to Winterton, 2 April 1890; Emma De Lamotta to Dear Friend, 31 March 1890; Emma De Lamotta to the Superintendent and Sunday School, Madison Avenue Baptist Church, 13 June 1890. Emma De Lamotta Biography File at ABAC, VF.

55. "Bureau of Information," *Home Mission Echo* (February 1894): 8; *Home Mission Echo* (October 1887): 2.

56. *Tidings*, June 1892, 3; WBHMS, *A Picture Gallery: Women's Baptist Home Mission Society* (Chicago: WBHMS, 1901), 3–4; WABHMS, *Eighth Annual Report*, 1886, 11; WABHMS, *Twenty-first Annual Report of the WABHMS with the Report of the Annual Meeting held in the Free Street Baptist Church, Portland, Maine, May 3–4, 1899* (Boston: C. H. Simonds, 1899), 22.

57. See "Questions for Mission Bands," *Home Mission Echo* (July 1885): 6; (February 1887): 11; (March 1887): 11; and in (May 1887): 11.

58. See Albert J. Raboteau, *Slave Religion: The "Invisible Institution" in the Antebellum South* (New York: Oxford University Press, 1978), 196–197; Walter H. Brooks, "The Priority of the Silver Bluff Church and Its Promotion," *Journal of Negro History*, 7 (April 1922): 172–196.

59. One such example of a multifaceted urban edifice in 1890 was the Nineteenth Street Baptist Church in Washington, D.C., led by the Reverend Walter H. Brooks. For discussion of this, see Walter H. Brooks, "Progress in the Number and Character of Church Edifices," *Home Mission Echo* (March 1898): 13.

60. "Gleanings from the Conference," *Tidings* (August 1888): 4.

61. See the reference to Reynolds and Dyer in dialogue in "Our Mission Schools," *Home Mission Echo* (February 1894): 6.

62. See A. E. Gray's reports in "Echoes from the Field," *Home Mission Echo* (February 1887):3–4 and (June 1887): 7.

63. Ibid., 7.

64. WABHMS, *Eighth Annual Report, 1886*, 4–5; "Annual Meeting," *Home Mission Echo* (June 1886): 3.

65. "Spelman Seminary," *Home Mission Echo* (April 1886): 2–3; for reprint of article from the *Spelman Messenger*, see "First Impression," in *Home Mission Echo* (December 1886): 4; also see reference to the extracts from the *Spelman Messenger* having been read at the northern women's meetings in *Home Mission Echo* (January 1888): 6.

66. *Home Mission Echo* (February 1888): 4–7.

67. *Home Mission Echo* (January 1888): 3.

68. For example, resolutions from the Kentucky black Baptist women's society were printed in *Home Mission Echo* (February 1888): 9–10; see also Mary Cook, "What the Colored Baptists Are Doing," *Home Mission Echo* (November 1890): 3–4.

69. Cook, "Oppression of the Colored Race," *Home Mission Echo* (August 1892): 3, NAACP, *Thirty Years of Lynching in the United States, 1889–1918* (New York, 1919; rpt. New York: Arno Press and the *New York Times*, 1969), 29.

70. "Earth Exchanged for Heaven," *Tidings* (February 1893): 4; for response to lynching in Mississippi, see report of Miss Scott in *Tidings* (August 1892): 10.

71. The resolution in protest of lynching formed part of a series of resolutions. Lynching followed intemperance and Mormonism. WABHMS, *Twenty-first Annual Report, 1899*, 24.

72. See Reynolds's discussion of integrated railroad cars in *Home Mission Echo* (June 1888): 3.

73. Rachel C. Mather, "Our Africa," *Home Mission Echo* (October 1887): 5.

74. See, for example, Robert Stuart MacArthur, *Current Questions for Thinking Men* (Philadelphia: American Baptist Publication Society, 1898), 381, 387.

75. Mather, "Our Africa," 5.

76. "Report of the Joint Meeting of the Women's Home Mission Societies," *Home Mission Echo* (July 1894): 3–4.

77. One article referred to immigrants as "the off-scourings of the whole earth" who "mass themselves in a thousand hiding places." See Mrs. J. Chapman, "Am I Needed," *Tidings* (April 1892): 12. The *Home Mission Echo* similarly highlighted a strong strain of anti-Catholicism when it warned: "To-day our country is in danger, dire and dreadful as the War of the Rebellion. Catholicism, Infidelity, Ritualism, are spreading darkness and desolation through our land." See *Home Mission Echo* (May 1885): 1. For attacks on Catholicism, parochial schools, and the liquor traffic in the *Home Mission Echo*, see "Editorial Notes Column—A Question of the Hour" (October 1888): 1–2; "Romanism and the Rum Traffic" (December 1890): 11; "Report of the Joint Meeting of the Women's Home Mission Societies" (July 1894): 3–4; and "Romanism in America" (April 1894): 6–7 and (April 1891): 2–3.

78. See generally Herbert G. Gutman, *Work, Culture, and Society in Industrializing America* (New York: Vintage Books, 1977). Also see Gutman's essays in Ira Berlin, ed., *Power and Culture: Essays on the American Working Class* (New York: Pantheon Books, 1987); Alan Trachtenberg, *The Incorporation of America: Culture and Society in the Gilded Age* (New York: Hill and Wang, 1982).

79. For discussion of peaceful gospel warfare see editorial column, "Our Country's Growth," *Home Mission Echo* (September 1888): 1–2; see report of Mrs. J. N. Chase of New Hampshire, in WABHMS, *Seventh Annual Report, 1885*, 34; also Margaret

McWhinnie, "Our Foreign Population, delivered at the Joint Meeting of the Women's
Home Mission Societies," *Home Mission Echo* (July 1894), 6–7.

80. Mather, "Our Africa," 5.

81. "Report of Miss Scott in Vicksburg," *Tidings* (July 1892): 9.

82. "Anglo-Africans," *Tidings* (March 1893): 7.

83. M. C. Reynolds, "The Work and the Workers," *Home Mission Echo* (November
1891): 6; also Chapman, "Am I Needed," 12.

84. Moore gave five "country pastors" money to spend two weeks at Leland
University in New Orleans and to spend a Sunday at a church she considered
intellectually enlightening. However, the black ministers arranged to speak at churches
that Moore deemed "ignorant African churches." Thus she persuaded the ministers
to abandon their plan and accompany her to the Sunday-school of the First Baptist
Church (white). See "An Interesting Incident," *Tidings* (May 1885): 2.

85. WABHMS, *Eighth Annual Report, 1886*, 37.

86. See reports from the states in WABHMS, *Seventh Annual Report, 1885*, 29,
38–39; WABHMS, *Eighth Annual Report, 1886*, 36–37.

87. WABHMS, *Eleventh Annual Report of the Woman's American Baptist Home
Mission Society with the Report of the Annual Meeting Held in Perkins Street Baptist
Church, Somerville, Mass., May 8, 1889* (Boston: C. H. Simonds, 1889), 22–23.

88. For Uxbridge women see reports from states in *Home Mission Echo* (January
1888): 7–9; for quilt see WABHMS, *Seventh Annual Report, 1885*, 27.

89. See, for example, "Self-Denial Week," *Home Mission Echo* (March 1888): 3 and
(May 1888): 3.

90. See the letter to the editor "My Dear Boy Friends," *Home Mission Echo* (June
1886): 9.

91. Fannie Allen, "A True Incident," *Tidings* (February 1892): 23–24.

92. See the column "Children's Corner," where the magazine's editor, Anna Sargent
Hunt, refers to herself as "Aunt Annie." Also note letters from children expressing
appreciation for learning about black children and children of other religions and
cultures. "Children's Corner," *Home Mission Echo* (September 1885): 7.

93. See Cousin Lulu to "Dear Young Friends," *Home Mission Echo* (February 1885):
4; also see reference to "Cousin Carrie," graduate of Spelman in the Class of 1888, in
Home Mission Echo (February 1888): 10; and Cousin Carrie, "Children's Exchange,"
Spelman Messenger, February 1888.

94. "Baby Department," *Baptist Woman's Era*, 15 October 1900; and "Children's
Column," *Home Mission Echo* (September 1885): 5.

95. Anna Julia Cooper, *A Voice from the South* (Xenia, Ohio, 1892; rpt. New York:
Negro Universities Press, 1969), 31.

5. Feminist Theology, 1880–1900

1. Peter Randolph, *From Slave Cabin to the Pulpit: The Autobiography of Rev. Peter
Randolph* (Boston: James H. Earle, Publisher, 1893), p. 89. Charles O. Boothe, *The
Cyclopedia of the Colored Baptists of Alabama* (Birmingham: Alabama Publishing
Company, 1895), 252; also see Jacqueline Jones, *Labor of Love, Labor of Sorrow: Black*

Women, Work, and the Family from Slavery to the Present (New York: Random House, 1985), 67.

2. Peter J. Paris, *The Social Teaching of the Black Churches* (Philadelphia: Fortress Press: 1985), 11–13.

3. Mary V. Cook, "Work for Baptist Women," in Edward M. Brawley, ed., *The Negro Baptist Pulpit* (Philadelphia: The American Baptist Publication Society, 1890), 271–285; American National Baptist Convention (hereafter ANBC), *Journal and Lectures of the Second Anniversary of the 1887 American National Baptist Convention, Held with the Third Baptist Church, Mobile, Ala., August 25–28, 1887* (n.p., n.d.), 57.

4. Rosemary Ruether and Eleanor McLaughlin, eds., *Women of Spirit: Female Leadership in the Jewish and Christian Traditions* (New York: Simon and Schuster, 1979), 19; also see this argument applied to white women during the Second Great Awakening in Carroll Smith-Rosenberg, "The Cross and the Pedestal: Women, Anti-Ritualism, and the Emergence of the American Bourgeoisie," in Smith-Rosenberg, *Disorderly Conduct: Visions of Gender in Victorian America* (New York: Oxford University Press, 1986), 129–164.

5. Rufus Perry traced the ancestry of black Americans to the biblical Cushites, who were the descendants of Cush, Ham's eldest son. According to Perry, the Cushites were the ancient Ethiopians and indigenous Egyptians whose history exemplified prowess in medicine, war, art, and religious thought. Identifying the Cushite leaders of the Bible, Perry considered the greatness of the African past to be the foundation stone of the African American's future. See Rufus L. Perry, *The Cushites, or the Descendants of Ham as Found in the Sacred Scriptures and in the Writings of Ancient Historians and Poets from Noah to the Christian Era* (Springfield, Mass.: Willey, 1893), 17–18, 158–161.

6. Caroline Walker Bynum, Stevan Harrell, and Paula Richman, eds., *Gender and Religion: On the Complexity of Symbols* (Boston: Beacon Press, 1986), 15–16.

7. Caroline Bynum argues similarly with regard to the appropriation and interpretation of symbols: "Even when men and women have used the same symbols and rituals, they may have invested them with different meanings and different ways of meaning." Ibid., 16; also Rita Felski, *Beyond Feminist Aesthetics: Feminist Literature and Social Change* (Cambridge, Mass.: Harvard University Press, 1989), 161–162, 179.

8. Marilyn Richardson, ed., *Maria W. Stewart: America's First Black Woman Political Writer* (Bloomington: Indiana University Press, 1987), 9.

9. Ibid., 70.

10. See Kathleen Berkeley's discussion of the Broughton case. Berkeley argues that the case was more than simply one of gender discrimination, but a power struggle between the white superintendent of schools and a black member of the school board. Kathleen C. Berkeley, "The Politics of Black Education in Memphis, Tennessee, 1868–1891," in Rick Ginsberg and David N. Plank, eds., *Southern Cities, Southern Schools: Public Education in the Urban South* (Westport, Conn.: Greenwood Press, 1990), 215–217.

11. Broughton was elected to office in the Woman's Convention, Auxiliary of the National Baptist Convention, U.S.A., when it was organized in 1900. She held the office of recording secretary in this organization, which represented more than one million black women across the United States. See National Baptist Convention,

Journal of the Twentieth Annual Session of the National Baptist Convention, Held in Richmond, Virginia, September 12–17, 1900 (Nashville: National Baptist Publishing Board, 1900), 195–196. See also Thomas O. Fuller, *History of the Negro Baptists of Tennessee* (Memphis: Haskins Print–Roger Williams College, 1936), 238.

12. Virginia Broughton, *Women's Work, as Gleaned from the Women of the Bible, and Bible Women of Modern Times* (Nashville: National Baptist Publishing Board, 1904), 3, 23, 36.

13. I. Garland Penn, *The Afro-American Press and Its Editors* (Springfield, Mass.: Willey, 1891), 367–374; G. R. Richings, *Evidences of Progress among Colored People,* 12th ed. (Philadelphia: Geo. S. Ferguson, 1905), 224–227; Charles H. Parrish, ed., *Golden Jubilee of the General Association of Colored Baptists in Kentucky* (Louisville: Mayes Printing Company, 1915), 284–285; State University Catalogue, 1883–1884, Simmons University Records, Archives Department, University of Louisville.

14. Brawley, ed., *The Negro Baptist Pulpit,* 271–286; ANBC, *Journal and Lectures, 1887,* 49.

15. Penn, *The Afro-American Press,* 376–381.

16. See Mary Cook's eulogy of Lucy Wilmot Smith in *Home Mission Echo* (January 1890): 4–5; Penn, *Afro-American Press,* 378–381; Woman's American Baptist Home Mission Society (herafter WABHMS), *Twelfth Annual Report of the Woman's American Baptist Home Mission Society with the Report of the Annual Meeting, Held in the First Baptist Church, Hartford, Connecticut, May 7–8, 1890* (Boston: C. H. Simonds, 1890), 26.

17. Gordon D. Kaufman, *Systematic Theology: An Historicist Perspective* (New York: Charles Scribner's Sons, 1968), 57.

18. Virginia W. Broughton, *Twenty Years' Experience of a Missionary* (Chicago: The Pony Press Publishers, 1907), 32.

19. *Minutes of the Baptist Women's Educational Convention of Kentucky. First, Second, Third, Fourth, Fifth Sessions, 1883–1887* (Louisville: National Publishing Company, Print, 1887), 13.

20. Miss M. O'Keefe to Mary Burdette, 4 April 1891, Mary Burdette File, Correspondence 1891–1898, WABHMS Archives, American Baptist Archives Center, Valley Forge, Pa.

21. See report of Mary Burdette, "Our Southern Field," *Tidings* (January 1894): 9.

22. Mary Cook stated: "As the Bible is an iconoclastic weapon—it is bound to break down images of error that have been raised. As no one studies it so closely as the Baptists, their women shall take the lead." ANBC, *Journal and Lectures, 1887,* 49.

23. See introduction by Sue E. Houchins, *Spiritual Narratives* (New York: Oxford University Press, 1988), xxxii. *Spiritual Narratives* includes Virginia Broughton's autobiography, *Twenty Years' Experience of a Missionary,* along with those of Maria Stewart, Jarena Lee, Julia A. J. Foote, and Ann Plato.

24. ANBC, *Journal and Lectures, 1887,* 53–54; also see the evaluation of woman's influence by black Baptist minister William Bishop Johnson, editor of *The National Baptist Magazine,* when he stated: "Man may lead unnumbered hosts to victory, he may rend kingdoms, convulse nations, and drench battlefields in blood, but woman with heavenly smiles and pleasant words can outnumber, outweigh, and outstrip the

noblest efforts of a generation." William Bishop Johnson, *The Scourging of a Race, and Other Sermons and Addresses* (Washington, D.C.: Beresford Printer, 1904), 78.

25. Broughton, *Women's Work*, 5–7.

26. Ibid., 11–16.

27. Ibid., 25.

28. Mary Cook described Mary, the mother of Jesus, as "non-excelled maternal devotion." See ANBC, *Journal and Lectures, 1887*, 47–48.

29. Broughton, *Twenty Years' Experience*, 48–51.

30. Ibid., 42–45, 48.

31. Representative of the cult of domesticity, Oldham's version of home life advocated woman's complete attentiveness to her husband's needs. See ANBC, *Journal, Sermons, and Lectures, of the Third Anniversary of the American National Baptist Convention, Held with the Spruce Street Baptist Church, Nashville, September 23–24, 1888* (n.p., n.d.), 88, 90.

32. ANBC, *Journal and Lectures, 1887*, 48; Broughton, *Women's Work*, 31–32; Brawley, ed., *Negro Baptist Pulpit*, 273.

33. Broughton, *Twenty Years' Experience*, 46–47. Sue Houchins argues that Broughton and women like her drew confidence to transcend prescriptive gender roles from belief in the "privileged nature of their relationship with God." See introduction by Houchins, *Spiritual Narratives*, xxxiii.

34. The argument that attempted to restrict Paul's words exclusively to "immoral" women of Corinth was used by both black and white advocates of greater church roles for women. See, for example, Frances Willard, *Women in the Pulpit* (Boston: D. Lothrop, 1888), 159, 164; ANBC, *Journal and Lectures, 1887*, 48–50.

35. ANBC, *Journal and Lectures, 1887*, 49–50.

36. Broughton restricted women in these three cases since none of the twelve apostles had been women. Otherwise, she sought to encourage women by noting that of the seventy who followed Jesus, "we are not sure they were all men." A classic rejoinder to those who shared Broughton's view on the twelve apostles was Frances Willard's statement that no black or Gentile had been among the twelve, but this did not restrict men of either group from seeking ordination to the ministry. See Broughton, *Women's Work*, 39–41; Broughton, "Woman's Work," *National Baptist Magazine* (January 1894): 35; Willard, *Woman in the Pulpit*, 35.

37. Olive Bird Clanton was raised in Decatur, Illinois, where she obtained a high school education. Her husband was elected secretary of the American National Baptist Convention in 1886. In a biographical sketch of Solomon Clanton, William J. Simmons, then president of the American National Baptist Convention, described Olive Clanton as "one of the most discreet, amiable, and accomplished women in the country." See William J. Simmons, *Men of Mark: Eminent, Progressive and Rising* (Cleveland: Geo. M. Rewell, 1887), 419–421; ANBC, *Journal and Lectures, 1887*, 56–57.

38. ANBC, *Journal and Lectures, 1887*, 46, 55.

39. ANBC, *Minutes and Addresses of the American National Baptist Convention, Held at St. Louis, Mo., August 25–29, 1886 in the First Baptist Church* (Jackson, Miss.: J. J. Spelman, Publisher, 1886), 68–74.

40. ANBC, *Journal and Lectures*, *1887*, 50–53, 55–56.

41. Ibid., 47; Broughton, *Women's Work*, 27–28.

42. ANBC, *Journal and Lectures*, *1887*, 55–56.

43. For discussions on the cult of motherhood and domesticity, as well as treatment of woman's unique qualities relative to man's, see the following: Ann Douglas, *The Feminization of American Culture* (New York: Alfred A. Knopf, 1977), 87–89; Barbara Welter, "The Cult of True Womanhood, 1820–1860," *American Quarterly*, 18 (Spring 1966): 151–174; Katherine Kish Sklar, *Catherine Beecher: A Study in American Domesticity* (New York: W. W. Norton, 1976), 134–137; Anne Firor Scott, *The Southern Lady: From Pedestal to Politics, 1830–1930* (Chicago: University of Chicago Press, 1970), 37; also see this discussion as part of the evolving themes in women's history in Linda K. Kerber, "Separate Spheres, Female Worlds, Woman's Place: The Rhetoric of Women's History," *Journal of American History*, 75 (June 1988): 9–39.

44. See Paula Baker, "The Domestication of Politics: Women and Political Society, 1780–1920," *American Historical Review*, 89 (June 1984): 620–647; Michael McGerr, "Political Style and Women's Power, 1830–1930," *Journal of American History*, 77 (December 1990): 864–885.

45. Willard, *Women in the Pulpit*, 54, 64; Douglas, *Feminization of American Culture*, 51–52.

46. Sydney E. Ahlstrom, *A Religious History of the American People* (New Haven: Yale University Press, 1972), 763–787; Arthur Meier Schlesinger, "A Critical Period in American Protestantism, 1875–1900," *Massachusetts Historical Society Proceedings*, 64 (1930–1932): 523–548; Richard Hofstadter, *Social Darwinism in American Thought, 1860–1915* (Philadelphia: University of Pennsylvania Press, 1944), 1–16, 88; Barbara Welter, "Something Remains to Dare," introduction to Elizabeth Cady Stanton et al., *The Woman's Bible* (1895; rpt. New York: Arno Press, 1974), v–xi.

47. The label "progressive orthodoxy," coined by the faculty of Andover Seminary in 1884, characterized the majority of evangelical liberals who sought to retain Christian doctrine as much as possible while allowing for adjustment when necessary. See Winthrop S. Hudson, *Religion in America: An Historical Account of the Development of American Religious Life*, 2nd ed. (New York: Charles Scribner's Sons, 1973), 269–274.; Martin E. Marty, *Modern American Religion*, vol. 1 (Chicago: University of Chicago Press, 1986), 17–43.

48. Mary Cook also encouraged the belief in a living, rather than static doctrine and argued that women's freedom would grow with the "vitalizing principles" of the Baptist denomination. Frances Willard's position was more extreme than Cook's, however. In order to discourage literalism, Willard presented a two-page chart that graphically revealed changing, ambivalent, and contradictory biblical references to women. Willard also rejected literalism's opposite tendency, or what she termed "playing fast and loose." ANBC, *Journal and Lectures*, *1887*, 49; Willard, *Woman in the Pulpit*, 17–38, 50.

49. Speaking of Robert Ingersoll's and Elizabeth Cady Stanton's views toward women and religion, Willard wrote: "Whether they perceive it or not, it is chiefly ecclesiasticism and not Christianity that Robert Ingersoll and Elizabeth Cady Stanton have been fighting; it is the burdens grievous to be borne that men have laid upon weak shoulders, but which they themselves would not touch with one of their fingers."

For a letter from T. DeWitt Talmage to Willard dated 2 March 1888, along with the testimony of many other supporters of woman's right to the clergy, see Willard, *Woman in the Pulpit*, 9–15, 52, 73–112, 129–172; also see Lillie Devereaux Blake, *Woman's Place Today: Four Lectures in Reply to the Lenten Lectures on "Women"* (New York: J. W. Lovell, 1883); Benjamin T. Roberts, *Ordaining Women* (Rochester: Earnest Christian Publishing House, 1891), 47, 49, 58, 115–119, 158–159.

50. See Matilda Jocelyn Gage, *Woman, Church, and State*, 2nd ed. (New York: The Truth Seeker Company, 1893); and Welter, "Something Remains to Dare," *Woman's Bible*, xxv–xxxiv; Aileen S. Kraditor, ed., *Up From the Pedestal: Selected Writings in the History of American Feminism* (Chicago: Quadrangle Books, 1968), 108–121.

51. Augustus H. Strong, *Philosophy and Religion* (New York: A. C. Armstrong and Son, 1888), 201.

52. Douglas, *Feminization of American Culture*, 9–13; Barbara Welter, "The Feminization of American Religion: 1800–1860," in Mary Hartman and Lois Banner, eds., *Clio's Consciousness Raised: New Perspectives in the History of Women* (New York: Harper and Row, 1974), 137–157.

53. See "Talmage's Sermon," *Baptist Headlight*, 25 January 1894. Carl Delos Case, *The Masculine in Religion* (Philadelphia: The American Baptist Publication Society, 1906), 31.

54. George Matheson, "The Feminine Ideal of Christianity," *Biblical World*, 12 (1898): 29–36, 90–97.

55. Willard, *Woman in the Pulpit*, 45–47, 72, 97.

56. Bederman notes that church membership remained more than 60 percent female for nearly two centuries and that the perceived crisis of a "feminized church" reflected in actuality the "gendered coding of contemporary languages of religion and of power." In short, feminized Protestantism was deemed acceptable to men during the era of laissez faire capitalism. It went hand in hand with the old middle-class virtues of hard work, thrift, and self-sacrifice. While these values served "an individualistic, producer-oriented middle class," they were rendered anachronistic to the emergent corporate capitalism of the Gilded Age. See Gail Bederman, "'The Women Had Charge of the Church Work Long Enough': The Men and Religion Forward Movement of 1911–1912 and the Masculinization of Middle Class Protestantism," *American Quarterly*, 41 (September 1989): 432–461; also T. Jackson Lears, *No Place of Grace: Anti-Modernism and the Transformation of American Culture 1880–1920* (New York: Pantheon Books, 1981), 104.

57. Twenty years before Matheson, a white Baptist minister, the Reverend Augustus Strong, stated that Christ had brought new respect to passive virtues at a time when the world had hitherto exalted only manly virtues. Strong's writings nonetheless insist on Christ's dominant masculinity. Strong incurred the ire of suffragists, since he opposed woman's suffrage and believed in woman's subordination to man in office based on biblical authority. See Strong, *Philosophy and Religion*, 400–416, 549–550. Another white Baptist minister, Jesse Hungate, denied woman's right to ordination, maintaining that the ministry was the divine calling of men. Hungate stressed the necessity of woman's subordination to her husband. Included in his book are the responses of seventy-two Baptist ministers who overwhelmingly agreed with Hungate's opposition to women in the clergy. See Jesse Hungate, *The Ordination of Women to*

the *Pastorate in Baptist Churches* (Hamilton, N.Y.: James B. Grant, University Bookstore, 1899), 4–5, 11, 13–14, 29–36, 46, 69–84, 101–102.

58. Case was pastor of the Hanson Place Baptist Church in Brooklyn, New York. He praised the religious expression of the YMCA for being a style representative of men and the workplace. See Case, *The Masculine in Religion*, 9–11, 22–29, 46–51, 59–78, 84–88, 113–120.

59. Such metaphors could present interesting consequences. For Virginia Broughton, they seemed to offer unambiguous masculine and feminine images: "By no title could our risen Lord endear himself more to women than that of bridegroom and thus it is he likens his return in the parable of the 'Ten Virgins.'" For the sexist, masculine bias of white Baptist Jesse Hungate, the common designation of the church as the "bride" of Christ led him to assert his demand for a manly Christianity, stating: "She is the church militant; who is also the conquering one." See Broughton, *Women's Work*, 43–44; Hungate, *Ordination of Women*, 35.

60. The argument that woman's status evolved with Christianity was advanced by critics for and against woman's rights. It put religious emphasis on the general impetus of Social Darwinism. The anti–women's rights group argued that Christianity's civilizing influence heightened differences between men and women. The higher the culture, the more women were removed from the hardening contact with labor alongside men. Women were able to confine their duties to home and family and thus became more refined and delicate. The black Baptist writers did not stress this particular theme as much as they argued the direct relation between Christianity and the sanctity of marriage and home life. They focused on women's victimization in non-Christian cultures in antiquity and the present. In non-Christian cultures, women were described as merchandise subject to barter, polygamy, and marriage without love or "delicacy." See ANBC, *Minutes and Addresses, 1886*, 69; ANBC, *Journal and Lectures, 1887*, 45–46; ANBC, *Journal, Sermons, and Lectures, 1888*, 89–90; also see Hofstadter, *Social Darwinism*, 24–29; Strong, *Philosophy and Religion*, 405–406; Hungate, *Ordination of Women*, 41–42; Case, *The Masculine in Religion*, 5–7.

61. The title of Joanna Moore's autobiography showed that she viewed her own work as surrogate to Christ's. See Joanna P. Moore, *In Christ's Stead* (Chicago: Women's Baptist Home Mission Society, 1895), 131–133, 139–140, 146.

62. Another comparison of Ida B. Wells with Esther in the Bible appeared in H. J. Moore, "Let America Beware," *National Baptist World*, 12 October 1894; [Mrs.] H. Davis, "A Moses Wanted," *National Baptist World*, 5 October 1894.

63. White Baptist women also spoke of the Christianization of family life as the cure for racial strife. See Moore, *In Christ's Stead*, 141; ANBC, *Minutes and Addresses, 1886*, 70; ANBC, *Journal and Lectures, 1887*, 52–53; Broughton, *Women's Work*, 21–23.

64. ANBC, *Journal and Lectures, 1887*, 48–49.

65. Broughton, *Women's Work*, 37–40, 43.

66. ANBC, *Minutes and Addresses, 1886*, 69; ANBC, *Journal and Lectures, 1887*, 48.

67. Penn, *Afro-American Press*, 380–381.

68. ANBC, *Journal and Lectures, 1887*, 49.

69. Broughton, *Women's Work*, 32.

70. Interestingly, at the women's rights conference in Rochester, N.Y., in 1878, Elizabeth Cady Stanton advocated that women relinquish the attitude of self-sacrifice and cultivate self-development instead. Frederick Douglass noted at that time that self-sacrifice and self-development were not inconsistent with each other. See Augustus Strong's reference to this exchange in Strong, *Philosophy and Religion*, 409; Brawley, *Negro Baptist Pulpit*, 11; Boothe, *Cyclopedia of Colored Baptists*, 253, 255; Anthony Binga, Jr., *Sermons on Several Occasions* (n.p., 1889), 121–123, 293.

71. George Fredrickson discusses "romantic racialism" within the context of the "benign" view of black distinctiveness. This view was upheld by romanticism, abolitionism, and evangelical religion and should be distinguished from anti-black sentiments which vilified blacks as beasts and unworthy of human dignity. See *The Black Image in the White Mind: The Debate on the Afro-American Character and Destiny, 1817–1914* (New York: Harper and Row, 1972), 101–115, 125–126; Everett C. Hughes et al., eds., *The Collected Papers of Robert Ezra Park* (Glencoe, Ill.: Free Press, 1950), 280, quoted in Stanford M. Lyman, *The Black American in Sociological Thought* (New York: Capricorn Books, 1973), 42.

72. Du Bois stated: "But while race differences have followed mainly physical race lines, yet no mere physical distinctions would really define or explain the deeper differences—the cohesiveness and continuity of these groups. The deeper differences are spiritual, psychical, differences—undoubtedly based on the physical but infinitely transcending them." W. E. B. Du Bois, "The Conservation of Races," in Philip S. Foner, ed., *W. E. B. Du Bois Speaks: Speeches and Addresses, 1890–1919* (New York: 1970), 77–79, 84.

73. W. E. Burghardt Du Bois, *The Gift of Black Folk: The Negroes in the Making of America* (New York: Washington Square Press, 1970), 178.

74. Blacks, more often than whites, counterposed a black ideal against white in distinguishing the two races. Outstanding black leaders such as W. E. B. Du Bois, Edward Wilmot Blyden, Benjamin Brawley, son of Baptist leader Edward M. Brawley, and Nannie H. Burroughs, the corresponding secretary of the Woman's Convention of the black Baptist church, expounded theories of "romantic racialism." See James McPherson, *Abolitionist Legacy: From Reconstruction to the NAACP* (Princeton, N.J.: Princeton University Press, 1975), 67–68, 344; Nannie H. Burroughs, "With All Thy Getting," *Southern Workman*, 56 (July 1927): 301.

75. ANBC, *Journal and Lectures, 1887*, 46–47, 49–50, 54–55, 57; Brawley, *The Negro Baptist Pulpit*, 285. Black Baptist minister William Bishop Johnson also used the warfare motif when addressing women, and he challenged them to fulfill their obligations to God "by going forth into the highways and hedges and compelling men to bow allegiance to Calvary's cross." Johnson, *Scourging of a Race*, 78–79.

76. Broughton, "Woman's Work," *National Baptist Magazine* (January 1894): 33.

77. Anthony Binga does not describe women outside the role of homemaker; William Bishop Johnson contended that men did not give women their proper estimation in society, and yet he also assigned to man the qualities of "understanding" and "mind," and to woman, "will" and "soul." See Binga, *Sermons*, 293; Johnson, *Scourging of a Race*, 76.

78. See the response of black club women to the *Virginia Baptist* articles in "Editorial—Woman's Place," *The Woman's Era*, 1 (September 1894).

79. Penn, *Afro-American Press*, 370, 378; Brawley, *Negro Baptist Pulpit*, 279–281; Simmons, *Men of Mark*, 39–63, 729–732, 1059–63; Richings, *Evidences of Progress*, 222–224.

80. J. Francis Robinson, "The Importance of Women's Influence in All Religious and Benevolent Societies," *National Baptist Magazine* (November-December 1899): 117, 120–121.

81. Douglas, *Feminization of American Culture*, 3–48, 130–139, 168–181.

82. Boothe, *Cyclopedia of the Colored Baptists*, 252; Simmons, *Men of Mark*, 730; DeBaptiste, "Ministerial Education," 243–246; Brawley, ed., *Negro Baptist Pulpit*, 5–9, 19–23.

6. The Coming of Age of the Black Baptist Sisterhood

1. The titles of the proceedings of the Woman's Convention show discrepancies in the first fourteen years. The journals of the Woman's Convention, which were bound and published with the journals of the National Baptist Convention, inconsistently use either 1900 or 1901 as the date for the women's first annual session, and thus meetings in 1907 and 1908 are both entitled the "Eighth Annual Assembly." Beginning in 1914 the Woman's Convention consistently used 1901 as the base year. National Baptist Convention (hereafter NBC), *Journal of the Twentieth Annual Session of the National Baptist Convention, Held in Richmond, Virginia, September 12–17, 1900* (Nashville: National Baptist Publishing Board, 1900), 10, 68.

2. The convention as a form of representative government did not escape E. C. Morris, president of the National Baptist Convention, U.S.A. He stated in 1916 that the convention was important "because it affords an opportunity to prove to the world that the black race is capable of self-government under democratic form." See NBC, *Journal of the Thirty-sixth Annual Session of the National Baptist Convention and the Sixteenth Annual Session of the Woman's Convention, Held in Savannah, Georgia, September 6–11, 1916* (Nashville: Sunday School Publishing Board, 1916), 40. For women's views on the convention as a form of self-government, see NBC, *Journal of the Twenty-seventh Annual Session of the National Baptist Convention and the Eighth Annual Assembly of the Women's Convention, Held in Washington, D.C., September 11–16, 1907* (Nashville: National Baptist Publishing Board, 1908), 187, 204; NBC, *Journal of the Eighth Annual Assembly of the Woman's Convention, Held in the First Baptist Church of Lexington, Kentucky, September 16–21, 1908* (Nashville: National Baptist Publishing Board, 1909), 246–247.

3. Black temperance leader and novelist Frances Ellen Watkins Harper delivered the speech "Woman's Political Future" in 1893, in which she asserted: "Through weary, wasting years men have destroyed, dashed in pieces, and overthrown, but to-day we stand on the threshold of woman's era, and woman's work is grandly constructive." See Bert James Lowenberg and Ruth Bogin, eds., *Black Women in Nineteenth-Century American Life* (University Park, Pa.: Pennsylvania State University Press, 1976), 245.

4. Beverly Washington Jones, *Quest for Equality: The Life and Writings of Mary Eliza Church Terrell, 1863–1957*, vol. 13, and Dorothy Salem, *To Better Our World: Black Women in Organized Reform, 1890–1920*, vol. 14, both found in the series edited

by Darlene Clark Hine, *Black Women in United States History: From Colonial Times to the Present* (Brooklyn: Carlson Press, 1990).

5. Quoting Ruffin is Jones, *Quest for Equality*, 19.

6. For the formation of the National Association of Colored Women, see ibid., 386–401; Salem, *To Better Our World*, 9–28; Beverly Guy-Sheftall, *Daughters of Sorrow: Attitudes Toward Black Women, 1880–1920*, vol. 11 in Hine, ed., *Black Women in United States History*, 26; Tulia K. B. Hamilton, "The National Association of Colored Women, 1896–1920" (Ph.D. dissertation, Emory University, 1978).

7. For example, at the conference in 1890 Jennie Watson of Ohio read a paper entitled "Intellectual Growth of Baptist Women"; Miss G. G. Gilbert of Kentucky spoke on "The Need of Women as Missionaries in the Churches"; Virginia Broughton (erroneously noted as Miss A. V. Broughton in the ANBC minutes) spoke on the subject "The Ideal Mother"; while Susie Stone "made an impressive address on 'Women's Work.'" The committee on women's work in 1890 was represented by the following states: Kentucky, Alabama, Texas, Tennessee, Missouri, Kansas, Mississippi, Washington, D.C., Illinois, and Ohio. American National Baptist Convention (hereafter ANBC), *Journal of the American National Baptist Convention: Three Sessions, 1889, Indianapolis, 1890, Louisville, 1891, Dallas* (Louisville: The Bradley and Gilbert Company Printers, 1892), 34. Also see Broughton's autobiography for confirmation of her reading the paper "The Ideal Mother" at the 1890 meeting, in Virginia W. Broughton, *Twenty Years' Experience of a Missionary* (Chicago: The Pony Press Publishers, 1907), 100.

8. Broughton, *Twenty Years' Experience*, 100.

9. Lewis G. Jordan, *Negro Baptist History U.S.A.* (Nashville: Sunday School Publishing Board, National Baptist Convention, 1930), 261.

10. ANBC, *Journal of the American National Baptist Convention, Seventh Annual Session, Held in the First African Baptist Church, Savannah, Georgia, September 15–18, 1892, and Eighth Annual Session, Held in the Vermont Avenue Baptist Church, Washington, D.C., September 16–19, 1893*, 47; NBC, *Journal of the Nineteenth Annual Session of the National Baptist Convention, U.S.A., Held in Nashville, Tennessee, September 13–16, 1899* (Nashville: National Baptist Publishing Board, 1899), 41–42; Joseph A. Booker, "National Federation of Negro Baptists," *National Baptist Magazine* (July 1896): 155–157.

11. "Woman's National Baptist Convention," *National Baptist Magazine* (October 1895): 235. Biographical information on Alice A. Bowie describes her as one of the "most faithful and successful missionaries" among black Baptist women. She was a graduate of black Baptist–owned and controlled Selma University in Alabama and worked as a school teacher for a number of years. She served as the educational secretary for the American National Baptist Convention. "Alice A. Bowie," *National Baptist Union*, 3 May 1902.

12. Broughton, *Twenty Years' Experience*, 100–101.

13. At the annual meeting of the Woman's Convention in 1909, field secretary Ella E. Whitfield briefly reviewed this history of the women's "beginning in Atlanta, dissolution in St. Louis and the glorious resurrection in Virginia, when Miss Nannie H. Burroughs came on the scene." NBC, *Journal of the Twenty-Ninth Annual Session of the National Baptist Convention and the Ninth Annual Session of the Woman's Auxiliary*

Convention, Held in Columbus, Ohio, September 15–20, 1909 (Nashville: National Baptist Publishing Board, 1909), 258; also NBC, Journal, 1900, 195–196.

14. NBC, Journal, 1900, 10, 68.

15. NBC, Journal of the Twenty-fifth Annual Session of the National Baptist Convention and the Sixth Annual Session of the Woman's Convention, Held in Chicago, Ill., October 25–30, 1905 (Nashville: National Baptist Publishing Board, 1905), 241.

16. NBC, Journal, 1900, 64; Theodore S. Boone, Negro Baptist Chief Executives in National Places (Detroit: A. P. Publishing Company, 1948), 31.

17. Jordan permitted Burroughs to designate his Louisville office as the official headquarters for the new women's convention. See "Thanks to the Foreign Mission Board," NBC, Eighth Annual Session of the WC, 1907, 203; also see NBC, Journal, 1900, 195; NBC, Journal of the Twenty-first Annual Session of the National Baptist Convention and the Second Annual Session of the Woman's Convention, Held in Cincinnati, Ohio, September 11–16, 1901 (Nashville: National Baptist Publishing Board, 1901), 20–21; for examples of the women's column in the Mission Herald, see "Sharps and Flats" (September 1910): 6 and "Open Letter to Women" (August 1911): 3.

18. Because of the birth of her son, Mary Cook Parrish was not present at the Richmond meeting in 1900 when the Woman's Convention was founded. See Journal of the Thirty-fifth Annual Session of the National Baptist Convention and the Fifteenth Annual Session of the Women's Convention, Held in Chicago, Illinois, September 8–12, 1915 (n.p.: Lisle–Carey Press, 1915), 163.

19. See letter from Emma B. Delaney to the Woman's Convention, dated 3 July 1904, in NBC, Journal of the Twenty-fourth Annual Session of the National Baptist Convention and the Fifth Annual Session of the Woman's Convention, Held in Austin, Texas, September 14–19, 1904 (Nashville: National Baptist Publishing Board, 1904), 358–361; NBC, Sixth Annual Session of the WC, 1905, 260, 300, 308; NBC, Journal of the Tenth Annual Session of the Woman's Convention, Held in New Orleans, Louisiana, September 14–19, 1910 (Nashville: National Baptist Publishing Board, 1910), 20, 23, 26; Broughton, Twenty Years' Experience, 102.

20. In 1910 six vice-presidents had been reelected for ten consecutive years as the representatives of their states: Mrs. C. M. Wells, Alabama; Mrs. Sophia C. Shanks, Arkansas; Mrs. M. E. Hamilton, Tennessee; Mrs. M. M. Buckner, Texas; Mrs. I. Miller, Texas; and Mrs. E. P. Fox, Virginia. At the close of its second decade, the WC boasted that the majority of its officers had retained their positions for twenty years: S. Willie Layten, president; Sylvia Bryant, first vice-president-at-large (she died on 11 January 1920, however); Virginia Broughton, recording secretary; and Nannie Burroughs, corresponding secretary. Mary Parrish had served as treasurer since 1908, Mrs. E. A. Wilson had served as statistician since the creation of the post in 1905, and E. E. Whitfield remained in the job of field secretary since its introduction in 1912. See [Mrs.] E. A. Wilson, Report to the Historian of the Woman's Convention, Auxiliary to the National Baptist Convention, Chicago, Illinois, August 14–25, 1930, 4–5.

21. NBC, Journal, 1900, 195–196.

22. NBC, Journal of the Twenty-second Annual Session of the National Baptist Convention, and the Third Annual Session of the Woman's Convention, Held in Birmingham, Alabama, September 17–22, 1902 (Nashville: National Baptist Publishing Board, 1902), 7.

23. NBC, *Journal, 1900*, 197–198.

24. Interview with Dorothy J. Moore, 11 December 1990, Philadelphia; also David L. Lyons, "Mrs. S. Willie Layten" and "Biographical Sketches of the Founders: The Phillips Family," unpublished manuscripts. See also Edward Guinn, *History of Shiloh Baptist Church*, Shiloh Baptist Church Archives, Philadelphia.

25. Boone, *Negro Baptist Chief Executives*, 29–30; Thomas O. Fuller, *History of the Negro Baptists of Tennessee* (Nashville: National Baptist Publication Board, n.d.), 201.

26. NBC, *Journal, 1901*, 19–21.

27. Nannie H. Burroughs to Booker T. Washington, 18 February 1896, Booker T. Washington Papers, Library of Congress (hereafter BTW Papers, LC).

28. Earl H. Harrison, *The Dream and the Dreamer* (Washington, D.C.: Nannie H. Burroughs Literature Foundation, 1956), 9–12.

29. Burroughs to Booker T. Washington, 14 November 1901, 24 January 1902, 10 September 1902, 11 September 1902, BTW Papers, LC.

30. NBC, *Third Annual Session of the WC, 1902*, 36; NBC, *Journal of the Twenty-third Annual Session of the National Baptist Convention and the Fourth Annual Session of the Woman's Convention, Held in Philadelphia, Pennsylvania, September 16–20, 1903* (Nashville: National Baptist Publishing Board, 1904), 26; Burroughs to Booker T. Washington, 6 October 1902, BTW Papers, LC.

31. NBC, *Journal, 1901*, 29, 59.

32. NBC, *Third Annual Session of the WC, 1902*, 20, 38; also Virginia Broughton writes in her autobiography that the "women took a decided stand to hold their organization intact." See Broughton, *Twenty Years' Experience*, 102.

33. NBC, *Journal, 1902*, 107; NBC, *Journal, 1903*, 82, 157.

34. See NBC, *Fourth Annual Session of the WC, 1903*, 301; NBC, *Journal of the Twelfth Annual Session of the Woman's Convention, Held in Houston, Texas, September 11–15, 1912* (Nashville: National Baptist Publishing Board, 1913), 25, 35, 59–61, 85; Samuel W. Bacote, *Who's Who among the Colored Baptists of the United States* (Kansas City, Mo.: Franklin Hudson Publishing Company, 1912), 101–103. See "Our Field Secretary" in NBC, *Journal of the Fortieth Annual Session of the National Baptist Convention and the Twentieth Annual Session of the Woman's Convention, Held in Indianapolis, Indiana, September 8–13, 1920* (Nashville: Sunday School Publishing Board, 1920), 326.

35. See, for example, in the secular black press, Woolford Damon, "Twenty-third Annual Session of the National Baptist Convention, at Philadelphia, Pa., Sept. 1903," *Colored American Magazine* (November 1903): 778–793, especially 782–793; see in *National Baptist Union* (hereafter *NBU*): N. H. Burroughs, "Woman's Department—Side Talk about the Convention," 4 October 1902; "News and Notes," 29 March 1902; "Woman's Department," 17 October 1903; and "National Convention of Baptist Women," 1 October 1910. The women's column in the *Mission Herald* was called "Sharps and Flats" and was edited by Nannie Burroughs. See N. H. Burroughs, "Sharps and Flats" (August 1911): 2.

36. NBC, *Fourth Annual Session of the WC, 1903*, 229; for reference to the size of the women's membership and discussion of it as a representative body, see also NBC, *Eighth Annual Session of the WC, 1907*, 187, 204; NBC, *Eighth Annual Assembly of the WC, 1908*, 246–247.

37. NBC, *Fifth Annual Session of the WC*, 1904, 338.

38. See the section "Woman's Day" in NBC, *Eighth Annual Assembly of the WC*, 1908, 249; also national leaders enhanced the budgets of many state and local societies. *The Slabtown Convention*, a one-act play written by Burroughs, netted churches and missionary societies more than $3,000 in 1909. The play carried a serious message in its humorous portrayal of a convention's attempt to carry out meaningful work, but unfortunately with the wrong methods. NBC, *Ninth Annual Session of the WC*, 1909, 273–275; Burroughs, *The Slabtown District Convention*, 21st ed. (Washington, D.C.: Nannie H. Burroughs Publications, 1974).

39. NBC, *Sixth Annual Session of the WC*, 1905, 256; also NBC, *Fifteenth Annual Session of the WC*, 1915, 223; N. H. Burroughs, "Sharps and Flats," *Mission Herald* (August 1911): 3.

40. NBC, *Third Annual Session of the WC*, 1902, 24; WC, 1908, 248–249; NBC, *Fifteenth Annual Session of the WC*, 1915, 222.

41. NBC, *Fifteenth Annual Session of the WC*, 1915, 212.

42. NBC, *Ninth Annual Session of the WC*, 1909, 273; NBC, *Tenth Annual Session of the WC*, 1910, 23.

43. NBC, *Eighth Annual Session of the WC*, 1907, 187.

44. See summary of report of M. Helen Adams, "What We Have Done through our Social Center," in NBC, *Fifteenth Annual Session of the WC*, 1915, 169.

45. See in *NBU*: "Miss Burroughs Contending for Her Rights," 14 March 1903; "Miss Nannie Burroughs Differs," 17 January 1903; N. H. Burroughs, "Woman's Department," 14 June 1902; N. H. Burroughs and V. W. Broughton, "Woman's Department," 2 August 1902; V. W. Broughton, "Woman's Department—Systematic Christian Giving Necessary to Success," 1 November 1902.

46. For women's expression of public solidarity, see the entire edition of the *National Baptist Union* devoted to the Woman's Convention: "Baptist Women's Edition," *NBU*, 8 August 1903. Also for editor's coverage of controversy, see in *NBU*: "Woman's Convention Top Heavy," 4 October 1902; "Give the Woman a Board," 3 January 1903; "Misunderstanding among the Women," 31 January 1903; "The Women's Board Explains," 21 February 1903; "President Layten Favors a Board," 14 March 1903.

47. See untitled editorial in *NBU*, 10 October 1903.

48. "The Baptist Controversy," *Crisis*, 12 (April 1916): 314–316; Walter H. Brooks, "Unification and Division Among Colored Baptists," ibid., 30 (May 1925): 20–22. For a full discussion of the roots of the split over the Publishing Board see Joseph H. Jackson, *A Story of Christian Activism: The History of the National Baptist Convention, U. S. A., Inc.* (Nashville: Townsend Press, 1978), 98–120.

49. NBC, *Fifteenth Annual Session of the WC*, 1915, 168.

50. NBC, *Eighth Annual Assembly of the WC*, 1908, 243.

51. Broughton, *Twenty Years' Experience*, 103.

52. See untitled column beginning "Ladies Auxiliary to the NBC held at the Union Baptist Church of which Rev. Proud is pastor." *The Baptist Woman's Era*, 15 September 1901.

53. Broughton, *Twenty Years' Experience*, 105.

54. The meeting in 1914 was housed at Convention Hall on Broad and Allegheny Streets in downtown Philadelphia. The NBC received mixed press in the *Philadelphia*

Tribune. Articles ranged from praise of the NBC's stand on racial equality and women's suffrage to attacks on the misconduct of some of the ministers present. See "National Baptist President Demands An Equal Chance," *Philadelphia Tribune*, 12 September 1914; also "Just Gone" and "National Conventions Establish Precedent" in ibid., 19 September 1914.

55. *Chicago Daily News*, 7 and 8 September 1915, clippings in Box 39, Illinois Writers Project, cited in James R. Grossman, *Land of Hope: Chicago, Black Southerners, and the Great Migration* (Chicago: University of Chicago Press, 1989), 92.

56. "National Baptist President Demands an Equal Chance," *Philadelphia Tribune*, 12 September 1914.

57. The U.S. Government Bureau of the Census appointed black Baptist minister Dr. William Bishop Johnson to coordinate the compilation of census information among black Baptists. The National Baptist Convention applauded the choice as "one of the best qualified men among us" and urged "our pastors and churches everywhere to give . . . immediate responses by sending our reports fully made out to the Census Bureau of the United States." See 1907 Minutes, NBC, 76. For statistics of religious denominations, see U.S. Department of Commerce and Labor, Bureau of the Census, *Special Reports: Religious Bodies, 1906*, vol. 1 (Washington, D.C.: Government Printing Office, 1910), 137–139; Bureau of the Census, *Religious Bodies, 1916*, Part I (Washington, D.C.: Government Printing Office, 1919), 40.

58. The emphasis on black history and dolls as a form of protest and resistance will be discussed in greater detail in Chapter 7. See *Crisis*, 2 (August 1911), inside back cover; NEW YORK Age (8 October 1908). At the 1914 convention in Philadelphia, the WC announced the formation of a "Girl's Dolls Club." The minutes noted that "in order to inculcate RACE PRIDE we have insisted that these clubs shall be NEGRO DOLL CLUBS so that we may teach every little girl the importance of having respect for her own race." NBC, *Journal of the Thirty-fourth Annual Session of the National Baptist Convention and the Fourteenth Annual Assembly of the Woman's Convention, Held in Philadelphia, Pennsylvania, September 9–15, 1914* (Nashville: National Baptist Publishing Board, 1914), 81.

59. In 1916 the National Baptist Convention reported a membership of 1,805,001 women and 1,128,237 men—leaving 5,341 of 2,938,579 who did not report their sex. See Bureau of the Census, *Religious Bodies, 1916*, Part 1, 40.

60. Letter of R. E. Pitts from Uniontown, Alabama, 21 September 1900, printed in *Baptist Woman's Era* (15 November 1900). In 1919 Pitts continued to serve as delegate from the Uniontown Association and was awarded a medal for bringing in the largest amount of revenue to the Woman's Convention for that year. See NBC, *Journal of the Thirty-ninth Annual Session of the National Baptist Convention and the Nineteenth Annual Session of the Women's Convention, Held in Newark, New Jersey, September 10–15, 1919* (Nashville: Sunday School Publishing Board, 1920), 221, 227.

61. NBC, *Eighth Annual Session of the WC, 1907*, 162.

62. NBC, *Tenth Annual Session of the WC, 1910*, 27, 67, 74.

63. NBC, *Fifth Annual Session of the WC, 1904*, 379; NBC, *Sixth Annual Session of the WC, 1905*, 306–307; NBC, *Tenth Annual Session of the WC, 1910*, 56–58.

64. White speakers, male and female, addressed the annual meetings of the WC. Representatives from white northern and southern Baptist women's organizations

periodically appeared on the program. In 1914 Dr. Thomas Jesse Jones of the U.S. Bureau of Education and Dr. Quay Roselle, representative of the social service commission of the Northern Baptist Convention, were listed among the speakers. NBC, *Journal, 1914*, 29.

65. NBC, *Sixth Annual Session of the WC, 1905*, 306; NBC, *Twelfth Annual Session of the WC, 1912*, 68; NBC, *Eighth Annual Session of the WC, 1907*, 203; NBC, *Fifteenth Annual Session of the WC, 1915*, 169-171; NBC, *Journal of the Eighteenth Annual Session of the Woman's Convention, Auxiliary to the National Baptist Convention, Held in St. Louis, Missouri, September 4-9, 1918* (Nashville: Sunday School Publishing Board, 1919), 179; NBC, *Nineteenth Annual Session of the WC, 1919*, 196, 200-201; NBC, *Twentieth Annual Session of the WC, 1920*, 334, 341, 350, 356.

66. The Woman's Convention gave each of its representatives $100 for the trip to the Baptist World Alliance, and this amount was supplemented by a number of individual donations. See Nannie Burroughs's report of the conference to the Woman's Convention, in NBC, *Sixth Annual Session of the WC, 1905*, 261-265; also for published proceedings of the World Baptist Congress and for reference and photograph of Nannie H. Burroughs along with her speech "Woman's Work," see *First Baptist World Congress: London, July 11-19, 1905* (London: Baptist Union Publication Department, 1905), xviii, 80-81, 325.

67. NBC, *Fourteenth Annual Assembly of the WC, 1914*, 155, 208-209.

68. U.S. Department of Commerce, Bureau of the Census, *Negro Population* (Washington, D.C.: Government Printing Office, 1918), 93.

69. Carole Marks, *Farewell—We're Good and Gone: The Great Black Migration* (Bloomington: Indiana University Press, 1989), 1-48, 60-67, 93-94, 110-115; Grossman, *Land of Hope*, 3-4, 13-20, 36.

70. Marks, *Farewell*, 21-24.

71. Florette Henri, *Black Migration: Movement North, 1900-1920* (Garden City, N.Y.: Anchor Press, 1975), 50-59, 68-69; Jacqueline Jones, *Labor of Love, Labor of Sorrow: Black Women, Work, and the Family from Slavery to the Present* (New York: Random House, 1985), 152-160.

72. Marks, *Farewell*, 145-147.

73. Robert H. Wiebe, *The Search for Order, 1877-1920* (New York: Hill and Wang, 1967), 165-168, 171, 173; Ellen Fitzpatrick, *Endless Crusade: Women Social Scientists and Progressive Reform* (New York: Oxford University Press, 1990), chap. 3.

74. In her annual report to the WC in 1912, Nannie Burroughs highlighted the work of white sociologists in urban areas and urged her sisters to form a Social Service Committee which could effect "real reform through a practical system of community education." NBC, *Twelfth Annual Session of the WC, 1912*, 40-41. See also NBC, *Fifteenth Annual Session of the WC, 1915*, 168-174, 197-205; NBC, *Sixteenth Annual Report of the Executive Board and Corresponding Secretary of the Woman's Convention, Auxiliary to the National Baptist Convention, Made at Savannah, Georgia, September 6-11, 1916*, 13-14; NBC, *Twentieth Annual Session of the WC, 1920*, 335-336. The WC also noted the pernicious impact of urban values upon hitherto "modest, industrious, honest . . . country girls" visited by "city cousins . . . who sow[ed] the seeds of restlessness and discontent." NBC, *Eighth Annual Session of the WC, 1907*, 191-192.

75. Charles Howard Hopkins, *The Rise of the Social Gospel in American Protestantism, 1865–1915* (New Haven: Yale University Press, 1940), 12–13, 318–326; also Ralph Luker, *The Social Gospel in Black and White: American Racial Reform, 1885–1912* (Chapel Hill: University of North Carolina Press, 1991).

76. See discussion of the institutional church for whites in Joan Jacobs Brumberg, *Mission for Life: The Story of the Family of Adoniram Judson, the Dramatic Events of the First American Foreign Mission, and the Course of Evangelical Religion in the Nineteenth Century* (New York: The Free Press, 1980), 189–195, 195–199, 200–214.

77. W. E. B. Du Bois's remarks are found in Philip S. Foner, ed., *W. E. B. Du Bois Speaks, 1890–1919* (New York: Pathfinder Press, 1970), 97; Fannie Barrier Williams, "Social Bonds in the 'Black Belt' of Chicago," *Charities*, 15 (7 October 1905): 41.

78. See David Wills, "Reverdy C. Ransom: The Making of an A.M.E. Bishop," in Randall K. Burkett and Richard Newman, eds., *Black Apostles: Afro-American Clergy Confront the Twentieth Century* (Boston: G. K. Hall, 1978), 196–197; Calvin Sylvester Morris, "Reverdy C. Ransom: A Pioneer Black Social Gospeler" (Ph.D. dissertation, Boston University, 1982).

79. For a discussion of Shiloh Baptist Church as an institutional church under the Reverend J. Milton Waldron, see Evelyn Brooks Higginbotham, "From Strength to Strength: The History of Shiloh Baptist Church of Washington, D.C., 1863–1988," in *From Strength to Strength: A Journey of Faith, 1873–1988*, ed. Madlyn Calbert (Washington: Shiloh Baptist Church, 1989), 44–57, Shiloh Baptist Church Archives, Washington, D.C.

80. The Nineteenth Street Baptist Church was also the church in which Nannie Burroughs held membership. See B. Henderson, "A Strong Pastor of a Strong Church," *Colored American Magazine*, 14 (January 1908): 20.

81. Nancy J. Weiss, *The National Urban League, 1910–1940* (New York: Oxford University Press, 1974), 11–12; Jesse Thomas Moore, Jr., *A Search for Equality: The National Urban League, 1910–1961* (University Park, Pa.: The Pennsylvania State University Press, 1981), 29–30, 268.

82. NBC, *Fifteenth Annual Report of the Executive Board and Corresponding Secretary of the Woman's Convention, Auxiliary to the National Baptist Convention, Made at Chicago, Illinois, September 8–12, 1915*, 38.

83. NBC, *Twelfth Annual Session of the WC, 1912*, 61–62. NBC, *Thirteenth Annual Report of the Executive Board and Corresponding Secretary of the Woman's Convention, Auxiliary to the National Baptist Convention, Made at Nashville, Tennessee, September 17–22, 1913*, 34; NBC, *Fifteenth Annual Report of the Executive Board and Corresponding Secretary of the WC, 1915*, 47–48.

84. NBC, *Fourteenth Annual Assembly of the WC, 1914*, 169–171.

85. NBC, *Twentieth Annual Session of the WC, 1920*, 320–321. The WC's advocacy of greater social service and less emotionalism should not be misinterpreted as a rejection of the black style of worship. The minutes of the annual meetings reveal that the women expressed their religion openly and freely within the black tradition. The minutes for 1912 reported fervent prayers, strong testimonies, and the singing of spirituals at the early morning prayer service led by the women from Louisiana and Georgia. At the annual meeting in 1914 "loud hallelujahs" followed Miss Porter's singing of "His Eye Is on the Sparrow and I Know He Watches Me." NBC, *Twelfth*

Annual Session of the WC, 1912, 20; NBC, *Fourteenth Annual Assembly of the WC, 1914*, 213.

86. NBC, *Journal of the Forty-first Annual Session of the National Baptist Convention and the Twenty-first Annual Session of the Woman's Convention, Held in Chicago, Illinois, September 7–12, 1921* (Nashville: Sunday School Publishing Board, 1921), 287.

87. For discussion of the convention as an "institute," see the speech of S. W. Layten in NBC, *Fifteenth Annual Session of the WC, 1915*, 201.

88. The minutes for 1915 note: "Social service work is being comprehended and the vital thing is instruction—how to ameliorate and prevent the evils of society, provide against the occurrence of those evils which are sapping so much of the vitality of our race. Remembering preventive work—is more important than rescue work." Ibid., 202.

89. Field secretary Ella Whitfield stated in her address to the convention in 1915: "This is a day of wonderful progress and efficiency is the watchword of the day." Also the report of the Child Welfare Committee for the same year stated: "Efficiency is the watchword of the age. Efficiency in every vocation, enterprise and phase of life—religious, social, industrial." Ibid., 173, 198.

90. NBC, *Fifth Annual Session of the WC, 1904*, 326; NBC, *Tenth Annual Session of the WC, 1910*, 42; NBC, *Twelfth Annual Session of the WC, 1912*, 90.

91. NBC, *Twelfth Annual Session of the WC, 1912*, 41–42. See also the section of Burroughs's report, "Too Much Reform," in NBC, *Sixteenth Annual Report of the Executive Board and Corresponding Secretary of the WC, 1916*, 30–31; NBC, *Ninth Annual Session of the WC, 1909*, 26, 40–42.

92. NBC, *Thirteenth Annual Report of the Executive Board and Corresponding Secretary of the WC*, 20.

93. See summary of report of M. Helen Adams, "What We Have Done through our Social Center," in NBC, *Fifteenth Annual Session of the WC, 1915*, 169; also NBC, *Fourteenth Annual Assembly of the WC, 1914*, 28–29, 173; NBC, *Fifteenth Annual Report of the Executive Board and Corresponding Secretary of the WC, 1915*, 35–38; NBC, *Twentieth Annual Session of the WC, 1920*, 312–313.

94. NBC, *Twelfth Annual Session of the WC, 1912*, 40–41; NBC, *Fourteenth Annual Assembly of the WC, 1914*, 30, 200, 202, 204, 212.

95. NBC, *Fifteenth Annual Report of the Executive Board and Corresponding Secretary of the WC, 1915*, 30–31.

96. NBC, *Eighteenth Annual Session of the WC, 1918*, 186–188; NBC, *Twentieth Annual Session of the WC, 1920*, 361–364.

97. Elizabeth Fee, "Venereal Disease: The Wages of Sin?" in Kathy Peiss and Christina Simmons with Robert A. Padgug, *Passion and Power: Sexuality in History* (Philadelphia: Temple University Press, 1989), 182–184.

98. Concern for child welfare was a central component of humanitarian progressivism. NBC, *Twelfth Annual Session of the WC, 1912*, 78–80; also for discussion of child-welfare reform, see Robyn Muncy, *Creating a Female Dominion in American Reform, 1890–1935* (New York: Oxford University Press, 1990), chap. 2; and Molly Ladd-Taylor, ed., *Raising a Baby the Government Way: Mothers' Letters to the Children's Bureau, 1915–1932* (New Brunswick, N.J.: Rugters University Press, 1986), 1–46.

99. NBC, *Fourteenth Annual Assembly of the WC, 1914*, 166–168; also see "Report of Committee on Child Welfare," NBC, *Fifteenth Annual Session of the WC, 1915*,

197. Commitment to progressive reform encouraged the women to address the socioeconomic conditions of their own people, but it also sparked a desire to learn about other ethnic groups. In 1915 they heard an address on working conditions in coal mines. They also learned about Italian laborers in construction camps and about the deplorable conditions of Italian and Polish children working in canneries. See, for example, brief summaries of the following addresses, which were presented to the Woman's Convention in its annual session in 1915: Lucille Payton, "Hard Coal and Breaker Boys"; Marie Johnson, "In the Construction Camp"; and Katherine M. Johnson, "Children in Canneries," in ibid., 173.

100. NBC, *Eighteenth Annual Session of the WC, 1918,* 144–145; NBC, *Twentieth Annual Session of the WC, 1920,* 383.

101. See Layten's presidential address to the Woman's Convention in September 1915 in NBC, *Fifteenth Annual Session of the WC, 1915,* 204–205; Theodore S. Boone, *A Social History of Negro Baptists* (Detroit: Historical Commission, National Baptist Convention, U.S.A., 1952), 60–62; S. W. Layten, "A Northern Phase of a Southern Problem," *A.M.E. Church Review,* 26 (March 1910): 315–325. Ellen Fitzpatrick discusses the work of Francis Kellor in *Endless Crusade,* 139.

102. Weiss, *National Urban League,* 18, 29–30.

103. Guichard Parris and Lester Brooks, *Blacks in the City: A History of the National Urban League* (Boston: Little, Brown, 1971), 7–10, 34.

104. Boone, *Negro Baptist Chief Executives,* 29–30.

105. NBC, *Sixth Annual Session of the WC, 1905,* 238–239, 243, 329; also NBC, *Eighth Annual Session of the WC, 1907,* 229.

106. Layten's Association for the Protection of Colored Women existed independently of the Philadelphia Travelers' Aid Society, but the society offered her program financial assistance and included Layten's work in its reports. See reports of the Philadelphia Association for the Protection of Colored Women between 1905 and 1914, especially the report for 1909, in Travelers' Aid Society Records, 1904–1972, Temple University Urban Archives.

107. NBC, *Ninth Annual Session of the WC, 1909,* 256; NBC, *Tenth Annual Session of the WC, 1910,* 17, 90; NBC, *Twelfth Annual Session of the WC, 1912,* 67; NBC, *Fifteenth Annual Session of the WC, 1915,* 204–205.

108. NBC, *Twelfth Annual Session of the WC, 1912,* 26.

109. See Chapter 3.

110. NBC, *Eighteenth Annual Session of the WC, 1918,* 141, 199; Mary V. Parrish, *Fourth Statistical Report of the National Association of Colored Women, August 7–8, 1914* (Louisville: American Baptist Press, n.d.), 1; National Association of Colored Women, *Tenth Biennial Convention of the National Association of Colored Women, 7–10 August 1916* (n.p.: C. A. Franklin Printer, 1916), 4, 6. The records of the Kentucky Federation of Colored Women's Clubs between 1918 and 1921 reveal that Mary V. Parrish was president of her state federation. *Kentucky Federation of Colored Women's Clubs, 1918–1919–1920–1921* (Louisville: American Baptist, 1924), 42, in Charles H. Parrish, Jr., Papers, Archives Department, University of Louisville.

111. For example, Miss F. C. Cobb delivered the speech "Lifting as We Climb" to the Woman's Convention in 1902. NBC, *Third Annual Session of the WC, 1902,* 4; NBC, *Sixth Annual Session of the WC, 1905,* 305; NBC, *Twelfth Annual Session of the WC, 1912,* 15; NBC, *Twentieth Annual Session of the WC, 1920,* 307.

112. W. E. B. Du Bois, *Efforts for Social Betterment among Negro Americans* (Atlanta: Atlanta University Press, 1909), 47–48.

113. The Bethesda Church Club supported both the American Baptist Home Mission Society and the National Training School for Women and Girls. Ibid., 50–51.

114. See E. C. Morris's annual address in 1914 for the NBC's endorsement of the Southern Sociological Congress. Also Mrs. M. W. Riddick, a delegate to the Woman's Convention in 1916, presented the paper "What the New South is Doing to be Saved," in which she identified the Southern Sociological Congress as "the greatest force now operating to change sentiment in favor of adjusting evils from which we suffer as a race." See NBC, *Journal, 1914*, 30; NBC, *Journal, 1913*, 32–33; NBC, *Sixteenth Annual Session of the WC, 1916*, 193.

115. In 1918 two presentations on racial subjects included "Mob-Violence—An Enemy of Both Races," by William O. Scroggs of Louisiana State University; and "Race Distinctions vs. Race Discriminations," by Judge Gilbert T. Stephenson of Winston-Salem, North Carolina. James E. McCulloch, ed., *The Call of the New South* (Nashville: Brandau-Craig-Dickerson Company, 1912), 7–8; McCulloch, ed., *Democracy in Earnest* (Nashville, 1918; rpt. New York: Greenwood Publishing Company, Negro Universities Press, 1969), 13–14, 24, 185–191, 201, 409, 413; Morton Sosna, *In Search of the Silent South: Southern Liberals and the Race Issue* (New York: Columbia University Press, 1977), 16–18.

116. See "Annual Address of Mrs. S. W. Layten, President of Woman's Convention," in NBC, *Fifteenth Annual Session of the WC, 1915*, 201.

7. The Politics of Respectability

1. In her cultural study of the Zion Christian Church of the Tshidi people of South Africa, Jean Comaroff defines "signifying practice" as the "process through which persons, acting upon an external environment, construct themselves as social beings." Jean Comaroff, *Body of Power, Spirit of Resistance: The Culture and History of a South African People* (Chicago: University of Chicago Press, 1985), 6.

2. Patricia Hill Collins, *Black Feminist Thought: Knowledge, Consciousness, and the Politics of Empowerment* (Boston: Unwin Hyman, 1990), 95.

3. Elizabeth A. Meese illustrates the dialogic quality of words in her discussion of the discursive negotiation between black and white feminists over conflicting representations of race, class, and sex. Extending her discussion (and specifically the following quote) to the study of black Baptist women permits a clearer understanding of the role of black women in the process of self-definition and in infusing words such as respectability and equality with meanings and intentions of their own. Meese writes: "Speakers designate me as they wish, to suit their intentions and interests. Unless I speak myself, language will not serve me, and only then does it throw me and the other(s) into a negotiating relationship so that we can bargain with each other and with language over our shared property, our respective investments in signification." See Elizabeth A. Meese, *(Ex)tensions: Re-figuring Feminist Criticism* (Urbana: University of Illinois Press, 1990), 130–131.

4. National Baptist Convention (hereafter NBC), *Journal of the Twenty-fifth Annual Session of the National Baptist Convention and the Sixth Annual Session of the*

Woman's Convention, Held in Chicago, Ill., October 25–30, 1905 (Nashville: National Baptist Publishing Board, 1905), 270.

5. See Bakhtin's analysis of the dialogic quality of language—what he calls a double-voiced discourse. Bakhtin observes: "The word in language is half someone else's. It becomes 'one's own' only when the speaker populates it with his [or her] own accent, when he [or she] appropriates the word, adapting it to his [or her] own semantic and expressive intention." M. M. Bakhtin, *The Dialogic Imagination: Four Essays*, ed. Michael Holquist, trans. Caryl Emerson and Michael Holquist (Austin: University of Texas Press, 1981), 293, 324; also for African Americans' appropriation of words for the purpose of resistance, see Evelyn Brooks Higginbotham, "African-American Women's History and the Metalanguage of Race," *Signs*, 17 (Winter 1992): 267.

6. Fraser asserts that "what is 'political'—call it 'discursive-political' or 'politicized'—contrasts both with what is not contested in public at all and with what is contested only in relatively specialized, enclaved, and/or segmented publics." Nancy Fraser, *Unruly Practices: Power, Discourse and Gender in Contemporary Social Theory* (Minneapolis: University of Minnesota Press, 1989), 166.

7. St. Clair Drake and Horace Cayton's discussion of the usage of respectability by blacks as a "front" connotes a certain level of insincerity in the manipulation of middle-class behavior—"it's not what you do that counts, but how you do it." They state: "The 'respectable,' 'educated,' and 'refined' believe in 'front,' partly because it is their accustomed way of life and partly in order to impress the white world." St. Clair Drake and Horace Cayton, *Black Metropolis: A Study of Negro Life in a Northern City* (New York: Harcourt Brace, 1945), 519.

8. For a discussion of respectability as an oppositional discourse for the purpose of black nationalist resistance in the late 1960s, see E. Frances White, "Africa on My Mind: Gender, Counter Discourse and African-American Nationalism," *Journal of Women's History*, 2 (Spring 1990): 76. Although not focusing on African Americans, a growing body of literature discusses respectability from the perspectives of gender, sexuality, and nationalism. For a gender analysis of "respectability" as orderliness and bodily self-control, see Iris Marion Young, *Justice and the Politics of Difference* (Princeton, N.J.: Princeton University Press, 1990), 136–138; also see the connection between respectability and nationalism (European, especially German) in George L. Mosse, *Nationalism and Sexuality: Respectability and Abnormal Sexuality in Modern Europe* (New York: H. Fertig, 1985), 4–5, 9–10; see also Dipesh Chakrabarty, "Postcoloniality and the Artifice of History: Who Speaks for 'Indian' Pasts?" *Representations*, 37 (Winter 1992): 11–17.

9. W. E. Burghardt Du Bois, *The Souls of Black Folk* (Greenwich, Conn.: Fawcett Publications, 1967), 21.

10. Madison Grant, *The Passing of the Great Race—Or the Racial Basis of European History*, 3rd ed. (New York: Charles Scribner's Sons, 1920), 10–12, 82–94, 99, 110; John Higham, *Strangers in the Land: Patterns of American Nativism, 1860–1925* (New York: Atheneum, 1978), 40–56, 97–105, 131–157.

11. For discussion of the headlines in the San Francisco *Chronicle*, see Herbert B. Johnson, *Discrimination against the Japanese in California: A Review of the Real Situation* (Berkeley: Courier Publishing Company, 1907), 15–16. See also Evelyn Nakanno Glenn, *Issei, Nisei, War Bride: Three Generations of Japanese-American Women in Domestic Service* (Philadelphia: Temple University Press, 1986), 30–31, 50–55. For

discrimination against Chinese Americans see Connie Young Yu, "The World of our Grandmothers," in Asian Women United of California, ed., *Making Waves: An Anthology By and About Asian American Women* (Boston: Beacon Press, 1990), 34–35; William F. Wu, *The Yellow Peril: Chinese Americans in American Fiction, 1850–1940* (Hamden, Conn.: Archon Books, 1978), 1–5, 30; Ronald Takaki, *Iron Cages: Race and Culture in Nineteenth Century America* (Seattle: University of Washington Press, 1982), 215–249.

12. Joel Williamson, *A Rage for Order: Black/White Relations in the American South since Emancipation* (New York: Oxford University Press, 1986), 190, 201, 207; August Meier and Elliot Rudwick, *From Plantation to Ghetto: An Interpretive History of American Negroes* (New York: Hill and Wang, 1966), 192; Otto Kerner, Chairman, *Report of the National Advisory Commission on Civil Disorders* (Washington, D.C.: Government Printing Office, 1968), 100–102.

13. The concept "rhetoric of violence" is taken from Teresa de Lauretis, who uses it in specific reference to rhetoric that attempts to excuse or explain wife beating. The implications of the concept's meaning, however, are useful for racial victimization as well. See Teresa de Lauretis, *Technologies of Gender: Essays on Theory, Film, and Fiction* (Bloomington: Indiana University Press, 1987), 31–48.

14. See Rogin's discussion of the film in his chapter, "'The Sword Became a Flashing Vision': D. W. Griffiths' *The Birth of a Nation*," in Michael Paul Rogin, *"Ronald Reagan," the Movie: And Other Episodes in Political Demonology* (Berkeley: University of California Press, 1987), 195–198, 219–224.

15. "Experiences of the Race Problem. By a Southern White Woman," *Independent*, 56 (17 March 1904), as quoted in Beverly Guy-Sheftall, *Daughters of Sorrow: Attitudes toward Black Women, 1880–1920*, vol. 11 in the series edited by Darlene Clark Hine, *Black Women in United States History: From Colonial Times to the Present* (Brooklyn: Carlson Publishing, 1990), 46; also see this theme discussed in Anne Firor Scott, "Most Invisible of All: Black Women's Voluntary Associations," *Journal of Southern History*, 56 (February 1990): 10.

16. See Sander L. Gilman, "Black Bodies, White Bodies: Toward an Iconography of Female Sexuality in Late Nineteenth-Century Art, Medicine, and Literature," in Henry Louis Gates, Jr., ed., *"Race", Writing, and Difference* (Chicago: University of Chicago Press, 1986), 223–240.

17. See Higginbotham, "Metalanguage of Race," 257–258.

18. See Neil R. McMillen, *Dark Journey: Black Mississippians in the Age of Jim Crow* (Urbana: University of Illinois Press, 1989), 205–206; also for discussion of the role of race in constructing and representing sexuality, see Higginbotham, "Metalanguage of Race," 251–274.

19. Guy-Sheftall, *Daughters of Sorrow*, 40–43.

20. Patricia Morton, *Disfigured Images: The Historical Assault on Afro-American Women* (New York: Praeger, 1991) 26–33.

21. Maggie Lena Walker frequently attended the WC's annual sessions, and in 1909 she donated $500.00 to the National Training School run by Nannie Burroughs. NBC, *Journal of the Twenty-Ninth Annual Session of the National Baptist Convention and the Ninth Annual Session of the Woman's Auxiliary Convention, Held in Columbus, Ohio, September 15–20, 1909* (Nashville: National Baptist Publishing Board, 1909), 290.

See also mention of Walker's financial advice to the WC in 1920. NBC, *Journal of the Fortieth Annual Session of the National Baptist Convention and the Twentieth Annual Session of the Woman's Convention, Held in Indianapolis, Indiana, September 8–13, 1920* (Nashville: Sunday School Publishing Board, 1920), 334, 341, 350, 356, and Elsa Barkley Brown, "Womanist Consciousness: Maggie Lena Walker and the Independent Order of Saint Luke," *Signs*, 14 (Spring 1989): 610. Gertrude Rush, who addressed the WC in 1919 and 1920, was one of only a handful of black women lawyers in the early twentieth century. The U.S. census of 1910 suggests a total of only two African American women employed as lawyers in that year. NBC, *Journal of the Thirty-ninth Annual Session of the National Baptist Convention and the Nineteenth Annual Session of the Woman's Convention, Held in Newark, New Jersey, September 10–15, 1919* (Nashville: Sunday School Publishing Board, 1920), 250; NBC, *Twentieth Annual Session of the WC, 1920*, 399; Department of Commerce, Bureau of the Census, *Negro Population, 1790–1915* (Washington, D.C.: Government Printing Office, 1918), 525. In 1925, in Des Moines, Rush and eleven black male lawyers founded the National Bar Association (N.B.A.), later to become the preeminent organization for the African American legal profession. Geraldine R. Segal, *Blacks in the Law: Philadelphia and the Nation* (Philadelphia: University of Pennsylvania Press, 1983), 18; S. Joe Brown, "Our Origin," *National Bar Journal*, 2 (September 1944): 161–164.

22. Eugene Genovese, in his study of slave culture, makes this point and argues further: "The doctrine, 'Render therefore unto Caesar the things which are Caesar's; and unto God the things which are God's' is deceptively two-edged." *Roll Jordan Roll: The World the Slaves Made* (New York: Random House, Pantheon Books, 1974), 165.

23. NBC, *Sixth Annual Session of the WC, 1905*, 270.

24. Burroughs, *NBU*, 10 October 1903; also Burroughs described "men and women who have come up from the ranks of the persevering poor, waging war against poverty." NBC, *Sixth Annual Session of the WC, 1905*, 269.

25. NBC, *Fifteenth Annual Report of the Executive Board and Corresponding Secretary of the Woman's Convention, Auxiliary to the National Baptist Convention, Made at Chicago, Illinois, September 8–12, 1915*, 46, 52, 54.

26. Pierre Bourdieu, *Outline of a Theory of Practice* (New York: Cambridge University Press, 1977), 94.

27. NBC, *Journal of the Tenth Annual Session of the Woman's Convention, Held in New Orleans, Louisiana, September 14–19, 1910* (Nashville: National Baptist Publishing Board, 1910), 35.

28. NBC, *Fifteenth Annual Report of the Executive Board and Corresponding Secretary of the WC, 1915*, 50.

29. NBC, *Sixteenth Annual Report of the Executive Board and Corresponding Secretary of the Woman's Convention Auxiliary to the National Baptist Convention, Savannah, Georgia, September 6–11, 1916*, 26.

30. Darlene Clark Hine, "Rape and the Inner Lives of Black Women in the Middle West: Preliminary Thoughts on the Culture of Dissemblance," *Signs*, 14 (Summer 1989): 912–920.

31. Virginia W. Broughton, "Need of Distinctive Literature," *NBU*, 13 December 1902.

32. NBC, *Journal of the Thirty-fourth Annual Session of the National Baptist Convention and the Fourteenth Annual Assembly of the Woman's Convention, Held in Philadelphia, Pennsylvania, September 9–15, 1914* (Nashville: National Baptist Publishing Board, 1914), 81; "The Negro or Colored Dolls," *National Baptist Review*, 1 January 1909; also see advertisement which reads "Dolls! 'Negro Dolls for Negro Children' Should be the Motto of all the Parents of Negro Children," in *National Baptist Review*, 12 December 1909.

33. NBC, *Fifteenth Annual Report of the Executive Board and Corresponding Secretary of the WC, 1915*, 12.

34. NBC, *Sixteenth Annual Report of the Executive Board and Corresponding Secretary of the WC, 1916*, 8–9. In 1910 the Woman's Convention noted: "There is not a week in which we do not receive a message from some woman or girl stating that she has read certain matter sent out by the organization, and that she wants to be enlisted in the army." NBC, *Tenth Annual Session of the WC, 1910*, 23.

35. W. E. Burghardt Du Bois, ed., *Efforts for Social Betterment among Negro Americans* (Atlanta: Atlanta University Press, 1909), 23–24.

36. Brian Harrison, *Peaceable Kingdom: Stability and Change in Modern Britain* (New York: Oxford University Press, 1982), 161.

37. Henry Louis Gates, Jr., "The Trope of a New Negro and the Reconstruction of the Image of the Black," *Representations*, 24 (Fall 1988): 137.

38. For representative works, see Booker T. Washington, ed., *A New Negro for a New Century: An Accurate and Up-to-Date Record of the Upward Struggles of the Negro Race* (New York, 1900; rpt. New York: AMS Press, 1973); also William Pickens, *The New Negro: His Political, Civil, and Mental Status, and Related Essays* (New York, 1916; rpt. New York: Negro Universities Press, 1969); W. E. Burghardt Du Bois and Augustus Granville Dill, eds., *Morals and Manners among Negro Americans* (Atlanta: Atlanta University Press, 1914).

39. NBC, *Ninth Annual Session of the WC, 1909*, 281.

40. Foucault's description of the effect of being constantly aware of one's own visibility is applicable to the black Baptist women's self-perceptions: "He who is subjected to a field of visibility, and who knows it, assumes responsibility for the constraints of power; he makes them play spontaneously upon himself; he inscribes in himself the power relation in which he simultaneously plays both roles; he becomes the principle of his own subjection." Michel Foucault, *Discipline and Punish: The Birth of the Prison*, trans. Alan Sheridan (New York: Vintage Books, 1979), 200, 202–203.

41. For discussion of this issue and also white women such as Frances Kellor and Jane Addams who were exceptions to the overall trend of disinterest toward black issues, see Ellen Fitzpatrick, *Endless Crusade: Women Social Scientists and Progressive Reform* (New York: Oxford University Press, 1990), 139.

42. NBC, *Journal of the Twenty-fourth Annual Session of the National Baptist Convention and the Fifth Annual Session of the Woman's Convention, Held in Austin, Texas, September 14–19, 1904* (Nashville: National Baptist Publishing Board, 1904), 324.

43. In the report of the corresponding secretary and the executive board in 1919, the Woman's Convention questioned the religious convictions of white women and of white Protestants in general and pointed to the contradiction in their spending

large sums of money for black education while failing to give a dollar to an anti-lynching fund or to promote, even verbally, anti-lynching laws. NBC, *Nineteenth Annual Session of the WC, 1919*, 233.

44. Fraser, *Unruly Practices*, 174.

45. S. W. Layten worked with Frances Kellor in the Association for the Protection of Colored Women. She also worked with Travelers' Aid, a white organization that met and aided newly arrived immigrants to the city. Her reports of work with black arrivals from the South were part of the Philadelphia branch of Travelers' Aid. S. W. Layten, "A Northern Phase of a Southern Problem," *A.M.E Church Review*, 26 (March 1910): 315–325; Frances A. Kellor, "Associations for Protection of Colored Women," *Colored American Magazine*, 9 (December 1905): 697; E. M. Rhodes, "The Protection of Girls Who Travel: A National Movement," *Colored American Magazine*, 13 (August 1909): 113–119.

In 1912 Virginia Broughton, the recording secretary of the Woman's Convention, was the first black person to be appointed by the Associated Charities of Memphis, Tennessee, to assist flood victims. The flooding of the Mississippi Valley had caused death and loss of property for blacks and whites alike. The Associated Charities emerged in response to the disaster and furnished food, clothes, fuel, and medical attention. As matron at Camp Crump, a refuge for black victims of the flood, Broughton assessed the needs of individuals and families and arranged for relief. NBC, *Journal of the Twelfth Annual Session of the Woman's Convention, Held in Houston, Texas, September 11–15, 1912* (Nashville: National Baptist Publishing Board, 1913), 94–95; Linda Gordon, "Black and White Visions of Welfare: Women's Welfare Activism, 1890–1945," *Journal of American History*, 78 (September 1991): 578–579.

46. The Home Mission Board of the male-run National Baptist Convention also took part in this plan. NBC, *Journal of the Twenty-first Annual Session of the National Baptist Convention and the Second Annual Session of the Woman's Convention, Held in Cincinnati, Ohio, September 11–16, 1901* (Nashville: National Baptist Publishing Board, 1901), 23–24; NBC, *Journal of the Twenty-second Annual Session of the National Baptist Convention, and the Third Annual Session of the Woman's Convention, Held in Birmingham, Alabama, September 17–22, 1902* (Nashville: National Baptist Publishing Board, 1902), 16–17, 29–30; NBC, *Journal of the Twenty-third Annual Session of the National Baptist Convention and the Fourth Annual Session of the Woman's Convention, Held in Philadelphia, Pennsylvania, September 16–20, 1903* (Nashville: National Baptist Publishing Board, 1904), 80–81, 295–296; NBC, *Sixth Annual Session of the WC, 1905*, 241–242.

47. NBC, *Fifth Annual Session of the WC, 1904*, 326–327; NBC, *Sixth Annual Session of the WC, 1905*, 241–242.

48. Jacquelyn Dowd Hall, *Revolt against Chivalry: Jessie Daniel Ames and the Women's Crusade against Lynching* (New York: Columbia University Press, 1979), 72–73.

49. NBC, *Fifth Annual Session of the WC, 1904*, 324; NBC, *Ninth Annual Session of the WC, 1909*, 256–257, 324; NBC, *Twelfth Annual Session of the WC, 1912*, 27.

50. NBC, *Ninth Annual Session of the WC, 1909*, 277.

51. Ibid., 276–278. In 1913 the WC minutes record no less concern for boys: "The fact is that thousands of Negro boys are made gamblers and criminals because they have no decent place to 'hang out' when they are not on duty. The preachers and

leaders in every city, should see to it that some place is provided. It may not be pretentious enough to call a Y.M.C.A., but it can be a Social Center, and can be made attractive." NBC, *Thirteenth Annual Report of the Executive Board and Corresponding Secretary of the Woman's Convention, Auxiliary to the National Baptist Convention, Made at Nashville, Tennessee, September 17–22, 1913*, 22.

52. NBC, *Twentieth Annual Session of the WC*, 1920, 334.

53. NBC, *Journal of the Forty-first Annual Session of the National Baptist Convention and the Twenty-first Annual Session of the Woman's Convention, Held in Chicago, September 7–12, 1921* (Nashville: Sunday School Publishing Board, 1921), 299. See also the section of Nannie Burroughs's address, "Two Evils," which condemned the "demoralizing" nature of Nickel-theatres. NBC, *Tenth Annual Session of the WC*, 1910, 38–39. The speech of Adele Crawford of Missouri, "Proper Amusements for Children," also condemned the pernicious impact of the nickelodeon, public dance hall, and private club. NBC, *Twelfth Annual Session of the WC*, 1912, 78–80.

54. Jane Addams, *The Spirit of Youth and the City Streets* (New York: Macmillan, 1916), 5–7, 87–88; Kathy Peiss, *Cheap Amusements: Working Women and Leisure in Turn-of-the-Century New York* (Philadelphia: Temple University Press, 1986), 178–184; also see Carroll Smith-Rosenberg, "Engendering the Political: Women and the Public Sphere," unpublished paper presented at the conference, "Jane Addams's Hull House in Context: A Centennial Exploration," University of Illinois–Chicago Circle, October 1989 (in author's possession).

55. Nannie Burroughs would not condone dancing—even under "wholesome influence"—and could see no air of respectability in it. NBC, *Fifteenth Annual Report of the Executive Board and Corresponding Secretary of the WC*, 1915, 37.

56. Jane Edna Hunter, *A Nickel and a Prayer* (Cleveland: Elli Kani Publishing Company, 1940), 133; Adrienne Lash-Jones, *Jane Edna Hunter: A Case Study of Black Leadership, 1910–1950*, vol. 12 in Hine, ed., *Black Women in United States History*; Darlene Clark Hine, "'We Specialize in the Wholly Impossible': The Philanthropic Work of Black Women," in Kathleen D. McCarthy, ed., *Lady Bountiful Revisited: Women, Philanthropy, and Power* (New Brunswick, N.J.: Rutgers University Press, 1990), 83.

57. See reports of black women with a strong emphasis on neat appearance and cleanliness in "Women's Baptist Home Mission Society," *Baptist Home Mission Monthly* (hereafter BHMM), 2 (October 1880): 203; and BHMM, 4 (July 1882): 206. See also a similar discussion in the newspaper of black women in Selma, "Lecture of Dr. L. I. Burwell," *Baptist Woman's Era*, 4 (15 June and 15 July 1900): 1.

58. NBC, *Thirteenth Annual Report of the Executive Board and Corresponding Secretary of the WC*, 1913, 21.

59. Foucault speaks of disciplinary punishment thus: "The workshop, the school, the army [for our purposes the black Baptist church] were subject to a whole micro-penalty of . . . behavior (impoliteness, disobedience), of speech (idle chatter, insolence), of the body ('incorrect' attitudes, irregular gestures, lack of cleanliness), of sexuality (impurity, indecency). At the same time, by way of punishment, a whole series of subtle procedures was used, from light physical punishment to minor deprivations and petty humiliations. It was a question both of making the slightest departures from correct behavior subject to punishment, and of giving a punitive

function to the apparently indifferent elements of the disciplinary apparatus." See Foucault, *Discipline and Punish*, 178.

60. Peter D. Goldsmith, *When I Rise Cryin' Holy: African-American Denominationalism on the Georgia Coast* (New York: AMS Press, 1989), 13, 50, 65.

61. See Church Minutes, January 1914 to February 1923, Shiloh Baptist Church Archives, Washington, D.C.; see also Lewis Newton Walker, "The Struggles and Attempts to Establish Branch Autonomy and Hegemony: A History of the District of Columbia Branch of the National Association for the Advancement of Colored People, 1912–1942" (Ph.D. dissertation, University of Delaware, 1979), 11–15.

62. Benjamin E. Mays, *Born to Rebel: An Autobiography* (New York: Charles Scribner's Sons, 1971), 15. Tera Hunter, in her study of domestic workers between 1861 and 1920, also gives examples of the surveillance of behavior on the part of blacks themselves. Domestic workers in Atlanta were among the women who founded and participated in the social reform organization, the Neighborhood Union. Hunter describes the women of the NU as church women and "moral crusaders," who worked to provide needed social services for Atlanta's black residents, while also fighting against drinking, prostitution, gambling, and other "immoral" behavior. The women formed vigilance committees, sometimes reporting immoral activity to the police or seeking out landlords for the eviction of "undesirables." See Tera W. Hunter, "Household Workers in the Making: Afro-American Women in Atlanta and the New South, 1861 to 1920" (Ph.D. dissertation, Yale University, 1990), 246–250.

63. Mary Douglas writes: "If we can abstract pathogenicity and hygiene from our notion of dirt, we are left with the old definition of dirt as matter out of place. This is a very suggestive approach. It implies two conditions: a set of ordered relations and a contravention of that order. Dirt then, is never a unique, isolated event. Where there is dirt there is a system. Dirt is the by-product of a systematic ordering and classification of matter, in so far as ordering involves rejecting inappropriate symbols." Mary Douglas, *Purity and Danger: An Analysis of the Concepts of Pollution and Taboo* (London: Ark Paperbacks, 1966), 34–35, 40.

64. NBC, *Fifth Annual Session of the WC*, 1904, 324.

65. Nannie H. Burroughs, "Some Straight Talk to Mothers," *National Baptist Union*, 13 February 1904.

66. NBC, *Twelfth Annual Session of the WC*, 1912, 48. Between 1910 and 1920 the Woman's Convention promoted the idea of a "better yards" movement. Speeches and papers presented at the annual gatherings reinforced this message. Delegates were told to form clean-up committees and "back and front yard" campaigns in their neighborhoods. In 1916, the report of the WC's executive board and corresponding secretary listed the following reasons for the "better yards movement": "First, the health and comfort of the family depends on it. Secondly, the real progress of the race is measured by it. It will remove the excuses given for segregation." NBC, *Sixteenth Annual Report of the Executive Board and Corresponding Secretary of the WC*, 1916, 9.

67. NBC, *Thirteenth Annual Report of the Executive Board and Corresponding Secretary of the WC*, 1913, 15–16. See also NBC, *Fourteenth Annual Assembly of the WC*, 1914, 161; NBC, *Journal of the Thirty-fifth Annual Session of the National Baptist Convention and the Fifteenth Annual Session of the Women's Convention, Held in Chicago, Illinois, September 8–12, 1915* (Philadelphia: The Lisle Carey Press, n.d.), 168; NBC, *Sixteenth*

Annual Report of the Executive Board and Corresponding Secretary of the WC, 1916, 9, 12–13.

68. Burroughs stated: "Let pastors and leaders teach their people to so conduct themselves at their work and on the streets and public carriers as to disarm racial antagonism and prejudice. We can change public sentiment and get a place among the efficient forces of society by our well-doing . . . The law-abiding, industrious man is always stronger than a lawless one." NBC, *Twelfth Annual Session of the WC, 1912*, 281; also see the tract "Travelers' Friend" in Du Bois, *Efforts for Social Betterment*, 23–24.

69. For a scholarly study of alley life in Washington, D.C., see Allen Borchert, *Alley Life in Washington: Family, Community, Religion, and Folklife in the City, 1850–1970* (Urbana: University of Illinois Press, 1980), 87–99.

70. NBC, *Thirteenth Annual Report of the Executive Board and Corresponding Secretary of the WC, 1913*, 15.

71. Peter Stallybrass and Allon White, *The Politics and Poetics of Transgression* (Ithaca, N.Y.: Cornell University Press, 1986), 191.

72. Brian Harrison quotes Wright in order to support his own discussion of the complex role of respectability in causing a number of social positions among working people. Quoting from Thomas Wright, *Our New Masters (1873)*, 2–3 is Harrison, *Peaceable Kingdom*, 159–160.

73. Carby describes blues culture and women blues singers as "breaking through the boundaries of respectability and convention." Hazel V. Carby, "It Jus Be's Dat Way Sometime: The Sexual Politics of Women's Blues," *Radical America*, 20 (1986): 20–21; also for a discussion of the oppositional sites, the "street" and the "home/church," and of the relationship between reputation and respectability for black women during the 1970s, see Roger D. Abrahams, "Negotiating Respect: Patterns of Presentation among Black Women," *Journal of American Folklore*, 88 (1975): 58–80.

74. James O. Horton observes that mainstream gender conventions were promoted by the black press in the antebellum North: "Black newspapers were clear in their support of the place reserved for the female sex in American society. In their pages were countless stories of the dire consequences that awaited those who did not accept and conform to the pattern, within the limits of their ability." James O. Horton, "Freedom's Yoke: Gender Conventions among Antebellum Free Blacks," *Feminist Studies*, 12 (Spring 1986), 56. Also see James Oliver Horton and Lois E. Horton, *Black Bostonians: Family Life and Community Struggle in the Antebellum North* (New York: Holmes and Meier, 1979), chap. 2; William Muraskin, *Middle-Class Blacks in White Society: Prince Hall Freemasonry in America* (Berkeley: University of California Press, 1979), 4–25; Jesse Bernard, *Marriage and Family among Negroes* (Englewood Cliffs, N.J.: Prentice-Hall, 1966), 28–33.

75. Stallybrass and White, *Politics and Poetics*, 89.

76. Mary Church Terrell, "The Duty of the National Association of Colored Women," *A.M.E Church Review* (January 1900). This essay along with others by Terrell is found in Beverly Washington Jones, *Quest for Equality: The Life and Writings of Mary Eliza Church Terrell, 1863–1954*, vol. 13 in Hine, ed., *Black Women in United States History*, 144.

77. NBC, *Sixth Annual Session of the WC, 1905*, 260.

78. NBC, *Fourth Annual Session of the WC*, 1903, 293; NBC, *Fifth Annual Session of the WC*, 1904, 323; NBC, *Twelfth Annual Session of the WC*, 1912, 69; NBC, *Fifteenth Annual Report of the Executive Board and Corresponding Secretary of the WC*, 1915, 46, 52, 54.

79. NBC, *Fifteenth Annual Report of the Executive Board and Corresponding Secretary of the WC*, 1915, 37.

80. The same report accuses middle-class elites of perceiving social service to be no more than a fad, a vehicle for "social prestige." The report sought to discourage acceptance of such elites as leaders of church work. "They are insincere; they are not doing anything practical; they are full of theories on the solution of great problems, but a poor, ragged, dirty, forsaken women [sic] is as objectionable to them as a leper." NBC, *Twelfth Annual Session of the WC*, 1912, 27–28.

81. NBC, *Fourteenth Annual Assembly of the WC*, 1914, 152.

82. NBC, *Journal of the Eighth Annual Assembly of the Woman's Convention Held in the First Baptist Church of Lexington, Kentucky, September 16–21, 1908* (Nashville: National Baptist Publishing Board, 1909), 243.

83. Even in southern areas churches bemoaned the rising spirit of secularism ("bootlegging enterprises, dance halls, and gambling parlors"). See, for example, Joe Trotter's discussion of this in southern West Virginia and also his overall discussion of the importance of black Baptist churches, as well as Baptist women's organizations, in race advancement. Joe William Trotter, *Coal, Class, and Color: Blacks in Southern West Virginia* (Urbana: University of Illinois Press, 1990), chap. 7, especially 186–187.

84. NBC, *Fifteenth Annual Report of the Executive Board and Corresponding Secretary of the WC*, 1915, 53.

85. E. Franklin Frazier, *Black Bourgeoisie* (New York: The Free Press, 1957), 80–81, 197–238. Bart Landry identifies the time period between 1915 and 1960 for Frazier's black middle class and observes the rise of a new type of black middle class beginning in the 1960s. The latter group, which still predominates, has had more opportunities because of civil rights legislation. However, Landry says of Frazier's negative assessment of the black bourgeoisie's values and lifestyle, which was similar in tone to the black Baptist women's: "There is no doubt that much of Frazier's criticism was valid, though black writers continue to debate the degree or extent of its accuracy." See Bart Landry, *The New Black Middle Class* (Berkeley: University of California Press, 1987), 61–62.

86. The Ewens posit: "The promise of the 'melting pot' . . . equated the utilization of consumer products not only with citizenship, but with a demonstrable and necessary transformation of the self." Stuart Ewen and Elizabeth Ewen, *Channels of Desire: Mass Images and the Shaping of American Consciousness* (New York: McGraw-Hill, 1982), 27, 54.

87. NBC, *Tenth Annual Session of the WC*, 1910, 39–40. For a similar critique, see NBC, *Thirteenth Annual Report of the Executive Board and Corresponding Secretary of the WC*, 1913, 22.

88. Griffin's paper was reproduced in the press. See Anna Griffin, "Don't Live on the Installment Plan," *National Baptist Union*, 21 November 1903. For a discussion of African Americans as consumers and as receptive to American mass culture, see Lizabeth Cohen, *Making a New Deal: Industrial Workers in Chicago, 1919–1939* (New York: Cambridge University Press, 1990), 147–154.

89. By the end of its first year the school had enrolled thirty-one students, who ranged in age from twelve to forty-three. In the following year enrollment had risen to eighty-three, sixty of whom were boarders. Twenty-four states and four foreign countries were represented in the student body. NBC, *Ninth Annual Session of the WC, 1909*, 283; NBC, *Journal of the Tenth Annual Session of the WC, 1910*, 43–47; NBC, *Journal of the Eleventh Annual Session of the Woman's Convention, Held in Pittsburgh, Pennsylvania, September 13–18, 1911* (Nashville: National Baptist Publishing Board, 1911), 45; National Training School for Women and Girls, Enrollment 1909–1910, Nannie Helen Burroughs Papers, Library of Congress (hereafter NHB, LC).

90. The school, today called the Nannie Helen Burroughs School, continues to operate on the same campus site in Washington, D.C. It is now a private school for elementary and secondary-age school children. During the years of this study, Burroughs remained in her position as corresponding secretary of the Woman's Convention while heading the National Training School. Nannie Helen Burroughs, "Woman's Department—Sharps and Flats: Sparks from the Secretary's Anvil," in *Mission Herald* (January 1907); also see Evelyn Brooks Barnett, "Nannie Burroughs and the Education of Black Women," in Sharon Harley and Rosalyn Terborg-Penn, eds., *The Afro-American Woman: Struggles and Images* (Port Washington, N.Y.: Kennikat Press, 1978), 97–108.

91. NBC, *Ninth Annual Session of the WC, 1909*, 276.

92. NBC, *Fifteenth Annual Session of the WC, 1915*, 288. In the women's column in the *National Baptist Union*, Burroughs wrote: "An idle woman is seldom a virtuous woman." See under section, "Chips from Our Woodpile," in the "Baptist Women's Edition," *National Baptist Union*, 8 August 1903.

93. According to the Bureau of the Census, slightly over half (1,051,137 out of 2,013,981) of the gainfully employed black women over ten years of age in 1910 worked in agricultural occupations. Of the remaining 962,844 black women in paid employment, 776,966, or 80.7 percent, were either laundresses or servants. Bureau of the Census, *Negro Population*, 523, 525.

94. In 1903 Burroughs observed: "We have always believed that our women who work at service for a living, ought to receive more attention at the hands of Christian women than they have." NBC, *Fourth Annual Session of the WC, 1903*, 313. The Training School identified its vocational course of study as preparing women for jobs as cooks, laundresses, chamber-maids, ladies' maids, nurses, housekeepers, dressmakers, stenographers, bookkeepers, and clerks. NBC, *Fifteenth Annual Session of the WC, 1915*, 288.

95. Both Elizabeth Clark-Lewis and Sharon Harley confirm the argument that black women migrated to Washington, D.C., for work as domestics. Elizabeth Clark-Lewis, "'This Work Had a End': African-American Domestic Workers in Washington, D.C., 1910–1940," in Carole Groneman and Mary Beth Norton, eds., *"To Toil the Livelong Day": America's Women at Work, 1780–1980* (Ithaca, N.Y.: Cornell University Press, 1987), 199; Sharon Harley, "For the Good of Family and Race: Gender, Work, and Domestic Roles in the Black Community, 1880–1930," *Signs*, 15 (Winter 1990): 338; see also "The National Training School," Report of the Corresponding Secretary, 1906, NHB Papers, LC.

96. NBC, *Thirteenth Annual Report of the Executive Board and Corresponding Secretary of the WC, 1913*, 15.

97. NBC, *Ninth Annual Session of the WC, 1909*, 286.

98. Ibid.

99. Burroughs insisted: "We so teach that each student is well qualified to work at some definite trade, and to perform the task so well that no one can really fill the place quite as satisfactorily and uniquely as she can fill it." NBC, *Eleventh Annual Session of the WC, 1911*, 47.

100. In 1920 Burroughs reported to the Woman's Convention that 200 students had graduated from the Training School. Although the school records are incomplete, they list eighty diplomas and eighty-four certificates awarded to students between 1911 and 1920. The records of students who graduated with diplomas or certificates reveal the preponderance of the trades department over the missionary and normal. Of the eighty diplomas awarded, only 13 percent went to students in missionary training, and only 9 percent to students in the normal department. Of the eighty-four certificates, 20 percent went to missionary students with 3 percent to normal. The trades department had awarded 78 percent of all diplomas and 77 percent of all certificates between 1911 and 1920. See "Graduates" in NHB Papers, LC; also NBC, *Eleventh Annual Session of the WC, 1911*, 47.

101. In a letter to Booker T. Washington in 1912, Burroughs stated that nine-tenths of the girls enrolled in her school would be unable to gain admission to the liberal-arts-oriented Howard University in Washington, D.C. Nannie H. Burroughs to Booker T. Washington, 2 September 1912, Booker T. Washington Papers, Library of Congress (hereafter BTW Papers, LC). She also shared speakers' platforms with him in promoting industrial education. See, for example, "Noted Negro Educator to Speak to Negro Gathering This Morning—Negro Woman Delivered Able and Forceful Address," *Atlanta Constitution*, 9 August 1902; Booker T. Washington, ed., *Tuskegee and Its People: Their Ideals and Achievements* (New York: D. Appleton and Company, 1905), 7–10.

102. The Training School's catalogs during the 1920s continued to emphasize industrial education rather than liberal arts: "The race is overstocked with teachers of academic subjects, but is in dire need of skilled artisans and qualified teachers of handicrafts." "National Training School for Women and Girls [Catalogue for calendar year 1928–1929]," NHB Papers, LC; Nannie H. Burroughs, "Ten Reasons Why We Should Have a Trade School for Negro Girls," Archibald H. Grimké Papers, Moorland-Spingarn Research Center, Howard University; Burroughs, "Industrial Education—Will It Solve the Negro Problem?" *Colored American Magazine* (March 1904):188–190; also Harrison, *Dream and the Dreamer*, 26, 35–36.

103. In a booklet entitled *Making Their Mark*, the Training School left a record of the achievements of some of its early alumnae and their activities after graduation. Graduates were identified by name and described in various capacities: domestic servants; dressmakers; typists and stenographers in a black university, insurance company, and orphan asylum; teachers of domestic science and commercial courses in high schools in Washington, D.C. and North Carolina; hairdressers and owners of beauty salons; printers; foreign missionaries; and wives and homemakers. Nannie

Burroughs, *Making Their Mark* (Washington, D.C.: National Training School for Women and Girls, n.d.), 9; also Washington, *Tuskegee*, 81.

104. U.S. Department of the Interior, Bureau of Education, *Negro Education: A Study of the Private and Higher Schools for Colored People in the United States*, vol. 2 (Washington, D.C.: Government Printing Office, 1917), 154.

105. In 1912 the Woman's American Baptist Home Mission Society strengthened the domestic science department at the National Training School by supplying a model home for the campus. The building was electrically lit and had a steam-heating plant in the basement. Its spacious floor plan contained a dining room, kitchen, and sun parlor on the second level, and four bedrooms and a bathroom on the third. The WABHMS donated the house on condition that black Baptists be responsible for furnishing it. The building was named the Mary G. Burdette Memorial Home after the first principal of the Missionary Training School in Chicago and long-time leader of white Baptist women in the Midwest. NBC, *Twelfth Annual Session of the WC, 1912*, 50–51; NBC, *Thirteenth Annual Report of the Executive Board and Corresponding Secretary of the WC, 1913*, 30.

106. Palmer notes that home economics, unlike the other sciences, made a distinction between the amateur and the professional, and also between the housewife-employer and the domestic employee. Phyllis Palmer, *Domesticity and Dirt: Housewives and Domestic Servants in the United States, 1920–1945* (Philadelphia: Temple University Press, 1989), 91; Thomas Woody, *A History of Women's Education*, vol. 2 (New York: The Science Press, 1929), 54, 56, 64–97.

107. Frederick W. Taylor, *Principles of Scientific Management* (New York: Harper and Row, 1911), chap. 1; "Taylor, Frederick Winslow," in Dumas Malone, ed., *Dictionary of American Biography*, vol. 18 (New York: Charles Scribner's Sons, 1936), 324; "Scientific Management" in Glenn Porter, ed., *The Encyclopedia of American Economic History: Studies of the Principal Movements and Ideas* (New York: Charles Scribner's Sons, 1980), 836–841; Bernard Doray, *From Taylorism to Fordism: A Rational Madness* (London: Free Association Books, 1988), 72–85; also for a study of Taylorized household training in Germany, see Mary Nolan, "'Housework Made Easy': The Taylorized Housewife in Weimar Germany's Rationalized Economy," *Feminist Studies*, 16 (Fall 1990): 549–577.

108. Palmer, *Domesticity and Dirt*, 89–100; Woody, *Women's Education*, 52–64.

109. NBC, *Sixth Annual Session of the WC, 1905*, 258.

110. David Katzman, *Seven Days a Week: Women and Domestic Service in Industrializing America* (New York: Oxford University Press, 1978), 229.

111. Quoted in Palmer, *Domesticity and Dirt*, 98.

112. See Foucault's discussion of discipline, especially his differentiation between moral "renunciations" and the increase of workers' utility. Foucault, *Discipline and Punish*, 211, 218, 222.

113. S. W. Layten argued that competent and efficient domestic servants created favorable public sentiment for blacks within the respective households in which they worked. S. W. Layten, "The Servant Problem," *Colored American Magazine*, 12 (January 1907): 15. See also NBC, *Sixteenth Annual Session of the WC, 1916*, 195. Burroughs in her executive report for 1905 argued that black domestic servants could

vindicate their race by "proving themselves industrious, upright, and honest." NBC, *Sixth Annual Session of the WC, 1905*, 267.

114. Burroughs referred to her school as the "School of the three B's," since the Bible, bathtub, and broom symbolized "righteous lives, clean bodies, and clean homes," respectively. NBC, *Ninth Annual Session of the WC, 1909*, 286; NBC, *Eleventh Annual Session of the WC, 1911*, 47.

115. In the section, "Don't Send Them to Us," Burroughs reported that the moral standard of the school demanded only the best girls, not "other peoples' neglected impossibles." See NBC, *Twelfth Annual Session of the WC, 1912*, 21–22, 43–44.

116. Palmer, *Domesticity and Dirt*, 147; for a similar discussion, see also Hunter, "Household Workers in the Making: Afro-American Women in Atlanta and the New South, 1861 to 1920," 201–204.

117. Harley, "For the Good of Family and Race," 340–341.

118. Clark-Lewis, "This Work Had a End," 198.

119. Burroughs's autobiographical notes are found in her own handwriting on the stationery of the Woman's Convention in the correspondence of the southern white Baptist leader Una Roberts Lawrence. Una Roberts Lawrence Papers, Southern Baptist Historical Library and Archives, Nashville, Tennessee.

120. NBC, *Twentieth Annual Session of the WC, 1920*, 337.

121. *Shiloh Herald*, 2 March 1924, in the Shiloh Baptist Church Archives, Washington, D.C.

122. NBC, *Tenth Annual Session of the WC, 1910*, 90; NBC, *Nineteenth Annual Session of the WC, 1919*, 220; NBC, *Twentieth Annual Session of the WC, 1920*, 336–337.

123. The National Association of Wage Earners appears to have concentrated its efforts on educational programs to inform the public, rather than on traditional trade unionist tactics. See letterhead on stationery, for example, Burroughs to Mrs. Terrell, Mary Church Terrell Collection, Moorland-Spingarn Research Center, Howard University; *Opportunity*, 2 (December 1924): 383; National Association of Wage Earners, NHB Papers, LC.

124. In 1912 Burroughs asked Booker T. Washington to recommend her school to the philanthropist Julius Rosenwald. She wanted Rosenwald to match half of the amount necessary for the erection of an industrial hall. Washington did not respond enthusiastically to her request, for he believed black Washingtonians to be the highest per capita recipients of philanthropy. Burroughs did not receive the funds from Rosenwald. See Burroughs to Booker T. Washington, 19 August 1912 and 2 September 1912; Booker T. Washington to Nannie H. Burroughs, 29 August 1912; and an unsigned letter from the Rosenwald Fund to Nannie H. Burroughs, 13 November 1912. BTW Papers, LC.

125. White contributors included the Woman's American Baptist Home Mission Society, the Emmeline Cushing Estate, the Phelps-Stokes Fund, and the Slater Fund. NBC, *Sixteenth Annual Report of the Executive Board and Corresponding Secretary of the WC, 1916*, 18–19; William Pickens, *Nannie Burroughs and the School of the Three B's* (New York: n.p., 1921), 11; also see NBC, *Ninth Annual Session of the WC, 1909*, 284; and see the Library of Congress's register for the Nannie Helen Burroughs Papers.

126. Whitfield Hall on the campus of the National Training School for Women and Girls was named in honor of Ella Ewell Whitfield, field secretary of the Woman's Convention, for her efforts in fund raising and winning friends for the school. See "Circular of Information for the Seventeenth Annual Session of the National Training School for Women and Girls, Incorporated, 1925–1926," 12, and also contribution slips in NHB Papers, LC.

127. Out of a total of $134,792.32 for the work of the Woman's Convention, $79,302.72 had been raised by the states for the Training School, and $55,489.60 had been raised for the convention's general fund and for missions between 1900 and 1920. NBC, *Twenty-first Annual Session of the WC, 1921*, 287–290.

128. Hunter, "Household Workers in the Making," chap. 4; Clark-Lewis, "'This Work Had a End,'" 203–212. For a discussion of similar efforts to organize black domestic servants during the 1910s and 1920s, see Rosalyn-Terborg Penn, "Survival Strategies among African-American Women Workers: A Continuing Process," in Ruth Milkman, ed., *Women, Work and Protest: A Century of US Women's Labor History* (New York: Routledge and Kegan Paul, 1985), 144–145.

129. Bonnie Thornton Dill, "'Making Your Job Good Yourself': Domestic Service and the Construction of Personal Dignity," in Ann Bookman and Sandra Morgen, eds., *Women and the Politics of Empowerment* (Philadelphia: Temple University Press, 1988), 41; also see Collins, *Black Feminist Thought*, 91–92; and Judith Rollins, *Between Women: Domestics and Their Employers* (Philadelphia: Temple University Press, 1985), 212–218, 225.

130. James C. Scott, *Domination and the Arts of Resistance: Hidden Transcripts* (New Haven: Yale University Press, 1990), 93–106.

131. NBC, *Thirteenth Annual Report, 1913*, 33.

132. NBC, *Fifth Annual Session of the WC, 1904*, 346; NBC, *Seventh Annual Report of the Executive Board and Corresponding Secretary of the Woman's Convention, Auxiliary to the National Baptist Convention, Made at Washington, D.C., September 1907*, 9–10; see also NBC, *Tenth Annual Session of the WC, 1910*, 37–38.

133. NBC, *Eighth Annual Assembly of the WC, 1908*, 268.

134. NBC, *Journal of the Eighteenth Annual Session of the Woman's Convention, Auxiliary to the National Baptist Convention, Held in St. Louis, Missouri, September 4–9, 1918* (Nashville: Sunday School Publishing Board, 1919), 169.

135. Representatives from the NAACP were often speakers at the annual meetings of the Woman's Convention. Judge Robert McMurdy, a representative of the NAACP from Chicago, spoke to the convention in 1915, and in 1919 John R. Shillady, secretary of the NAACP, was a speaker. NBC, *Fifteenth Annual Session of the WC, 1915*, 170; see also NBC, *Fourteenth Annual Assembly of the WC, 1914*, 173, 178; NBC, *Nineteenth Annual Session of the WC, 1919*, 243–244.

136. NBC, *Sixth Annual Session of the WC, 1905*, 269; NBC, *Eighteenth Annual Session of the WC, 1918*, 168; NBC, *Nineteenth Annual Session of the WC, 1919*, 233.

137. NBC, *Nineteenth Annual Session of the WC, 1919*, 232, 261; "Meetings," *Crisis*, 19 (December 1919): 85.

138. NBC, *Twentieth Annual Session of the WC, 1920*, 319–320. For a discussion of the NAACP's campaign against lynching during this time period, see also Robert

L. Zangrando, *The NAACP Crusade against Lynching, 1909–1950* (Philadephia: Temple University Press, 1980), 22–71.

139. NBC, *Eighteenth Annual Session of the WC, 1918*, 140, 142, 160–161, 168–169, 191.

140. NBC, *Nineteenth Annual Session of the WC, 1919*, 232, 261.

141. Records of the War Department, General and Special Staffs, Military Intelligence Division, "Black Radicals (Church of God)," from Record Group 165, National Archives. I would like to thank Gerald R. Gill for alerting me to this material.

142. NBC, *Ninth Annual Session of the WC, 1909*, 256–257; NBC, *Twelfth Annual Session of the WC, 1912*, 39.

143. NBC, *Ninth Annual Session of the WC, 1909*, 256–257.

144. NBC, *Twelfth Annual Session of the WC, 1912*, 93.

145. S. W. Layten emphasized women's suffrage for racial progress and for facilitating progressive-reform legislation. See S. W. Layten to Mary Church Terrell, June 1916, Mary Church Terrell Papers, LC; Burroughs, "Black Women and Reform," *Crisis*, 10 (August 1915): 187; and Rosalyn Terborg-Penn, "Woman Suffrage: 'First because We Are Women and Second because We Are Colored Women,'" *Truth: Newsletter of the Association of Black Women Historians* (April 1985), 9.

146. NBC, *Nineteenth Annual Session of the WC, 1919*, 250.

147. NBC, *Nineteenth Annual Session of the WC, 1919*, 203, 209, 211; NBC, *Twentieth Annual Session of the WC, 1920*, 305, 316.

148. NBC, *Twentieth Annual Session of the WC, 1920*, 305, 338–339; also see Rosalyn Terborg-Penn, "Discrimination against Afro-American Women in the Woman's Movement, 1830–1920," in Harley and Terborg-Penn, eds., *The Afro-American Woman*, 22–27.

149. NBC, *Twentieth Annual Session of the WC, 1920*, 338–340, 383.

150. NBC, *Twenty-first Annual Session of the WC, 1921*, 282. Evelyn Brooks Higginbotham, "In Politics to Stay: Black Women and Party Politics in the 1920s," in Louise A. Tilly and Patricia Gurin, eds., *Women, Politics, and Change* (New York: Russell Sage, 1990), 208–212; Theodore S. Boone, *Negro Baptist Chief Executives in National Places* (Detroit: A. P. Publishing Company, 1948), 30–31.

151. "Miss Burroughs Given an Ovation," *National Baptist Union*, 28 June 1902.

152. I owe this discussion of the relational character of charismatic leadership to James Scott's analysis. Scott observes: "It is the cultural and social expectations of followers that exercise a controlling or at least limiting influence over the would-be charismatic figure. . . . The role of heroine in this case is to a large extent scripted in advance offstage by all members of the subordinate group, and the individual who fills that role is that one who somehow—through anger, courage, a sense of responsibility, or indignation—summons the wherewithal to speak on behalf of others to power." Scott, *Domination and the Arts of Resistance*, 20, 221.

153. NBC, *Fourteenth Annual Assembly of the WC, 1914*, 179.

Index

Abbey, Dr. Charlotte, 178
ABHMS. *See* American Baptist Home Mission Society
Abolitionism, 91, 106, 111, 114, 146, 269n71
Adams, Emma, 104
Adams, M. Helen, 177, 178
Addams, Jane, 175, 284n41; *The Spirit of Youth*, 199–200
Africa, 48, 242n48
African Americans, 3, 5, 9, 10, 16, 19, 56; and political participation, 12; history of, 14, 106; cultural differences among, 43; on school faculties, 51; upward mobility for, 63, 96, 119, 243n65; self-perceptions of, 142; individual behavior of, 196. *See also* Nationalism, black
African Methodist Episcopal Church, 6, 11, 53, 58, 233n15, 234n29
African Methodist Episcopal Zion Church, 11, 233n15
Afro-American Life Insurance Company, 174
Ahlstrom, Sydney, 137
Alabama Baptist University. *See* Selma University
Allen, Fannie, 117–118
Alvord, John W., 54
American Baptist Home Mission Society (ABHMS), 25, 26, 27, 28, 42, 44, 46, 69, 72; and education of freedpeople, 30, 91–92, 98, 239n29, 240n33; schools of, 21–24, 29, 39, 43, 50–53, 55, 56, 57, 58, 59, 60, 61, 62, 91, 108, 239n28; and missionary training, 35, 36; policies of, 49, 54, 113; financial support of, 90, 92, 280n113; view of African Americans, 112; annual reports of, 238n16

American Baptist (Louisville), 61, 76, 78
American Baptist Publication Society, 66, 247n26
American Home Economics Association, 215
American Missionary Association (Congregationalist), 90
American National Baptist Convention (ANBC), 65, 147, 156; women delegates to, 64, 124, 125, 126, 130, 132, 133, 134, 135, 144–145, 153, 154, 250n59; officers of, 251n63, 265n37
American Social Hygiene Association, 179
ANBC. *See* American National Baptist Convention
Anderson, Benedict, 49, 234n25
Anderson, James, 55
Anthony, Susan B., 227
Anti-Catholicism, 112–113, 261n77
Arkansas Baptist College, 58, 95, 249n53
Armstrong, Annie, 197
Assimilation, 40, 115, 187, 194–204, 205
Associated Charities, 197
Atlanta Baptist College. *See* Morehouse College
Atlanta Baptist Female Seminary. *See* Spelman Seminary
Atlanta University, 18
Ayer, Reverend Charles, 21

Baker, Houston, 236n42
Bakhtin, Mikhail, 16, 236n45, 281n5
Baptist College (Macon, Missouri), 74. *See also* Western College
Baptist Foreign Mission Convention, 64, 65, 153
Baptist Headlight (Topeka, Kansas), 77, 139
Baptist Journal (St. Louis), 76

Baptist Leader (Selma, Alabama), 77
Baptist Teacher, 247n26
Baptist Tribune (South Carolina), 76
Baptist Vanguard (Arkansas), 77
Baptist Woman's Era (Alabama), 63, 78, 118, 166
Baptist Women's Educational Convention of Kentucky, 59–61, 78, 126
Baptist Women's Missionary League, 156
Barber, Max J., 169
Barkley, Anna, 93–94
Barrett, L. G., 104
Battey, E. B., 30
Becker, Charles, 51
Bederman, Gail, 141, 267n56
Beecher, Henry Ward, 137
Bellah, Robert N., 9
Benedict Institute (South Carolina), 21, 22, 51, 109
Bennett, Nora, 94
Berger, Peter, 8, 233n20
Berkeley, Kathleen, 263n10
Bethel Institutional Church (Jacksonville, Florida), 174
Bible: and women's rights, 2, 70, 120–121, 122–123, 125, 127, 128–129, 138, 139, 149, 153; and literacy, 19, 22, 44, 73; study of, 35, 38, 45, 69, 70, 71, 93, 127, 253n88; interpretation of, 122–124, 125, 126–128, 132, 143, 264n22; feminine symbolism in, 142; and racial equality, 186; and respectability, 216
Bible and Normal Institute (later Howe Institute; Memphis), 70, 72, 93
Bible Bands, 69, 70, 71–72, 93, 99, 127, 253n88
Biblical World (University of Chicago Divinity School), 140
Binga, Anthony, 23, 145, 269n77
Birth of a Nation, The (film), 189
Bishop College (Marshall, Texas), 51, 57–58
Black Baptists, number of, 6–7, 232n15, 233n17
Blair Bill, 55
Blake, Lille Devereaux: *Woman's Place Today*, 138
Blyden, Edward Wilmot, 269n74
Booker, Reverend Joseph A., 249n49
Boothe, Reverend Charles Octavius, 62, 120, 145
Bothwell, Miss L. J., 241n46
Bourdieu, Pierre, 192–193
Bowie, Alice A., 63, 65, 155, 271n11
Boyd, Richard H., 65, 160, 164, 194
Brawley, Benjamin, 269n74
Brawley, Mrs. Edward, 63

Brawley, Reverend Edward McKnight, 44, 51, 61, 145, 249nn49,52, 251n63, 269n74
Brooks, Reverend Walter H., 23, 53, 56, 65, 85 (ill.), 147, 174, 182, 247n26
Broughton, John, 124, 131–132
Broughton, Virginia, 69, 101, 103–104, 143, 144, 155, 157, 160, 271n7; as missionary, 70, 72–73, 95, 99; popularity of, 71; and Woman's Convention, 72, 85 (ill.), 263n11, 272n20, 273n32; on women's movement, 79, 252n83; as feminist theologian, 124–125, 126, 127, 128, 131, 132, 133, 135, 142, 263n10, 265nn33,36, 268n59; *Women's Work, as Gleaned from the Women of the Bible*, 125, 128–129, 146–147; children of, 130; marriage of, 131–132; rivalry with Nannie Burroughs, 163; description of NBC meeting, 164–165; on black history, 194; on black women's dress, 200; as leader, 228–229; and flood relief, 285n45
Bryant, Sylvia, 85 (ill.), 157, 272n20
Buckner, Mrs. M. M., 272n20
Bullock, Penelope, 11
Burdette, Mary, 86 (ill.), 95, 115, 127, 257n16, 292n105
Burroughs, Jennie, 217, 218
Burroughs, Nannie Helen: and Woman's Convention, 84 (ill.), 85 (ill.), 150, 157, 158–159, 160, 161, 162, 176, 177, 178, 271n13, 272nn17,20, 276nn66,74, 286n53; speeches of, 150, 152, 155, 156; and Virginia Broughton, 163; on ordinary women, 164, 208–209; on clergy, 175–176; and Nineteenth Street Baptist Church, 182, 277n80; and politics of respectability, 191, 195, 200, 218–219, 283n24, 286n55, 288n68; "Straight Talk to Mothers," 202; speech on alley reform, 203; and WC annual reports, 206, 207, 223; and National Training School, 211–221, 233n19, 282n21, 290n90, 291nn100,101, 293nn114,115,124, 294n126; on manual labor, 214, 215, 217; family background of, 217–218; and organized labor, 218–219, 221; on segregation, 222–223; on prayer, 224; and World War I, 225–226, 235n33; on women's suffrage, 226, 227; popularity of, 228; papers of, 233n19, 293n119; on "romantic racialism," 269n74; *The Slabtown Convention* (one-act play), 274n38; quoted, 290nn92,94, 291n99
Butler, Selena Sloan, 66
Bynum, Caroline, 123, 263n7

Carby, Hazel, 13, 204, 288n73
Carnegie, Andrew, 89
Case, Carl Delos: *The Masculine in Religion*, 141, 268n58
Catt, Carrie Chapman, 227
Cayton, Horace, 281n7
Central City College (Macon, Georgia), 57
Chase, Calvin, 237n3
Chesterton, Gilbert, 10, 233n24
Christian Home and Training School for Women, 72
Christianity, 191, 202, 227, 266n49; feminization of, 139–142; "tough," 141; and status of women, 144, 148, 268n60; and family life, 268n63
Chronicle (San Francisco), 188
Church, black: and women, 1–18, 50, 58, 153, 184, 229, 235n36; rise of, 2; after Reconstruction, 4–7; as public sphere, 7–13; legacy of resistance in, 15–18; dialogic model of, 16; and collective self-help, 47, 49, 50, 96; influence of, 50, 204; and bourgeois values, 96–97; and reform, 171–180, 236n47; institutional, 173–174, 277nn76,79; role of, 233n20, 289n83
Civil rights, 48, 100, 191, 221–229, 289n85
Civil Rights Act (1875), 5
Civil Rights Movement, 229
Civil War, 3, 19, 21, 30, 50, 53, 91, 93, 114, 120, 139, 146; and freedpeople, 21, 43, 92, 98, 143; preaching before, 45
Clanton, Olive Bird, 133–134, 265n37
Clanton, Reverend Solomon T., 133, 249n49, 265n37
Clark, James, 37
Clarke, William Newton, 137
Clark-Lewis, Elizabeth, 217, 221
Class, 20, 40, 42–46, 51, 187; and status differentiation, 204–211
Clubwomen, 16–17, 151–152, 182, 205, 206, 207, 280n113
Cohen, Lizabeth, 97
Cole, Anna Russell, 183
Coles, Reverend J. J., 64
Collins, Patricia Hill, 186
Colored American Magazine, 174, 228
Comaroff, Jean, 280n1
Commercialism, 210–211
Conservatism, 15, 203–204
Convention movement, 19–20, 48, 121, 148, 153, 175, 205, 251n63, 252n74
Conventions: definition of, 2–3; women's, 58–63, 68–80, 99–100, 124, 127, 151
Cook, Mary V. (Mary V. Parrish), 62, 64, 78, 85 (ill.), 99, 103, 116, 119, 143, 169,

182–183; quoted, 60, 68, 79, 128, 129, 144, 208, 259n38; marriage of, 63, 156; early life of, 88–89, 125; on lynching, 110; and feminist theology, 124, 126, 129–130, 131, 132–133, 134, 135–136, 264n22, 265n28, 266n48; and women's conventions, 169, 248n37, 264n16, 272nn18,20; and social reform, 179
Cooper, Anna J., 123–124, 237n3, 248n41; *A Voice from the South*, 13, 19, 67–68, 119
Cooperation, interracial, 89–119, 197, 198; and exchange of letters, 105, 110
Crawford, Adella, 179
Crisis, 102, 166, 224, 226
Crittenden, Lizzie, 127
Crummel, Alexander, 237n3
Culture: black, 15, 42–46, 47, 108, 113–114, 115, 194, 200, 201, 236n42, 244n74, 288n73; consumer, 185; of dissemblance, 194; and women's rights, 268n60; slave, 283n22

Davis, Mrs. H., 143
De Lamotta, Emma, 35, 38, 81 (ill.), 103, 105
Delaney, Emma B., 156, 272n19
de Lauretis, Teresa, 189, 282n13
Democracy, 48, 186, 225
de Staël, Madame, 143
Dill, Bonnie Thornton, 221
Dinkins, Charles, 249n52
Dinkins, Pauline (Mrs. Charles), 63, 249n52
Discrimination: racial, 5, 120, 152, 203, 227; gender, 120, 188, 263n10
Disfranchisement, 4, 47, 55, 76, 89, 197, 226
Dix, Reverend Morgan J., 138
Dixon, Thomas: *The Clansman*, 189
Douglas, Ann, 139; *The Feminization of American Culture*, 148
Douglas, Mary, 287n63
Douglass, Frederick, 9, 269n70
Drake, St. Clair, 58, 281n7
Du Bois, W. E. B., 48, 183, 188, 221, 228, 269n74; *Darkwater*, 1; on black church, 7, 18, 173; on higher education, 20, 237n3; on motherhood, 100; "The Conservation of Races," 146, 269n72; *The Gift of Black Folk*, 146; *Efforts for Social Betterment*, 195
Dunbar, Paul Lawrence, 170
Dyer, Carrie, 104, 108, 244n79

Earle, Victoria: *Aunt Lindy*, 13
Ebenezer Baptist Church (Richmond), 23, 120

Education, 1–2, 13, 19, 202, 244n75; higher, 19–46, 55, 89, 100, 154, 182; liberal arts, 20, 237n3; for women, 20–46, 136, 152, 182, 214, 248n41; Christian, 30; religious, 34, 176, 177; and public schools, 55, 113, 247n25; and upward mobility, 63, 119, 208; denial of, to blacks, 123; sex, 178; kindergarten, 180, 184. *See also* Training; *individual colleges*
Emancipation, 43, 53, 107
Empowerment, 2, 3, 19, 45, 46, 56, 128, 166, 185
Evers, Medgar, 229
Ewen, Elizabeth, 210, 289n86
Ewen, Stewart, 210, 289n86

Fee, Elizabeth, 178, 179
Felski, Rita, 123
Fireside School, 101, 169
First African Baptist Church (St. Simon's Island), 201
Fisk University, 23, 69, 124, 173
Flinn, Victor, 181
Flowers, Mary, 101, 169
Foster, Susie C., 157
Foucault, Michel, 196, 201, 284n40, 286n59, 292n112
Fox, Mrs. E. P., 272n20
Fraser, Nancy, 50, 187, 234n27, 245n6, 281n6
Frazier, E. Franklin, 5, 7, 11; *Black Bourgeoisie*, 210, 236n41, 289n85
Fredrickson, George, 145, 269n71
Freedman, Estelle, 79
Freedmen of the Presbyterian Church: Board of Missions to, 90
Freedmen's Aid Society (Methodist Episcopal Church), 90
Freedmen's Bureau, 54
Freedmen's education societies, 90–91
Freeman, Alice, 109
Free Speech and Headlight, 11, 234n29
Friendship Baptist Church (Atlanta), 22, 31, 32, 155, 240n36
Frierson, Mrs. H. E., 182
Frye, R. T., 168
Fuller, Thomas, 253n88
Fund raising, 2, 9, 17, 59, 77, 157, 160, 161, 184, 220

Garland, Elizabeth A., 64
Gates, Henry Louis, Jr., 195
Gazette (Georgia), 37
Gender consciousness, 8, 50, 67–73, 79, 151, 154, 166; double-, 142–147
General Association of Kentucky, 60, 63
Genovese, Eugene, 15, 283n22

Genung, Hattie E., 105
Gilbert, Miss G. G., 271n7
Giles, Harriet, 22, 33, 34, 35, 36, 39, 83 (ill.), 105, 237n6, 240n39, 241n45, 242n51, 243n62
Gilman, Sander, 190
Gladden, Washington, 137
Glenn, G. R., 36, 245n9
Goins, Mary E., 85 (ill.)
Goldsmith, Peter, 201
Gordon, J. D., 57, 247n30
Gordon, Nora, 37, 38
Gramsci, Antonio, 47, 245n1
Grant, Madison: *The Passing of the Great Race*, 188
Gray, Mrs. A. E., 108–109
Griffin, Anna, 210–211, 289n88
Griffin, Elizabeth V., 36
Griggs, Reverend Sutton, 44, 65
Guadalupe College, 57
Guy-Sheftall, Beverly, 190
Gwaltney, John Langston, 236n42

Habermas, Jürgen, 10, 234nn26,27,28, 245n6
Hall, Jacquelyn Dowd, 198
Hamer, Fannie Lou, 229
Hamilton, Mrs. M. E., 272n20
Hampton Institute, 241n45
Harlan, Louis, 246n12
Harper, Frances Ellen Watkins, 100, 143, 237n3, 270n3; *Iola Leroy*, 13, 100–101
Harper's Bazaar, 77
Harrison, Brian, 195, 288n72
Hartshorn, Rachel, 116
Hartshorn Memorial College (Richmond), 23–24, 28, 45, 104, 108, 111, 116, 244n79
Haygood, Dr. Atticus G., 241nn45,46
Haynes, George Edmund, 170, 180
Henri, Florette, 172
Hine, Darlene Clark, 193–194
Hobsbawm, Eric, 18
Holmes, Willis Anthony, 68
Home Mission Echo, 103, 106, 107, 110, 118, 240n39, 248n37, 264n16
Hooper, Governor Ben (Tennessee), 184
Hope, John, 170
Hope (Louisiana), 99–100, 101, 169
Horton, James O., 288n74
Houchins, Sue E., 128, 265n33
Hovey, Mrs., 108
Howard, Annie, 103
Howard, Oliver O., 51
Howard University, 23, 51, 59, 60, 170, 177, 291n101
Hudson, Winthrop, 137–138
Humphrey, Rosella, 38, 39
Hungate, Jesse, 267n57, 268n59

Hunt, Anna Sargent, 103, 111, 262n92
Hunter, Jane Edna, 200
Hunter, Tera, 221, 287n62

Immigrants, 40, 112, 113, 133, 171, 175, 188, 189, 197, 217, 261n77
Industrialization, 172
Ingersoll, Robert, 137, 266n49
Institutional Church and Settlement House, 173–174
International Congress of Women, 198
Isaac, Reverend I. W. D., 163

Jackson, Helen, 94, 98
Jasper, John, 43
Johnson, Amelia E., 47, 66–67, 251n68; *Clarence and Corinne*, 13, 66; *The Hazely Family*, 13, 66
Johnson, James Weldon, 170
Johnson, Reverend Harvey, 66, 147
Johnson, Reverend William Bishop, 264n24, 269nn75,77, 275n57
Jones, Dr. Sophia, 34, 241n46
Jones, Dr. Thomas Jesse, 276n64
Jones, Emma King, 70
Jones, Eugene Kinkle, 170, 181
Jones, Jacqueline, 30, 42, 54, 244n68
Jordan, Lewis G., 154, 156, 159, 160, 272n17
Joy, 66, 251n68
Judson Memorial Church (New York City), 173

Kaufman, Gordon, 126
Kelley, Emma Dunham: *Megda*, 13
Kellor, Frances, 180, 181, 284n41, 285n45
King, G. M. P., 22, 52–53, 246n13
King, Martin Luther, Jr., 229, 240n41
Kortrecht school (Memphis), 124

Landry, Bart, 289n85
Langston, John Mercer, 51
Lawrence, Una Roberts, 293n119
Laws: anti-lynching, 1, 225, 285n43; segregation, 1, 4, 98, 164, 222–223; civil-rights, 4; child-labor, 226; labor, 227
Layten, Sarah Willie, 85 (ill.), 157–158, 170, 180, 182, 184, 285n45; and National Baptist Convention, 160, 163; as leader, 181, 197, 198, 202, 228–229, 272n20, 279nn101,106; on self-indulgent youth, 199; and World War I, 225; on Great Migration, 227; on domestic servants, 292n113; and women's suffrage, 295n145
Layton, Julia Mason, 64–65
Lee, Jarena, 123
Leland University, 21, 22, 238n18

LeMoyne College (Memphis), 158
Levine, Lawrence, 244n71
Lincoln, C. Eric, 16
Literacy, 11, 19, 42, 44–45, 54, 71, 73, 89, 99
Literature: racist, 191; "distinctive," 194, 201; tract, 195, 198
Litwack, Leon, 53
Logan, Rayford, 4
Long, Charles, 233n24
Love, Reverend Emmanuel K., 57, 65, 247n26
Lynching, 4, 11, 18, 76, 78, 110–111, 143, 198, 222, 224, 225, 227, 285n43; week of prayer against, 224

MacVicar, Malcolm, 28, 35, 57, 238n16, 242n52
Madison Avenue Baptist Church (New York City), 105
Mamiya, Lawrence, 16
Marks, Carole, 171
Martin, Hardie, 79
Martin, Sandy D., 231n5
Martineau, Harriet, 143
Mason, Anna M., 52
Mather, Rachel, 111–112, 114
Matheson, George, 140, 267n57
Mayo, Amory Dwight, 36
Mays, Benjamin, 12, 201
McCulloch, James E., 183
McDowell, Mary, 182
McEwen, Alice E., 77
McEwen, Reverend A. N., 77
McLaughlin, Eleanor, 122
McMillen, Neil, 190
McMurdy, Judge Robert, 294n135
McPherson, James, 90–91, 111, 238n15, 245n7
Mead, Sidney E., 10, 233n24
Meese, Elizabeth A., 280n3
Men and Religion Forward Movement, 141
Methodist Episcopal Church, 6, 233n15
Mial, S. A., 257n22
Migration, black, 27, 102, 171–172, 180, 181, 185, 189, 227
Miller, Mrs. I., 272n20
Ministers, black, 15, 40–42, 49, 53, 59, 107, 145, 246n18; attitude toward women, 3, 70–71, 98, 147; training of, 21, 22, 41; preaching style of, 43–44, 115–116; and women's state conventions, 68, 70, 175, 252n74; and reform, 175–176
Missionaries, 34, 38, 39, 40, 44, 64, 156, 248n36; Yankee, 43, 54, 102, 116–117; women, 50, 69, 70, 75, 77, 90–95, 97, 104, 109, 114, 117, 121, 124–125, 186

Missionaries *(continued)*
198; letters of, 110; and children, 117–
118. *See also* Training: missionary
Missionary societies, 17, 68, 75–76, 90, 161,
162, 164, 181
Mission Herald, 156, 161
Mitchell, Edward C., 238n18
Mitchell, Robert, 160
Moore, Joanna P., 69, 70, 97–102, 143;
quoted, 93, 107–108, 258nn31,32,34; and
black ministers, 115–116, 262n84; *In
Christ's Stead,* 258n30, 268n61
Morehouse, Henry, 23, 25, 26–27, 32, 36,
39–40, 51, 55, 57
Morehouse College, 21, 23, 25, 57, 170,
201, 245n9
Morgan, T. J., 27, 28–29, 39, 57, 113,
238n18, 241n44, 242n48
Morris, Harriet, 77
Morris, Reverend Elias Camp, 65, 160, 164,
167, 244n72, 249n49, 270n2, 280n114
Morton, Patricia, 190
Moses, Wilson, 48
Moss, Thomas, 110
Mossell, Gertrude: *The Work of the Afro-
American Woman,* 13
Mount Holyoke College, 28
Mt. Zion Baptist Church (Stanton, Tennes-
see), 70
Murray, Gertrude, 38

NAACP. *See* National Association for the
Advancement of Colored People
NACW. *See* National Association of Colored Women
Nashville Institute, 21
Natchez Seminary, 21
National American Woman Suffrage Association, 136
National Association for the Advancement
of Colored People (NAACP), 102, 163,
166, 170, 201, 225, 294n135; and civil
rights, 221, 223; campaign against lynching, 224, 294n138
National Association of Colored Women
(NACW), 16–17, 125, 152, 158, 170,
198, 200; and Woman's Convention, 182–
183, 206, 207, 219, 224; formation of,
271n6
National Association of Wage Earners, 219,
221, 293n123
National Baptist Convention, U.S.A.
(NBC), 2, 124, 147, 148–149, 153, 158,
164; membership of, 6–7, 65–66, 166,
232n15, 275n59; masculine bias of, 8;
publications of, 11–12; formation of, 65,

79, 232n6; and Woman's Convention,
150–151, 159, 160; founding meeting of,
155; Foreign Mission Board of, 156–157,
159, 161; incorporation of, 164; meetings
of, 164–165, 167, 170, 171, 235n32,
250n62, 270n1, 274n54; and Negro dolls,
194, 275n58; cooperationists of, 251n63;
and self-government, 270n2; Home Mission Board of, 285n46. *See also National
Baptist Union; Woman's Convention*
National Baptist Convention of America
(unincorporated), 164
National Baptist Educational Convention
(NBEC), 64, 65, 153, 154
National Baptist Foreign Mission Conven-
tion, 64, 154, 231n5, 232n6
National Baptist Magazine, 11, 66, 79, 147,
155, 166, 235n31, 264n24
National Baptist Publishing Board, 164
National Baptist Union, 161, 163, 191–192,
228, 274n46
National Baptist World (Wichita), 76, 77, 143
National Bar Association (N.B.A.), 283n21
National Council of Women, 138
Nationalism, black, 10, 48, 49, 66, 245nn2, 5
National League for the Protection of Col-
ored Women (NLPCW), 158, 163, 180,
181, 197, 279n106, 285n45
National League of Republican Colored
Women, 227
National Training School for Women and
Girls, 159, 177, 211–221, 290n90,
293n114, 294n126; Domestic Training
Class at, 86 (ill.), 187; Missionary Train-
ing Class at, 85 (ill.); basketball team at,
87 (ill.); and Woman's Convention, 162,
197; funding for, 220, 280n113, 282n21,
293nn124,125, 294nn126,127; enrollment
of, 290n89; and industrial education,
291n102; graduates of, 291nn100,101,103
National Urban League, 158, 170, 174, 180,
181
NBC. *See* National Baptist Convention,
U.S.A.
NBEC. *See* National Baptist Educational
Convention
The Negro Baptist Pulpit, 44, 125, 145
Neily, Lizzie, 257n22
Nelson, Alice Dunbar, 170
Nelson, Amanda V., 64
Neuhaus, Richard, 8, 233n20
Newspapers, 11, 76, 235n30. *See also individ-
ual newspapers*
Nicholson, Joseph, 12
Nightingale, Reverend Taylor, 234n29
Nineteenth Amendment, 218, 219

NLPCW. *See* National League for the Protection of Colored Women
Normal schools, 36, 42
Northern Baptist Convention, 6, 166

O'Keefe, Mary, 127
Oldham, Mrs. G. D., 130–131, 265n31
Oliphant, Laurence, 139
Orthodoxy: and gender, 122, 149, 288n74; progressive, 266n47
Osborne, Lulu, 103, 118
Our Women and Children, 78

Packard, Sophia B., 22, 33, 34, 38, 83 (ill.), 92, 93, 105, 237n6, 240n39, 241n45, 243n63
Palmer, Phyllis, 214, 216–217, 292n106
Paris, Peter, 121
Park, Robert, 146
Parks, Rosa, 229
Parrish, Mary V. (Mrs. Charles H. Parrish). *See* Cook, Mary V.
Parrish, Reverend Charles H., 63, 125, 147, 156, 249n49
Paternalism, 46, 49, 53–54, 66, 92, 94
Patriotism, 9, 114, 115
Paul, Alice, 227
Peck, Jennie, 85 (ill.), 98
Penn, I. Garland: *The Afro-American Press and Its Editors*, 14, 78, 251n68
Perry, Reverend Rufus: *The Cushites, or the Descendants of Ham as Found in the Sacred Scriptures*, 122, 263n5
Pettigrew, Belle, 30, 259n37
Philadelphia Tribune, 166, 274n54
Phillips, Ulrich B., 191
Phillips, William H., 157
Pitts, Rebecca, 166–167, 275n60
Pollard, Eliza, 62–63, 76, 77, 78
Pollard, Robert T., 63, 249n49
Population, black, 102, 171–172
Potsdam Normal School, 36
Poverty, 1, 13, 97, 116
Preachers, 40–42, 43; women, 2. *See also* Ministers
Presbyterian Church, 17
Press, black. *See* Newspapers
Progressive Party, 226
Progressivism, secular, 172–180
Prohibition, 226
Protestantism, 91, 113, 114, 137; feminized, 267n56
Pruitt, Mrs. L. D., 226
Public sphere, concept of, 10–11
Purce, Mrs. Charles, 63, 249n52
Purce, Reverend Charles L., 249nn49,52

Quarles, Reverend Frank, 22, 23, 237n6

Rabinowitz, Howard, 32, 43, 240n36
Race: perceptions of, 145–146; and romanticism, 269n71
Race relations, 1, 4, 39, 48, 107, 183, 184, 187, 192
Racial consciousness, 5–6, 10, 13, 48, 49, 50, 56, 65, 67, 79, 145, 152, 154
Racism, 28, 46, 49, 51, 115, 121, 146, 207, 213; and the church, 1; post-Reconstruction, 4; and respectability, 15; and convention movement, 18, 167, 186; and reform, 152, 187–188; "scientific," 188; and suffrage movement, 227. *See also* Social Darwinism
Randolph, Peter, 120
Ransom, Reverend Reverdy, 173
Rape, 189, 190, 193
Reconstruction, 4, 5, 19, 48, 89, 90, 92, 232nn8,11; schools during, 54
Reform, Progressive-era, 17, 171–180, 258n27, 279n99; and vital statistics, 178; child welfare in, 178, 179, 278nn89,98; sex education in, 178; and venereal disease, 178–179; and race relations, 187; and alley cleanup, 203, 288n69; and elitism, 208, 289n80; and women's suffrage, 226
Religion, 19, 31, 107, 119, 208; civil, 9, 10, 233nn21,24, 234n24; in public sphere, 10–11, 233n22, 234n26; and gender differences, 123, 141; fundamentalist, 137; feminization of, 148, 267n56; slave, 232n12. *See also* Church, black
Respectability, 145, 211, 288n73; politics of, 14–15, 185–229, 258n26, 280n3, 281nn7,8, 286n57; and professionalism, 216
Reynolds, Mary, 108, 111
Rhodes, James Ford, 190–191
Rice, Jessie, 109
Richardson, Marilyn, 123
Richmond Theological Institute, 21, 23, 51, 239n28
Riddick, Mrs. M. W., 280n114
Roberts, Benjamin T.: *Ordaining Women*, 138
Robinson, Dr. E. G., 239n28
Robinson, Minnie, 119
Robinson, Mrs. C. J., 155
Robinson, Reverend J. Francis, 147–148
Rockefeller, John D., 32, 89, 173
Rockefeller, Laura Spelman, 32
Roger Williams University, 51
Rogin, Michael, 189
Roman Catholic Church, 6, 7

Roosevelt, Theodore, 226
Roselle, Dr. Quay, 276n64
Rosenwald, Julius, 89, 293n124
Ruether, Rosemary, 122
Ruffin, Josephine St. Pierre, 152
Rush, Gertrude, 191, 226–227, 283n21

Sale, George, 25–26, 240n33
Schools: struggle over, 50–55; Sabbath, 54,
    246n21, 248n36; black private, 54–55;
    public, 54–55, 247n25; mothers' training,
    95, 97, 99, 100–101, 179. *See also* Educa-
    tion; *individual colleges*
Scott, Amelia, 114
Scott, Emmett J., 111170
Scott, James, 221, 237n49, 295n152
Scroggs, William O., 280n115
Seeley, Elizabeth, 61
Segregation, 4–5, 11, 47, 51, 89, 119, 193,
    222–223, 225, 232n10
Self-determination, racial, 3, 53–55, 153,
    157, 166, 174, 186, 191, 209, 229,
    251n63, 280n3
Self-help, racial, 5, 18, 61–62, 188, 195,
    197, 209, 211, 221, 232n11, 259n46; and
    philanthropy, 89
Selma University (Alabama Baptist Univer-
    sity), 61, 62, 63, 77, 103, 119,
    249nn46,52, 250n54, 251n63, 271n11
Separatism, 47–80; strategies of, 73–80
Sexism, 15, 28, 121, 123, 144, 152, 167,
    186, 268n59
Sexuality, black, 189–190, 282n18, 286n59
Shanks, Sophia, 74, 272n20
Shaw, Anna Howard, 138, 227
Shaw University (Raleigh), 21, 30, 104,
    239n28
Shillady, John R., 294n135
Shiloh Baptist Church (Washington, D.C.),
    174, 201, 219, 246n13, 277n79
Simkins, Frances Butler, 191
Simmons, Reverend William J., 59–60, 62,
    68, 78, 88, 125, 247n26, 248n40, 249n49,
    265n37; and ANBC, 64, 132, 147, 153,
    154; death of, 154–155; and ABHMS,
    251n63
Slater Fund, 34, 241nn45,46
Slavery, 26, 30–31, 41, 146, 189, 190, 195,
    244n76; and conventions, 3; and the
    church, 5, 47, 53, 96; and illiteracy, 19,
    22, 113; and work ethic, 33; and secret
    schooling, 54; and the Bible, 122, 123.
    See also Abolitionism
Smith, Lucy Wilmot, 62, 64, 78, 124, 126,
    129, 134–135, 143, 144, 156, 264n16
Smith, Mrs. Lillie, 175
Smith-Hughes Act, 215

Smyth, Newman, 137
Sneed, Charles, 63
Sneed, Lavinia, 63, 78
Social Darwinism, 115, 137, 169, 188, 192,
    268n60
Social Gospel movement, 172–173, 174, 201
Social welfare, 2, 8, 9
Southern Baptist Convention, 6, 166, 197
Southern Sociological Congress, 183–184,
    280n114
Spelman Messenger, 66, 100, 109, 118
Spelman Seminary (Atlanta), 22–23, 30, 31–
    40, 93, 103, 105, 108, 155, 240n35,
    241n47, 243nn62,63; Model School of,
    35–36; trustees of, 57; Missionary Train-
    ing Department of, 81 (ill.); and training
    of teachers, 82 (ill.), 242n52, 245n9;
    Union Hall at, 83 (ill.); and domestic
    training, 241n44; financing of, 241n45;
    annual reports of, 242n48; and exclusion
    of black doctors, 245n9
Stallybrass, Peter, 203–204, 206
Stanton, Elizabeth Cady, 137, 266n49,
    269n70; *The Woman's Bible,* 138–139
State University at Louisville, Kentucky
    (Simmons University), 59–61, 89, 119,
    125, 251n63; faculty of, 62, 63, 64, 104,
    156; graduates of, 88, 126, 240n42,
    249n52; Model School of, 126; organiza-
    tion of, 248n36
Stephenson, Judge Gilbert T., 280n115
Stereotypes, racial, 189, 190, 191, 196, 223
Steward, Mamie, 62, 63, 75, 182
Steward, William, 63
Stewart, Maria, 120, 123, 124
Stewart, Maria, 120, 123, 124
Stone, Susie, 271n7
Strong, Augustus, 139, 267n57
Superstition, 44, 108, 113
Supreme Court, 5, 189, 232n10
Swarthmore News, 224

Talbert, Mary, 170
Talented Tenth, female, 19–46, 51, 55–58,
    82 (ill.), 96, 213
Talmage, T. De Witt, 138, 139–140
Taylor, Frederick, 215
Teachers, 37–39, 40–42, 50–51, 75, 94, 104,
    109, 242n51, 243n55; salaries of black
    women, 244n68. *See also* Training: teacher
Tefft, Lyman, 28
Temperance, 38, 43, 45, 63, 66, 78, 99, 143,
    193, 194, 196
Terrell, Mary Church, 206–207
Theology: feminist, 120–149; liberal, 136–
    142, 266n47
Tidings, 106, 107, 110, 114, 118
Tilman, W. H., 108

Tilton, Theodore, 146
Training: industrial, 26, 31, 33, 45, 54, 211, 213, 237n3; domestic, 33–34, 97, 99, 212, 214–215, 241n44; of nurses, 34, 241n46, 245n9; missionary, 35, 239n24; teacher, 35–36, 242n52; theological, 71, 239n23; of mothers, 97, 99, 100–101, 152
Travelers' Aid, 197, 279n106, 285n45
Traver, Mary, 244n75
Trotter, Joe, 289n83
Truth, Sojourner, 123, 143
Tubman, Harriet, 18
Turner, Henry McNeil, 248n38
Turner, Nat, 18
Tuskegee Institute, 52, 214
Two Republics, 30
Tyler, Amanda, 63
Tyler, Reverend Manfield, 63

University of Chicago, 28, 29
University of Michigan, 29, 34
Upton, Lucy, 35, 243n62
Urbanization, black, 171, 172, 185, 189

Vassar College, 28, 30, 42, 103
Violence, racial, 47, 89, 101, 119, 152, 189, 224, 282n13
Virginia Baptist, 147
Virginia Baptist State Convention, 23, 58
Virginia Baptist Theological Seminary, 58
Virginia Union University, 44, 58, 217
Voice of the Negro, 169
Voting rights, 1, 4, 12, 226. *See also* Women's suffrage

WABHMS. *See* Woman's American Baptist Home Mission Society
Waldron, John Milton, 174, 201, 277n79
Walker, C. J., 169
Walker, Maggie Lena, 169, 170, 191, 282n21
Wallace, Mrs. M. B., 75–76
Walls, Carrie, 37, 118
Wanamaker, John, 171
Washington, Booker T., 52, 89, 158, 213, 214, 228, 246n12, 291n101, 293n124; and W. E. B. Du Bois, 20, 48; Atlanta Compromise speech of, 25; and Woman's Convention, 159, 220, 221, 226
Washington, James Melvin, 10; *Frustrated Fellowship*, 3
Washington, Maggie, 52
Washington, Margaret Murray, 214
Watkins, Professor Daniel, 124
Watson, Jennie, 271n7
Wayland Seminary, 21, 22, 52, 53, 103, 246n13

WBHMS. *See* Women's Baptist Home Mission Society
WC. *See* Woman's Convention
Weatherford, W. D., 183–184
Wellesley College, 28, 30, 103, 108–109, 243n62
Wells, Ida B., 11, 78, 110, 143, 169–170, 234n29, 254n108, 268n62; *On Lynchings*, 13
Wells, Mrs. C. M., 272n20
Wells-Barnett, Ida. *See* Wells, Ida B.
Welter, Barbara, 139
Western College (Macon, Missouri), 58
Wheeler, Edward, 18
Whipple, Helen, 68
White, Allon, 203–204, 206
White, Charles, 239n29
White, Lizzie, 109
White, William J., 22
White League, 101
White supremacy, 101, 186, 189
Whitfield, Ella E., 161, 220, 271n13, 272n20, 278n89, 294n126
Willard, Frances, 137, 138, 139, 143, 265n36, 266n48; *Woman in the Pulpit*, 140–141
Williams, Fannie Barrier, 16–17, 173
Williams, Lillie, 53
Williams, Mary E., 52–53
Wilson, Mrs. E. A., 85 (ill.), 272n20
Wilson, Woodrow, 189, 225, 235n33
Woman's American Baptist Home Mission Society (WABHMS; New England), 31, 35, 92, 103, 104, 109, 235n35, 237n6, 293n125; and teacher training, 36, 39, 242n48; Bureau of Information of, 105–106; protest against lynching, 110–111; history of, 240n35; and National Training School, 292n105. *See also* American Baptist Home Mission Society
Woman's Convention (WC), 8, 12, 150–151, 156–162, 163, 164, 165, 167, 185–186; officers of, 85 (ill.); annual meetings of, 165–171, 175, 176, 178, 186, 191, 199, 205–206, 208, 219, 270n1, 271n13, 275n64; 1907 program of, 167–168; and reform, 172, 175–176, 180, 181–182, 183–184, 187, 278n88; settlement house (Centre) of, 177, 178; and class, 187, 192, 205, 207; and respectability, 193, 195, 197, 198, 200, 214, 220, 287n66; on morals of youth, 199; annual reports of, 205–208, 284n34; and labor, 211, 212, 218, 279n99; and training servants, 217, 220; seven-point manifesto (1913) of, 222; and segregation, 222–223; and NAACP, 223–224; in World War I, 225; and

Woman's Convention (WC) *(continued)*
women's suffrage, 226, 227; and religion,
277n85, 284n43; speakers at, 294n135.
See also National Training School for
Women and Girls

Woman's Missionary Union, 198

Women: college-educated black, 20–46, 94,
126, 180, 183; as homemakers, 29, 39,
100, 131, 142, 143, 215, 269n77; working, 29, 134–136; professional, 40–42;
quest for equality, 50, 80; and public
speaking, 68, 133; "Bible," 94; influence
of, 128–132, 135, 136–137; and motherhood, 129–130, 143, 180, 192, 202,
266n43; and marriage, 130; ordination of,
133, 138, 140, 267n57; and religion, 136;
emancipation of, 148; and child care,
152, 184; sexuality of black, 189–190; representation of black, 190–191, 202;
black, as servants, 212, 214, 215, 216,
290nn93,94,95; and reform, 226, 235n39;
and self-development vs. self-sacrifice,
269n70

Women's Baptist Home and Foreign Missionary Convention (North Carolina), 95,
257n22

Women's Baptist Home Mission Society
(WBHMS; Midwest), 69, 70, 92, 93, 94,
95, 98–99, 101, 103, 235n35, 239n24,
244n75

Women's Christian Temperance Union, 76,
198

Women's rights, 13, 18, 100, 119, 154, 157,
185, 186, 226, 267n49, 268n60; and the
Bible, 2, 22; 1878 conference on, 269n70

Women's suffrage, 12, 13, 76, 126, 136, 148,
152, 185, 226, 267n57, 275n54

Wood, Ione, 78

World Baptist Congress, 170–171, 276n66

World War I, 171, 179, 182, 185, 225, 227

Wright, Thomas, 204, 288n72

Yates, Josephine Silon, 183

Young Men's Christian Association, 88, 184,
248n36, 268n58, 285n51

Young Women's Christian Association, 35,
88, 200, 248n36